TASTE,
EXPERIENCE,
AND
FEEDING

TASTE, EXPERIENCE, AND FEEDING

ELIZABETH D. CAPALDI
AND
TERRY L. POWLEY

American Psychological Association
Washington, DC

Published by
American Psychological Association
1200 Seventeenth Street, NW
Washington, DC 20036

Copies may be ordered from
APA Order Department
P.O. Box 2710
Hyattsville, MD 20784

Designed by Paul M. Levy
Typeset by BG Composition, Baltimore, MD
Printed by BookCrafters, Chelsea, MI
Technical editing and production coordinated by
Linda J. Beverly

Library of Congress Cataloging-in-Publication Data

Taste, experience, and feeding / edited by Elizabeth D. Capaldi and
  Terry L. Powley.
    p. cm.
    "This volume is the result of a conference held at Purdue
University . . . April 7 and 8, 1989 . . . sponsored by the American
Psychological Association and the Department of Psychological
Sciences and the School of Humanities, Social Science, and Education
at Purdue"—Pref.
    Includes bibliographical references and index.
    ISBN 1-55798-091-8
    1. Food habits—Psychological aspects—Congresses. I. Capaldi,
Elizabeth D. II. Powley, T. L. (Terry L.) III. American
Psychological Association. IV. Purdue University. Dept. of
Psychological Sciences. V. Purdue University. School of
Humanities, Social Science, and Education.
TX357.T34 1990   90-1129
613.2′01′9—dc20

Printed in the United States of America
First edition

CONTENTS

PART SIX: SOCIAL CONTEXT OF FOOD PREFERENCES

CONTRIBUTORS

Linda M. Bartoshuk, *Yale School of Medicine*
Gary K. Beauchamp, *Monell Chemical Senses Center*
Gundeep Behl, *Brown University*
Ilene L. Bernstein, *University of Washington*
L. L. Birch, *University of Illinois at Urbana-Champaign*
Robert C. Bolles, *University of Washington*
David Booth, *University of Birmingham*
Michel Cabanac, *Laval University*
Elizabeth D. Capaldi, *University of Florida*
Adam Drewnowski, *University of Michigan*
C. Peter Herman, *University of Toronto*
Jacques Le Magnen, *College de France*
Lewis P. Lipsitt, *American Psychological Association*
Cynthia L. Meachum, *University of Washington*
Patricia Pliner, *University of Toronto*
Janet Polivy, *University of Toronto*
Terry L. Powley, *Purdue University*
Barbara J. Rolls, *The Johns Hopkins University School of Medicine*
Neil E. Rowland, *University of Florida*
Paul Rozin, *University of Pennsylvania*
Anthony Sclafani, *Brooklyn College*
Thomas R. Scott, *University of Delaware*
Harvey P. Weingarten, *McMaster University*
Charles J. Wysocki, *Monell Chemical Senses Center*

FOREWORD

Federal research agencies stopped regularly supporting investigator-initiated "state-of-the-art" research conferences in scientific psychology well over a decade ago. Yet over that same period, scientific psychology has continued to both grow and diversify into many new areas. Thus there have been relatively few opportunities for investigators in new and promising research areas to convene in special settings to discuss their findings.

The American Psychological Association (APA), as part of its continuing efforts to enhance the dissemination of scientific knowledge in psychology, undertook a number of new initiatives designed to foster scientific research and communication. In particular, the APA Science Directorate, in 1988, initiated the Scientific Conferences Program.

The APA Scientific Conferences Program provides university-based psychological researchers with seed monies essential to organizing specialty conferences on critical issues in basic research, applied research, and methodological issues in psychology. Deciding which conferences to support involves a competitive process. An annual call for proposals is issued by the APA Science Directorate to solicit conference ideas. Proposals from all areas of psychological research are welcome. They are then reviewed by qualified psychologists, who forward substantive suggestions and funding recommendations to the Science Directorate. At each stage, the criteria used to determine which conferences to support include relevance, timeliness, and comprehensiveness of the topics, and qualifications of the presenters. In 1988, seven conferences were funded under the APA Science Directorate program's sponsorship, and seven conferences were funded in 1989. We expect to fund several more in 1990, at an annual program expense of $90,000 to $100,000.

The APA Scientific Conferences Program has two major goals. The first is to provide, by means of the conferences, a broad view of specific topics (and, when appropriate, to provide for interdisciplinary participation). The second goal is to assure timely dissemination of the findings presented by publishing a series of carefully crafted scholarly volumes based, in part, on each conference. Thus the information reaches the audiences at each conference as well as the broader psychological and scientific communities. This enables psychology and related fields to benefit from the most current research on a given topic.

This volume presents findings presented at the April 1989 conference, "Taste, Experience, and Feeding." Research in this areas focuses on a variety of topics including how positive consequences affect taste preferences, the physiological basis of taste, and how human obesity is affected by taste. Researchers who use different perspectives, methods, and subjects in the study of taste, experience, and feeding were brought together to exchange ideas and explore new research directions.

This volume is representative of what we at the American Psychological Association believe are a number of exceptional volumes that give readers a broad sampling of the diverse and outstanding research now being done in scientific psychology. We hope you will enjoy and be stimulated by this book and the many others to come.

A list of the conferences funded through this program follows:

Researching Community Psychology: Integrating Theories and Methodologies, September 1988

Psychological Well-Being in Nonhuman Captive Primates, September 1988

Psychological Research on Organ Donation, October 1988

Arizona Conference on Sleep and Cognition, January 1989

Socially Shared Cognition, February 1989

Taste, Experience, and Feeding, April 1989

Perception of Structure, May 1989

Suggestibility of Children's Recollections, June 1989

Best Methods for the Analysis of Change, October 1989

Conceptualization and Measurement of Organism-Environment Interactions, November 1989

Cognitive Bases of Musical Communication, April 1990

Conference on Hostility, Coping/Support, and Health, November 1990

Psychological Testing of Hispanics, February 1991

Study of Cognition: Conceptual and Methodological Issues, February 1991

Virginia E. Holt
Manager, Scientific Conferences Program
Science Directorate, APA

ACKNOWLEDGMENTS

This volume is the result of a conference held at Purdue University in West Lafayette, Indiana on April 7 and 8, 1989. The conference was sponsored by the American Psychological Association and the Department of Psychological Sciences and the School of Humanities, Social Science, and Education at Purdue. In addition to the participants whose papers comprise this volume, there were many researchers who attended the conference and enriched the papers herein by their comments and discussion. These included the formal discussants: Kent Berridge, University of Michigan; Art Campfield, Hoffmann-LaRoche; Robert Frank, University of Cincinnati; and Michael Tordoff, Monell Chemical Senses Center.

PREFACE

There has been a recent surge of work on taste, experience, and feeding. This development reflects several factors, including behavioral work on taste aversion which has led to a concern with how positive consequences can affect taste preferences, progress in understanding the physiological basis of taste, as well as a practical concern with human obesity and how it is affected by taste and experiential factors. With this growth in experimental interest, common questions and related issues have often been pursued within different subspecialties. To promote dialogue among researchers from these separate specializations, the American Psychological Association and Purdue University jointly sponsored a 3-day conference. The meeting brought together and stimulated productive interchanges among investigators who use different perspectives, methods, and experimental subjects in the study of the various aspects of taste, experience, and feeding.

The chapters in this book stem from papers given at the conference. This volume has been divided into six parts, each dealing with a different aspect of taste and feeding. The first part of this volume deals with the current perspective of and approach to feeding used by most researchers. As Bolles puts it, the focus has shifted from a concern with the internal stimulus that produces feeding to the importance of the hedonics of food in feeding and to other nonhomeostatic factors that influence feeding (chapter 1, this volume). He discusses three organizers of feeding behavior: circadian cycle, the cost of obtaining a meal, and the hedonics of the available food. In chapter 2, Weingarten stresses the importance of experience in determining food intake and makes the point that biological mechanisms can only be understood by analyzing the role of learning in feeding behavior. Concluding this section, Cabanac presents his theory that sensory pleasure may be the mechanism by which physiological homeostasis is achieved (chapter 3, this volume).

Taste perception is the focus of the second part. In chapter 4, Scott describes how the responses of taste neurons are modified by experience and by physiological need. This provides a mechanism that underlies some of the phenomena described in later chapters. Bartoshuk (chapter 5, this volume) then discusses how the senses of both taste and smell contribute to flavor perception and the similarities and differences between taste and smell.

The third part of this volume deals with the genetic and the developmental aspects of taste and feeding. Lipsitt in chapter 6, describes taste and ingestion studies done on infants whose sucking-tasting-ingestion systems have not yet been affected by experience. In chapter 7, Rowland reviews the evidence for innate and learned aspects of sodium salts intake (NaCl in particular). Olfaction is studied from a developmental and experiential framework by Beauchamp (chapter 8, this volume). This part concludes with Birch's review of current evidence regarding the contribution of learning and experience to the dramatic changes that occur in the control of food intake during the first few years of children's lives (chapter 9, this volume).

Learning and feeding are the concerns of chapters 10, 11, 12, and 13 in part four. In chapter 10, Sclafani presents clear evidence that conditioned flavor preferences can be produced by the association of nutrients with flavors. Capaldi (chapter 11, this volume) then demonstrates that conditioned flavor preferences can be produced by the hunger level under which the flavor is consumed and the preference is often greater for a flavor consumed when the subject is not very hungry. The role that food aversion learning plays in producing changes in food intake is discussed by Bernstein in chapter 12 (this volume). Finally, Booth (chapter 13, this volume) provides an excellent overview of the many ways in which learning and experience can affect food preferences and food intake.

Part five concerns work done with taste preferences, food consumption, and human obesity. Rolls (chapter 14, this volume) reviews the work done on sensory-specific satiety and food preferences and food intake. Pliner, Herman, and Polivy discuss the role of food palatability in obesity in chapter 15 (this volume). Drewnowski reviews the current evidence suggesting that individual differences in reaction to tastes may be very important in obesity studies in his chapter (chapter 16, this volume). Le Magnen discusses the role of endogenous opiates in the sensory stimulation to eat or not eat in the final chapter of part five (chapter 17, this volume).

Rozin's chapter on social influences and feeding makes up the sixth and final part of this volume. There is a general consensus that in humans these social factors are immensely important; Rozin reviews the data supporting this view in chapter 18. The mechanism of these effects, however, is still unknown.

We hope this volume will stimulate research on taste, experience, and feeding. The factors discussed in the following chapters are important and we now need to concentrate on understanding how they operate. We hope to reconvene ten years from now and find that the progress we hope and expect in understanding has indeed occurred.

Elizabeth D. Capaldi
University of Florida

Terry L. Powley
Purdue University

PART ONE

BACKGROUND AND THEORY

CHAPTER 1

A FUNCTIONALISTIC APPROACH TO FEEDING

ROBERT C. BOLLES

It appears that we have turned a corner. Until recently most of the people who worked on the problem of feeding usually approached it in one way, but now many of us approach it from a quite different direction. I want to say something about this change in direction. First I will sketch how it used to be and where everyone thought they were going, and then I will discuss where we seem to be going now. I will indicate why it is to our credit that we made the change, and I suggest that this new direction be called a functionalistic approach. Let us start with a little story.

THE TRADITIONAL APPROACH

Once upon a time, about 80 years ago, there was a famous physiologist named Walter B. Cannon. One day while he was puttering around in his laboratory he noticed that Mr. Washburn, the young man who was working with him, was not his normal self. Washburn was usually calm and efficient, but on this particular day he seemed irritable and distracted. Cannon wondered if the lad was alright. Then the great scientist noticed that Washburn's stomach was rumbling, and that observation promptly lead him to a grand new scientific advance. Perhaps, Cannon hypothesized, the young man was merely hungry. But rather than let the poor fellow go off to lunch, Cannon seized the opportunity to do an experiment. Washburn swallowed a balloon (after all, he was the student), that was connected by a tube to a recording device. To add to his troubles, Washburn was also supposed to push a button whenever he felt a hunger sensation. Cannon and Washburn (1912) were soon able to report that hunger, or what they called a hunger pang, was nothing but the sensation of stomach contractions. Hunger *was*

3

stomach contractions, nothing more, nothing less. That became the definition, and it was accepted by a lot of people, both psychologists and physiologists.

There are two important implications of Cannon's approach to hunger that we need to look at more closely. One implication is that for Cannon hunger was basically a physiological matter that had very little to do with the psychology of eating. Cannon's objective view of Washburn's problem that day was very different from Washburn's personal view of it. The famous physiologist wanted to find a bodily basis for hunger; for him hunger had to be a body state. For the young man, his hunger was much more psychological; what he wanted was to go over to the student union, meet a friend, and enjoy a hamburger. In fairness to Cannon I should note that he admitted that eating was controlled by two kinds of mechanisms, one being his newly-found "hunger," and the second a host of factors that he lumped together and called "appetite." He said that appetite was not a proper thing for the physiologist to study because it was so psychological. Hunger, as he defined it, was perfectly safe ground for the scientist.

These events were unfolding just as John B. Watson was preparing to launch his behavioristic revolution. Watson's revolution was enormously successful, and its success, like that of all successful uprisings, was due to the fact that the majority of us wanted what the new movement promised. Those in the discipline were ready to become mechanistic; we wanted it. Psychology had been overwhelmed by the complexities of introspectionism, and by too much mentalism. Behaviorism eliminated all such problems. The behavioristic program promised simplicity and clarity. Cannon's ideas were in the same spirit. Science should not concern itself with what Washburn plans and wishes were on that fateful day. We should not care what, when, where, or with whom he wanted to eat. Cannon's approach made all those psychological complexities disappear. It simplified hunger enormously to make it a body problem rather than a psychological problem.

Unfortunately, in just a few years a variety of evidence showed up to convince everyone that stomach contractions did not constitute the true stimulus for hunger. For example, the first bite of food stops the contractions, but whets rather than appeases one's appetite. A number of such seemingly fatal difficulties did not seriously damage the concept, however. The negative evidence was only taken to mean that Cannon had not found the right body stimulus. The mechanistic approach was still right, the only thing wrong was the little detail of what the correct stimulus was. For 50 years now we have looked everywhere for it. For a time it seemed that the magic stimulus was glucostatic. Somewhere there were sugar receptors that sent messages when blood sugar was low. This was how the body told the brain that it needed energy. That stimulus, if we could only find it, would be the hunger signal. Then for a while it seemed that the missing stimulus was lipostatic. Fats go into or come out of fat cells because of hormonal mediators, and it was thought that perhaps these hormones also signaled hunger when they reached appropriate receptors in the brain.

Then we went through a phase when we became obsessed with the receptors, that is, where the hypothetical stimulus was received, rather than with where it came from. It seemed that hunger stimuli, as well as satiety stimuli, made contact with the brain in the hypothalamus. A lot of researchers made lesions there to show that that was the place. The focus of research had shifted, but Cannon's old paradigm was still in place. The physiological problem was unchanged: Find the stimulus and find its receptor. The only psychological part of the problem were some unimportant details such as how the animal finds food, and what, when, and how much does it eat.

A second implication of Cannon's approach was illustrated in our little story when the great scientist showed some concern for his young assistant's well being. Cannon got us started on all this when he noted that Mr. Washburn was not functioning normally. Some stimulus from his body had to be "intruding" on his mind and disrupting his normally rational behavior. The idea that various body states can disrupt ordinary rationality arose long ago. In 1649, when René Descartes was worrying about how the mind and body interact, he was concerned about the body disrupting the mind, and he put his worries into the wonderful monograph "Passions of the Soul." Descartes told us that if, in an emotional state, the agitations around the heart were strong enough, they could spread to the head where they make themselves known as an emotional feeling (Descartes, 1649/1911). More importantly, this emotional agitation can disrupt a person's normal rationality. Thus disturbed states of body, such as strong emotions, interfere with the mind. We know them as intrusions upon, or afflictions of, our minds. That was the original concept.

Then early in the present century, the perspective began to shift as we started to think about motivation as an organizing or propelling force. McDougall (1932) said that in the absence of any emotion we would lie around inertly, like a watch with a broken mainspring. Freud (1915) maintained that the function of the nervous system is to rid itself of stimulation. If there were no potential disruptions, the nervous system would have nothing to do. Hull (1943) argued that because behavior is a product of both habit and drive, there would be no behavior at all if there were no drive (i.e., no state of bodily disturbance). Most psychologists shifted over from the earlier Cartesian model to the new rule that body states were important in the expression of behavior.

There is another way in which the body has been assumed to be important in motivated behavior. It is widely held that our thoughts, feelings, and behavior all serve the ultimate biological purpose of keeping the body hemostatic. There is an imperative to get sufficient food, water, oxygen, or whatever. If we do not keep these essentials in proper balance the consequences would be too serious to contemplate. We simply have to eat, drink, breath, and so on. There are normal levels for these essentials, and if the organism falls much below or rises much above these obligatory norms, then an "error signal" that stimulates the brain will be generated. If this sounds like Cannon again, it should, because homeostasis was one of his favorite concepts. Eventually, some problems with the concept appeared. It was discovered, for example, that animals sometimes eat when they have no need for food, and that they sometimes stop eating when they are still in deficit. It was also discovered in the 1950s that animals tend to explore, play, and be active when there is clearly no vital homeostatic basis for such behaviors. A kitten will not die if it fails to play like a kitten, but it plays with so much zest and vigor that one might think it to be a matter of survival.

A serious fault of the traditional approach is that it was entirely devoted to studying the physiological state of hunger; it had almost nothing to say about the behavior of eating. Eating was no more than a behavioral index of hunger, only one of many indices, such as blood sugar level, that could indicate the physiological state of an animal. To insure that there could be no doubt that the animals were hungry, we typically restricted their access to food to such a degree that they lost 15% of their normal body weight. Interestingly, such skinny rats still show strong tendencies to explore, play, and be active, but by and large they do seem to want to eat. What is a 15% weight loss like? In human terms, it is like starting with a average-sized woman of 140 pounds, and restricting her food so that she drops to a slender 120 pounds. Without knowing anything at all about this subject, we can predict one thing for sure about her: She is hungry. She wakes up hungry, she remains hungry after the skimpy meal we give her, she goes to bed hungry, and then she probably dreams about food. This is the basic preparation that has been used to study hunger. Researchers in the old tradition earnestly believed that by studying the behavior of starving rats they could explain everything important about feeding behavior. Moreover, they were ready to extend this kind of explanatory model to account for all motivated behavior.

I can sum up the traditional approach in one sentence: Certain states of need, such as hunger, are life-threatening departures from happy, healthy normality, and these states produce stimuli from the body that disrupt our well-ordered existence and move us to action.

A NEW DIRECTION

Because psychologists were so busy looking for the appropriate motivating stimuli, they could not attend to other matters or other aspects of motivated behavior. They could not see, for example, that when an animal is ready to eat, it *wants* food. Furthermore, when it is in an experimental situation where it has been fed, the animal *expects* food. In addition to that, it expects the particular kind of food it has been getting there. We recall how his monkeys became very upset when Tinklepaugh (1928) shifted them from the expected banana to the surprising lettuce.

I have not heard anyone at this conference say that hunger is just a stimulus, or that we should be searching for such a stimulus. On the contrary, we have been talking about expectancies, hedonics, preferences, meal patterns, and many other psychological aspects of feeding. We have been talking about all sorts of things that we avoided for many years while we looked for motivating stimuli. Another part of the picture that has changed is the idea that all the motivating forces—emotion, hunger, the different kinds of arousal—disrupt our normal, rational existence. Hunger used to be viewed as something of a crisis, which had to be dealt with immediately. Moreover, we thought of ourselves being the innocent victims of these physiological disturbances. They were something that happened to us, something external that intruded. Such disturbances might come from our bodies, but they were still intrusions on the psyche.

Now we think of it somewhat differently. Rozin (chapter 18, this volume) has observed that for many people, eating is a major source of pleasure. Many folks do not enjoy their employment, poverty, home, family situation, sex life, or social status. But everyone enjoys food. Many people organize their lives around eating. In many American subcultures the family life is organized around the kitchen table. The family gathers for dinner not because they all happen to be suffering from stomach contractions at the same time, but because dinner gives them an opportunity to talk, visit, and share. Sometimes a dinner date provides a wonderful way to make a new friend or to commune with an old one. In all of these social situations dinnertime is not a matter of remedying a disturbance, but a way of organizing the social situation.

In the past, we have been obliged to think of hunger in homeostatic terms: If you don't eat, you will shrivel up and die. There are, unfortunately, countries where that happens all too often. However, I doubt that many of us in the more prosperous nations eat because we would perish if we didn't. Actually, most of us in the developed nations are overweight. We can afford ample food, we like to eat our food, and so we eat a lot of it. This is also true of most rats in developed countries. Most rats do not run around hoping to find a scrap of food. Urban rats know where there is tons of garbage, and rural rats stay close to a silo where there is food for an eternity. Most of the time neither *Homo sapiens* nor *Rattus norvegicus* is in serious peril from hunger. The old seriousness of hunger was part of the mechanistic and behavioristic tradition, typified by Cannon's and Watson's approach, which sought to dismiss all psychological considerations and reduce everything to the physiological.

A particularly interesting aspect of the new perspective is that while we used to be concerned with the body state of hunger, now we are more interested in eating as a kind of behavior. To look at hunger we had to have a depleted body state so we could locate the stimulus that makes the machine move. But when we start to look at eating behavior, we can use our familiar behavioral tools. We can focus on how an individual's feeding behavior depends upon learning, motivation, attitudes, values, social factors, and a host of other things that psychologists like to work on. I think it is exciting that the participants of this conference were not talking about hunger but about feeding behavior. We have moved from the narrow, constraining business of hunger to the free, open space of eating behavior. We have turned a corner.

THE ORGANIZATION OF EATING

Eating is so important that we have to expect it to be multiply determined, and organized in many different ways. I will outline here three different sets of factors that can play an important part in organizing feeding. These are the circadian cycle, the cost of obtaining a meal, and the hedonics of available food.

Everyone organizes their eating into some kind of circadian pattern. Some people eat a hearty breakfast, skip lunch, and then get the other half of their calories at dinner. Other people skip breakfast, grab a snack for lunch, and get nearly all of their calories at dinner. Some people split their dinner into two parts, an early part consisting of "tea," tapas, or martinis, and a later part involving food. But there is an important invariant amidst this variety of patterns: Any given individual is almost sure to be firmly locked into their own pattern, whatever it may be. I do not think I know anyone who skips breakfast half the time, eats a big lunch half the time, and frequently skips dinner. Almost everyone holds true to some fixed pattern.

The major factor that determines when you will eat your next meal is not your blood sugar level, stomach rumblings, or something happening in your hypothalamus; the major determinant is your wristwatch. Somebody sticks their head in your doorway and says "How about lunch?" Do you make a quick check of your body state? No, you consult your wristwatch. Even people with feeding disorders typically show temporally organized feeding patterns. Thus the restraining anorectic usually eats when the other people in the family do, even if their regularly scheduled meal may contain only 100 calories. Habitual bingers nearly always have a special time, often but not necessarily in the evening, when they do their bingeing and purging.

It might be argued that everything in our lives is run by the clock, so that the regularity of our meals does not mean much. Alright, we can check our animal friends. Even though they don't usually have regular working hours, they still demonstrate regular diurnal patterns of behavior. Like us, different animals show different patterns. Some animals eat at dusk and dawn while others eat in the early evening. Some birds eat only in the morning, while others nibble all day long, and an owl will prowl at night. Most animals can adjust their feeding pattern to arbitrary circumstances. If you feed your dog once a day, say when you come home from work, the dog will be happy with that, and will be there full of love to greet you when you get home. If you let your dog eat ad libitum, it will adjust to that just as well, and probably love you just as much.

Many other behaviors are also temporally patterned. Some animals drink mostly in conjunction with their meals. Others gather at the water hole in the early morning and late afternoon. Rats generally do all their mating in the evening, marmots mate in the morning, cats do it without regard to time because they are so dependent upon other stimuli.

It might be argued that all this temporal patterning is shaped by weather, predatory pressures, and other factors that have little to do with eating per se. Alright, we can check some animal experiments. Richter (1927) was the first to show that rats given one meal a day very quickly came to anticipate mealtime each day. Richter's animals showed anticipation by exaggerated running in activity wheels in the hours just before their regular mealtime, but anticipation has also been demonstrated in Skinner boxes and other kinds of apparatus. The form of the anticipatory behavior depends on what stimulus support is present. An interesting feature of the anticipation is that it seems to be inherently tied to the animal's endogenous biological rhythm. Bolles and Stokes (1965) worked with rats that had been born and reared in a 29-hr environment, and then when mature, put on a 29-hr feeding cycle. There animals failed to show any anticipation of the regular meal, in either wheel running or bar pressing. We obtained similar negative results with rats born, reared, and tested on a 19-hr cycle. The effect appears to be intrinsically connected with the natural 24-hr cycle.

Imagine a young woman student who lives in a dormitory and dines every evening at 5:30 sharp. She skips dinner on Friday, however, because she has a 7 o'clock date. Around 5:30, her accustomed time of eating, she is hungry enough to start eating the furniture. But she survives until her date arrives, and is able to wait until 9:00 to finally eat. She does not perish from hypoglycemia during the delay. She will actually lose much of her ferocious appetite over the long delay, because what makes her hungry is the time of day and not her metabolism. I found the same sort of thing in rats (Bolles, 1965); their zest for food began to decline after 24 hrs after the last big meal.

Thus the anticipation of a daily meal seems to be intimately linked with the organism's biological clock. The same is true with two meals a day. Bolles and Moot (1973) fed rats two regular meals a day, and found that both meals were anticipated. Some years ago, Kathleen Chambers and I did some preliminary work with rats that had lab chow continuously available but were given a sugar solution once a day. We thought that if anticipatory activity depended on some temporal conditioning mechanism, and if it reflected learned incentive motivation, then we should have gotten sugar anticipation. But we did not get it, and I have held up publishing anything on the phenomenon until I understood it better. I'm sure we could get it in humans. Suppose you eat ice cream at 9:30 for a couple of evenings. You are likely to get hooked very quickly on 9:30 ice cream, and be pretty uncomfortable trying to break the habit. You will miss your snack and feel deprived, even though you are full, above your mean weight, and still hyperglycemic from dinner.

A second major factor that organizes eating behavior is how much it costs to obtain a meal. About 20 years ago I spent a sabbatical with George Collier. Rutgers was short of offices so I occupied a corner of George's large office. We talked a lot and solved quite a number of problems, but the solution of one particular problem eluded us. The problem was that when rats live in a Skinner box they generally take about 12 meals a day, but Richter (1922) had reported that in his complex apparatus, which required rats to get up and go to where the food was, they took only about six meals a day. Collier started worrying about the discrepancy. He thought about African lions who make a kill every two or three days, and he thought about street pigeons who seemed to nibble at bits of something all day long, in effect, taking countless small meals. After I had gotten out of George's way, he figured it out. If there is a large effort or biological cost involved, then the animal will eat just a few large meals. On the other hand, if the biological cost of a meal is small, that is, food is abundant, then the animal will eat many small meals. The number of meals a day is inversely related to how much a meal costs. The cost of a meal depends upon who the animal is and what it eats; it also depends upon the lifestyle. A big predator eats wonderfully nutritious, high calorie, well-balanced food, but it has to do a lot of work and take a lot of risks to get such good food. So it goes for large prey once in a while. The bird that eats bugs or seeds is getting good food too, but the food comes in small packets and is widely scattered. So the bird may be obliged to eat a large number of tiny meals a day. The herbivore has a similar problem, it has abundant food right underfoot, but it has to eat tons of greenery because vegetation is so low in calories. Everything depends on the lifestyle.

In the laboratory, Collier, Hirsch, and Hamlin (1972) simulated the biological cost of food by making rats press a bar on different schedules to get a meal. They found a strong inverse relationship between the cost of a meal in bar presses and the number of meals taken per day. When the rat was required to make in the order of 4,000 bar presses to get food, it ate once a day. Comparable results have now been obtained with several species and under a variety of experimental conditions, so the basic rule about the cost of a meal has considerable generality. Collier's work is important for several reasons. It gives us a way to look at species differences in feeding patterns. It focuses our attention on the relationship between the animal and its habitat. It makes us think about the quality of food, its caloric value, and so on. It leads us to think about animal lifestyles. In short, it forces us to think about feeding behavior in functional terms.

A third factor that organizes feeding behavior is the hedonics of food. Several of the conference participants have referred to how good a food tastes, and have used that concept to account for how avidly their subjects consumed some food. This sort of an account is both very old and very new. The basic notion that we do (or eat) what gives us pleasure comes from early Greek philosophy, and so is very old. But contemporary animal psychologists and experimentalists who work with human subjects share a behavioristic background, and for many years, behaviorism totally rejected any idea of hedonism. It was too subjective and unscientific. So hedonistic thinking among experimental psychologists is very new. Perhaps none of us at this point is entirely comfortable with this new way of thinking. I will try to clear up a couple of potential problems; perhaps that will make some of us a little more comfortable.

One potential problem was encountered in a series of studies by P. T. Young (e.g., Young & Greene, 1953). When rats were given consumption tests with different concentrations of sugar water, they drank more of the dilute solutions over a 24-hr period, but more of the concentrated solutions on a very short test. Thus there was an ambiguous relationship between how good a sweet solution tastes and how much of it is taken. What Young discovered here is that intake is not a one-dimensional thing, it depends upon hedonics, yes, but also upon other factors, some of which are physiological. The animal cannot eat too much of the concentrated solution without getting into satiation trouble, insulin trouble, caloric surplus, gastric distension, and other problems. A number of physiological mechanisms put the brakes on further consumption. The rat likes 32% sucrose for hedonic reasons (it tastes marvelous), but will not drink very much of it. The rat will drink a lot of 8% sucrose because it tastes pretty good and there are no adverse consequences; it can consume a lot of this isotonic concentration without encountering osmotic problems, surplus calories, or any of the troublesome effects of consuming highly concentrated solutions. We have much the same thing in our own experience. Most of us would admit that candy tastes better than spaghetti. But while most of us would happily eat 1,000 calories of spaghetti for dinner, how many of us could eat 1,000 calories of candy bars (four bars) in one sitting? Young's reaction to the problem was that it was no problem, rather it presented a whole new set of physiological variables to experiment with. I agree.

A second potential problem for modern hedonism is the matter of circularity. Why is the animal eating so much of some particular food? Because it tastes good. How do we know it tastes good? Because the animal is eating so much of it. The argument certainly is circular, but then any such explanatory argument is going to be circular. Explanations in terms of reinforcement, for example, go around in just the same tail-chasing manner. Why is that rat pressing the bar so much? The circle is still there, although it is not so patent if we can get reinforcement effects in different situations, at different times, or with different animals. In short, the problem of circularity is eased if the explanatory principle has some generality, and the more generality it has the better it is going to look. The most important dimension of generality, however, is the size of the community of people who use the explanatory concept. If we could all agree that food pellets are reinforcers, that would be wonderful because then we would all sound like scientists. But if you say food pellets are reinforcers and I say they are incentive motivators, we are back to circles again. Circularity is not a problem, the problem is getting the community to accept an explanatory principle.

Having dispatched those potential difficulties, I can state the first postulate of hedonism: An animal will eat a food if it tastes good. Cabanac (chapter 3, this volume) observes that a given food can taste good or not so good depending on the immediate circumstances. He reports that the relevant circumstances change as the animal continues eating that food. Thus when an animal begins to eat a particular food it has a high hedonic value; it tastes good. But as the animal continues to eat it, it loses hedonic value; it tastes less good. When the momentary hedonic value declines to the point where the food does not taste good at all, the animal stops eating it.

This termination of eating is something different from satiety, however, because the animal may continue eating other foods or even the same food in a new form (Mook, 1988). This sort of dissociation is one reason why we really do not want to think of satiety being some sort of demotivating force that inhibits ingestion. I really don't think we want to think about satiety at all. To do so invites us to return to the old ways, of searching for satiety stimuli and receptor sites, back where we came from. I think it better to look at the behavior. One thing we have discovered about ingestive behavior is that animals quickly learn to eat less of a food that supplies more calories, even though they may like it more. Young and Greene (1953) found this effect with innate sugar preferences, and Booth, Lovett, and McSherry (1972) found it with learned preferences based on flavors arbitrarily assigned to different calorie-valued foods. Booth's argument was that a high-calorie food quickly produces satiety, which then conditions satiety-inducing effects on the taste and other stimulus properties of the food. When the animal encounters it the next time, it will eat less of it because its level of satiety will have been increased. A separate preference test showed that when hungry, the animal did prefer the flavors paired with rapid satiation, the high-calorie flavors.

While Booth's basic effect seems clear, the interpretation of it as a conditioning phenomenon has been a little cloudy. It was not clear whether satiety was a response that got conditioned, a stimulus whose motivational properties got transferred to the arbitrary flavor stimulus, or just how it should be handled. Moreover, in the past 20 years conditioning theory has changed a good deal so that it has become mainly a matter of predictive relationships. Does a high-calorie flavor "predict" satiety, and that is why the animal eats less of it? Booth's learned satiety phenomenon does not fit comfortably into the conditioning paradigm, and so we have one more reason for not thinking about satiety. Let us approach the problem as a hedonist would, and see if we cannot straighten it out.

John Garcia (1989) has argued that there is another kind of conditioning, something quite different from the Pavlovian variety. He has proposed that it involves not the attachment of a "conditioned response" to an arbitrary stimulus, but rather a change in the hedonic value of the stimulus. If the stimulus was initially neutral, then it will begin to acquire the hedonic value of events that follow. It is hedonic shift learning, rather than the learning of a new response. In Garcia's own experiments the consequence is typically illness and so the shift in the hedonics of the taste of a food is usually from neutral or positive to negative. That is the Garcia effect. But we have found that the mechanisms can work the other way around. In Booth's laboratory, and in my own, we used positive aftereffects and we found that an arbitrary flavor, which is experimentally associated with caloric relief for a hungry animal, came very quickly to be preferred. There was an upward shift in hedonic value of the flavor.

There remains the other part of the phenomenon, namely, that although the animal likes the stimulus properties of the good food very much, it also learns to eat less of it. There is, indeed, something like Booth's conditioned satiety (although we do not want to call it that). Mehiel and Bolles (1988) have suggested a possible mechanism. We proposed that the secretion of the digestive hormone cholecystokinin (CCK) is conditionable, and that highly preferred, high-calorie foods release more CCK. We have discovered the candy bar again! You love the way it tastes, but it very quickly turns you off. The turnoff occurs not because of direct postingestional effects, such as osmotic problems and the secretion of insulin, but because, through prior conditioning, the taste of it releases so much CCK.

The hedonic point of view is new and unfamiliar, but it looks as though it might enrich our understanding of feeding behavior. It promises to be an important factor in the organization of consummatory behavior.

It is much too early to know if my suggested CCK mechanism has any validity, whether hedonic shift learning makes any sense, or whether the hedonic approach to these matters will be useful. But however these specific issues turn out, it is clear that we have turned a corner, and that suddenly we can see entirely new, inviting vistas ahead.

References

Bolles, R. C. (1965). Consummatory behavior in rats maintained aperiodically. *Journal of Comparative and Physiological Psychology, 60,* 239-243.

Bolles, R. C., & Moot, S. A. (1973). The rat's anticipation of two meals a day. *Journal of Comparative and Physiological Psychology, 83,* 510-514.

Bolles, R. C., & Stokes, L. W. (1965). Rat's anticipation of diurnal and a-diurnal feeding. *Journal of Comparative and Physiological Psychology, 60,* 290-294.

Booth, D. A., Lovett, D., & McSherry, G. M. (1972). Postingestive modulation of the sweetness preference gradient in the rat. *Journal of Comparative and Physiological Psychology, 78,* 485-512.

Cannon, W. B., & Washburn, A. L. (1912). An explanation of hunger, *American Journal of Physiology, 29,* 441-454.

Collier, G., Hirsch, E., & Hamlin, P. (1972). The ecological determinants of reinforcement. *Physiology & Behavior, 9,* 705-716.

Descartes, R. (1911). *Passions of the soul.* In E. S. Haldane & G. R. T. Ross (Eds.), *Descartes, philosophical writings.* Cambridge, England: Cambridge University Press. (Original work published in 1649).

Freud, S. (1915). Instincts and their vicissitudes. In J. Strachey (Ed.), *Sigmund Freud: Collected papers.* New York: Basic Books.

Garcia, J. (1989). Food for Tolman: Conditioning and cathexis in concert. In T. Archer & L. Nilsson (Eds.), *Aversion, avoidance, anxiety: Perspectives on aversively motivated behavior.* Hillsdale, NJ: Erlbaum.

Hull, C. L. (1943). *Principles of behavior.* New York: Appleton.

McDougall, W. (1932). *The energies of man.* London: Methuen.

Mehiel, R. & Bolles, R. C. (1988). Learned flavor preferences based on calories are independent of initial hedonic value. *Animal Learning and Behavior, 16,* 383-387.

Mook, D. G. (1988). On the organization of satiety. *Appetite, 11,* 23-39.

Richter, C. P. (1922). A behavioristic study of the activity of the rat. *Comparative Psychology Monographs, 1*(Whole No. 2).

Richter, C. P. (1927). Animal behavior and internal drives. *Quarterly Review of Biology, 2,* 307-343.

Tinklepaugh, O. L. (1928). An experimental study of representative factors in the monkey. *Journal of Comparative Psychology, 8,* 197-236.

Young, P. T., & Greene, J. T. (1953). Quantity of food ingested as a measure of relative acceptability. *Journal of Comparative and Physiological Psychology, 46,* 288-294.

CHAPTER 2

LEARNING, HOMEOSTASIS, AND THE CONTROL OF FEEDING BEHAVIOR

HARVEY P. WEINGARTEN

It used to be fashionable to ask whether learning and experience were important in the control of food intake. This question is no longer controversial. The evidence that experience and learning are critical in all aspects of ingestive behavior is overwhelming. For example, learning is a potent mechanism for eliciting meals: Meals motivated by learned controls are as large or larger than meals elicited by potent pharmacological insults or direct application of neuro-transmitters to the brain (Weingarten, 1985). The ability of animals to select appropriately from an array of foods—the problem of diet selection—cannot be adequately understood until the importance of experience in this process is recognized (Galef, Kennett, & Wigmore, 1984; Sclafani, this volume; Tordoff, Tepper, & Friedman, 1987). Studies of meal termination provide innumerable demonstrations of conditioned satiety in rats and humans (Booth, 1985). Although bold assertions—such as "satiety is a conditioned reflex" (Booth 1977; Stunkard, 1975)—heralding the exclusivity of experience in the control of food intake are premature, it appears that experience plays an important role in determining when animals initiate and terminate meals and how much they eat at those meals. Anyone denying the importance of learning in the control of ingestion has been either negligent in the reading of the literature or blind to anything associated with experience.

This presentation, and the data described herein, were supported by funds from the Natural Sciences and Engineering Research Council of Canada. I thank Michel Bédard for permission to reveal our hitherto unpublished data. Address correspondence and reprint requests to Dr. H.P. Weingarten, Department of Psychology, McMaster University, Hamilton, Ontario, Canada L8S 4K1.

We should recognize that in spite of the view that learning and experience are important controllers of ingestion, and the orientation of the contributions to this volume, only a small portion of the research on ingestive behavior examines the contribution of these variables. I reviewed all of the articles with food intake as a dependent variable in three primary journals over the years 1980 through 1988. These articles were then classified according to the categories listed in Table 1. Only 48 or 5% of the 942 articles reviewed dealt with learning and experience in any way. These numbers suggest that experimental consideration of learning and experience was a minor concern of those interested in understanding the physiology of eating. Ironically, more people investigated glucostatic controls of eating—a theory textbooks insist we no longer believe in—than the role of experience.

Thus the issue is not whether learning can control eating, but why we should pursue a learning or experiential analysis of ingestion. This is the question I will address in this chapter. I suggest two important reasons for exploring the role of these variables in ingestive behavior:

1. Studies of the role of experience provide powerful preparations for analyzing food intake control systems.
2. Studies of the role of experience are critical to elucidate how energy stores are regulated.

LEARNING AS A MEANS OF ANALYZING FOOD INTAKE CONTROL MECHANISMS

Two of my laboratory experiments illustrate how preparations developed to analyze the role of learning can be exploited for the more general purpose of studying mechanisms—especially biological ones—underlying feeding behavior.

Postingestive Consequence Conditioning

When organisms eat they form associations between a sensory property of the food (e.g., its taste) and the subsequent postingestive consequences of the ingested nutrient (Young, 1957). This learning is termed *taste to postingestive consequence conditioning*. Taste to postingestive consequence associations are believed to direct food selection and influence meal size. To analyze the mechanisms underlying this learning it is necessary to possess a clear marker for the presence of a learned association between a food's taste and its postingestive consequences. Some assume that a food preference is sufficient to index a taste to postingestive consequence association (e.g., Tordoff et al., 1987). However, this evidence is indirect. The data below establish a direct behavioral marker of a taste to postingestive consequence association.

This analysis depends upon a feature of sham feeding first described by Davis and Campbell (1973) and presented in greater detail by Mook, Culberson, Gilbert, and McDonald (1983). This characteristic, illustrated in Figure 1, is a

Table 1

CLASSIFICATION OF FEEDING-RELATED ARTICLES BY TOPIC FOR YEARS 1980–1988 INCLUSIVE

Journal	Neural Controls	Peptides	Pharmacological/ Hormonal Controls	Glucostatic Controls	Palatability	Learning & Experience	Unclassified[a]	Total
Physiology & Behavior	110	112	81	63	56	27	180	629
Appetite	32	15	23	12	50	10	81	223
JCPP/Behavioral Neuroscience	33	5	13	1	8	11	19	90
TOTAL	175	132	117	76	114	48	280	942
%	19	14	12	8	12	5	30	

[a]Unclassified denotes that the article did not conform to any of the other categories.

Acquisition Sham Feeding:

18% Sucrose

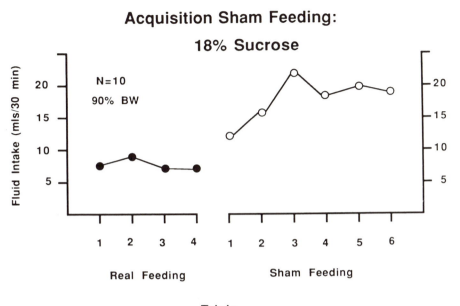

Figure 1 Thirty-min intakes of rats normal and sham feeding 18% sucrose. Trials were on successive days. Rats were maintained at 90% and libitum body weight. Note the reduced intake on the first sham feeding trial, and the gradual elevation of the same feeding response with additional sham feeding trials. Data shown are group means (*N*=10).

gradual rise in the magnitude of sham feeding with repeated sham feeding opportunities. There are many reasons why rats might take small meals upon initial exposure to sham feeding: the novelty of the testing situation or surprise at the absence of postingestive events. We present two experiments, however, that confirm that attenuated sham feeding upon initial exposure must be considered an associative learning phenomenon and that this event is the behavioral assay for a taste to postingestive consequence association (Weingarten & Kulikovsky, 1989).

If attenuated sham feeding represents a nonassociative phenomenon that nonselectively competes with a large feeding response on an initial trial, it should be observed regardless of the food animals experience on the first sham feed. In contrast, if the reduction of sham feeding reflects an associative learning-based expectation of postingestive consequence, it should be apparent with only those foods with which the animal has had normal feeding experience. This was tested using the protocol shown in Table 2. In Phase 1, both groups received extensive sham feeding experience with 36% sucrose flavored with either almond or lemon. The animals' normal feed was either almond-flavored (Group 1) or lemon-flavored (Group 2) sucrose for six trials in Phase 2. During Phase 3, both groups sham fed both lemon- and almond-flavored sucrose. The results, shown in Figure 2, indicated that a gradual rise in sham feeding was seen only when rats were eating foods with which they had normal feeding experience. When they sham

Table 2

PROTOCOL FOR STIMULUS SPECIFICITY STUDY

Group	Phase 1	Phase 2	Phase 3
1	$SF_{A\&L}$	NF_A	$SF_{A\&L}$
2	$SF_{A\&L}$	NF_L	$SF_{A\&L}$

Note. SF = sham feed; NF = normal feed; A = almond-flavored 36% sucrose; L = lemon-flavored 36% sucrose.

fed a food with which they had no postingestional experience, the level of sham feeding was asymptotic, even on the first trial.

A second experiment, summarized in Table 3, provides additional confirmation that an initial, attenuated sham-feeding response marks a taste to postingestive consequence association. This experiment relied on the associative learning phenomenon of latent inhibition. Latent inhibition refers to a reduced capacity to form a conditioned stimulus (CS)-unconditioned stimulus (US) association because of prior exposure to the CS alone. Operationally, latent inhibition is produced by exposing an animal repeatedly to the CS in the absence of the US. Then, the animal is provided with CS-US pairings appropriate to establish a CS-US association and, as a consequence of the latent inhibition pretreatment, a reduced level of learning is revealed. Sham feeding is ideal for this experimental

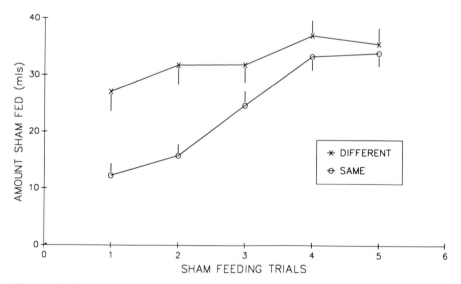

Figure 2 Change in the magnitude of sham feeding with repeated sham feeding experience during Phase 3 of the stimulus specificity experiment. SAME refers to trials where rats sham fed the same food that they normally fed in Phase 2. DIFFERENT refers to trials where rats sham fed the flavored food they did not normally feed in Phase 2. Data shown are group means ($N=16$). An attenuated sham feeding response is restricted to foods the rats fed on normally (i.e., experienced its postingestive effects).

Table 3

PROTOCOL FOR LATENT INHIBITION STUDY

Group	Phase 1	Phase 2	Phase 3
CONDITION	SF_A	NF_L	SF_L
LATENT INHIBITION	$SF_{A\&L}$	NF_L	SF_L
CONTROL	SF_A	SF_A	SF_L

Note. SF = sham feed; NF = normal feed; A = almond-flavored 36% sucrose; L = lemon-flavored 36% sucrose.

maneuver because the CS (i.e., taste) can be presented in the absence of the US (i.e., postingestive consequence) by simply allowing the animal to sham feed (cannula open). Good CS-US pairings are provided during normal feeding (cannula closed) when the animal experiences both the CS and US. The goal of this experiment was to see whether latent inhibition eliminated the attenuated sham feeding response on initial trials. If so, this would support the idea that rats form an association between a food's taste and its postingestive consequences during normal feeding, and that reduced sham feeding is the marker of that association. Three groups of rats were tested. The first group (CONDITION) sham fed almond-flavored 36% sucrose in Phase 1. In Phase 2, they received two normal feeding trials in which to associate the flavor of lemon with its postingestive events. During Phase 3, the presence of this association was investigated by allowing animals to sham feed lemon-flavored sucrose for the first time. Based upon the previous experiment, we expected an attenuated sham feeding response.

The second group of rats (LATENT INHIBITION) were exposed to lemon sham feeding in Phase 1. In Phase 2, they received the identical opportunity as the CONDITION animals to form a lemon to postingestive consequence association. In Phase 3, the sham feeding response to lemon was measured. If the reduced sham feeding on initial trials reflects an associative learning process, the LATENT INHIBITION rats should have been impaired in their ability to form a lemon to postingestive consequence association in Phase 2. In addition, if reduced sham feeding reflects a taste to postingestive consequence association, the LATENT INHIBITION rats should have shown no reduction of eating on the first sham feed in Phase 3.

The CONTROL group provided the expected magnitude of sham feeding of animals that have had no experience with lemon-flavored sucrose. The results, presented in Figure 3, demonstrated that LATENT INHIBITION animals showed no attenuation of sham feeding in Phase 3. These data indicate that during normal feeding, rats form associations between the taste of a food and its postingestive consequence, and that an attenuated initial sham intake is the behavioral marker for the existence of that association.

It is now possible to use this behavioral marker to examine the properties and mechanisms of taste to postingestive consequence conditioning. For example,

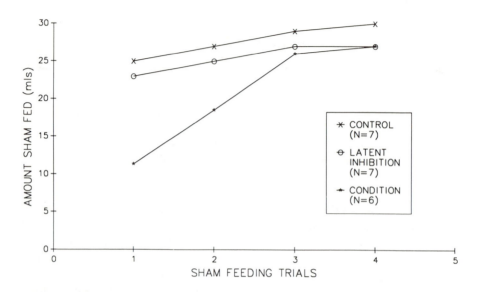

Figure 3 Change in the magnitude of sham feeding in Phase 3 of the latent inhibition study. Data shown are group means ±1 SEM. Note that rats that have been subjected to a latent inhibition procedure showed no reduction of sham feeding on the initial trial.

it is not known which postingestive consequences become associated with taste (although nutrient utilization in the liver may be relevant [Tordoff et al., 1987]). Sham feeding permits the systematic replacement of discrete postingestive events such as intraportal, systemic, or central infusions of various substances, and observing which of these are sufficient to support a taste to postingestive consequence association.

Conditioned Feeding Studies

Conditioned feeding uses standard Pavlovian conditioning procedures to teach an association between a neutral cue (a CS such as a tone or light) and food. After this conditioning, exposure to the food-associated cue elicits a robust and reliable eating response even in sated rats (Weingarten, 1984). Conditioned feeding is ideal for dissecting behavioral and physiological controls of eating because—in a single test session—it reveals the entire repertoire of responses associated with the feeding bout. Specifically, when the CS is on, but prior to the presentation of food, the animal exhibits the *appetitive phase* of eating. These behaviors are manifest in anticipation of eating, are presumed to reflect the animal's motivation to eat, and are measured by the amount of time rats poke their heads into the food cup in the anticipation of a meal and the latency to eat once the food is presented. Once the meal is delivered, the *consummatory phase* of eating can be measured with all of its indices, the most important of which is meal size. The current feeding literature is fixated on the consummatory phase of eating and meal size. With rare exceptions (e.g., Cox & Smith, 1987), there is no consideration of the appetitive phase of eating. This is especially ironic because contemporary physiological psychology has also emphasized the importance of gut afferents in the control of food intake. Yet, when the role of gut afferents was initially considered (e.g., Cannon & Washburn, 1912) these events were presumed to reflect motivation to eat and were not considered to be involved in the control of meal size per se.

Conditioned feeding can be used to demonstrate that the failure to consider both phases of meal taking provides a distorted view of feeding behavior controls. For example, Michel Bédard and I examined the ability of food-associated conditioned cues to promote ingestion in the light and dark phases of the day-night cycle. These data are shown in Figure 4. Given the habit of nocturnal eating in the rat, it is not surprising that rats appeared more motivated to eat in the dark than in the light; they showed more anticipatory nosepoking and a shorter latency to eat in the dark than the light. Importantly, however, once the animals actually made contact with the food, the duration of eating and the total amount eaten were equivalent in the day and the night. Measurements of meal size only would fail to reveal a day or night difference in eating control when one is clearly evident.

In an extensive study, Weingarten and Martin (1989) examined further the relationship between, and mechanisms mediating, appetitive and consummatory phases of eating. For example, making animals averse to the signalled food does not affect appetitive responding but dramatically diminishes consumption. Opiate antagonism reduces consumption but has no impact on appetitive responding. Conversely, dopamine antagonism reduces appetitive behavior but has no impact on meal size once the meal is initiated. These examples confirm that the commonly used term hunger incorporates at least two distinct processes mediated by different physiological mechanisms. The present emphasis on the appetitive/consummatory distinction is of no surprise to anyone familiar with historical analyses of motivated behavior (e.g., Craig, 1913). However, contemporary analyses of food intake have largely forgotten about appetitive components of eating and our understanding of ingestive behavior will be inadequate until consideration of appetitive mechanisms is resurrected. The conditioned feeding paradigm is ideal for such studies.

THE RELATIONSHIP BETWEEN LEARNING AND REGULATION

I also suggest that studies of learning are critical to our understanding of energy regulation. Demonstrations that learning and experience affect ingestion are not the final aims in the analysis of food intake control systems. The ultimate problem is to understand how the organism controls its eating to maintain energy homeostasis and, thus to survive. Ever since Claude Bernard ushered in the modern era of regulatory studies, maintenance of appropriate energy stores and flux has been recognized as one of the great and essential regulations accomplished by the body.

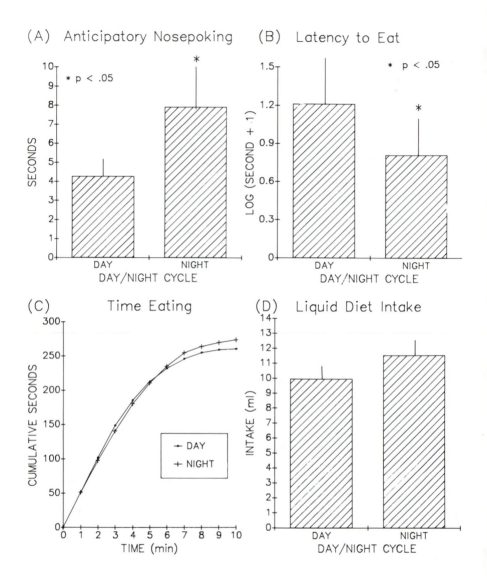

Figure 4 Comparison of appetitive and consummatory responses to a food-associated conditioned stimulus presented in the day or in the night. Appetitive phase measures anticipatory nosepoking (A) and latency to eat (B). Consummatory phase measures time spent eating (C) and diet intake (D). Appetitive measures are elevated in the dark reflecting an enhanced food motivation even though the actual meal sizes in the day and in the night were not different.

Almost all feeding conferences impose either an implicit or explicit distinction between experiential and regulatory controls of eating. This dichotomy, I believe, represents a fundamental misunderstanding of the nature of regulatory systems. Regulation of energy could not occur without the assistance of learning. The logic behind this assertion is revealed by a brief review of the architecture of regulatory systems. My presentation of regulation, and my use of terms has been shaped by Houk (1988) and Horrobin (1970). An excellent presentation of arguments similar to the ones I express here is in Davis (1980) and Hogan (1980).

Figure 5A represents the backbone of any regulated system, the negative feedback loop. The response which is defended is the regulated variable. Negative feedback accomplishes regulation by detecting the regulated variable (or some correlate of it), computing whether the level of that variable is appropriate and, if not, activating effector mechanisms to correct the imbalance. Negative feedback models have dominated analyses of food intake control. It is often assumed that the body monitors energy availability and when a state of depletion is sensed, hunger is activated and meals are initiated. As a consequence of eating, calories are absorbed and the state of energy depletion is redressed. Although different theories of meal initiation differ in their candidate for the regulated variable and location of the sensor, almost all share the negative feedback conceptualization of how meals are controlled and energy regulation accomplished (i.e., Weingarten, 1985).

Negative feedback may be sufficient to explain temperature regulation in a house (the classic example), but, it is inadequate to explain how complex biological functions like energy or temperature homeostasis. There are several fundamental limitations of regulation based on negative feedback. First, systems based on negative feedback are unstable because they require error in the regulated variable before corrections are initiated. Second, regulation controlled by negative feedback tends to be slow. Finally and most importantly, the behavior of many physiological regulated events does not conform to a negative feedback model. For example, a change in internal body temperature (the regulated temperature variable) is almost never seen when an organism moves from a warm environment to a cold environment even though this is the predicted result if temperature regulation was mediated solely by negative feedback. The analysis of many regulated biological systems yields the necessary conclusion that features in addition to negative feedback are necessary to explain the observed properties of the regulation.

One of these additional features is the feedforward loop shown in Figure 5B. Feedforward contains a disturbance detector which detects the presence of factors or forces which disturb the regulated variable. The key advantage conferred by feedforward is to permit the regulated system to compensate for anticipated perturbations prior to them having any impact on the regulated variable. Feedforward increases the speed and stability of regulation. In the case of body temperature, disturbance detectors in the skin detect changes in environmental temperature and activate thermoregulatory mechanisms to compensate for antici-

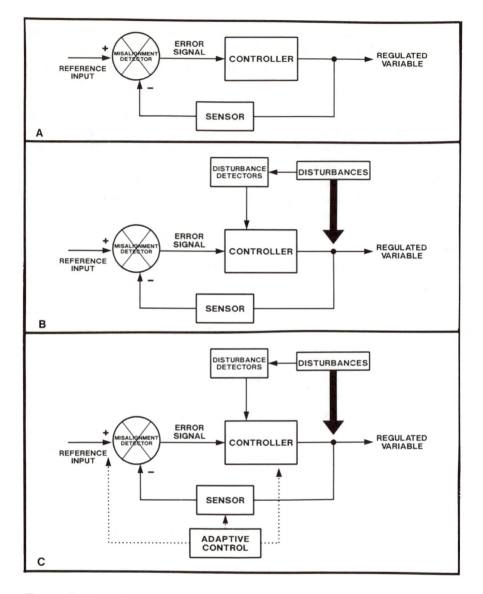

Figure 5 The architecture of regulated systems. (A) Negative feedback; (B) The addition of feedforward; (C) The addition of adaptive controls.

pated disturbances of internal temperature prior to any changes in the internal temperature itself.

The incorporation of feedforward in a homeostatic system does raise some problems. The major one is the possibility that the disturbance detector will activate compensatory responses in expectation of a disturbance which is never actually encountered. In these situations, feedforward can induce an error in the regulated variable. To protect against this possibility, many feedforward loops in biological systems activate only small, compensatory adjustments.

The emphasis on cybernetics in the late 1950's made it clear that feedback and feedforward were still insufficient to explain regulation of complex acts. A third level of control was required. This was termed adaptive control. Adaptive control is the process by which a regulatory system learns about its environment and uses that information to adjust its own regulatory machinery to permit more effective regulation. The mechanisms by which adaptive control amend the regulatory system are often unclear. As indicated in Figure 5C, adaptive control may adjust sensitivity of sensors, the reference input, or effector mechanisms. Adaptive control can also be anticipatory; for example, an organism can activate effector mechanisms in advance of any change of the regulated variable because it has learned to expect some perturbing event. The operational distinction between adaptive control and feedforward is the necessity for learning. Feedforward is often assumed to be hard-wired and, therefore, functions on the very first exposure to a disturbance. In contrast, the emergence of adaptive control requires experience with the environment and learning about disturbances and their consequences. Thus, adaptive controls become manifest only after several trials. Classical conditioning is the type of learning often used to model the development of adaptive control.

The following thought experiment illustrates in a concrete way the relationship between these three levels of regulation and the maintenance of homeostasis. Consider the problem of Canadians who are required to thermoregulate in the cold of winter. There are three possible ways to solve this problem of thermoregulation, each corresponding to one of the regulatory levels described. One could rely exclusively on negative feedback: An individual could venture outside and when a drop of internal temperature was sensed, initiate behavioral or physiological thermoregulation. Alternatively, one might rely on feedforward: Upon venturing outside and sensing one's skin getting cold, an individual might activate thermoregulation in anticipation of an actual drop in internal temperature. Finally, one could rely on adaptive control: An individual recognizing that it is February in Canada, emits thermoregulatory responses (i.e., dressing appropriately) in order to maintain body temperature at some appropriate level.

Although the example I used to illustrate adaptive control was laced with heavy doses of cognition, one should recognize that adaptive control requires neither consciousness nor cognition. Robots demonstrate adaptive control over mechanisms regulating movement. For a more relevant example, consider the following experiment. Rats were trained to sham feed in a distinctive environment. They then normal fed in that environment for the first time. On that day, we observed an approximate doubling of meal size, compared to normal feeds on subsequent days (Weingarten & Kulikovsky, 1989). What accounted for the excess eating on the first normal feed? Presumably, the animal received all of the inhibitory postingestive feedback on that trial (in fact, more than the usual amount because meal size was so high). Yet, the rat failed to register those satiety signals or chose to minimize them because of the previous sham feeding history. With additional normal feed experience, the rat's behavior was once again sensitive to these internal signals. The experience-induced shift in responsiveness to identical internal signals was a manifestation of adaptive control—the mechanisms controlling meal size adapted to take into account recent experience.

It is impossible to generate an exact percentage reflecting contribution of negative feedback, feedforward, and adaptive control to the regulatory process. It is quite likely that all three interact to maintain homeostasis. However, these two things are apparent. First, behavior is often necessary for biological homeostasis. Curt Richter (1942–1943) argued this exact point eloquently and forcefully many years ago. Second, it would be impossible for humans to regulate as well as they do, and to exploit the range of environments they do, were it not for the presence of adaptive controls of regulation. It becomes clear from this discussion that learning is not dichotomous with regulation. Rather, learning is essential for regulation and, in fact, may be one of the primary mechanisms by which homeostasis is achieved. We should not presume that adaptive controls of regulation operate via idiosyncratic or unique physiological mechanisms. Rather, the more parsimonious view is that adaptive controls exploit exactly the same pathways and mechanisms which physiologists steeped in the negative feedback tradition have identified as important.

References

Booth, D. A. (1977). Satiety and appetite are conditioned responses. *Psychosomatic Medicine, 39,* 79–81.

Booth, D. A. (1985). Food-conditioned eating preferences and aversions with interoceptive elements: Conditioned appetites and satieties. *Annals New York Academy of Sciences, 443,* 22–42.

Cannon, W. B., & Washburn, A. L. (1912). An explanation of hunger. *American Journal of Physiology, 29,* 441–454.

Cox, J. E., & Smith, M. J. (1987). Dose-dependent interaction between cholecystokinin and sham feeding. *Behavioral Brain Research, 26,* 109–117.

Craig, W. (1913). Appetites and aversions of constituents of instinct. *Biological Bulletin, 34,* 91–107.

Davis, J. D. (1980). Homeostasis, feedback and motivation. In F. M. Toates, & T. R. Halliday (Eds.), *Analysis of motivational processes.* New York: Academic Press, 23–37.

Davis, J. D., & Campbell, C. S. (1973). Peripheral control of meal size in the rat: Effect of sham feeding on meal size and drinking rate. *Journal of Comparative and Physiological Psychology, 83,* 379–387.

Galef, B. G., Kennett, D. J., & Wigmore, S. W. (1984). Transfer of information concerning distant foods in rats: A robust phenomenon. *Animal Learning and Behavior, 12,* 292–296.

Hogan, J. A. (1980). Homeostasis and behavior. In F. M. Toates & T. R. Halliday (Eds.), *Analysis of motivational processes* (pp. 3–21). New York: Academic Press.

Horrobin, D. F. (1970). *Principles of biological control.* Aylesbur, England: Medical and Technical Publishing Co. Ltd.

Houk, J. C. (1988). Control strategies in physiological systems. *Federation of American Societies for Experimental Biology Journal, 2,* 97–107.

Mook, D. G., Culberson, R., Gelbert, R. J., & McDonald, K. (1983). Oropharyngeal control of ingestion in rats: Acquisition of sham-drinking patterns. *Behavioral Neuroscience, 97,* 574–584.

Richter, C. (1942–1943). Total self-regulatory functions in animals and human beings. *Harvey Lecturers, 38,* 63–103.

Stunkard, A. (1975). Satiety is a conditioned reflex. *Psychosomatic Medicine, 37,* 383–387.

Tordoff, M. G., Tepper, B. J., & Friedman, M. I. (1987). Food flavor preferences produced by drinking glucose and oil in normal and diabetic rats: Evidence for conditioning based on fuel oxidation. *Physiology & Behavior, 41,* 481–487.

Weingarten, H. P. (1984). Meal initiation controlled by learned cues: Basic behavioral properties. *Appetite, 5,* 147–158.

Weingarten, H. P. (1985). Stimulus control of eating: Implications for a two-factor theory of hunger. *Appetite, 6,* 387–401.

Weingarten, H. P., & Kulikovsky, O. (1989). Taste to postingestive consequence conditioning: Is the rise in sham feeding with repeated experience a learning phenomenon? *Physiology & Behavior, 45,* 471–476.

Weingarten, H. P., & Martin, G. P. (1989). Mechanisms of conditioned meal initiation. *Physiology & Behavior, 45,* 735–740.

Young, P. T. (1957). Physiologic factors regulating the feeding process. *American Journal of Clinical Nutrition, 5,* 154–161.

CHAPTER 3

TASTE: THE MAXIMIZATION OF MULTIDIMENSIONAL PLEASURE

MICHEL CABANAC

It is generally assumed that a motivated behavior is oriented by the incentives received by the subjects (Nutin, 1975; Toates, 1986). In the case of physiological function, it has been shown that the wisdom of the body is to seek pleasure and avoid displeasure (Cabanac, 1971). Relations exist between pleasure and usefulness and between displeasure and harm or danger. For example, the pleasure aroused by a skin thermal stimulus can be predicted from the subject's deep body temperature (Attia, 1984; Cabanac, 1981). A hypothermic subject will experience pleasure when stimulated with heat and displeasure when stimulated with cold. The opposite takes place in a hyperthermic subject. Pleasure is observable only in transient states—when the stimulus helps the subject to return to normothermia. As soon as the subject returns to normothermia, all stimuli lose their strong pleasure component and tend to become indifferent. Sensory pleasure and displeasure thus appear to be especially well-suited as motivators of thermoregulatory behavior. In one study (Cabanac, Massonnet, & Belaiche, 1972), subjects' preference switched from hot water to cold water when deep body temperature evolved from hypo- to hyperthermia and reciprocally. In this case, pleasure was so dependent on body temperatures that it was possible to produce simple mathematical models predicting the preferred skin temperature of the subject (Figure 1).

Pleasurable tastes and flavors show an identical behavior pattern. Alimentary flavors are pleasurable during hunger and become unpleasant or indifferent during satiety. Measurement of human ingestive behavior confirms this relationship between behavior and pleasure. Human subjects tend to consume stimuli that they report to be pleasant and avoid stimuli that they report to be unpleasant

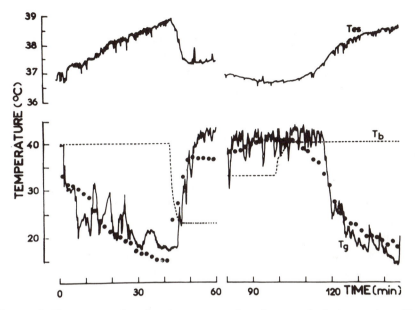

Figure 1 Time course of preferred temperature based on core body temperature. Time course of body core temperature (Tes), bath temperature (Tb), and preferred temperature (Tg) of a subject immersed up to the chin in water. Preferred temperature was recorded in a glove perfused with thermostated water on the subject's left hand. The subject's right hand commanded the thermostat regulating the temperature of the water flowing into the glove. The dots indicate the theoretical temperature preferred by the subject as computed periodically from the bath temperature, core temperature, and the following model: Tpref = −0.3 Tbath (Tes −36.3) + 44. All temperatures in degrees Celsius.

This shows that it is possible to predict from physiological variables the pleasure aroused by a temperature applied to a subject's skin. From "Preferred Skin Temperature as a Function of Internal and Mean Skin Temperature" by M. Cabanac, M. Massonnet, and R. Belaiche, 1972, *Journal of Applied Physiology; 33*, p. 701. Copyright 1972 by American Psychological Society. Reprinted by permission.

(Fantino, 1984). This preference shows a qualitative influence: Human subjects ingest what they like. Pleasure shows a quantitative influence also: The amount eaten is a function of alimentary restrictions and increases after dieting when negative alliesthesia has disappeared. The result is that pleasure scales can be used to judge the acceptability of food.

Comparable results were obtained in rat studies. Grill & Norgren (1978) observed that rats display a facial mimic in response to gustatory stimuli. When a palatable stimulus was injected into the rat's mouth, the animal responded with a characteristic facial pattern including chewing, opening the upper lip, licking, and so on. On the other hand, the rat responded to an unpleasant, bitter taste with opening the lower lip, rubbing its chin on the floor, drooling, and so forth. This response, which can be dissociated from ingestion, is therefore an open loop situation (Berridge & Grill, 1984). In a series of experiments Grill and Norgren

(1978) showed that the rat's mimic was not invariably linked to the stimulus. On the contrary, rats responded with opposite mimics to a given stimulus when their internal state was manipulated. Sucrose aroused ingestive mimics in naive rats while pairing sweet sensation with lithium chloride sucrose aroused aversive mimics (Berridge, Flynn, Schulkin, & Grill, 1984; Berridge, Grill, & Norgren, 1981; Grill & Norgren, 1978). This technique was also used to study the influence of glucose gastric loads on the palatability of sucrose. In the minutes following infusion of glucose into the stomach, rats changed their initially positive responses to sucrose to aversive responses (Figure 2). Thus rats present the whole pattern of gustatory alliesthesia, short- and long-term, and negative and positive. The results of psychological studies of pleasure on humans can therefore be extended with little risk of error to animals. It can also be accepted that sensory pleasure is adapted to the defence of homeostasis in animals.

Thus the seeking of pleasure and the avoidance of displeasure lead to homeostatic behaviors. Pleasure therefore indicates a useful stimulus and simultaneously motivates the subject to approach the stimulus. Both a reward and a

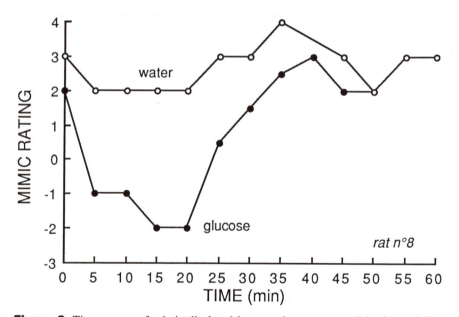

Figure 2 Time course of mimic displayed by a rat in response to injections of 50 μl sucrose solution. A sucrose solution was injected every 5 min into the rat's mouth. At time zero the rat received 5 ml intra gastric of either pure water (o), or water containing 1 g glucose (•). The response was estimated by an observer unaware of the nature of the gastric load and quantified as +1, +2, and so on when 1, 2, and so forth ingestive signs were displayed, and as −1, −2, and so forth when 1, 2, and so on aversive signs were displayed. Data from "Postingestive Alliesthesia: The Rat Tells the Same Story" by M. Cabanac and L. LaFrance, 1990, *Physiology & Behavior, 47*, pp. 539–543. Copyright 1990 by Pergamon Press Inc.

motivation, pleasure leads to optimization of life mechanisms. One great advantage of this mechanism is that it does not take a high level of cognition to produce a behavior adapted to biological goals. As soon as a stimulus is discriminated, the affective dimension of the sensation aroused tells the subject, animal or human, that the stimulus should be sought or be avoided.

In daily life, however, a stimulus rarely comes alone; a motivation is seldom solitary. On the contrary, a subject must constantly rank simultaneous motivations. One basic postulate of ethology is that behavior tends to satisfy the most urgent need of the subject (Baerends, 1956; Tinbergen, 1950), but nothing is said on why a subject ranks conflicting motivations in a given order. Since pleasure leads to optimization of behavior in situations where only one motivation is present it may be hypothesized that maximization of pleasure might lead to the solution of conflicts of motivations, also. To verify that hypothesis the following must be demonstrated: subjects placed in situations of conflict tend to maximize their sensory pleasure, and maximizing their sensory pleasure is consistent with optimizing behavior.

MAXIMIZATION OF MULTIDIMENSIONAL SENSORY PLEASURE

The assumption that subjects tend to maximize their total sensory pleasure was recently verified, in the case of taste, when subjects were placed in bidimensional sensory spaces (Cabanac & Ferber, 1987). The rating of pleasure aroused by stimuli was compared with the actual behavior choice displayed by the subject (Figure 3). The stimuli were presented in matrices. In these experiments, the subjects were invited to rate their pleasure in one dimension of the matrix of stimuli in one session, and then in the second dimension in a second session. This situation has been extensively studied by Drewnowski and his colleagues (Drewnowski, Bellisle, Aimez, & Remy, 1987; Drewnowski, Brunzell, Sande, Iverius, & Greenwood, 1985; Drewnowski & Greenwood, 1983; Drewnowski, Halmi, Pierce, Gibbs, & Smith, 1987) by combining fat and sweet in a matrix of stimuli and recording the bidimensional pleasure aroused in controls and various patients. In two additional sessions, the subjects were invited to select their preferred stimulus while manipulating one dimension of the matrix.

A combination of sweet gustatory stimuli was thus pitted against sour stimuli. In a matrix, 25 gustatory stimuli combined 5 sucrose concentrations in small cups (0.15 to 2.35 mole/1) with 5 sour concentrations of the samples (pH 1.8 to 5.7)(Cabanac & Ferber, 1987). Four sessions took place on 4 different days at the same time of day. Throughout the first session, the 25 stimuli were tasted for 5 sec each and the subjects gave an estimate of the magnitude of their pleasure or displeasure in response to one dimension of the matrix (e.g., sweetness). Similarly, throughout the second session, the same stimuli were tasted again and the subjects rated their pleasure or displeasure in response to the second dimension of the matrix (e.g., sourness). For the third session, however, the subjects were invited to mix samples, this to allow a behavioral choice in one

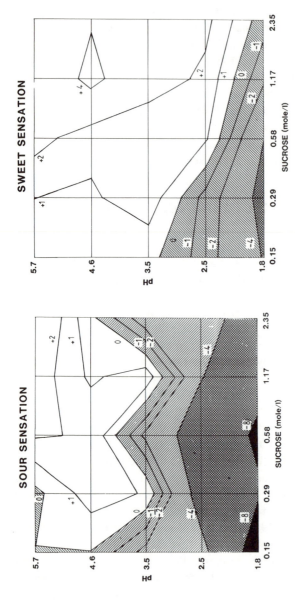

Figure 3 Mean ratings maps of pleasure and displeasure aroused by sweet and sour samples. Left: Three-dimensional map of the mean ratings (indicated by the number on the isohedonic lines) showing the pleasure (+) and the displeasure (−) aroused by the sourness of the 25 samples combining five pH (ordinates) with five sucrose concentrations (abscissae). The 25 stimuli were the nodes on the grid. The isohedonic curves were obtained by interpolation between the nodes on the matrix and the mean of six subjects. Right: Same as left map, but here the subjects rated the pleasure (+) and the displeasure (−) aroused by the sweetness of the same 25 samples as in the left map. From "Sensory Pleasure and Preference in a Two-Dimensional Sensory Space," by M. Cabanac and C. Ferber, 1987, *Appetite*, 8, pp. 18–19. Copyright 1987 by Academic Press Inc. (London) Ltd. Reprinted by permission.

dimension of the matrix, the other being imposed (e.g., they could mix sucrose and water ad libitum for each of five imposed sour concentrations). For the last session, the subjects could adjust the previously imposed dimension, the other previously adjustable dimension being now imposed (e.g., they could modify the sourness of the five imposed sucrose concentrations).

The results of the first two sessions showed that pleasure and displeasure resulted from a two-dimensional combination of the taste modalities offered. The results of the last two sessions showed that the subjects tended to maximize their sensory pleasure. Their operant choices coincided with the ratings obtained in the first two sessions (Figure 4). Whether a dimension of the matrix was imposed or operantly adjustable made no difference on the results; the subjects tended to maximize sensory pleasure in the imposed dimension as well as in the adjustable dimension. The subjects, therefore, maximized their pleasure in the bidimensional space offered when two dimensions were independent. This means that they tended to maximize the algebraic sum of pleasures aroused by the combination of stimuli.

In itself, this result is interesting, but one may question its significance when a cost is involved, that is, when maximizing the pleasure of one sensory dimension implies increasing the displeasure of another sensation. To answer this question subjects were again placed in a bidimensional sensory space, but they had to make a trade-off. The perception aroused by a thermal environment was pitted against the perception aroused by walking on a treadmill (Cabanac & LeBlanc, 1983). Dressed in swim suits and shoes, the subjects walked at 3 km.h^{-1} on a treadmill placed in a climate chamber. In the first series of measurements, the slope of the treadmill was varied from 0 to 24%, and the ambient temperature from 25°C to 5°C. Both treadmill slope and ambient temperature were imposed on subjects who gave quantitative ratings of the pleasure or displeasure evoked by the ambient temperature and by the exercise. Figure 5 shows the isohedonic line of indifference obtained as the algebraic sum of the two ratings. Thus this is a bidimensional map of pleasure and displeasure in the bidimensional sensory space explored. In the second series of measurements, either slope or ambient temperature was imposed by the experimenter and the subjects could manipulate the other. The results showed that the subjects adjusted reciprocally exercise intensity and ambient temperature. When a steep slope was imposed, they selected low ambient temperature, and when a level slope was imposed, they selected lukewarm ambient temperature. Their behavior was reciprocal when the treadmill slope was adjustable. Figure 5 also shows the superimposed results of both series of measurements in this experiment. It is quite striking that the dots showing the selected experimental conditions in the quasi-steady states at the end of the 1-hr sessions are located in the clear areas indicative of bidimensional pleasure. The subjects' operant behavior was therefore guided by the tendency to minimize displeasure (or maximize pleasure).

There is evidence that animals also tend to maximize pleasure in multidimensional sensory spaces (i.e., when a cost is involved). Wild animals are

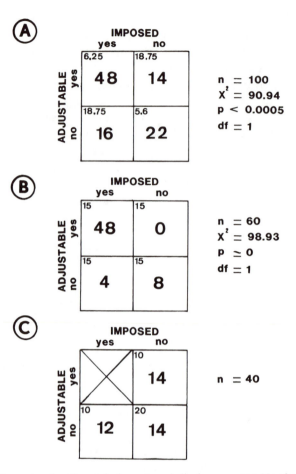

Figure 4 Two-dimensional ratings of pleasure and displeasure. (A) Numbers of cases when the subjects finally produced a sample at pH, or temperature, and sucrose concentration considered maximally pleasant (yes) or not maximally pleasant (no). Rows refer to the free variable that the subjects could manipulate. Columns refer to the imposed variable: $n=100$; $x^2=90.94$; $p=0.0005$; $df=1$ (n = number of choices; χ^2 = chi square; df = degree of freedom; p = probability). (B) Out of the 100 possible choices in A, the ratings for maximal pleasure of sourness (and temperature) and maximal pleasure of sweetness coincided in 60 cases. This shows the distribution of these cases. Since the theoretical frequency of the yes × yes box was only 3.8, χ^2 test was performed by comparing observed distribution, not with theoretical frequency but with 25% (i.e., 15): $n=60$; $\chi^2=98.93$; $p=0$; $df=1$. (C) In 40 cases maximal pleasure with adjustable and imposed variables did not coincide. This shows the actual distribution of these cases; $n=40$. In all boxes the large figure is the frequency observed, and the small figure in the top left-hand corner is the theoretical frequency of the repartition random. Altogether, the results show that the subjects manipulated the solutions so as to reach the maximal bidimensional pleasure. From "Sensory Pleasure and Preference in a Two-Dimensional Sensory Space" by M. Cabanac and C. Ferber, 1987, *Appetite, 8*. p. 24. Copyright 1987 by Academic Press Inc. (London) Ltd. Reprinted by permission.

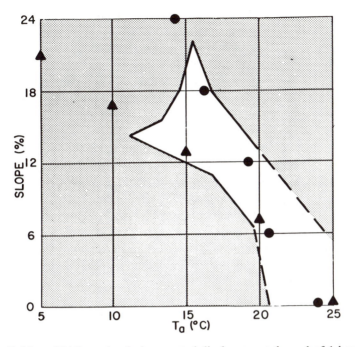

Figure 5 Map of bidimensional pleasure and displeasure at the end of 1 hour exercise sessions. The effects of different combinations of ambient temperature and work intensity on 10 subjects were measured. An isohedonic zero line separates negative area, bidimensional displeasure (shaded), from positive area, bidimensional pleasure (white). The isohedonic line is interrupted in lower right corner because information was not obtained on six of the subjects. Black dots show mean behavioral choice when subjects could manipulate either slope (▲) or ambient temperature (Ta) (●) . Behavioral choice tended to remain in area of bidimensional pleasure. From "Physiological Conflict in Humans: Fatigue vs Cold Discomfort" by M. Cabanac and J. LeBlanc, 1983, *American Journal of Physiology, 244,* p. R626. Copyright 1983 by The American Physiological Society. Reprinted by permission.

capable of coping with nutritional stress by substituting various responses (King & Murphy, 1985). It is likely that the behavior displayed by pigs which prefer feeding to thermoregulating (Ingram & Legge, 1970), steers which prefer thermoregulating to feeding. (Malecheck & Smith, 1976); and sheep which prefer drinking to feeding (Squires & Wilson, 1971), are examples of animals optimizing—from the point of view of cost—their behavioral responses to stressful farm environments.

Recently, Stricker and Verbalis (1988) have shown how rats alternate drinking pure water and salted water in response to their need for water and their need for salt. Thus behavior is alternately serving both motivations. One may hypothesize that such a perfect adaptation of behavior to physiological need is achieved through pleasure. It is possible to obtain empirical evidence showing that animals will seek sensory pleasure and succeed in trading off some amount of displeasure for it. In the obstruction method, the strength of a motivation is measured not as a motor response, or a consumption of a reward, but rather as the decision made by an animal to overcome a resistance to obtain a reward (Warden, 1931). Such a situation can be explored in the laboratory under conditions close to nature. Rats were trained for several weeks to feed each day from 10:00 in the morning to 12:00 noon. During the same period, they learned that once a week additional highly palatable food was available to them, but at 16 m from their warm shelter and in a very cold environment of $-15°C$ in turbulent air. Although regular laboratory chow was available ad libitum in their warm shelter, rats invariably ran to the cold feeder to obtain the highly palatable food. With such foods, the animals took as much as half their nutrient intake in an environment potentially lethal to them (Cabanac & Johnson, 1983). For less palatable foods, the rats went only once or twice to the feeder, and stayed for a short time. Thus the animals faced the painful cold not out of necessity, since food was provided in their warm shelter, but for the pleasure of ingesting a palatable bait (Figure 6). This also shows that there existed a quantitative matching of the pleasure of food with the displeasure of enduring cold. Such a result can be interpreted in light of the experiments done on humans by stating that the rats exercised their freedom to increase their algebraic sum: alimentary pleasure minus cold displeasure.

Thus pleasantness is both a sign of a useful stimulus and a motivation to approach this stimulus when it is needed. The reverse is also true with unpleasant stimuli. The greatest advantage of pleasure is that it shortcuts any other cognitive analysis by the subject, any rationalization as to cause and effect. Thus further cognition may improve behavior, but is not necessary: Subjects can adjust perfectly to their environment without any information other than sensory pleasure.

The experiments reported above were limited to physiological motivations and conflicts. One may question whether it is possible to extend the conclusions to domains other than biology. The notion of *behavioral final common path* is especially enlightening from this perspective. Paraphrasing the image of the motoneuron final common path of all motor responses, McFarland and Sibly (1975) pointed out that behavior is also a final common path on which all motivations converge. This image incorporates all motivations into a unique category since behavior must satisfy not only physiological motivation, but also social, moral esthetical, ludic, and so forth in a time-sharing pattern. Indeed, it is often the case that behaviors are mutually exclusive; one cannot work and sleep at the same time. Therefore, the brain, which is responsible for the behavioral response, must rank priorities and determine trade-offs in the decisions concerned with allocating time among competing behaviors. It can be accepted that the brain operates this ranking system by using a common currency (McFarland, 1985). Thus moral or esthetical motivations must share a common currency with physiological motivations. It may be hypothesized that pleasure is a common currency of nonphysiological motivation, and that a subject will respond to the motivation

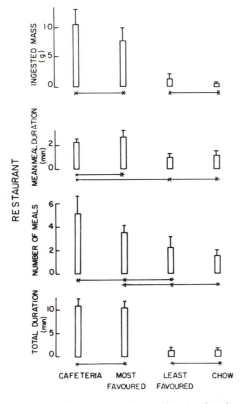

Figure 6 Feeding characteristics of rats when offered cafeteria diet, the most and the least favored bait of each animal, and lab chow at $-15°C$ and 16 m from their warm home. The rats had water and chow ad libitum in their homes. Bars above columns indicate S. E. (standard error); x—x lines join columns that are not significantly different. This shows that rats ventured in the cold to forage for palatability. From "Analysis of a Conflict between Palatability and Cold Exposure in Rats" by M. Cabanac and K. G. Johnson, 1983, *Physiology & Behavior, 31*, p. 252. Copyright 1983 by Pergamon Press Inc. Reprinted by permission.

that will provide the greatest additional pleasure for given cost. Such a hypothesis was verified experimentally.

Money was used as a nonphysiological motivation and pitted against two physiological motivations: cold discomfort in a climatic chamber (Johnson & Cabanac, 1983), and pain from isometric contraction in the thighs (Cabanac, 1986). In these experiments, human volunteers earned money for duration of exposure to these unpleasant sensations. Thus the longer they withstood cold discomfort or pain, the more money they earned. In several sessions, the rate of money reward was varied. The sensation, as described by the ratings given by the subjects, increased linearly with time. It was found that the subjects tolerated higher discomfort or pain for a longer time when the monetary reward was higher. This finding conformed with the common sense expectation. In addition, it experimentally measured and demonstrated that an unpleasant sensation was reliably and quantitatively matched against money, a nonphysiological motivation. The relationship between reward and duration of tolerated displeasure was logarithmic. It can be assumed that the subjects decided to end a session at the time the displeasure of the sensation became greater than the pleasure of the monetary reward. This result opens up the field of all other motivations to the hypothesis that decisions involving nonphysiological motivations are made by following the tendency to maximize pleasure.

Thus pleasure seems to be at the center of behavior. Both a result of useful behavior and a motivation, pleasure is the key to optimal behavior. This paramount importance of pleasure in life leads to the hypothesis that pleasure is not only useful but also necessary, and that the lack of pleasure is a source of stress.

Recent experimental studies have presented problems without solutions to animals that could do nothing to improve their situation. Such a situation is pathogenic and the animal develops apathy, depression, disease, impairment of the immune system (Seligman, 1975), and impairment of future learning in that situation (Maier & Seligman, 1976). Many examples are found in recent works (Oliverio & Puglisi-Allegra, in press). This experimental evidence is confirmed by the epidemiological information available on humans; pathology is closely correlated to helplessness (Levi, in press). It may be hypothesized that situations where subjects are unable to solve their problems can be equated to their incapacity to obtain pleasure. If this were the case, pleasure would be not only the key to optimal behavior and the answer to conflicts of motivations, but also a necessary experience the absence of which is pathogenic. The response of subjects to noise tends to confirm this hypothesis.

Noise is a cause of stress; it disturbs biological parameters (Blois, Debilly, & Mouret, 1980) and can result in obesity and diabetes (Metz, Brandenberger, & Follenius, 1978). In a noisy environment subjects tend to eat more (Fantino & Goillot, 1986).

Ten healthy adult subjects were offered sucrose and sodium chloride stimuli, and were invited to rate on a magnitude scale the pleasure aroused (Ferber & Cabanac, 1987). Five sucrose and five sodium chloride solutions were used. Their concentrations were 0.15, 0.30, 0.58, 1.17, and 2.35 M/l; they were presented in a random order to avoid the effect of increasing or decreasing concentration (Mattes & Lawless, 1985). The stimuli were presented at room temperature, mean temperature during the experiment was 20.6 ± 0.41°C. Each sample (10ml) was presented in a plastic cup. It was tasted for 5 sec then expectorated. After rating the sample, the subjects rinsed their mouths well and observed a 3-min pause before the next stimulus.

During the experiment, the subjects wore a set of headphones connected to a tape recorder. Two minutes of unpleasant noise had been obtained from an electronic synthesizer and reproduced on an endless tape. The sound level of the recorder had previously been calibrated. Two sound levels were selected. The first at about 70 dB, the second at about 90 dB. Since pleasantness might have a positive influence, the subjects brought their own preferred music cassettes. In two control sessions the subjects received, through headphones, either silence or pleasant music of their choice at 90 dB. Twenty minutes before tasting the first sample, the subjects received unpleasant noise through their headphones so that during the measurements the situation would be comparable to that in a public cafeteria. The four different conditions of the noise environment were presented in a random order to each subject.

Figure 7 shows the mean rating for the pleasure aroused by the various concentrations of sucrose and displeasure aroused by sodium chloride under the four environmental conditions. It can be seen that sucrose was more pleasant with 90 dB and music, especially for high concentrations of sucrose. No significant modification was noted concerning salt. The mean hedonic rating given by the ten subjects for all the sucrose stimuli in one mean was significantly higher for 90 dB ($p < 0.002$) and music ($p < 0.003$) than for the control without sound. This is therefore a case of positive alliesthesia; the subjects tended to compensate for the displeasure aroused by the unpleasant noise.

As a general conclusion, it is proposed that animals and humans estimate the optimality of a behavior from the amount of pleasure aroused by the behavior. The law of effect would thus act not only as a learning process, but also as a way

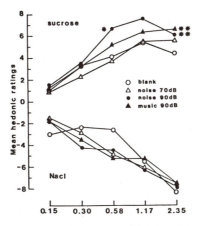

Figure 7 Mean ratings given by ten subjects to various molar concentrations of sucrose and sodium chloride, expressing pleasure (positive ordinates) and displeasure (negative ordinates). The Wilcoxon matched-pairs signed-rank test was used to judge the significance of the differences between the control (blank tapes) and experimental variables: **$p < 0.02$; *$p < 0.05$ (two tailed). Environmental variables included the playing of a blank tape (o), unpleasant noise at 70 dB (△), unpleasant noise at 90 dB (•), and preferred music (▲). Loud noise increased the reported pleasure aroused by sweet stimuli, but did not influence salt sensation. From "Influence of Noise on Gustatory Affective Ratings and Preference for Sweet or Salt" by C. Ferber and M. Cabanac, 1987, *Appetite, 8,* p. 232. Copyright 1987 by Academic Press Inc. (London) Ltd. Reprinted by permission.

for living organisms to know that they are producing an optimal behavior. Maximization of pleasure may thus be the link between physiology and behavior, and be the key to the problem of physiological optimization without the implication of animal cognition, identification, rationality, and even memory. The seeking of pleasure is sufficient to activate an appropriate behavior. This central place of pleasure in animal behavior is now being postulated when interpreting experimental results (Baldwin, 1985) and field observations (Hladik, 1977), or recognized from theoretical considerations (Bindra, 1978; Lester, 1984). The great advantage of pleasure, both as a motivation and as a key to optimization, lies in its versatility. Pleasure renders unnecessary instinctual, rigid, stimulus-response programs and environment-linked behaviors, and opens an infinite register of possible responses.

In situations of conflicting motivations, pleasure serves as common currency—with additive properties—for the ranking of emergencies and the resulting trade-offs. At this stage it is not possible to answer the question of the phylogenic origin of pleasure and the question of the phylogenic correlation between pleasure and behavior. Lower species depend on behavior and have only limited autonomic capability to achieve the short-term stability of their autonomic functions. Yet, lower species still manage to optimize. If lower species rely so heavily upon their behavior, it can be expected that rationality plays a modest part in the determination of behavior.

Taste is an important source of pleasure. Responsible for the most basic behaviors, this pleasure plays its part in the permanent concert which operates the behavioral final common path. The case of taste hints that pleasure is not only useful, but also necessary and that the lack of pleasure can be the source of stress. If this is the case, pleasure would be not only the key to optimal behavior and the answer to conflicts of motivations, but also a necessary experience the absence of which is pathogenic.

References

Attia, M. (1984). Thermal pleasantness and temperature regulation in man. *Neuroscience and Biobehavioral Reviews 8*, 335–343.

Baldwin, B. A. (1985). Neural and hormonal mechanisms regulating food intake. *Proceedings of the Nutrition Society, 44*, 303–311.

Baerends, G. P. (1956). Aufbau des tierischen Verhaltens. In W. Kukenthal & T. Krumback (Eds.), *Handbuch der Zoologie*. De Gruyter abd Co., Berlin, Teil 10 Lfg 7.

Berridge, K. C., Flynn, F. W., Schulkin, J., & Grill, H. J. (1984). Sodium depletion enhances salt palatability in rats. *Behavioral Neuroscience, 98*, 652–660.

Berridge, K. C., & Grill, H. J. (1984). Isohedonic tastes support a two dimensional hypothesis of palatability. *Appetite, 5*, 221–231.

Berridge, K. C., Grill, H. J., & Norgren, R. (1981). Relation of consummatory responses and preabsorptive insulin release to palatability and learned taste aversions. *Journal of Comparative and Physiological Psychology, 95*, 363–382.

Bindra, D. (1978). How adaptive behavior is produced: A perceptual-motivational alternative to response-reinforcement. *The Behavioral and Brain Science, 1*, 41–91.

Blois, R., Debilly, G., & Mouret, J. (1980). Daytime noise and its subsequent sleep effects. In: Noise as a public health problem. *Proceedings of the American Speech Language and Hearing Association, 10,* 425–432.

Cabanac, M. (1971). Physiological role of pleasure. *Science, 173,* 1103–1107.

Cabanac, M. (1981). Physiological signals for thermal comfort. In K. Cena & J. A. Clark (Eds.), *Bioengineering thermal physiology and comfort.* (pp. 181–192). Amsterdam: Elsevier Scientific Publishing Company.

Cabanac, M. (1986). Money versus pain: Experimental study of a conflict in humans. *Journal of Experimental Analysis of Behavior, 46,* 37–44.

Cabanac, M., & Ferber, C. (1987). Sensory pleasure and preference in a two-dimensional sensory space. *Appetite, 8,* 15–28.

Cabanac, M., & Johnson, K. G. (1983). Analysis of a conflict between palatability and cold exposure in rats. *Physiology & Behavior, 31,* 249–253.

Cabanac, M., & Lafrance, L. (1990). Post-ingestive alliesthesia: The rat tells the same story. *Physiology & Behavior, 47,* 539–543.

Cabanac, M., & LeBlanc, J. (1983). Physiological conflict in humans: Fatigue vs cold discomfort. *American Journal of Physiology, 244,* R621–R628.

Cabanac, M., Massonnet, M., & Belaiche, R. (1972). Preferred skin temperature as a function of internal and mean skin temperature. *Journal of Applied Physiology, 33,* 699–703.

Drewnowski, A., Bellisle, F., Aimez, P., & Remy, P. (1987). Taste and bulimia. *Physiology & Behavior, 41,* 621–626.

Drewnowski, A., Brunzell, J. D., Sande, K., Iverius, P. H., & Greenwood, M. R. C. (1985). Sweet tooth reconsidered: Taste responsiveness in human obesity. *Physiology & Behavior, 35,* 617–622.

Drewnowski, A., & Greenwood, M. R. C. (1983). Cream and sugar: Human preferences for high-fat foods. *Physiology & Behavior, 30,* 629–633.

Drewnowski, A., Halmi, K. A., Pierce, B., Gibbs, J., & Smith, G. P. (1987). Taste and eating disorders. *American Journal of Clinical Nutrition, 46,* 442–450.

Fantino, M. (1984). Role of sensory input in the control of food intake. *Journal of the Autonomic Nervous System, 10,* 347–359.

Fantino, M., & Goillot, E. (1986). Hyperphagie induite par le stress chez l'homme [Stress-induced hyperphagia in man] *Cahiers de Nutrition et de Diététique, 21,* 51.

Ferber, C., & Cabanac, M. (1987). Influence of noise on gustatory affective ratings and preference for sweet or salt. *Appetite, 8,* 229–235.

Grill, H. J., & Norgren, R. (1978). Chronically decerebrate rats demonstrate satiation but not bait shyness. *Science, 201,* 267–269.

Hladik, C. M. (1977). A comparative study of the feeding strategies of two sympatric species of leaf monkeys: *Presbytis senex* and *Presbytis entellus*. In T. H. Clutton-Brock (Ed.), *Primate Ecology* (pp. 323–353). New York: Academic Press.

Ingram, D. L., & Legge, K. F. (1970). The thermoregulatory behavior of young pigs in a natural environment. *Physiology & Behavior, 5,* 981–987.

Johnson, K. G., & Cabanac, M. (1983). Human thermoregulatory behavior during a conflict between cold discomfort and money. *Physiology & Behavior, 30,* 145–150.

King, J. R., & Murphy, M. E. (1985). Periods of nutritional stress in the annual cycles of endotherms: Fact or fiction. *American Zoologist, 24,* 955–964.

Lester, N. P. (1984). The "feed drink" decision. *Behavior, 89,* 200–219.

Levi, L. (in press). Approaches to stress in man. In A. Oliverio & S. Puglisi-Allegra (Eds.), *Psychobiology of Stress.* Norwell, MA: Kluwer Academic Publishers.

Maier, S. F., & Seligman, M. E. P. (1976). Learned helplessness: Theory and evidence. *Journal of Experimental Psychology, 105,* 3–46.

Malecheck, J. C., & Smith, B. S. (1976). Behavior of range cows in response to winter weather. *Journal of Range Management, 29,* 9–12.

Mattes, R. D., & Lawless, H. T. (1985). An adjustment error in optimization of taste intensity. *Appetite, 6,* 103–114.

McFarland, D. (1985). *Animal behavior.* London: Pitman Publication Ltd.

McFarland, M., & Sibly, R. M. (1975). The behavioral final common path. *Philosophical Transactions of the Royal Society,* (Series B), *270,* 265–293.

Metz, B., Brandenberger, G., & Follenius, M. (1978). Endocrine responses to acoustic stresses. In I. Assenmacher & D. S. Farner (Eds.), *Environment Endocrinology* (pp. 262–269). Berlin: Springer,.

Nutin, J. (1975). *Iraité de psychologie expérimentale: Vol. V* [Textbook of experimental psychology] (3ème édition). Paris: Presses Universitaires de France.

Oliverio, A., & Puglisi-Allegra, S. (Eds.). (in press). *Psychobiology of stress.* Norwell, MA: Kluwer Academic Publishers.

Seligman, M. E. P. (1975) *Helplessness: On depression, development and death.* San Francisco, CA: Freeman.

Squires, V. R., & Wilson, A. D. (1971). Distance between food and water supply and its effect on drinking frequency and food and water intake of Merino and Border Leicester sheep. *Australian Journal of Agriculture, 22,* 283–290.

Stricker, E. M., & Verbalis, J. G. (1988). Hormones and behavior: The biology of thirst and sodium appetite. *American Scientist, 76,* 261–267.

Tinbergen, N. (1950). The hierarchical organization of mechanisms underlying instinctive behavior. *Symposia of the Society for Experimental Biology, 4,* 305–312.

Toates, F. (1986). *Motivational Systems.* Cambridge, U.K.: Cambridge University Press.

Warden, C. J. (1931). *Animal motivation: Experimental studies on the albino rat.* New York: Columbia University Press.

PART TWO

TASTE PERCEPTION

CHAPTER 4

THE EFFECT OF PHYSIOLOGICAL NEED ON TASTE

THOMAS R. SCOTT

The acquisition of nutrients is among the most basic yet complex of biological functions. It requires the selection of a diverse set of macro- and micronutrients from a broader range of substances that do not satisfy physiological needs or are disruptive of biochemical processes. What guides the behavior of foragers and predators as they seek to satisfy their various chemical requirements? From a distance, perhaps vision or olfaction. The final arbiter of the decision to swallow or reject, however, is taste.

Stimuli presented to the taste system are rarely treated neutrally; they carry an hedonic tag. Taste differs from the nonchemical senses which, during wakefulness, are constantly and often dispassionately analyzing the external world. The taste system is presented with potential foods discretely and is called upon to determine their individual acceptability. To discharge this responsibility, the taste system incorporates or maintains intimate contact with the neural substrates of hedonic appeal. Its message must provide a dimension on which the physiological value of a potential food can be determined for subsequent hedonic coloring by higher-order neurons. It is certainly more than coincidence that the two most primitive biological behaviors—feeding and sex—appear to offer the most intense and universal pleasure to animals.

Complicating the effective acquisition of nutrients is the constant flux of physiological needs. In just hours, the decision of which chemicals are acceptable, and the hedonic appreciation that guides that decision, may be subject to modification as the dangers of malnutrition weigh against those of toxicity. This balance may reverse once again after feeding. In order to provide chemical analyses and to drive the hedonic processes on which feeding is based, taste signals must reflect physiological changes.

This chapter summarizes recent evidence demonstrating that the taste and visceral afferent systems act in concert to guide feeding. The sense of taste evaluates stimuli along a physiological dimension of nutrition versus toxicity and this evaluation is susceptible to modification according to individual experience and momentary physiological need.

THE AFFERENT CODE FOR TASTE

The relation between the sense of taste and the metabolic state of the organism is established at its most fundamental level by this finding: The afferent code for taste quality is based on a dimension of physiological welfare. Both the spatial distribution of neural activity across the cells involved with taste and the time course of that activity serve to separate nutrients from toxins (Scott & Mark, 1987). This distribution of chemicals along a nutrient-toxicity dimension correlates quite well with the rat's acceptance–rejection behavior in short-term licking tests and with attributions of pleasure or revulsion by human subjects in psychophysical studies (Schiffman & Erickson, 1971). Through the taste system, the consumption of nutrients is encouraged by the arousal of positive hedonics; the rejection of toxins by negative hedonics.

It is not surprising that the taste system evolved to protect its host from ingesting toxins through the unpleasant sensation that humans label bitterness, or that it motivates the organism to consume carbohydrates through positive sensations labeled sweetness. Animals who preferred the taste of toxins would have contributed little to subsequent gene pools. What is less expected is that the perceptions we derive from this system are organized not according to the physical characteristics of the stimuli, as they are in nonchemical senses, but to the physiological consequences of ingestion. By analogy, the visual system may be instrumental in permitting us to avoid predators and detect prey, but predator and prey are not coded as such in the optic nerve, except perhaps in quite primitive animals. This distinction reinforces the unique quality of taste as the final determinant of which substances physically enter the body and reaffirms its role in recognizing both the external and internal environments.

There is ample behavioral evidence that the hedonic value of a taste stimulus is monitored in the hindbrain. Acceptance–rejection reflexes are readily identifiable across a wide phylogenetic and ontogenetic range (Steiner, 1979) and remain essentially constant with only the caudal brainstem intact (Grill & Norgren, 1978a, 1978b). Steiner concluded that facial expressions are adaptive both in dealing with the chemical—swallowing if appetitive, clearing the mouth if aversive—and in communicating its hedonic dimension to other members of the species. The hedonic monitor is innate, is located in the brainstem (Pfaffmann,

During preparation of this chapter, the author was supported by research grants from the National Institutes of Health, the National Science Foundation, and the Campbell Institute. Dr. Barbara K. Giza helped organize the references and Ms. Judy A. Fingerle typed the manuscript.

Norgren, & Grill, 1977) and is neurally intact in humans by the seventh gestational month (Steiner, 1979). Thus the neural organization on which the hedonics of feeding may be based and the reflexive behavior commensurate with the ultimate hedonic appreciation is incorporated in the rat's hindbrain gustatory code.

PLASTICITY IN THE GUSTATORY CODE
The preceding section argues that the taste system is organized to perform a general differentiation of toxins from nutrients, that this is accomplished at a lower-order neural level, and that the analysis incorporates or directly influences powerful hedonic experiences. while providing a broad and effective system for maintaining the biochemical welfare of the species, this organization does not recognize idiosyncratic allergies or the needs of the individual, nor is it sensitive to changes in individual needs over time. To serve these requirements, the taste code must be plastic.

Plasticity Based on Experience
An animal's experience has a pronounced and lasting effect on its behavioral reactions to taste stimuli. The gustatory experiences of suckling rats establish taste preferences that persist into adulthood (Capretta & Rawls, 1974). Preferences also develop through association of a taste with positive reinforcement, in particular with a visceral reinforcement such as occurs with the administration of a nutrient of which the animal has been deprived (Revusky, Smith, & Chalmers, 1971). Gustatory preferences can also be established in humans and other animals by familiarity through constant exposure (Domjan, 1976). However, the most reliable effect of experience on subsequent preference is obtained from the establishment of a conditioned taste aversion (CTA). This is an especially efficient form of conditioning in which an intense aversion may be developed through the single pairing of a novel taste (the conditioned stimulus or CS) with gastrointestinal malaise (the unconditioned stimulus or US) (Garcia, Kimmeldorf, & Koelling, 1955). The aversion to a conditioned taste solution is so readily established, so potent, and so resistant to extinction that the CTA protocol has become a standard tool for studying physiological processes and taste-related behavior (Smotherman & Levine, 1978).

The neural substrates of conditioned taste aversions have been investigated in scores of experiments, most of which have involved ablating selected structures and testing the ability of subjects to retain former CTA's or to develop subsequent aversions. Although these studies have implicated the cortex, amygdala, hippocampus, thalamus, olfactory bulb, and area postrema as having some involvement in aversion learning, only amygdaloid and hypothalamic participation seems unequivocal. Rarely have recordings been made from neurons of conditioned animals to determine the effects of a CTA on taste-evoked activity. Aleksanyan, Buresova, and Bures (1976) reported that the preponderance of hypothalamic activity evoked by saccharin in rats shifted from the lateral to the ventromedial nucleus with the formation of a saccharin CTA. DiLorenzo (1985) recorded the responses evoked by a series of taste stimuli in the pontine parabrachial nucleus of rats, then paired the taste of NaCl with gastrointestinal malaise and repeated the recordings. The response to NaCl increased significantly and selectively in a subset of gustatory neurons.

Chang and Scott (1984) recorded single unit gustatory-evoked activity from the nucleus tractus solitarius (NTS) of three groups of rats: unconditioned (exposed only to the taste of the saccharin CS with no induced nausea), pseudoconditioned (experienced only the US, nausea, with no gustatory referent), and conditioned (taste of saccharin CS paired with gastrointestinal malaise). Comparisons were performed among the groups' responses to an array of 12 stimuli— including the saccharin CS, a more concentrated saccharin solution, saccharides, salts, acids, and an alkaloid—through which alterations in the entire gustatory code resulting from this taste-learning experience could be evaluated. Chang and Scott reported that the CS evoked a significantly larger response from conditioned animals than from control animals, and that the effect was limited to the 30% of neurons that showed a sweet-sensitive profile of responsiveness. Temporal analyses of the activity evoked from this subgroup of saccharin-sensitive neurons revealed that nearly the entire increase in discharge rate was attributable to a burst of activity that diverged from control group levels 600 ms following stimulus onset, peaked at 900 ms, and returned to control levels by 3,000 ms (Figure 1). Thus the major consequence of the conditioning procedure was to increase responsiveness to the saccharin CS through a well-defined peak of activity. The same enhanced response and temporal pattern was evoked to a lesser extent by other sweet stimuli (fructose, glucose and sucrose), thus providing a likely neural counterpart to generalization of the aversion.

Since a range of taste stimuli was used in this study, the effect of an increased response to the CS and related chemicals could be evaluated in terms of taste quality. The pattern of activity evoked by saccharin was altered by the conditioning procedure. How did the new pattern relate to those of other chemicals? Correlation coefficients between the patterns evoked by each pair of stimuli were calculated and organized into a correlation matrix. This served as the basis for multidimensional similarity spaces which were constructed in three dimensions from the response profiles of unconditioned and conditioned rats (Figure 2). In a normally functioning taste system (Figure 2A), the stimulus arrangement was similar to that seen by others (Doetsch & Erickson, 1970). The basic distinction between sweet and nonsweet chemicals was apparent, as was the precise arrangement of stimuli within the nonsweet group. The four Na-Li salts were virtually indistinguishable by the neural patterns they elicited and the complex sweet-salty-bitter taste of concentrated (0.25M) sodium saccharin was represented appropriately between the sweet and nonsweet clusters. The consequence of the conditioning procedure was to disrupt this clear organization (Figure 2B). The relative similarity among nonsweet qualities was reduced and the sharp

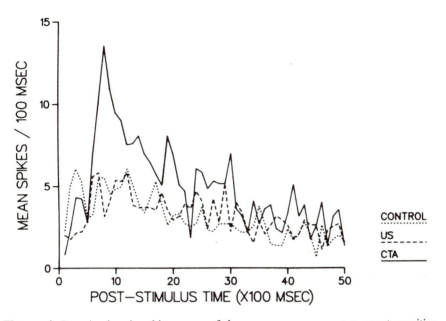

Figure 1 Poststimulus time histograms of the mean responses among sweet–sensitive neurons to 0.0025 M NaSaccharin in the three groups of rats. The enhanced activity during the first three seconds of evoked response in conditioned subjects may represent the increased salience of the saccharin taste for these animals. From "Conditioned Taste Aversions Modify Neural Responses in the Rat Nucleus Tractus Solitarius" by F-C. T. Chang and T. R. Scott, 1984, *Journal of Neuroscience, 4*, p. 1857. Copyright 1984 by Oxford University Press. Reprinted by permission.

distinction between sweet and nonsweet was blurred. Moreover, the relative increased in similarity between sweet and nonsweet chemicals was differential, with the greatest increase occurring between the saccharin CS and bitter quinine. The rearrangement caused quinine to be as close to the sweet CS as it was to the acids, a finding that would be quite aberrant in a normally functioning taste system. This may offer a neural concomitant to the increasingly similar behavioral reaction evoked by quinine and sweet chemicals to which an aversion has been conditioned (Grill & Norgren, 1978a).

There are several implications of these findings for the interrelationship of taste and ingestion. First, they reinforce the reports by Aleksanyan et al. (1976) and DiLorenzo (1985) that the responses of brainstem and indeed hindbrain taste neurons are subject to modification by experience. Secondly, conditioned aversions, which in humans affect primarily the hedonic evaluation of the CS rather than its perceived quality, caused a rearrangement of the neural taste space that was based on responses from the NTS of rats. This suggests that the hindbrain neural code in rats combines sensory discrimination with an hedonic component. Finally, activity in these intact animals was modified in ways appropriate for

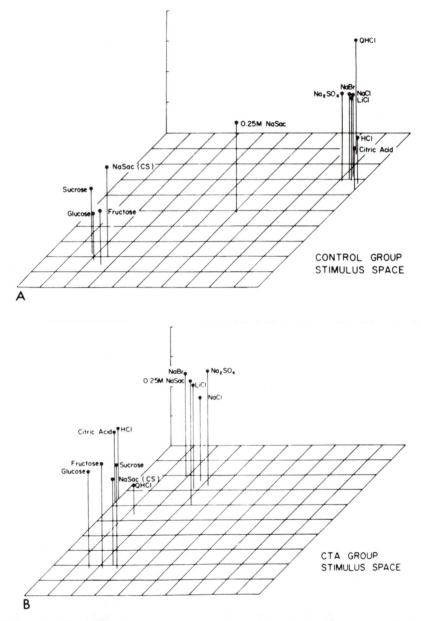

Figure 2 Three-dimensional spaces representing relative similarities among stimuli as determined from neural responses in the control group (A) and the CTA group (B). NaSac (CS) is fixed at the same coordinates in each space. From "Conditioned Taste Aversions Modify Neural Responses in the Rat Nucleus Tractus Solitarius" by F-C. T. Chang and T. R. Scott, 1984, *Journal of Neuroscience, 4,* p. 1859. Copyright 1984 Oxford University Press. Reprinted by permission.

mediation of the behavioral aversion, yet decerebrate rats—rats with NTS and its vagal afferents intact—were incapable of learning or retaining a CTA (Grill & Norgren, 1978a). This implies hypothalamic or amygdaloid involvement in the processes expressed in NTS, given the association of these areas with motivation and hedonics, their required integrity for aversion learning to proceed (Kemble & Nagel, 1973), and their close, reciprocal anatomical relationship with NTS. A direct test of this implication, however, refuted it. Mark and Scott (1988) treated decerebrate rats with the same conditioning protocol as in the Chang and Scott study and, based on facial reactions, confirmed the failure of these animals to develop aversions to the saccharin CS. Subsequent recordings from the NTS, however, disclosed a peak of evoked activity to the CS with virtually the same amplitude and time course as was reported in intact rats. Thus the source of modification must be located caudal to the colliculi (the plane of decerebration). Selective vagotomies and lesions of nuclei such as area postrema and dorsal motor nuclei may be required to identify that source.

Plasticity Based on Need

An animal's physiological condition is closely related to its choice of foods. The "body wisdom" demonstrated in cafeteria studies by Richter (1942) appears to result from taste-directed changes in food selection. Compensatory feeding behavior has been shown in cases of experimentally induced deficiencies of thiamine (Seward & Greathouse, 1973), threonine (Halstead & Gallagher, 1962), and histidine (Sanahuja & Harper, 1962). It is presumed that the physiological benefits of dietary repletion are paired with the taste that preceded those benefits, creating a conditioned taste preference by which the associated hedonic value of the taste is enhanced. Since physiological needs are in constant flux, the hedonic value of a taste experience must be quite labile.

Long-Term Needs: The Case of Sodium

A constant and perhaps innate preference exists for sodium. Mammals evolving in sodium-deficient environments seek out and consume salt wherever it is found and, when salt is plentiful, consume more than they need. Both rats and humans select sodium salts in their diets even when sodium replete (Denton, 1976). This preference becomes exaggerated under conditions of salt deficiency. Humans depleted by pathological states (Wilkins & Richter, 1940) or by experimental manipulations (McCance, 1936) often show a pronounced craving for salt. Rodents subjected to uncontrolled urinary sodium loss following adrenalectomy (Richter, 1936), dietary sodium restrictions (Fregley, Harper, & Radford, 1965), or acute loss of plasma volume (Jalowiec & Stricker, 1970) show sharp increases in salt consumption. This compensatory response to the physiological need for salt results from a change in the hedonic value of tasted sodium. Concentrations of NaCl that had been evaluated negatively and rejected under conditions of sodium repletion evoke a positive hedonic response and acceptance when the organism is deprived. This hedonic change has been thought to result from the decreased gustatory sensitivity to salt that accompanies sodium depletion. Contreras and Frank (1979) analyzed the responses of single fibers in the chorda tympani nerve to NaCl in both replete and sodium-deficient rats. Depletion was accompanied by a specific reduction in salt responsiveness among the 40% of fibers that were most sodium-responsive. This decreased sensitivity may result in the observed shift in the acceptance curve to higher concentrations.

This intensity-based interpretation has been recast recently by Jacobs, Mark, and Scott (1988). Recording from central taste neurons in the NTS, these researchers confirmed a moderate, overall reduction in responsiveness to sodium in salt-deprived rats. Separate analyses of activity among different neuron types, however, revealed that the responsiveness of the salt-sensitive group of cells was profoundly depressed and that this effect was partially offset by a remarkable increase in activity among sugar-sensitive cells. The net effect was to transfer the burden of coding sodium from salt- to sugar-sensitive neurons. This implies not so much a change in perceived intensity as a change in perceived quality in sodium-deficient rats: Salt should now taste sweet or, if sweetness is only a human construct, good to the animal. Multidimensional spaces based on the responses of replete and sodium-deprived rats confirm shifts in the neural code for sodium and lithium salts toward those of sucrose and fructose (Figure 3). This interpretation explains the eagerness with which deprived rats consume sodium, an avidity usually reserved for the ingestion of sugars.

Short-Term Needs: The Effects of Satiety

Whereas the appreciation of micronutrient or sodium deficiency occurs over a period of days, the availability of macronutrients, notably glucose, is of almost hourly concern. There must be an accommodation of the decision to accept a food, and in the hedonic evaluation that drives this decision, as energy needs become more acute. Common experience reinforces the results of psychophysical studies: Foods become more palatable with deprivation and less palatable with satiety (Cabanac, 1971). The following evidence suggests that these effects are also mediated by alterations in gustatory afferent activity.

In mammals the term satiety encompasses a complex of physical and biochemical mechanisms that may operate through independent neural channels. It is clear that alterations in gustatory activity are involved in this process. Glenn and Erickson (1976) recorded multiunit activity from the NTS of freely fed rats as they induced gastric distension and observed a pattern of differential modification in taste responsiveness. Distension severely depressed activity evoked by (in descending order) sucrose, NaCl, HCl, and finally quinine, the responses to which were unmodified. Relief from distension reversed the effect over a 45-min period. When rats were deprived of food for 48–72 hrs, however, the influence of distension on taste was lost, suggesting that the modulating processes may be sensitive to the overall nutritive state of the animal.

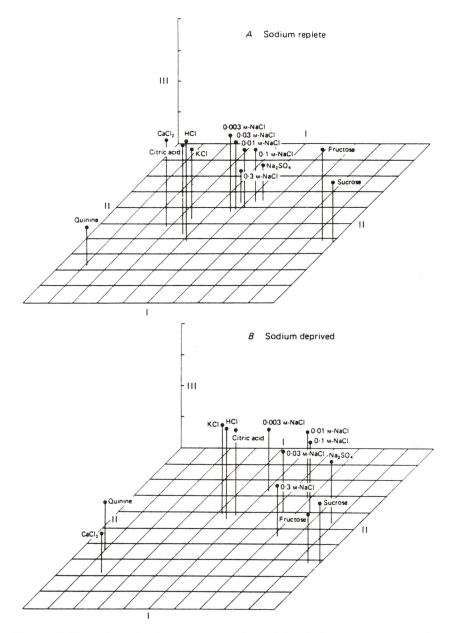

Figure 3 Three-dimensional spaces representing relative similarities among stimuli as determined from neural responses in sodium-replete (A) and sodium-deprived (B) rats. From "Taste Responses in the Nucleus Tractus Solitarius of Sodium-Deprived Rats" by K. M. Jacobs, G. P. Mark, and T. R. Scott, 1988, *Journal of Physiology, 406,* p. 406. Copyright 1988 by The Physiological Society. Reprinted by permission.

Giza and Scott have investigated the effects of other satiety factors on taste-evoked activity in the NTS. Multiunit responses to taste stimuli were recorded before and after intravenous loads of 0.5 g/kg glucose or another vehicle were given (Giza & Scott, 1983). The glucose infusion had a selectively suppressive effect on taste activity. Elevated blood glucose was associated with a significant reduction in gustatory responsiveness to glucose, with a maximum effect occurring 8 min after the intravenous load. Recovery took place over 60 min as blood glucose approached normal levels. Responsiveness to NaCl and HCl was suppressed to a lesser degree and for a briefer period, quinine-evoked responses were unaffected. Similarly, an intravenous administration of 0.5 U/kg insulin resulted in a transient suppression of taste activity evoked by glucose and fructose (Giza & Scott, 1987b). Therefore, hyperglycemia and modest hyperinsulinemia, both of which result in depression of food intake, are associated with reductions in the afferent activity evoked by hedonically positive tastes. These findings imply that the pleasure that sustains feeding is reduced, making termination of the meal more likely.

If taste activity in NTS is influenced by the rat's nutritional state, then intensity judgments should change with satiety. Psychophysical studies of human subjects, while not fully consistent among themselves, generally do not support this position. Humans typically report that the hedonic value of appetitive tastes declines with satiety, but that intensity judgments are affected to a lesser extent or not at all (Rolls, Rolls, Rowe, & Sweeney, 1981). There are at least three levels of ambiguity that cloud the interpretation of these conflicting results: species differences—rats versus humans, neural level—electrophysiological data are from the hindbrain while psychophysical responses presumably reflect a cortical influence, and the possible effects of barbiturate anesthetics on the rats. A resolution of the implied conflict requires an analysis of both the rat's intensity perceptions and the human's taste-evoked activity in the hindbrain.

To examine intensity perception in the rat, conditioned taste aversions were formed to 1.0M glucose and the degree of behavioral generalization from this to a range of other concentrations was measured (Scott & Giza, 1987). Hyperglycemic rats reacted to glucose concentrations as if they were 50% less intense than did conditioned animals with no glucose load (Giza & Scott, 1987a). Thus the neural suppression in the hindbrain that results from an intravenous glucose load appears to be manifested in the perception of reduced intensity.

While it is reassuring that the rat's behavior conforms to the implications of its neural responses, the original conflict with psychophysical results remains unresolved. To complete the puzzle, information is needed on the influence of satiety on taste-evoked activity at various synaptic levels of the human. The closest available approximation to these data may be supplied by subhuman primates. First the response characteristics of taste neurons in the NTS of cynomolgus monkeys were defined (Scott, Yaxley, Sienkiewicz, & Rolls, 1986). Then the activity of small clusters of these cells was monitored as mildly food-deprived monkeys were fed to satiety with glucose (Yaxley, Rolls, Sienkiewicz, & Scott,

1985). Satiety was measured behaviorally as the monkeys progressed from avid acceptance to active rejection of glucose, typically after consuming 200–300 ml (Figure 4, bottom of each frame). Despite the effects of gastric distension and elevated blood glucose and insulin levels this procedure was designed to cause, the responsiveness of NTS neurons to the taste of a range of solutions, including glucose, was unmodified (Figure 4, top of each frame). These results are in marked contrast to those reported in anesthetized rats, where similar physiological manipulations caused a reduction in responsiveness to sugars of up to 50% (Giza & Scott, 1983; Glenn & Erickson, 1976).

The same approach has been extended to single neurons in cortical taste areas of the frontal operculum (Rolls, Scott, Sienkiewicz, & Yaxley, 1988) and anterior insula (Yaxley, Rolls, & Sienkiewicz, 1989) with similar results. Thus it appears that the decreased acceptance and reduced hedonic value associated with satiety do not result from a decrement in gustatory responsiveness at any level up to and including primary gustatory cortex, but is related to sensory quality independent of physiological state.

This situation changed when neurons of the macaque monkey's orbitofrontal cortex (OFC) were studied (Rolls, Yaxley, Sienkiewicz, & Scott, 1985). Taste-responsive cells showed vigorous activity to preferred solutions when the monkey was deprived. As satiety increased—and acceptance turned to rejection—the responsiveness declined to near spontaneous rate (Figure 5). There was no change in the activity elicited by other stimuli, however, even those to whose qualities the taste of the satiating stimulus would readily generalize. Thus the effects that are apparent in the rat's hindbrain are not manifested in the macaque until the afferent signal reaches an advanced stage of cortical processing in the OFC. There the association between a stimulus and its reward value could occur, depending on the need state of the monkey. Separate populations of neurons have also been identified in the monkey's lateral hypothalamic area that responded to the taste of preferred foods if the animal was hungry (Burton, Rolls, & Mora, 1976). As in OFC, the induction of satiety suppressed this activity. The electrophysiological evidence supports the position that gustatory incentives for initiation and maintenance of feeding may be modulated by momentary physiological needs. In primates, however, this influence is evident only after several stages of synaptic processing, including cortical relays at which the quality–intensity evaluation is held independent of hedonic appreciation. It would not be surprising if the macaque had the same ability as humans to evaluate the sensory aspects of food separately from its appeal. Thus a resolution to the conflict between rat electrophysiological and human psychophysical data lies not in whether hedonic evaluations are part of the gustatory neural code, but in the neural level at which the interaction occurs.

CONCLUSION

I propose that the sense of taste is like a Janus head placed at the gateway to the city. One face is turned outward to its environment, to warn of and resist the

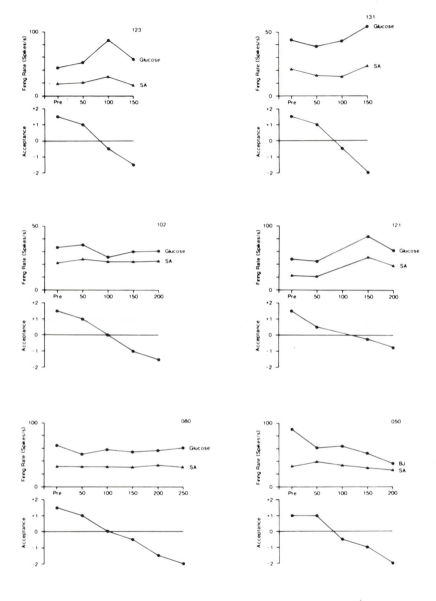

Figure 4 The spontaneous activity (SA) and multiunit neural responses (spikes/sec)
Each graph represents the results of a separate experiment during which the monkeys
data in each frame is a behavioral measure of the acceptance of the satiating solution on a
satiating solution that was used, either glucose or BJ (black currant juice). From "Satiety
Monkey" by S. Yaxley, E. T. Rolls, Z. J. Sienkiewicz, and T. R. Scott, 1985, *Brain*
permission.

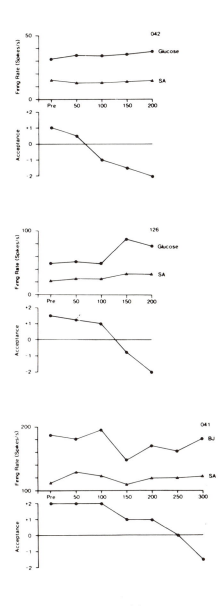

Volume Ingested (ml)

evoked from the NTS by the taste solutions on which the monkeys were fed to satiety. consumed the satiating solution in 50-ml aliquots. Represented below the neural response scale of +2.0 (avid acceptance) to −2.0 (active rejection). Each graph is labeled with the Does Not Affect Gustatory Activity in the Nucleus of the Solitary Tract of the Alert *Research, 347,* p. 90. Copyright 1985 by Elsevier Science Publishers BV. Reprinted by

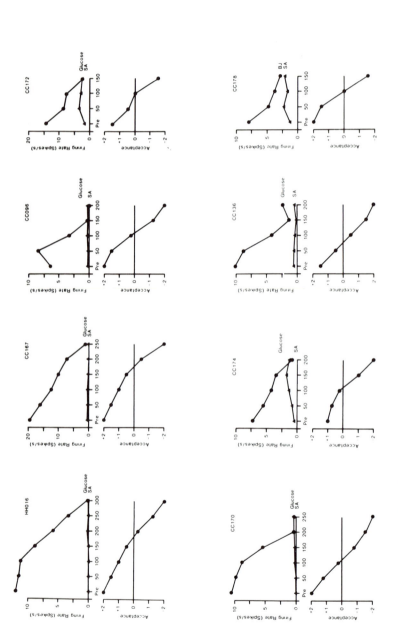

Figure 5 The spontaneous activity (SA) and responses derived form single neurons in the orbitofrontal cortices of monkeys fed to satiety. At this level of processing, discharge rate is related to the level of satiety rather than the purely sensory aspects of a stimulus. Each graph represents the results of a separate experiment during which the monkeys consumed glucose or black currant juice (BJ) in 50 ml aliquots. Below the neural response data is a measure of the monkeys' acceptance ($+2.0$) or rejection (-2.0) of the satiating solution.

incursion of chemical perils while recognizing and encouraging the receipt of required goods. The other face looks inward to monitor the effects of the admitted wares on the city's activity and to remain current with its needs.

The outward face of taste signals the quality and intensity of chemicals through a spatiotemporal code, both the spatial and temporal aspects of which are organized on a dimension of physiological welfare. This analysis offers the first approximation of the appropriateness of consuming a chemical. The capacity to perform it is genetically endowed and, one supposes, derives from evolutionary pressures to avoid chemicals that are toxic and to consume those that provide nutrients. We are, after all, the progeny of those who, among other things, selected wisely from the chemicals in their environment. Because this analytical process is inherent to the structure and function of the taste system, it is applicable to all members of a species at all times. It forms the first layer of what may be seen as a three-tiered system that underlies the concept of body wisdom.

The second layer which, with the third, requires both faces of taste, permits fine adjustments to the inherited code, and tailors it to the physiology of the individual. A deficient enzyme may render a normally nutritious substance indigestible: its ingestion causes nausea, vomiting, and diarrhea. Hormonal abnormalities may lead to an electrolyte imbalance, causing abnormal dietary needs. The experience resulting from these situations—a conditioned aversion in the former, conditioned preferences in the latter—alters gustatory responsiveness in a manner appropriate to accommodate the idiosyncrasy. Thus a chemical that generates a response pattern similar to those of preferred tastes in the naive rat may assume negative characteristics after its ingestion is associated with malaise. Conditioning occurs on a time scale that relates to visceral rather than operant processes. In tandem with neophobic reactions, it serves to limit the harm of ingesting a toxin to that caused by a single, mild exposure. Whereas the effects of conditioning apply only to the individual, the mechanism that permits this extraordinarily powerful association between taste and physiological consequences is inherent to the structure of the gustatory-visceral complex and thus affects all members of the species.

The third tier involves short-term fluctuations in sensitivity that promote or inhibit feeding and which encourage consumption of a nutritionally replete diet. Positive hedonics are suppressed by satiety factors such as gastric distension, hyperglycemia, and moderate hyperinsulinemia. Thus a ready endogenous energy supply reduces the reinforcing value of food and discourages further feeding. Conversely, the need for sodium arouses enhanced responsiveness to salt among taste neurons whose activity is associated with positive hedonics, thereby encouraging salt consumption.

The taste system evaluates substances at the interface between discrimination and digestion. It combines the qualities of rapid stimulus identification and spatiotemporal coding associated with the exteroceptive senses with the slower recognition and still mysterious codes of the visceral senses. The result is a system that reduces the diverse and frequently hostile environment to a chemical subset that effectively satisfies the complex and changing requirements of the individual's internal milieu.

References

Aleksanyan, A. A., Buresova, O., & Bures, J. (1976). Modification of unit responses to gustatory stimuli by conditioned taste aversion in rats. *Physiology & Behavior, 17,* 173–179.

Burton, M., Rolls, E., & Mora, F. (1976). Effects of hunger on the response of neurons in the lateral hypothalamus to the sight and taste of food. *Experimental Neurology, 51,* 668–677.

Cabanac, M. (1971). Physiological role of pleasure. *Science, 173,* 1103–1107.

Capretta, P. J., & Rawls, L. H. (1974). Establishment of a flavor preference in rats: Importance of nursing and weaning experience. *Journal of Comparative and Physiological Psychology, 86,* 670–673.

Chang, F-C. T., & Scott, T. R. (1984). Conditioned taste aversions modify neural responses in the rat nucleus tractus solitarius. *Journal of Neuroscience, 4,* 1850–1862.

Contreras, R., & Frank, M. (1979). Sodium deprivation alters neural responses to gustatory stimuli. *Journal of General Physiology, 73,* 569–594.

Denton, D. A. (1976). Hypertension: A malady of civilization? In M. P. Sambhi (Ed.), *Systemic Effects of Antihypertensive Agents* (pp. 577–583). New York: Stratton Intercontinental Medical Books.

DiLorenzo, P. M. (1985). Responses to NaCl of parabrachial units that were conditioned with intravenous LiCl. *Chemical Senses, 10,* 438.

Doetsch, G. S., & Erickson, R. P. (1970). Synaptic processing of taste-quality information in the nucleus tractus solitarius of the rat. *Journal of Neurophysiology, 33,* 490–507.

Domjan, M. (1976). Determinants of the enhancement of flavored-water intake by prior exposure. *Journal of Experimental Psychology: Animal Behavior Processes, 2,* 17–27.

Fregley, M. J., Harper, J. M., & Radford, E. P., Jr. (1965). Regulation of sodium chloride intake by rats. *American Journal of Physiology, 209,* 287–292.

Garcia, J., Kimmeldorf, D. J., & Koelling, R. A. (1955). Conditional aversion to saccharin resulting from exposure to gamma radiation. *Science, 122,* 157–158.

Giza, B. K., & Scott, T. R. (1983). Blood glucose selectively affects taste-evoked activity in the rat nucleus tractus solitarius. *Physiology & Behavior, 31,* 643–650.

Giza, B. K., & Scott, T. R. (1987a). Blood glucose level affects perceived sweetness intensity in rats. *Physiology & Behavior, 41,* 459–464.

Giza, B. K., & Scott, T. R. (1987b). Intravenous insulin infusions in rats decrease gustatory-evoked responses to sugars. *American Journal of Physiology, 252,* R994–R1002.

Glenn, J. F., & Erickson, R. P. (1976). Gastric modulation of gustatory afferent activity. *Physiology & Behavior, 16,* 561–568.

Grill, H. J., & Norgren, R. (1978a). The taste reactivity test: I. Mimetic responses to gustatory stimuli in neurologically normal rats. *Brain Research, 143,* 263–279.

Grill, H. J., & Norgren, R. (1978b). The taste reactivity test. II. Mimetic responses to gustatory stimuli in chronic thalamic and chronic decerebrate rats. *Brain Research, 143,* 281–297.

Halstead, W. C., & Gallagher, B. B. (1962). Autoregulation of amino acids intake in the albino rat. *Journal of Comparative and Physiological Psychology, 55,* 107–111.

Jacobs, K. M., Mark, G. P., & Scott, T. R. (1988). Taste responses in the nucleus tractus solitarius of sodium-deprived rats. *Journal of Physiology, 406,* 393–410.

Jalowiec, J. E., & Stricker, E. M. (1970). Restoration of body fluid balance following acute sodium deficiency in rats. *Journal of Comparative and Physiological Psychology, 70,* 94-102.

Kemble, E. D., & Nagel, J. A. (1973). Failure to form a learned taste aversion in rats with amygdaloid lesions. *Bulletin of the Psychonomic Society, 2,* 155-156.

Mark, G. P., & Scott, T. R. (1988). Conditioned taste aversions affect gustatory activity in the NTS of chronic decerebrate rats. *Neuroscience Abstracts, 14,* 1185.

McCance, R. A. (1936). Experimental sodium chloride deficiency in man. *Proceedings of the Royal Society of London Series B, 119,* 245-268.

Pfaffmann, C., Norgren, R., & Grill, H. J. (1977). Sensory affect and motivation. *Annuals of the New York Academy of Science, 290,* 18-34.

Revusky, S. H., Smith, M. H., & Chalmers, D. V. (1971). Flavor preferences: Effects of ingestion contingent intravenous saline or glucose. *Physiology & Behavior, 6,* 341-343.

Richter, C. P. (1936). Increased salt appetite in adrenalectomized rats. *American Journal of Physiology, 115,* 155-161.

Richter, C. P. (1942). Total self-regulatory function in animals and human beings. *The Harvey Lectures, 38,* 63-103.

Rolls, B. J., Rolls, E. T., Rowe, E. A., & Sweeney, K. (1981). Sensory specific satiety in man. *Physiology & Behavior, 27,* 137-142.

Rolls, E. T., Scott, T. R., Sienkiewicz, Z. J., & Yaxley, S. (1988). The responsiveness of neurons in the frontal opercular gustatory cortex of the monkey is independent of hunger. *Journal of Physiology, 56,* 876-890.

Rolls, E. T., Yaxley, S., Sienkiewicz, Z. J., & Scott, T. R. (1985). Gustatory responses of single neurons in the orbitofrontal cortex of the macaque monkey. *Chemical Senses, 10,* 443.

Sanahuja, J. C., & Harper, A. E. (1962). Effect of amino acid imbalance on food intake and preference. *American Journal of Physiology, 202,* 165-170.

Schiffman, S. S., & Erickson, R. P. (1971). A psychophysical model for gustatory quality. *Physiology & Behavior, 7,* 617-633.

Scott, T. R., & Giza, B. K. (1987). A measure of taste intensity discrimination in the rat through conditioned taste aversions. *Physiology & Behavior, 41,* 315-320.

Scott, T. R., & Mark, G. P. (1987). The taste system encodes stimulus toxicity. *Brain Research, 414,* 197-203.

Scott, T. R., Yaxley, S., Sienkiewicz, Z. J., & Rolls, E. T. (1986). Gustatory responses in the nucleus tractus solitarius of the alert cynomolgus monkey. *Journal of Neurophysiology, 55,* 182-200.

Seward, J. P., & Greathouse, S. R. (1973). Appetitive and aversive conditioning in thiamine-deficient rats. *Journal of Comparative Physiology, 83,* 157-167.

Smotherman, W. P., & Levine, S. (1978). ACTH and ACTH4-10 modification of neophobia and taste aversion responses in the rat. *Journal of Comparative and Physiological Psychology, 92,* 22-23.

Steiner, J. E. (1979). Human facial expressions in response to taste and smell stimulation. In H. W. Reese & L. Lipsett (Eds.), *Advances in Child Development, Vol. 13* (pp. 257-295). New York: Academic Press.

Wilkins, L. & Richter, C. P. (1940). A great craving for salt by a child with corticoadrenal insufficiency. *Journal of the American Medical Association, 114,* 866-868.

Yaxley, S., Rolls, E. T., & Sienkiewicz, Z. J. (1989). The responsiveness of neurons in the insular gustatory cortex of the macaque monkey is independent of hunger. *Physiology & Behavior, 42,* 223-229.

Yaxley, S., Rolls, E. T. Sienkiewicz, Z. J., & Scott, T. R. (1985). Satiety does not affect gustatory activity in the nucleus of the solitary tract of the alert monkey. *Brain Research, 347,* 85-93.

CHAPTER 5

DISTINCTIONS BETWEEN TASTE AND SMELL RELEVANT TO THE ROLE OF EXPERIENCE

LINDA M. BARTOSHUK

The hedonics of the chemical senses require a consideration of some sensory issues. First, when a change in intake occurs, it may be the result of a hedonic or a sensory change. Distinguishing between the two requires a variety of experimental approaches (Bartoshuk, 1980). For example, we know that depriving a rat of NaCl will cause the animal to consume NaCl avidly when it has the opportunity. Richter (1936) originally attributed this phenomenon to increased sensory acuity for NaCl but now, most would argue for a hedonic change: NaCl becomes more palatable as a result of deprivation (Cabanac, 1971; Kriekhaus, 1970; Kriekhaus & Wolf, 1968). In general, when a hedonic change appears to have occurred, a sensory control is required to insure that the change was truly hedonic. That is, before we can conclude that the palatability of a taste has changed, we must be certain that the sensory experience itself has not changed.

Another reason to consider sensory issues concerns differences between taste and smell. The hedonic properties of these two senses are not the same. Analyses of hedonic changes to food may profit from an appreciation of these differences.

Although we speak of "tasting" food, other oral sensory experiences are also stimulated when we eat. These include olfaction, touch, heat, cold, and pain. In particular, olfaction and taste combine to produce flavor. The common use of taste to refer to flavor or to all of the sensations elicited by foods and beverages, produces confusion in the scientific literature as well as in everyday conversation. A possible origin of this confusing usage will be discussed in the anatomy section below. In the following section, "taste" refers only to taste per se.

QUALITIES EXPERIENCED

The "four basic tastes" refer to sweet, salty, sour, and bitter. Although a variety of other quality names have been proposed for taste (e.g., metallic, alkaline, umami), none have been accepted by large numbers of chemosensory investigators. These four taste quality names share a very interesting characteristic. They are abstract terms that can be used as metaphors in sentences that do not refer to the sense of taste at all. For example, we can say "Mary is sweet," or "John is bitter" and the meaning is clear.

Olfactory quality names have very different characteristics. First, there are many more olfactory qualities than there are taste qualities. Experts have been unable to agree on a set of "basic smells." Second, olfactory names are concrete. That is they tend to name the object that emits the odor (e.g., minty, smokey, vanilla, lemon).

Independence of Qualities

The idea of four basic tastes originated in 19th century taste psychophysics in Europe. One of the psychophysicists of that era, Kiesow, believed that these taste qualities were analogous to colors in vision. His views were very influential, possibly because his German mentor was Wundt, who taught many American psychologists who later wrote influential texts. However, a Swedish psychophysicist, Öhrwall (1901), maintained that the four taste qualities were independent of one another and should be considered four separate senses. He based this idea on a variety of taste phenomena showing that taste qualities could be manipulated independently of one another. From a modern point of view, Öhrwall turns out to have been correct on many of the empirical issues that interested these two great figures in the history of psychophysics. Öhrwall (1901) and McBurney (1986) have both noted that the four taste qualities can be considered in the same way we consider the skin senses. Touch, temperature, and pain are all skin senses yet we treat them as separate modalities. Sweet, salty, sour, and bitter are all tastes but we can consider them as separate modalities.

Incidentally, this psychophysical controversy had its parallel in the neurophysiology of taste. The early belief that there were no taste fiber types (Pfaffmann, 1955) has given way to an acceptance of fiber types (Frank, 1973; Pfaffmann, 1974; Scott & Chang, 1984) that may mediate the four basic tastes experienced by human subjects.

The olfactory qualities have not shown the same kinds of independence among them that led to the early ideas about separate modalities in taste. This independence in taste may be responsible for the analytic nature of taste mixtures (discussed below).

Hedonic Tone

Good and bad are so intimately associated with taste and smell that we have special words for the experiences (e.g., repugnant, foul). The immediacy of the pleasure makes it seem absolute and thus inborn. This turns out to be true for taste but not for smell.

The pleasure associated with sweet and the displeasure associated with bitter are present at birth in humans (Steiner, 1977) and other species (Ganchrow, Oppenheimer, & Steiner, 1979; Hall & Bryan, 1981; Jacobs, Smutz & Dubose, 1977). Developmental work showed that the ability to taste NaCl develops after birth in some species (Mistretta & Bradley, 1978). When NaCl can be tasted, dilute NaCl concentrations appear to be pleasant (Beauchamp & Cowart, 1985).

The pleasure and displeasure associated with olfactory experiences do not appear to be present in human infants. Lipsitt and Engen (cited in Engen, 1982) presented two-year-olds and their mothers with odors including both good and bad ones as judged by the mother. The toddlers did not show the affect that their mothers did. One of the difficulties in this area is that there are so many distinct qualitative sensations in olfaction that no one experiment can sample them all. Thus even though the two-year-old children in the Lipsitt and Engen study were indifferent to the odorants tested, the possibility remains that some odorants might have produced affect.

Certain studies in the pheromone literature seem to suggest that some odors are intrinsically attractive to some species; however, there is also evidence that suggests that this attractiveness is learned. (Beauchamp, Doty, Moulton, & Mugford, 1976; Fillion & Blass, 1986). The affect associated with taste and smell can be modified by experience but again taste and smell show interesting differences.

Unpleasant odors can be rendered less unpleasant by simple exposure to them (Cain & Johnson, 1978). But, bitter taste does not become less unpleasant by simple exposure (Pfaffmann, 1959; Zellner, Berridge, Grill, & Ternes, 1985).

Conditioned aversions are produced when a flavor is experienced in association with nausea (Pelchat, Grill, Rozin, & Jacobs, 1983; Pelchat & Rozin, 1982). True taste aversions form easily in rats (Palmerino, Rusiniak, & Garcia, 1980) but not in humans. Humans form conditioned aversions to many foods and beverages (Bernstein & Webster, 1980; Garb & Stunkard, 1974; Logue, Ophir, & Strauss, 1981) associated with nausea. An analysis of the foods to which these aversions occur, however, suggests that these aversions are much more likely to be formed to the olfactory components of the flavor rather than to the taste components of the flavor (Bartoshuk & Wolfe, 1990). This makes sense. If the purpose of a conditioned aversion is to prevent future ingestion of a suspect food, then smell, which is perceived before the food enters the mouth, is a better warning cue than taste.

Conditioned preferences are formed when olfactory stimuli are paired with pleasurable or beneficial experiences (e.g., sweet taste, calories). A variety of odors can be rendered more palatable in this way within a single experimental session (e.g., Booth, Lee, & McAleavey, 1976; Zellner, Rozin, Aron, & Kulish, 1983).

Attempts have been made to render bitter substances more palatable through conditioning. Rats will temporarily increase intake of bitter solutions when those solutions provide the only source of water; however, rats will avoid the bitter solutions when water itself becomes available (Pfaffmann, 1959; Zellner et al., 1985). Rats will consume bitter SOA (sucrose octa acetate) when it is paired with a desirable substance like polycose (Scalfani & Vigorito, 1987), and they will consume bitter morphine for the positive affect produced by the morphine (Zellner, et al, 1985). The latter study utilized the facial expression measure of palatability developed by Grill and his colleagues (e.g., Grill & Berridge, 1985). After long-term consumption of morphine (9 months), the rat's facial expressions suggested that the morphine had increased in palatability. However, the duration of this phenomenon is unknown. Zellner et al. (1985) noted that human subjects fail to show even this modest change in palatability. We do not come to like the taste of bitter medications even if they make us feel better (Rozin & Vollmecke, 1986).

Cabanac (1971) coined the term *alliesthesia* to describe changes in palatability produced by changing the state of the body. For example, the consumption of sugar diminishes the palatability of sweetness (Cabanac, Minaire, & Adair, 1969), while injection of insulin increases it (Jacobs, 1958; Mayer-Gross & Walker, 1946; Rodin, Wack, Ferannini, & DeFronzo, 1985). The palatability of NaCl is also related to body state. In fact, in rats and in some people, the need for sodium is associated with a craving for saltiness (Henkin, Gill & Bartter, 1963; Richter, 1936, 1942–1943; Schulkin, 1986).

Thus the effect of olfaction is labile and affected by associations between odors and their consequences. The effect of the sweet and salty tastes is more robust but is affected by bodily needs for sugar and salt.

ANALYTIC VERSUS SYNTHETIC VERSUS HOLISTIC PROCESSING

Early in the history of sensory psychophysics, psychophysicists became interested in the nature of sensory combinations (e.g., mixtures). Vision provides the classic example of synthetic mixing. This means that when the eye receives two different wavelengths, the perceived color is a synthesis of the two that does not contain the components. For example, when we mix red and green we see yellow.

Audition provides the classic example of analytic mixing. This means that when the ear receives two different frequencies (provided that they are not too close together), we hear both pitches. This is easily demonstrated by playing high and low notes on the piano. Each note is recognizable.

The status of taste mixtures, however, is controversial. Historically, taste has been assumed to be analytic since the components of simple taste mixtures are identifiable. Yet, some authors describe taste mixtures as synthetic. Their argument is based on the empirical finding that subjects can fail to perceive all of the components in a taste mixture (Erickson & Covey, 1980). However, this fails to consider mixture suppression (Szczesiul, Grill, & Bartoshuk, 1987). When substances with different qualities and perceived intensities are mixed, the weaker qualities may be suppressed (Bartoshuk, 1975; Lawless, 1979; Pangborn, 1960). This is not synthesis.

Two component olfactory mixtures can be analytic (Laing, Panhuber, Willcox, & Pittman, 1984). However, a consideration of analysis and synthesis does not completely describe what happens in olfactory mixtures. Like more complex perceptual experiences, we can group parts of an olfactory array and respond to them as a whole. In fact, this appears to be how we process most olfactory experiences. Cain (1987) suggested that we form templates of complex olfactory arrays. In this way, we recognize specific olfactory arrays holistically. Thus we can respond to a large number of olfactory experiences that contain some elements in common. This allows us to make impressive discriminations among the odors emitted by a variety of objects.

Taste is an analytic sense tuned to simple, specific sensations. Olfaction contains many more sensory elements than taste. We can respond to these elements analytically, but more typically we group them into meaningful wholes and respond to that whole.

Anatomy

Taste buds are found on the roof of the mouth at the boundary between the hard and soft palates and on the edges of the tongue. Moving from the edge of the tongue to the center of the tongue, the density of taste buds diminishes. The center of the tongue is virtually devoid of taste buds. We are not subjectively aware of this distribution, however.

This failure to localize taste seems to occur because the brain uses touch to obtain localization information. That is, when taste sensations occur along with touch sensations in the mouth, the brain localizes the taste to the areas touched. Stroking from the tip of the tongue to the center with a cotton swab saturated in a strong taste solution demonstrates this phenomenon. The taste sensation will seem to follow the path of the cotton swab (Baroshuk et al., 1987).

Olfactory sensations are mislocated even more severely. The olfactory receptors are located at the top of the nasal cavity, just under the eyes. If we inhale a pungent agent like horseradish, we can feel the path the volatiles take on their way to the olfactory receptors because tactile receptors in the lining of the nose are- stimulated. However, during normal eating, olfactory volatiles are pumped from the mouth into the nasal cavity where they make their way to the olfactory receptors. There are no localization cues so the entire experience is localized to the mouth where touch is experienced (Cain, 1978). Other sensations coming from receptors in the oral cavity (taste, temperature, pain) may also aid in this localization (Rozin, 1982).

Pathologies

Olfaction

The olfactory system is, unfortunately, easy to damage. The olfactory nerve divides into small nerve bundles which pass through small holes in a fragile bone on their way to the brain. Head injuries can fracture this bone, severing the olfactory neurons. Although they are capable of regeneration, the holes in the bone appear to become occluded with scar tissue so that the olfactory neurons which regenerate in the periphery cannot find their way back to the brain. In addition to trauma, the olfactory nerve appears to be vulnerable to damage from viruses and toxins (possibly by direct invasion of the nerve). Finally, polyps can grow inside the nose and occlude the olfactory cleft, the small opening through which odorants must pass to reach the receptors. This vulnerability of the olfactory system results in both anosmia (total inability to smell) and hyposmia (reduced ability to smell).

Taste

The taste system initially appeared to be very robust, but this turned out to be a consequence of its redundancy. We now know a variety of ways in which the taste system is damaged; however, this damage is localized to portions of the gustatory system and the patients experience no subjective taste loss.

The failure to experience subjective taste loss results from two factors. First, when taste is abolished in one area, taste intensities appear to increase on the remaining areas. This was demonstrated by temporarily abolishing taste on the front of one side of the tongue with a dental anesthetic (Ostrum, Catalanotto, Gent, & Bartoshuk, 1985). Taste intensities of a variety of stimuli perceived by whole mouth taste testing were either unchanged or increased. This phenomenon was originally observed by Halpern and Nelson (1965) in the rat. Neural responses from the back of the tongue actually increased when the nerve innervating the front of the tongue was anesthetized. Halpern and Nelson interpreted this as being a release of inhibition. That is, nerves innervating various areas of the tongue appear to exert inhibition on one another (possibly in the central nervous system). When one nerve is temporarily anesthetized, it no longer contributes to the overall taste experience or inhibits the other nerves.

Additional evidence for this interpretation came under an unusual opportunity to study a case of Ramsey-Hunt's Syndrome. This disorder is caused by the same virus that causes chicken pox. Many years after the original infection, the virus (still present in the body) reactivates and damages a variety of cranial nerves on one side of the body. In one individual (Bartoshuk, Pfaffmann, & Catalanotto, 1989; Pfaffmann & Bartoshuk, 1989) taste was completely lost on the left side. The patient had no subjective awareness of loss. Localized testing showed that the patient's tastes were perceived to be unusually intense on the unaffected right side. Since the taste nerve regenerates, taste function began to return after an interval. As the affected side improved, the unaffected side showed decrements in perceived taste intensity. We suggest that as the affected nerves regenerated, they regained their ability to inhibit the other side.

The second factor preventing patients from experiencing localized taste losses is the localization illusion noted previously. In the patient with Ramsey-Hunt's Syndrome, painting with a cotton swab from the unaffected to the affected side caused taste to invade the damaged area (Bartoshuk, Pfaffmann, & Catalanotto, 1989).

Thus olfaction is much more vulnerable to subjective losses than taste. Taste loss is usually localized to specific areas and the taste system is organized to compensate for these losses. This raises the interesting question of the purpose of the redundancy of the taste system.

Genetic Variation

Both taste and smell contain examples of genetic variation. This sensory variability can be mistaken for hedonic variability without careful sensory testing.

Taste

Some individuals do not taste certain bitter compounds (e.g., phenylthiocarbamide [PTC], and 6-n-propylthiouracil [PROP]). This "taste blindness" has been known for several decades (Bartoshuk, 1979; Fischer, 1967; Fox, 1932; Harris & Kalmus, 1949; Lawless, 1980). Those who are taste blind carry two recessive genes for this trait. They are called *nontasters*. *Tasters* may be either heterozygous or homozygous for the dominant gene. Nontasters are now known to perceive reduced sweetness in some sweet compounds including sucrose (Gent & Bartoshuk, 1983) as well as reduced bitterness in some bitter compounds including KCl (Bartoshuk, Rifkin, Marks, & Hooper, 1988).

Olfaction

Androstenone does not smell the same to all individuals. Some do not perceive it at all, others perceive a floral odor, and still others perceive a urinous order (Gilbert & Wysocki, 1987). A variety of other odorants show similar variations in the intensity of the perceived odor. The genetic contribution to this variation is not known.

HOW WE PERCEIVE MACRO- AND MICRONUTRIENTS

Macronutrients

Protein molecules and fat molecules have essentially no taste and no smell. The flavors that are apparently associated with the proteins and fats that we eat come from small amounts of other substances (e.g., bacon fat is flavored by volatiles mixed with the fat). Carbohydrates include both sugar and starch. Some sugars have sweet tastes (e.g., sucrose, glucose, fructose), but starch has no taste to humans. Starch (at least the shorter starch chains consisting of four glucose molecules) does have a taste, however, to some nonhuman species (Scalfani & Mann, 1987).

Micronutrients

The tastes and/or smells of most vitamins are present in very small quantities in food and are usually not perceived. There is no taste or odor cue that labels the presence of vitamins in food. On the other hand, some minerals present in foods as salts are of sufficiently high enough concentrations to permit them to be tasted. For example, when the minerals sodium and potassium are present as salts, they taste salty and, in the case of potassium, bitter as well to many individuals depending on their genetic status for PTC/PROP tasting (Bartoshuk, et al., 1988).

Antinutrients

It is useful to think of poisons as antinutrient because they interact with the body's chemistry. Although there are many exceptions, poisons tend to taste bitter. This bitter taste and the negative affect it produces presumably evolved to protect organisms from poisons with which they have had no prior experience.

Selecting a Healthy Diet

If our chemical senses are not atuned to nutrients, how do we select a healthy diet? Taste provides some direct nutritional guidance that requires no learning. Both sugar and salt will become more palatable when the body needs them. Olfaction directs our food choices after we learn the consequences of ingestion. We process the smell of a particular food holistically. The palatability of that smell is determined by the previous consequences of ingesting that food. It should be noted that taste plays an additional role. Taste cues (as well as textural cues, etc.) become incorporated into the whole sensory complex that is used to identify a food.

References

Bartoshuk, L. M. (1975). Taste mixtures: Is mixture suppression related to compression? *Physiology & Behavior, 14,* 643–649.

Bartoshuk, L. M. (1978). History of taste research. In E. C. Carterette & M. P. Friedman (Eds.), *Handbook of Perception, Vol. 6A. Tasting and Smelling* (pp. 3–18) New York: Academic Press.

Bartoshuk, L. M. (1979). Bitter taste of saccharin: Related to the genetic ability to taste the bitter substance 6-*n*-propylthiouracil (PROP). *Science, 205,* 934–935.

Bartoshuk, L. M. (1980). Preference changes: Sensory versus hedonic explanations. In J. H. A. Kroeze (Ed.), *Preference behaviour and chemoreception* (pp. 367–370). London: Information Retrieval, Ltd.

Bartoshuk, L. M., Desnoyers, S., Hudson, C., Marks, L., O'Brien, M., Catalanotto, F. C., Gent, J., Williams, D., & Ostrum, K. M. (1987). Tasting on localized areas. In S. Roper & J. Atema (Eds.), *Olfaction and taste IX: Annals of the New York Academy of Sciences: Vol. 510.* (pp. 166–168).

Bartoshuk, L. M., Pfaffmann, C., & Catalanotto, F. (1989, June). Why is taste loss so often unnoticed? Poster presented at the meeting of the American Psychological Society, Washington, DC

Bartoshuk, L. M., Rifkin, B., Marks. L. E., & Hooper, J. E. (1988). Bitterness of KCl and benzoate: Related to PTC/PROP. *Chemical Senses, 13,* 517–528.

Bartoshuk, L. M. & Wolfe, J. M. (1990, April). Conditioned "taste" aversions in humans: Are they olfactory aversions? Paper presented at the meeting of the Association for Chemoreception Sciences, Sarasota, FL.

Beauchamp, G. K., & Cowart, B. J. (1985). Congenital and experiential factors in the development of human flavor preferences. *Appetite, 6,* 357–372.

Beauchamp, G. K., Doty, R. L., Moulton, D. G., & Mugford, R. A. (1976). The pheromone concept in mammalian chemical communication: A critique. in R. L. Doty (Ed.), *Mammalian olfaction, reproductive processes and behaviour* (pp. 143–160). New York: Academic Press.

Bernstein, I. L., & Webster, M. M. (1980). Learned taste aversions in humans. *Physiology & Behavior, 25,* 363–366.

Booth, D. A., Lee, M., & McAleavey, C. (1976). Acquired sensory control of satiation in man. *British Journal of Psychology, 67,* 137–147.

Cabanac, M. (1971). Physiological role of pleasure. *Science, 173,* 1103–1107.

Cabanac, M., Minaire, Y., & Adair, E. R. (1969). Influence of internal factors on the pleasantness of a gustative sweet sensation. *Communications in Behavioral Biology, Part A, 1,* 77–82.

Cain, W. S. (1978). History of research on smell. In E. C. Carterette and M. P. Friedman (Eds.), *Handbook of perception, Vol. VIA. Tasting and Smelling* (pp. 197–229). New York: Academic Press.

Cain, W. S. (1987). Taste vs. smell in the organization of perceptual experience. In J. Solms, D. A. Booth, R. M. Pangborn, & O. Raunhardt (Eds.), *Food acceptance and nutrition* (pp. 63–77). New York: Academic Press.

Cain, W. S. & Johnson, F. (1978). Lability of odor pleasantness: Influence of mere exposure. *Perception, 7,* 459–465.

Engen, T. (1982). *The Perception of odors.* Orlando, FL: Academic Press.

Erickson, R. E., & Covey, E. (1980). On the singularity of taste sensations: What is a taste primary? *Physiology & Behavior, 25,* 79–110.

Fillion, T. J. & Blass, E. M. (1986). Infantile experience with suckling odors determines adult sexual behavior in male rats. *Science, 231,* 729–731.

Fischer, R. (1967). Genetics and gustatory chemoreception in man and other primates. In M. R. Kare & O. Maller (Eds.), *The chemical senses and nutrition* (pp. 61–81). Baltimore, MD: The Johns Hopkins Press.

Fox, A. L. (1932). The relation between chemical constitution and taste. *Proceedings of the National Academy of Sciences, 18,* 115–120.

Frank, M. (1973). An analysis of hamster afferent taste nerve response functions. *Journal of General Physiology, 61, 588–618.*

Ganchrow, J. R., Oppenheimer, M., & Steiner, J. E. (1979). Behavioral displays to gustatory stimuli in newborn rabbit pups. *Chemical Senses and Flavour, 4,* 49–61.

Garb, J. L., & Stunkard, A. J. (1974). Taste aversions in man. *American Journal of Psychiatry, 131,* 1204–1207.

Gent, J. F., & Bartoshuk, L. M. (1983). Sweetness of sucrose, neohesperidin dihydrochalcone, and saccharin is related to genetic ability to taste the bitter substance 6-*n*-propylthiouracil. *Chemical Senses, 7,* 265–272.

Gilbert, A. N., & Wysocki, C. J. (1987). The smell survey results. *National Geographic, 172,* 515–525.

Grill, H. J., & Berridge, K. C. (1985). Taste reactivity as a measure of the neural control of palatability. *Progress in Psychobiology and Physiological Psychology, 11,* 1–61.

Hall, W. G., & Bryan, T. E. (1981). The ontogeny of feeding in rats: IV. Taste development as measured by intake and behavioral responses to oral infusions of sucrose and quinine. *Journal of Comparative and Physiological Psychology, 95,* 240–251.

Halpern, B. P., & Nelson, L. M. (1965). Bulbar gustatory responses to anterior and to posterior tongue stimulation in the rat. *American Journal of Physiology, 209,* 105–110.

Harris, H., & Kalmus, H. (1949). The measurement of taste sensitivity to phenylthiourea (PTC). *Annals of Eugenics, 15,* 24–31.

Henkin, R. I., Gill, J. R., & Bartter, F. C. (1963). Studies on taste thresholds in normal man and in patients with adrenal cortical insufficiency: The role of adrenal cortical steriods and of serum sodium concentration. *Journal of Clinical Investigation, 42,* 727–735.

Jacobs, H. L. (1958). Studies on sugar preference: I. The preference for glucose solutions and its modification by injections of insulin. *Journal of Comparative and Physiological Psychology, 51,* 304–310.

Jacobs, H. L., Smutz, E. R., & DuBose, C. N. (1977). Comparative observations on the ontogeny of taste preference. In J. M. Weiffenbach (Ed.), *Taste and development: The genesis of sweet preference* (pp. 99–107). Bethesda, MD: U.S. Dept. of Health, Education, and Welfare.

Krieckhaus, E. E. (1970). "Innate recognition" aids rats in sodium regulation. *Journal of Comparative and Physiological Psychology, 73,* 117–122.

Kriekhaus, E. E., & Wolf, G. (1968). Acquisition of sodium by rats: Interaction of innate mechanisms and latent learning. *Journal of Comparative and Physiological Psychology, 65,* 197–201.

Laing, D. G., Panhuber, H., Willcox, M. E., & Pittman, E. A. (1984). Quality and intensity of binary odor mixtures. *Physiology & Behavior, 33,* 309–319.

Lawless, H. T. (1979). Evidence for neural inhibition in bittersweet taste mixtures. *Journal of Comparative and Physiological Psychology, 93,* 538–547.

Lawless, H. (1980). A comparison of different methods used to assess sensitivity to the taste of phenylthiocarbamide (PTC) *Chemical Senses, 5,* 247–256.

Logue, A. W., Ophir, I., & Strauss, K. & E. (1981). The acquisition of taste aversions in humans. *Behavior, Research, & Therapy, 19,* 319–333.

Mayer-Gross, W., & Walker, J. W. (1946). Taste and selection of food in hypoglycaemia. *British Journal of Experimental Pathology, 27,* 297–305.

McBurney, D. H. (1986). Taking the confusion out of fusion. In H. L. Meiselman & R. S. Rivlin (Eds.), *Clinical measurement of taste and smell* (pp. 50–65). Lexington, MA: Collamore Press.

Mistretta, C. M. & Bradley, R. M. (1978). Taste responses in sheep medulla: Changes during development. *Science, 202,* 535–537.

Öhrwall, H. (1901). Die modalitäts- und qualitatsbegriffe in der sinnesphysiologie und deren bedeutung. [Modality and quality concepts in sensory physiology and their significance]. *Skandinavian Archiv für Physiologie, 11,* 245–272.

Ostrum, K. M., Catalanotto, F. A., Gent, J. F., & Bartoshuk, L. M. (1985). Effects of oral sensory field loss of taste scaling ability. *Chemical Senses, 10,* 459.

Palmerino, C. C., Rusiniak, K. W., & Garcia, J. (1980). Flavor-illness aversions: The peculiar roles of odor and taste in memory for poison. *Science, 208,* 753–755.

Pangborn, R. M. (1960). Taste interrelationships. *Food Research, 25,* 245–256.

Pelchat, M. L., & Rozin, P. (1982). The special role of nausea in the acquisition of food dislikes by humans. *Appetite, 3,* 341–351.

Pelchat, M. L., Grill, H. J., Rozin, P., & Jacobs, J. (1983). Quality of acquired responses to tastes by *Rattus norvegicus* depends on type of associated discomfort. *Journal of Comparative Psychology, 97,* 140–153.

Pfaffmann, C. (1955). Gustatory nerve impulses in rat, cat, and rabbit. *Journal of Neurophysiology, 18,* 429–440.

Pfaffmann, C. (1959). The sense of taste. In J. Field (Ed.), *Handbook of Physiology:*

Sec. 1: Neurophysiology: Vol. 1 (pp. 507–533). Washington, DC: American Physiological Society.

Pfaffmann, C. (1974). Specificity of the sweet receptors of the squirrel monkey. *Chemical Senses and Flavor, 1,* 61–67.

Pfaffmann, C. P., & Bartoshuk, L. M. (1989, April). A case of unilateral taste loss. Paper presented at the 11th annual meeting of the Association for Chemoreception Sciences, Sarasota, FL.

Richter, C. P. (1936). Increased salt appetite in adrenalectomized rats. *American Journal of Physiology, 115,* 155–161.

Richter, C. P. (1942–1943). Total self-regulatory functions in animals and human beings. *Harvey Lecture Series, 38,* 63–103.

Rodin, J., Wack, J., Ferrannini, E., & DeFronzo, R. A. (1985). Effect of insulin and glucose on feeding behavior. *Metabolism, 34,* 826–831.

Rozin, P. (1982). "Taste-smell confusions" and the duality of the olfactory sense. *Perception and Psychophysics, 31,* 397–401.

Rozin, P., & Vollmecke, T. A. (1986). Food likes and dislikes. *Annual Reviews of Nutrition, 6,* 433–456.

Schulkin, J. (1986). Behavioral dynamics in the appetite for salt in rats. In B. de Caro, A. N. Epstein, & M. Massi (Eds.), *The physiology of thirst and sodium appetite* (pp. 497–502). New York: Plaenum.

Sclafani, A., & Mann, S. (1987). Carbohydrate taste preferences in rats: Glucose, sucrose, maltose, fructose, and polycose compared. *Physiology & Behavior, 40,* 563–568.

Sclafani, A., & Vigorito, M. (1987). Effects of SOA and saccharin adulteration on polycose preference in rats. *Neuroscience and Biobehavioral Reviews, 11,* 163–168.

Scott, R. R., & Chang, F. (1984). The state of gustatory neural coding. *Chemical Senses, 8,* 297–314.

Steiner, J. (1977). Facial expressions of the neonate infant indicating the hedonics of food-related chemical stimuli. In J. M. Weiffenbach (Ed.), *Taste and development: The genesis of sweet preference* (pp. 173–188). Bethesda, MD: U.S. Department of Health, Education, and Welfare (HEW).

Szczesiul, R., Grill, H., & Bartoshuk, L. M. (1987 August–September). Recognition of components in taste mixtures: Analytic or synthetic? Poster presented at the annual meeting of the American Psychological Association, New York, NY.

Zellner, D. A., Rozin, P., Aron, M., & Kulish, C. (1983). Conditioned enhancement of human's liking for flavor by pairing with sweetness. *Learning and Motivation, 14,* 338–350.

Zellner, D. A., Berridge, K. C., Grill, H. J., & Ternes, J. W. (1985). Rats learn to like the taste of morphine. *Behavioral Neuroscience, 99,* 290–300.

PART THREE

GENETIC AND DEVELOPMENTAL ASPECTS

CHAPTER 6

TASTE-MEDIATED DIFFERENCES IN THE SUCKING BEHAVIOR OF HUMAN NEWBORNS

LEWIS P. LIPSITT AND GUNDEEP BEHL

Human newborns have self-regulatory capabilities which enable them to execute appropriate patterns of behavior necessary for ingestion. These include mouthing, head turning, sucking, swallowing, and respiring in cycles which promote avoidance of choking and other annoyances. The self-regulatory mechanisms entailed in this process seem to be mediated by the pleasures of the sensation. In feeding, behaviors that enhance savoring experiences derived from substances entering the mouth, particularly those associated with a sweet taste, are probably crucial to the process. Studies reported here document the capacities of human infants to respond to differences in the taste qualities of substances. Some of these studies may be considered "reactive," in that they demonstrate differential responsivity to the delivery of different taste substances. Other studies are of a "proactive" nature, involving delivery of the substances contingent upon the baby's own responses. Concomitant adjustments in aspects of the sucking behavior depending upon the hedonic value or attractiveness of the stimulus take place. Thus babies slow down their sucking maneuvers with increasing sweetness of the fluid, up to an optimal concentration level, but take fewer rest periods and invest more sucks per burst of sucking. This optimizes intake of the most palatable substances by leaving the savory substance for a longer time on the tongue and promoting more sucks over a longer period of time (Lipsitt, 1974; Lipsitt, Reilly, Butcher, & Greenwood, 1976). The history of such studies is reviewed briefly to reflect that relatively little attention has been accorded these rather complex but interesting and life-sustaining processes in human infants. We conclude that sucking and other ingestion-associated behaviors are under the control of a variety of conditions, including hunger and, perhaps most importantly, the hedonic disposition and pleasure-promoting character of the human newborn. Approach and avoidance behavior of the human infant, mediated by the pleasures and annoyances of sensation, is key to understanding the nature of basic learning processes, as well as cognitive elaborations on these.

HISTORICAL BACKGROUND

When in the developmental span of human infancy does gustatory sensitivity first occur, and what are the limits of those capabilities at successive ages? Morphological studies suggest that the physiological apparatus is available very early in fetal life (Peiper, 1963). Bradley (1972) has noted the appearance of taste buds in 7–8-week-old human fetuses and found that those receptors mature structurally as early as 14 weeks of gestation.

In an effort to discover the taste capacities of mammals during fetal development, and the underlying neural apparatus permitting such sensory sensitivity, Bradley and Mistretta (1973) addressed the functional characteristics of the in utero taste buds in sheep. They recorded responses from the chorda tympani nerve and the tractus solitarius while chemically stimulating the tongue of the fetal sheep. The development of taste receptors of these animals follows much the same chronological path as humans. Salts and acids were found to elicit a higher frequency neural discharge than chemicals which taste sweet or bitter to man. These responses were similar to those of newborn and adult lambs.

To explore whether behavioral responses to taste stimuli could be obtained in utero, Mistretta and Bradley (1977) monitored fetal swallowing by implanting an electromagnetic flow transducer in the esophagus of sheep fetuses. After obtaining baseline data, attempts to increase or decrease swallowing by injecting sweet or bitter chemicals respectively led to inconsistent results. Thus they were unable to determine whether the fetus can respond differentially to such taste stimuli in utero although they established that the taste buds of sheep are responsive to chemical stimuli from 80 days of gestational age to term.

Many studies lead to the conclusion that in the first few hours of life, humans are capable of detecting even subtle changes in gustatory stimulation, and show a pronounced preference for sweet tasting stimuli (Peiper, 1963). In the earliest reported work, Kussmaul (1859) noted sucking movements to a saturated

This chapter is dedicated to the memory of Professor Curt Richter, pioneer in the study of developmental psychobiology. A friend of the neonate laboratory and of the Brown University Child Study Center from which this manuscript was generated, Curt Richter's work on taste and ingestion, and on human development, has been an inspiration. This work has been supported by the March of Dimes Birth Defects Foundation, the Mailman Family Foundation, the American Psychological Foundation, the Hasbro Corporation, and the W. T. Grant Foundation. We thank Bernice Reilly, RN, for her many years of devoted service to the Brown University newborn behavior laboratory at Women and Infants Hospital of Rhode Island.

sugar solution, and grimaces to solutions of quinine sulphate, salt, and tartaric acid in human newborns.

Similar results confirming differential behavioral effects were obtained by Preyer (1882). He found that even on the first day of life, a quinine solution (bitter) evoked a wry facial reaction that was considerably different from the facial reaction evoked by a sugar solution (sweet). The "sour" expression to an acetic acid solution differed from both these "bitter" and "sweet" reactions. He concluded that of all reactions in the newborn, those to gustatory stimuli are the most highly developed, and differential gustatory qualities are distinguished by the neonate, evoking different reflex movements.

In marked contrast to the foregoing findings, Shinn (1893–1899), on the basis of her numerous observations of one child, reported that the newborn is extremely unresponsive to taste stimuli. This would not warrant mention in view of the other strong evidence to the contrary in the history of the study of neonatal taste and from recent findings, except that Shinn's observations make salient the importance of individual differences in sensory attributes and responsivity of the human neonate.

Peterson and Rainey (1910) observed that the facial reactions of 76 neonates to a concentrated salt solution, a 1% solution of acetic acid, a syrup of unspecified strength, and a tincture of gentian could be differentiated and that they bore great resemblance to those of adults. These investigators found that the simple appearance of sucking movements cannot be taken as evidence of satisfaction, since salt, sour, and bitter stimuli often produce such sucking motions together with facial expressions of dissatisfaction.

One of the first studies sensitive to the intricate interrelationships among the several psychobiological systems associated with taste and ingestion, such as sucking, swallowing, respiration, and heart rate, was that of Canestrini in 1913. By using direct measures of cardiovascular and respiratory responses, the reactions of 35 infants, from 1–14 days old, to different taste solutions were studied. The sweet solution produced a quieting, calming effect shown by a lowering of the respiratory and circulatory rates. Salt produced restlessness shown by respiratory disruption and pulse increases, and by cessation or interruption of sucking movements. Sour and bitter solutions yielded breathing irregularities as well as fontanelle action greater than the responses caused by sweet and salt.

Eckstein (1927) graphically recorded the sucking responses of prematures, normal neonates, and older infants to taste stimuli of varying concentrations. Almost all infants, including the prematures, made similar differential responses to the same stimuli, with bitter almost without exception being followed by inhibition of the sucking reflex.

A classic investigation of neonatal taste was conducted by Pratt, Nelson, and Sun (1930). Testing 28 infants an average of eight times from birth to 15 days of age, they observed differential responses to sugar, salt, quinine, and citric acid, with distilled water being used as a control stimulus. Bodily movements were recorded by a stabilimeter and polygraph, and supplementary records of sucking behavior and facial reactions were also obtained. The babies showed some reaction to all of the nonwater stimuli about 85% of the time, with sucking occurring on approximately 30% of the stimulations. Although frequency and intensity of response to gustatory stimuli are dependent upon intensity, and it is thus not very meaningful to compare responsivity across qualitative boundaries, Pratt and his colleagues noted that the overall sucking reactions to the various stimuli were: 49% to sugar, 36% to salt, 32% to water, 22% to quinine, and 7% to citric acid. The reactions to water were taken to imply that newborns react not only to taste but also to the presence of something in the mouth, and thus response to water should perhaps be taken as the "basal level." Body movements occurred most to citric acid (25% of the time), and least to water (on 15% of the occasions). Comparing these results to adult reactions showed that the citric acid solution, which seemed weak to adults, produced a strong reaction in the infants. Conversely, the quinine solution which seemed strong to the adults produced a relatively weak aversive response in the newborns.

Another early investigation employing well-controlled procedures was conducted by Jensen (1932) using a specially constructed nursing bottle with a calibrated nipple connected to a manometer which registered responses on a kymograph. Among the gustatory stimuli administered, only salt solutions were found to impair or cause cessation of the sucking response, with higher concentrations causing vigorous avoidance movements and crying. Jensen made the interesting observation that moderately satiated babies show better taste discrimination than very hungry infants. The suggestion, which might be beneficially pursued further, is that competing stimulation, perhaps both interoceptive and exteroceptive, may have critical influences upon the discriminative responses of the infant.

Shirley (1933) observed facial and bodily reactions of 14 newborns to bitter, salt, sour, and sweet stimuli. While the infants sucked contentedly on the sweet applicator, reactions to the first three stimuli were mainly those of rejection.

Detailed observations were made by Stirnimann (1936) of 100 neonates after applying gustatory solutions to their tongues by means of a nipple-shaped cotton piece. Variable reactions corresponding to the four principal taste sensations were reported, with sucking responses following not only stimulations with sugar, but also those with salt, citric acid, and quinine. Crying among infants was noted at times when sugar-soaked applicators were removed from their mouths. Thus both positive and negative hedonic behavior, with respect to ingestion, are clearly in evidence in the newborn.

The ability of infants to discriminate among sweet solutions has been generally confirmed by several studies. Desor, Maller, and Turner (1973) observed that the volume of sugar solutions ingested by neonates was greater than the volume of water ingested in the same time period. Moreover, ingestion of .20 M and .30 M solutions was greater than .05 M and .10 M solutions, thus showing the newborn's capability of discriminating between various concentrations of solutions. These preferences paralleled adult ratings of the sweetness of the sugar solutions. The infants also discriminated between types of sugars, showing a preference for sucrose and fructose over glucose and lactose. Nowlis and Kessen (1976) obtained similar results with two concentrations of sucrose (.058 M and .117 M) and glucose (.227 M and .555 M), using anterior tongue pressure changes during sucking as the dependent measure.

Preference is usually obtained for the sweeter of two fluids, when comparisons are made of various sucking parameters in newborns. When comparisons are made across qualitatively different fluids, the perceived sweetness of the two fluids offered should control preference. Two studies (Dubignon & Campbell, 1969; Kron, Stein, Goddard, & Phoenix, 1967) have reported that milk formula elicited more sucking than solutions of 5% sugar (dextrose or corn syrup). The presumption may be made that the milk formula was sweeter than the sugar solution offered, and that a 10% or 12% sugar solution might well be preferred over the same milk formula. Casual evidence from our laboratory suggests that a 10% sucrose solution is "equivalent" in palatability to commercial formula available in the U.S., and that a 12% solution might well provoke preference for the sucrose solution over the commercial lactose solutions. Studies need to be conducted on the relative palatabilities of mother's milk (which is not of constant sweetness), commercial formula, and various dilutions of sucrose and lactose.

The foregoing review does not make possible entirely unequivocal statements regarding the gustatory capabilities of newborns. However, it does indicate that infants manifest positive reactions to sweet solutions, and that salt, sour, and bitter solutions may give negative reactions, depending on their concentrations. Salt solutions tend to interrupt the sucking response, whereas sugar solutions evoke and sustain it.

RECENT STUDIES

In the last 15–20 years of laboratory studies investigating gustation in the newborn, much attention has been directed toward quantifying the positive and negative hedonic reactions to various tastes. This work has entailed the development of measures that could be relatively easily elicited and recorded, as through the use of a polygraph and related instrumentation. Thus specific aspects of the baby's sucking and other mouthing responses have yielded information presumably reflecting the savory quality of the intra-oral stimuli. Heart rate has also been used as a measure of the infant's autonomic responsivity to changing tastes (Lipsitt, 1977; Lipsitt, Reilly, Butcher, & Greenwood, 1976).

The Phenomenon of Avidity

Of special interest at this time is the concept of avidity. We suppose that it is possible to define in a variety of ways the "zest" or "enthusiasm" with which the infant sucks to obtain whatever fluid is available contingent upon his or her sucking behavior. Most of the remaining presentation will be devoted to the work of one laboratory, the Brown University Infant Behavior Laboratory located at the Women and Infants Hospital of Rhode Island, where we have chosen to concentrate on such parameters as the infant's response speed, the number of sucks which the baby invests in per given unit of time, and some indication of the autonomic nervous system involvement in the stimulus-savoring process. We have presumed that the economy of the feeding process would follow some universal rules that guide the foodsearch and ingestive behavior of other mammals (Collier, Hirsch, & Hamlin, 1972). We also assumed that the infant's oral behaviors would have some commonalities with other self-regulatory systems in which the optimization of comfort or pleasure prevails, as in behavioral thermoregulation (Weiss & Laties, 1961). Indeed we (Lipsitt & Kaye, 1965) have demonstrated previously that the mere shape of the nipple sucked, in the absence of any fluid reinforcement, was related to optimal and nonoptimizing sucking behavior. Moreover, sucking behavior is affected appreciably through conditioning procedures; when infants are reinforced for sucking, their behavior changes (Lipsitt & Kaye, 1965) to maximize the delivery of sweet fluid according to the constraints of the environmental manipulations (Kaye, 1967).

Polygraphic studies have yielded information about the discriminative capacities of newborns, and the effects on the subsequent taste reactions of the infant. These studies capitalize upon the concept of avidity, defining this attribute in terms of the baby's behavior changes occurring when opportunities to suck vary in the generated stimulus feedback. Thus on some occasions, the baby is enabled to suck for plain, distilled water, on other occasions for 5% sucrose and, on still other occasions, 15% sucrose. Our interest centered on the polygraphically recorded, quantifiable alterations in the pattern of sucking, as reflected in, for example, numbers of sucks per minute, speed of sucking within bursts, and the number and length of rest periods engaged in by the infant. In these experiments (e.g., Lipsitt, 1974; Lipsitt, 1977; Lipsitt et al., 1976), the infant sucked on a nipple which contained several small tubes allowing different taste stimuli to be presented without removing the nipple during the tests.

The amount of sucking and fluid ingestion was controlled by the infant, since the drops of fluid were presented contingent on sucks of a preset criterion amplitude. The possibility of differential responsivity to the taste stimuli being affected by postingestional consequences was controlled by presenting, for example, only .02 ml of fluid for each criterion response. Fluid deliveries, or the occurrence of a criterion suck during no-fluid conditions, were recorded by a polygraph event marker.

The typical finding of these studies was that sucking patterns for different fluids were closely related not only to whether fluid was offered (a finding reported by Wolff in 1968) but to the tastes of the fluids. The sweetness of the fluid was in fact critically determinative for understanding and predicting the sucking behavior of the newborn. Nonnutritive sucking (i.e., sucking for no fluid, as on a pacifier) characteristically entailed short bursts (6–8 sucks) of rapid sucking separated by relatively long pauses of about 15 sec. When presented with distilled water, the newborn slowed down its sucking within bursts, which were defined as a succession of sucks in which no inter-suck interval was longer than

2 sec, and invested more sucks per burst (e.g., 10–15), taking shorter and fewer rest periods between bursts. Further, when 5% sucrose was presented to the newborn, the sucking bursts became still longer, the sucking rate within bursts became slower still, and the baby commenced to take still fewer and shorter pauses. This pattern continued as the sucrose concentration was increased to 15%, so that the infant actually sucked more times per minute even while sucking at slower rates within bursts, since shorter and fewer rest pauses were taken.

Changes in heart rate were also found to accompany these changes in sucking. While the sucking rate within bursts decreased with increasing concentrations of the sweet fluids, the heart rate increased, up to a level of about 15% sucrose. This effect cannot be attributed to a change in blood sugar level since the change in heart rate was observed in the very first burst of sucking after the introduction of increased concentration of sucrose, even within the first few sucks of the burst. Moreover, since the rate of activity decreased during sucking for sweet fluids (the pacification phenomenon), the associated energy expenditure might be expected to be less than that under nonnutritive or no-fluid conditions, rendering the associated increase in heart rate paradoxical, unless we consider factors other than hunger and satiation.

In one of our early studies documenting change in several sucking parameters as a function of reinforcing stimulus feedback, Lipsitt et al. (1976) showed that over a 24-hour test-retest period the number of sucks invested per burst, number of sucks per minute, inter-suck interval, and mean number and mean length of inter-burst interval were of acceptable stability, (i.e., the 24-hour test-retest correlations were statistically reliable, although of differential magnitude for different sucking parameters). Moreover, we were able to show that heart rate was also a stable, individual difference variable, and that this stability held whether the infant was sucking for water or for sucrose. The sweeter the substance, however, the more stable was the heart rate recorded within bursts of sucking. Because heart rates rose to a higher level within sucking bursts when sucking for sweeter fluids, even though sucking slowed down within those bursts for sweeter fluids, we concluded that a savory process must be mediating both the slowing of the sucking rate within bursts to the sweeter fluid and the otherwise paradoxical higher heart rates during those bursts. The "excitement" of the baby in the presence of the optimally sweet substance was reflected in both slow sucking and high heart rates.

Crook and Lipsitt (1976), and Crook (1977) studied the effect of the magnitude of the incentive fluid per suck on the patterns of sucking behavior. The collapsibility of the sweetness and magnitude of the drop as joint determinants of the incentive value was documented. It was found that with increasing size of the drops (.06 ml as opposed to .03 ml) received contingent upon their criterion responses, newborns slowed down their sucking behavior within bursts, took shorter and fewer rest periods between bursts, invested higher average numbers of sucks per burst, sucked more times per minute, and had higher heart rates within bursts.

The Crook studies thus showed that the response parameters moved consistently in the same directions for increasing magnitudes of the drops with sweetness held constant, as for increasing sweetness of the drops when magnitude of the drop was held constant in previous studies. The construct of "incentive motivation," as propounded by Hull (1931, 1943) and Spence (1956) is helpful in understanding the mechanisms through which these common effects for sweetness and magnitude have been obtained in infants. In the theory of Hull, and elaborated by Spence and his successors, incentive motivation variables relate to the quality, and presumably the hedonic value, of the reinforcer delivered contingent upon the organism's response. Increasing delays of reinforcement and diminishing sizes of rewarding food supplies reduce the incentive motivational value of engaging in the instrumental task, and can thereby impair performance. Schedules of reinforcement, amount of delay of reinforcement, magnitude of rewards, and so on are all incentive motivation parameters, which is to say they are events that force or modulate self-regulatory behavior (Richter, 1942–43), and thus relate to persistence, efficacy, or adequacy of performance.

Reinforcement Contrast Effects

A further example of the interesting ways in which incentive motivation affects sucking in the human newborn was seen in a dissertation carried out in the Brown University laboratory by Bosack (1973). He compared the sucking behavior of human newborns (mean age 73 hours) under nutritive and nonnutritive sucking conditions using several fixed-ratio schedules of reinforcement. Nutritive sucking was found to produce higher overall sucking rates but lower within-burst rates. Burst lengths were longer during nutritive than nonnutritive sucking, with fewer bursts per unit time occurring during nutritive sucking. Bosack pointed out that although the within-burst sucking rate was lower during the nutritive conditions, the babies "compensated" by sucking longer and pausing less often, thereby obtaining more fluid reinforcement than if the sucking pattern were the same as that during the nonnutritive condition. This "negative contrast effect" was manifested in a sharp response decrement when fluid delivery was terminated following nutritive sucking as compared to nonnutritive sucking rates which were not preceded by fluid delivery.

The influence of one reinforcer in enhancing or diminishing the effectiveness of a second reinforcer in a similar situation is termed *reinforcement contrast*. Kobre and Lipsitt (1972) documented this phenomenon by studying the effects of previous taste experiences upon the infant's response during a subsequent taste experience. The study subjects were 25 newborns (mean age 70 hours) who had a mean sucking rate of at least 30 sucks per minute. A total of 20 min of responding was recorded for each infant, in four 5-min successive periods. The infants received one of five reinforcement regimens for the 20-min period.

The first group (Suc-Suc) received only 15% sucrose throughout. The second group (H_2O-H_2O) received water throughout. The third group (Suc-H_2O)

received 15% sucrose and water in that order, alternated twice in 5-min units. A fourth group (NF-NF) received no fluid throughout the four 5-min periods, and a fifth group (Suc-NF) received 15% sucrose alternated with no fluid in 5-min periods.

The mean sucking rate during the four 5-min periods for the first three groups is shown in Figure 1. The mean sucking rate for sucrose alone (55/min) and for water alone (46/min) were found to remain relatively constant across all four periods, with that for sucrose being significantly higher than that for water. The mean sucking rate in the alternation group which was high during the first sucrose period, dropped sharply when water was introduced, doubled when the subjects were shifted back to sucrose, and decreased again to the lowest level when the subjects were shifted once more to water.

In order to test for positive contrast, mean rates during period 3 of the Suc-Suc and Suc-H_2O groups were compared. A small increase in sucrose responding by subjects shifted from water to sucrose, when compared with those subjects

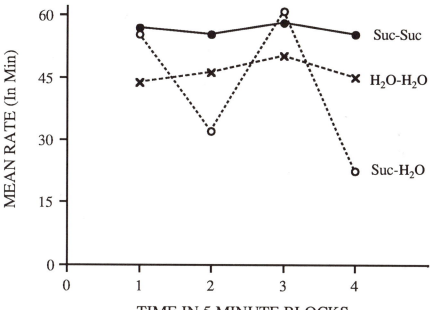

Figure 1 Mean sucking rate over four 5-min blocks for each of the three groups: sucrose alone (Suc-Suc), water alone (H_2O-H_2O), and sucrose and water alternated twice (Suc-H_2O). $N=5$ in each group. Standard deviations for each of the successive graph points for each of the groups were as follows: (a) Suc-Suc, 5.38, 8.41, 4.23, 3.95; (b) H_2O-H_2O, 6.75, 6.48, 5.58, 4.89; and (c) Suc-H_2O, 6.04, 16.33, 5.38, 9.73. From "A Negative Contrast Effect in Newborns" by K. R. Kobre and L. P. Lipsitt, 1972, *Journal of Experimental Child Psychology, 14*, p. 85. Copyright 1972 by Academic Press. Reprinted by permission.

maintained on sucrose throughout, was in the positive contrast direction, but the increase was not statistically significant. To test for negative contrast, the mean rates of the H_2O-H_2O and Suc-H_2O groups were compared during periods 2 and 4 in which both groups received water. During both of these periods, mean sucking rates of the Suc-H_2O group were significantly below those of the H_2O-H_2O group. Thus a negative contrast effect with newborns was documented.

Sucrose and no-fluid alternation led to comparable results. The mean sucking rates of the NF-NF group and the Suc-NF group during the four periods are shown in Figure 2. The mean rate of the NF-NF group increased after the first period from 32 sucks/min to about 44 sucks/min during the next three periods. In the alternation group, the mean rate was high during the sucrose periods (55 sucks/min) and dropped in half when no fluid was delivered (29 sucks/min), with the response rate during the no-fluid conditions (periods 2 and 4) being significantly below that of the NF-NF group.

Kobre and Lipsitt concluded that the observed negative contrast effect must be a reinforcement phenomenon rather than a peripheral sensory effect, since any

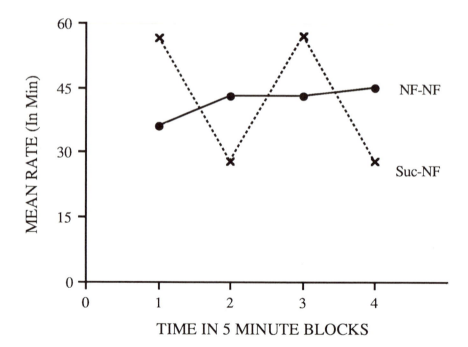

Figure 2. Mean sucking rate over four 5-min blocks for each of two groups: no-fluid (NF-NF), and sucrose and no-fluid alternated twice (Suc-NF). $N=5$ in each group. Standard deviations for each of the successive graph points for each of the groups were as follows: (a) NF-NF, 18.11, 18.00, 15.14, 9.16; and (b) Suc-NF, 12.53, 14.13, 12.03, 10.08. From "A Negative Contrast Effect in Newborns" by K. R. Kobre and L. P. Lipsitt, 1972, *Journal of Experimental Child Psychology, 14,* p. 87. Copyright 1972 by Academic Press. Reprinted by permission.

persistent effect of sucrose on the taste receptors would be expected to enhance rather than depress responding during no-fluid conditions.

Thus when newborns have experience in sucking for sucrose, an immediate subsequent experience with water "turns them off." Their apparent "aversion" for the water is displayed by a marked reduction in the instrumental behavior that would result in delivery of that fluid (Lipsitt & Werner, 1981).

Effect of Salt Stimulation

In order to determine if developmental changes in salt taste responses occur, Mistretta and Bradley (1983) stimulated the anterior tongue in sheep fetuses, young lambs, and adults of the species. They recorded from the whole chorda tympani by dissecting its constituent bundles and then recording from its separate bundles sample responses from the entire nerve fiber population. The stimuli used were 0.5 M NH_4Cl, KCl, NaCl, and LiCl, and a 0.05–0.75 M concentration series of the first three salts. The results suggested that during development there are changes in neurophysiological salt responses from the primary afferents that innervate taste receptors on the anterior tongue. In fetuses beginning the last third of gestation, NaCl and LiCl were found to elicit much smaller response magnitudes from the chorda tympani than NH_4Cl and KCl. For the remainder of the gestational period and postnatally, the NaCl and LiCl responses gradually increased in magnitude relative to NH_4Cl and KCl. Finally, in adulthood, similar response magnitudes were elicited by NaCl, LiCl, and NH_4Cl, while KCl was a relatively less effective taste stimulus. Ultrastructural studies of taste buds at different ages showed the presence of microvilli on taste bud cell apices, and tight junctions between cells in the youngest fetuses studied, thereby implying that initial stimulus-receptor membrane contacts were similar to those in adults.

The results of the Mistretta and Bradley study suggested that the essential mechanism of salt taste stimulation does not change developmentally. Rather, the composition of the taste membrane alters as it matures, so that relative changes occur in response to various salts. In other words, different membrane components interact with the various monochloride salts, and taste receptors contain different proportions of these various membrane components at different developmental stages. Mistretta and Bradley proposed that a changing neural substrate underlies salt taste function, and that the developmental changes occur in both prenatal and postnatal life. That there are both constitutional transitions and experientially modifiable taste propensities in mammals presents interesting challenges for further research on the development and manifestation of affinities and aversions with respect to food substances.

Beauchamp (1987) has suggested that human sensitivity to salt and, therefore, the preference for it, may mature after birth. The support for this suggestion comes from a study by Beauchamp, Cowart, and Moran (1986) in which the responses of infants and children to saline solutions at several ages after birth were noted. A cohort of 54 healthy infants falling under three age groups (2.5–

3.9 months, 4.0–5.3 months, and 5.4–6.7 months) were tested for their acceptance of both salt (0.10 M and 0.20 M) and sucrose (0.20 M and 0.40 M) solutions relative to plain water. In a standard intake test, the infants were presented briefly with taste solutions, of which they could consume as much as they wanted. The consumed volume was taken as an index of the subjects' preferences. Subjects in all three age groups consumed more sweetened than unsweetened solution. The results showed a developmental shift in NaCl acceptability but not in sucrose acceptability; in fact, in the latter case there was a trend toward change in the opposite direction of that observed for NaCl. The youngest group of infants did not differentially ingest plain and salt water, while both groups of older infants exhibited a greater acceptance of saline solutions than of water.

Following the reasoning that most adults do not find salt solutions pleasant or ordinarily consume them, Beauchamp et al. (1986) conducted a second experiment with older children to study the possibility of a further developmental change in the acceptability of salt. This time, 34 children divided into two age groups (7–23 months and 31–60 months) were tested using NaCl solutions (0.17 M and 0.34 M) and deionized water. The results revealed a second developmental trend in salt water acceptance. The younger group consumed more of the 0.17 M NaCl solution than water, while the intake of 0.34 M NaCl did not differ from that of water. The older group, on the other hand, rejected both concentrations of NaCl.

Crook (1978) studied the effects, in the Brown University laboratory, of intraoral fluid stimulation on the nonnutritive sucking rhythm of newborn infants. It was demonstrated that when such stimulation occurred during a pause in the rhythm, a burst of sucking was potentiated. Moreover, taste properties of the stimulus were reflected by the length of the potentiated burst. A comparison with distilled water showed that sucrose solutions potentiated longer bursts, while shorter bursts were potentiated by salt solutions. The burst lengthening and shortening effects of sucrose and salt stimulations, respectively, were recorded as a function of concentration. As expected, high concentrations of sucrose did not lengthen sucking bursts as dramatically as moderate concentrations, as shown in Figure 3. For groups receiving as their experimental stimuli water, 0.1 M, 0.3 M, and 0.6 M NaCl, there was little difference in the degree of shortening between the three NaCl groups (Crook, 1978) (Figure 4). On the basis of these results, Crook suggested that newborns are equipped with a "sweet tooth," and find salt solutions "hedonically negative."

Ganchrow, Steiner, and Daher (1983) orally stimulated 23 neonates with distilled water, 0.1 and 1.0 M sucrose, 0.15 and 0.15 M urea, and 0.0001 M quinine hydrochloride. The facial expressions of the infants were videotaped and later decoded for specific features in a double-blind setting. The presence of some features was noted for all stimulations, while other components were found to be consistently associated with a specific taste quality. Facial reactions to low concentrations of sucrose were judged to be more pleasant than water, while

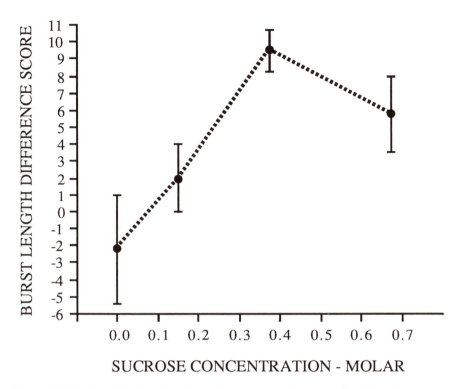

Figure 3 The burst lengthening effect of sucrose stimulation as a function of concentration. The mean length of bursts containing a water stimulus is subtracted from the mean length of bursts containing a sucrose stimulus for each subject. Group means and ± 1 standard error are shown. From "Taste Perception in the Newborn Infant" by C. K. Crook, 1978, *Infant Behavior and Development, 1,* p. 63. Copyright 1978 by Ablex Publishing Corporation. Reprinted with the permission of Ablex Publishing Corporation.

facial reactions to low considerations of urea were judged to be less pleasant than water. Increased concentration led to an increased separation of these estimates from water. On the basis of their results, the authors concluded that the human gustofacial response is an innate response of the nervous system sensitive to changes in stimulus quality and intensity.

Maller and Desor (1974) tested 102 male and 102 female newborn infants, varying in age from 17–83 hours, for their response to salty, bitter, and sour taste qualities. Each baby was offered water for 3 min and a sapid solution for 3 min, with a 2-min rest period between presentations. The concentrations of the solutions ranged from .003–.2 M saline, .03–.18 M urea, and .001–.012 M citric acid. The differences between the ingested volumes of sapid solutions and water were subjected to analyses of variance, which yielded the conclusion that the infants did not distinguish among bitter, sour, or salty solutions and water.

The newborns' indifference may be attributable to the solutions being too low in concentration for detection. Another possibility is that the infants perceived

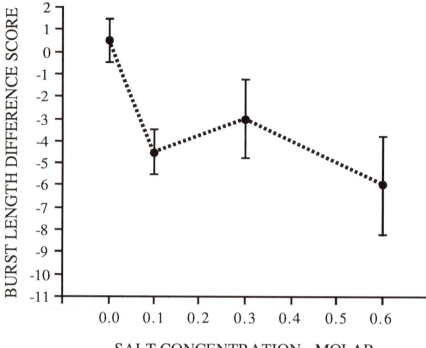

SALT CONCENTRATION - MOLAR

Figure 4 The burst shortening effect of salt stimulation as a function of concentration. The mean length of water potentiated bursts is subtracted from the mean length of salt potentiated bursts for each subject. Group means and ± 1 standard error are shown. From "Taste Perception in the Newborn Infant" by C. K. Crook, 1978, *Infant Behavior and Development, 1,* p. 65. Copyright 1978 by Ablex Publishing Corporation. Reprinted with the permission of Ablex Publishing Corporation.

the taste differences, but manifested no preferential responding. The design of the study could not differentiate among possible explanations. Therefore, Desor, Maller, and Andrews (1975) conducted two clarifying experiments. In Experiment 1, they used stronger solutions than those previously, and tested 48 infants 21–82 hours of age. The infants were offered bottles containing either sterile water or one of the following solutions: .24 or .48 M urea; .024 or .048 M citric acid. The results shows that these newborns did not vary the volume they ingested as a function of the presence and concentration of either urea or citric acid. Thus the indifference noted in the previous study persisted even in the face of higher concentrations of taste stimuli.

Experiment 2 was conducted to control for the possibility that aversions to sour, salty, and bitter are present in the human newborn but not demonstrable when water is used as the standard of comparison, since water in itself may be an aversive rather than a neutral stimulus for newborns. A sucrose solution was used as the standard fluid, its concentration being high enough to ensure a baseline ingestion rate above that of water, while being as mild as possible to prevent obscuring the taste of the compounds added to it. The test fluids were sterile water, 0.07 M sucrose to which one of the following compounds was added: .05, .10, .15, .20 M sodium chloride; .18, .24, .48 M urea; .001, .003, .006, .012, .024 M citric acid.

As expected, the standard fluid, .07 M sucrose, was ingested in greater quantities than water (Figure 5). An evaluation by analyses of variance showed no difference in the amount consumed between the sugar solution and the mixtures containing sodium chloride or urea. Further, the concentration of these mixtures had no effect on total volume intake. However, the addition of citric acid suppressed intake of the sucrose solution, and the effect did not vary according to the concentration of citric acid added. This aversion to sour had not been observed previously when water was used as the standard of comparison. On the basis of these results, the authors concluded that water is apparently aversive to newborns. By actively varying the volume they ingest, newborn infants show their preference for sweet stimuli and their aversion to sour stimuli, and appear to be indifferent to bitter and salty stimuli.

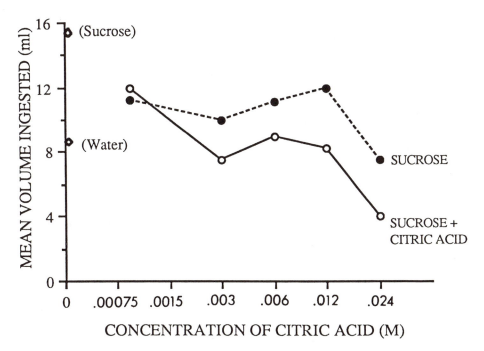

Figure 5 Mean volumes of .07 M sucrose with and without citric acid ingested by newborns offered different concentrations of citric acid (*n* = 12). From "Ingestive Responses of Human Newborns to Salty, Sour, and Bitter Stimuli" by J. A. Desor et al., 1975, *Journal of Comparative and Physiological Psychology, 89,* p. 968. Copyright 1975 by American Psychological Association. Reprinted by permission.

Fetal Sucking and Swallowing

Liley (1972) noted that measures of fetal swallowing over two consecutive 48–72 hour periods showed consistency and therefore, investigation of other influences on fetal swallowing is possible. One such investigation was conducted by DeSnoo in 1937 (cited in Liley, 1972). Following the reasoning that a particular prenatal disorder, polyhydramnios, was due to inadequate fetal swallowing and that the remedy would be to make the fluid more attractive to the fetus, DeSnoo injected saccharin into the amniotic cavity. With the exception of one fetus that had an esophageal atresia, DeSnoo noted clinical improvement in all the polyhydramniotics so treated. Liley extended DeSnoo's investigation, by studying the effect of both a pleasant and an aversive stimulus on fetal swallowing. He used 2.5 gm saccharin for the former, but only on two subjects; and lipiodol, an iodinated poppy seed oil, for the latter. The injection with saccharin led to inconsistent results, but lipiodol was found to consistently depress fetal swallowing.

It is a rather exciting prospect that the sucking and swallowing behavior of fetuses may be, as seen in the work of both DeSnoo and Liley, of immense importance in regulating the amount and quality of amniotic fluid. The fetus may truly be said to save its own life by altering its sucking behavior and ingestion. The fetus and the maternal environment interact and reciprocate. When the fluid is sweeter, the baby sucks more; when not so sweet, or when bitter, the infant sucks less. Existing knowledge about neonatal sucking behavior, particularly the extent to which it is under the control of stimulus feedback, suggests we should not be surprised at the relevance of behavior for the survival of the fetus. After all, newborns are constantly saving their own lives through ingestion. Before artificial feeding, babies without an adequate sucking response were almost surely destined to die in infancy.

Sucking Behavior as a Model of Biological Self-Regulation

We have seen that the oral ingestive behavior of the newborn is complex. Such behavior depends on the shape of the nipple or other object which elicits it, and on the quality, amount, and spacing of the fluid delivered contingent on the sucking behavior of the baby.

Although complex, neonatal sucking behavior yields to understanding in terms of antecedents, such as the nature of perinatal events, which are determinants of the multiple parameters involved in sucking and ingestion. By the same token, sucking behavior of the newborn can be seen as an index and measure of the extent to which perinatal hazards may have worked to impair neurobehavioral responsivity. Furthermore, the oral behaviors of the newborn are vital, and can be manipulated in ways that will enhance the probability of survival of the child, as well as reveal the importance of learning processes in the infant's psychobiological history.

Finally, the oral, approach-to-goal behaviors of the very young child serve as a proving ground for the development of other self-regulatory human behaviors. A model for numerous other patterns of behavior involving interactions of congenital and experiential determinants, the early developmental mechanisms of oral ingestive behavior (particularly those processes connecting behavior with response consequences and which determine the nature of subsequent behavior) enable the learning of a larger lesson. The sucking behavior of a baby has pleasant consequences which determine subsequent behavior. The perpetuation of behavior is of still further consequence. What one does makes a difference, in fairly lawful, interesting ways.

References

Beauchamp, G. K. (1987). The human preference for excess salt. *American Scientist: Jan–Feb,* 27–33.

Beauchamp, G. K., Cowart, B. J, & Moran, M. (1986). Developmental changes in salt acceptability in human infants. *Developmental Psychobiology, 19,* 17–25.

Bosack, T. N. (1973). Effects of fluid delivery on the sucking response of the human newborn. *Journal of Experimental Child Psychology, 15,* 77–85.

Bradley, R. M. (1972). Development of the taste bud and gustatory papillae in human fetuses. In Bosma, J. F. (Ed.), *The third symposium on oral sensation and perception: The mouth of the infant* (pp. 37–162). Springfield, IL: CC Thomas.

Bradley, R. M., & Mistretta, C. M. (1973). The gustatory sense in foetal sheep during the last third of gestation. *Journal of Physiology, 231,* 271–282.

Canestrini, S. (1913). Uber das Sinnesleben des Neugeborenen. *Monogr. Gesamtgeb. Neurol. Psychiat., 5,* 1–104.

Collier, G., Hirsch, E., & Hamlin, P. H. (1972). The ecological determinants of reinforcement in the rat. *Physiology and Behavior, 9,* 705–716.

Crook, C. K. (1977). Taste and the temporal organization of neonatal sucking. In J. M. Weifenbach (Ed.), *Taste and development: The genesis of sweet preference* (DHEW Publication No. (NIH) 77-1068, pp. 146–160). Washington, DC: U.S. Department of Health, Education, and Welfare.

Crook, C. K. (1978). Taste perception in the newborn infant. *Infant Behavior and Development, 1,* 52–69.

Crook, C. K. & Lipsitt, L. P. (1976). Neonatal nutritive sucking: Effects of taste stimulation upon sucking rhythm and heart rate. *Child Development, 47,* 518–522.

Desor, J. A., Maller, O., & Andrews, K. (1975). Ingestive responses of human newborns to salty, sour, and bitter stimuli. *Journal of Comparative and Physiological Psychology, 89,* 966–970.

Desor, J. A., Maller, O., & Turner, R. G. (1973). Taste in acceptance of sugars by human infants. *Journal of Comparative and Physiological Psychology, 84,* 496–501.

Dubignon, J., & Campbell, D. (1969). Discrimination between nutriments by the human neonate. *Psychonomic Science, 16,* 186–187.

Eckstein, A. (1927). Zur Physiologie der Geschamacksempfindung und des Saugreflexes bei Sauglingen. *Z. Kinderheilk, 45,* 1–18.

Ganchrow, J. R., Steiner, J. E., & Daher, M. (1983). Neonatal facial expressions in response to different qualities and intensities of gustatory stimuli. *Infant Behavior and Development, 6,* 473–484.

Hull, C. L. (1931). Goal attraction and directing ideas conceived as habit phenomena. *Psychological Review, 38,* 487–506.

Hull, C. L. (1943). *Principles of behavior: An introduction to behavior theory.* New York: Appleton-Century-Crofts.

Jensen, K. (1932). Differential reactions to taste and temperature stimuli in newborn infants. *Genetic Psychology Monographs, 12,* 363–479.

Kaye, H. (1967). Infant sucking behavior and its modification. In L. P. Lipsitt & C. C. Spiker (Eds.), *Advances in child development and behavior, Vol. 3* (pp. 1–52). New York: Academic Press.

Kron, R. E., Stein, M., Goddard, K. E., & Phoenix, M. D. (1967). Effect of nutrient upon the sucking behavior of newborn infants. *Psychosomatic Medicine, 29,* 24–32.

Kussmaul, A. (1859). *Utersuchungen uber das Seelenleben des Neugenborenen Menschen.* Tubingen, Germany: Moser.

Kobre, K. R., & Lipsitt, L. P. (1972). A negative contrast effect in newborns. *Journal of Experimental Child Psychology, 14,* 81–91.

Liley, A. W. (1972). Disorders of amniotic fluid. In N. S. Assali (Ed.), *Pathophysiology of gestation: Vol. 2. Fetal-placental disorders* (pp. 157–206). New York: Academic Press.

Lipsitt, L. P. (1974). The synchrony of respiration, heart rate, and sucking behavior in the newborn. In J. C. Sinclair & J. B. Warshaw (Eds.), *Mead Johnson Symposium on perinatal and developmental medicine: Biologic and clinical aspects of brain development, 6* (pp. 67–72).

Lipsitt, L. P. (1977). Taste in human neonates: Its effects on sucking and heart rate. In J. M. Weiffenbach (Ed.), *Taste and development: The genesis of sweet preference* (DHEW Publication No. (NIH) 77-1068, pp. 125–142). Washington, DC: U.S. Department of Health, Education, and Welfare.

Lipsitt, L. P. & Kaye, H. (1965). Change in neonatal response to optimizing and nonoptimizing sucking stimulation. *Psychonomic Science, 2,* 221–222.

Lipsitt, L. P., Reilly, B. M., Butcher, M. J., & Greenwood, M. M. (1976). The stability and interrelationships of newborn sucking and heart rate. *Developmental Psychobiology, 9,* 305–310.

Lipsitt, L. P., & Werner, J. S. (1981). The infancy of human learning processes. In E. S. Gollin (Ed.), *Developmental plasticity* (pp. 101–133). Orlando, FL; Academic Press.

Maller, O. & Desor, J. A. (1974). Effect of taste on ingestion by human newborns. In J. Bosma (Ed.), *Fourth symposium on oral sensation and perception: Development in the fetus and infant* (pp. 279–291). Washington, DC: U.S. Government Printing Office.

Mistretta, C. M., & Bradley, R. M. (1977). Taste in utero: Theoretical considerations. In J. M. Weiffenbach (Ed.), *Taste and development: The genesis of sweet preference* (DHEW Publication No. (NIH) 77-1068, pp. 51–69). Washington, DC: U.S. Department of Health, Education, and Welfare.

Mistretta, C. M., & Bradley, R. M. (1983). Neural basis of developing salt taste sensation: Response changes in fetal, postnatal, and adult sheep. *Journal of Comparative Neurology, 215,* 199–210.

Nowlis, G. H., & Kessen, W. (1976). Human newborns differentiate differing concentrations of sucrose and glucose. *Science, 191,* 865–866.

Peiper, A. (1963). *Cerebral function in infancy and childhood.* New York: Consultants Bureau.

Peterson, F., & Rainey, L. H. (1910). The beginnings of mind in the newborn. *Bulletin of the Lying In Hospital City of New York, 7,* 99–122.

Pratt, K. C., Nelson, A. K., & Sun, K. H. (1930). *The behavior of the newborn infant* (Contributions to Psychology, Vol. 10). Columbus: Ohio State University Press: Ohio State University Studies.

Preyer, W. (1882). *The Mind of the Child* (H. W. Brown, Trans.). New York: Appleton.

Richter, C. P. (1942–43). Total self-regulatory functions in animals and human beings. *Harvey Lecture Series, 38,* 63–103.

Richter, C. P. (1943). The self-selection of diets. *Essays in biology: In honor of Herbert M. Evans.* University of California Press.

Shinn, M. W. (1893–1899). Notes on the development of a child. *Berkeley: University of California Publications, 1,* 424. Berkeley, CA: University Publication Series.

Shirley, M. M. (1933). *The first two years: A study of twenty-five babies: Intellectual development, 2.* Minneapolis, MN: University of Minnesota Press.

Spence, K. W. (1956). *Behavior theory and conditioning.* New Haven: Yale University Press.

Stirnimann, F. (1936). Le gout et l'odorat du nouveau-né [Taste and odor in the newborn]. Revue français de pediatriques, *12,* 453–485.

van den Boom, D. C. (1988). *Neonatal irritability and the development of attachment: Observation and intervention.* Unpublished doctoral dissertation, University of Leiden, The Netherlands.

Weiss, B. & Laties, V. (1961). Behavioral thermoregulation. *Science, 133,* 1338–1344.

Wolff, P. (1968). The serial organization of sucking in the young infant. *Pediatrics, 42,* 943–956.

CHAPTER 7

SODIUM APPETITE

NEIL E. ROWLAND

It has often been argued that the appetite for sodium is innate, and that this distinguishes it from various acquired appetites (Denton, 1982). In this chapter, I will review the respective evidence for innate and learned aspects of intake of sodium salts, and NaCl in particular. Studies on the mechanism of sodium intake have mainly used animals that are sodium-depleted, and their intake is usually termed *sodium appetite*. These animals show a strong preference for some salty commodities over unsalted counterparts and exhibit enhanced preference for sodium. Many studies, including those on humans, do not involve obvious physiologic need for sodium, and so the intake is more accurately termed *a preference*. Thus it appears that one of the most important questions in the understanding of NaCl consumption involves elucidation of factors that influence need-free preference.

SODIUM PREFERENCE

Humans
Several studies have described the development of liking for NaCl in humans (see Beauchamp, 1987; Cowart & Beauchamp, 1986 for reviews). At birth, infants show little evidence for discrimination (in sucking tests) between water and dilute NaCl. It has been suggested that mechanisms for NaCl taste are immature at this time because by 4 months of age, infants show a preference for NaCl solutions over water. At some time between about 2 and 5 years of age, the preference for salt solutions becomes an aversion, and salty foods are preferred instead. Thus salt preference is gradually acquired.

The suggestion here is that humans like salty foods and dislike salty water. The reverse, a preference for NaCl in fluids but not in foods, has been reported in many animal species (Rowland & Fregly 1988a). It could be argued that the mechanisms differ between animals and humans, but it is more parsimonious to regard the human pattern as culturally determined. For example, water in deserts is frequently brackish, and this mildly salty water is preferred by the Bedouin because it assuages thirst more effectively than either pure water or extremely salty water (Paque, 1980). Paque argues that this is a manifestation of human salt appetite, but also notes that the intakes of both salt and water are minimized by dietary and social practices; excessive salt intakes are actively avoided. It is this delicate balance of diet and hydromineral balance, in a net state of what many would consider deficit, that have allowed the Bedouin to live in the Sahara desert.

People of many cultures add salt only to certain foods (often those that are relatively bland) and not to others (often those that are sweet). At an early age, children learn that salt is good with some foods (e.g., soups, crackers) and not with others (e.g., ice cream, beverages). Sweet and salty are psychologically "opponent processes." For example, the Bedouin use the term "sweet water" for water from low-salt wells to contrast it with brackish water wells (Paque, 1980). We rarely (if ever) talk about a mixed taste of sweet and salt and in "sports drinks" (a rare example of voluntary intake of salty fluid in the USA) the salt taste is almost completely masked. Another example of "mixing" tastes is salting watermelon, which may have originated with the physiologic need for both salt and fluid by farm workers stranded in the heat all day.

Once established, salt habits and preferences appear to be permanent, although the preferred amounts of salt can be modulated by alteration of dietary salt intake. Humans that are restricting their dietary sodium intake prefer low concentrations of NaCl in food than prior to restriction (Bertino, Beauchamp, & Engelman, 1983). Thus recent dietary history combines with genetic, learned, and cultural factors to determine current preference for NaCl.

Animals

The preference of animals for NaCl is determined in intake tests using reference samples and test samples presented either sequentially (one bottle) or simultaneously (two bottles). For rats, Richter (1939) originally described an inverted U-shaped preference/aversion function for varying concentrations of NaCl in solution. The ascending limb stretches from the preference threshold (the lowest concentration at which the intake of NaCl exceeds the intake of water) to the maximum preference (most preferred) concentration of about 0.15 M. The descending limb starts at NaCl concentrations exceeding 0.15 M. This function has been observed in several strains of rats and in several test paradigms (Midkiff, Fitts, Simpson, & Bernstein, 1985; Richter, 1939; Rowland & Fregly 1988a).

Developmental Factors

Rats as young as 6 days of age show a preference for NaCl solutions over water, but they reject only extremely concentrated solutions. This suggests that their gustatory mechanisms are only crudely developed at this time. By 18 days of age, they reject less concentrated (but still hypertonic) solutions, and the adult-like preference aversion function is not fully developed until 3–4 weeks of age (Bernstein & Courtney, 1987; Moe, 1986).

Thus while developmental data from humans suggest sequential processes of acceptance then rejection, in rats there is an age-related increase in the acceptance of low (<0.15 M) concentrations of NaCl and a simultaneous decrease in the acceptance of concentrated (>0.3 M) solutions. The reasons for these "normal" developmental shifts in rats are not understood at this time. Rats that are raised during most of their gestational and lactational periods on high sodium diets have increased preferences for hypertonic NaCl solutions and salty foods after weaning (Bird & Contreras, 1987). Furthermore, low levels of dietary salt during a critical period (on or before embryonic day 8) produce decreased chorda tympani responses in the weaned offspring (Hill 1987; Hill & Przekop, 1988). Decreased responsiveness of salt-specialist taste fibers of the chorda tympani may then allow for increased acceptance of high concentrations of salt (Contreras, Kosten, & Frank, 1984; Scott, this volume), although this may not be always be the case (Bird & Contreras, 1987; Moe, 1986).

Genetic Factors

This analysis is complicated by behavioral findings that the classic two-limb preference/aversion function is not found in all strains of rats but instead has an important genetic component. Rats of both the Fischer 344 (F344) inbred (Midkiff et al, 1985) and outbred Dahl salt-sensitive (S; develop high blood pressure with a high sodium intake) and salt-resistant (R) sublines do not show a preference for any concentration of NaCl (Ferrell, Lanou, & Gray, 1986; Rowland & Fregly, 1990). Bernstein (1988) reported that Fischer 344 rats showed a substantial intake of NaCl solutions in "towel tests" at 10 days of age, but by weaning (20–24 days) they showed the aversion characteristics of adults. Further studies on the development of salt preference need to be performed in these salt-shy strains. I should add that the outbred Dahl S rats, originating from Brookhaven, in contrast to the lines later inbred by Rapp, do not become markedly hypertensive at the levels of NaCl intake in preference studies, and it is unlikely that they are self-restricting intake to avoid hypertension. Further, the avoidance of NaCl is evident in the R sublines as well as F344 strain, both of which are resistant to salt-induced hypertension.

A similar lack of preference for NaCl has been observed in many strains of mice as well as hamsters (Carpenter, 1956; Hoshishima, Yokoyama, & Seto, 1962; Rowland & Fregly, 1988a). In many of the above examples, it has also been determined that the taste responses to sweet, sour, and bitter are similar between species and strains, independent of their preference for salt. The behavioral development of salt preference (or aversion) has not been investigated in most of these species or strains. Depending upon the ages at which strain differences start to emerge, it would be of interest to determine whether humans also show genetic and/or marked individual differences. This could be accomplished by measuring the developmental shifts in salt acceptance in children of suitably different populations or cultures.

In contrast to humans, rats of salt-preferring strains such as Wistar and Sprague-Dawley do not show a spontaneous preference for salty foods (Beauchamp & Bertino, 1985). Additionally, it is not easy to produce a robust increase in this low basal preference for salty foods during states of sodium depletion (Bertino & Tordoff, 1988; Galef, 1986; Grimsley & Starnes, 1979). Thus the study of the basis for spontaneous preference for NaCl is restricted to a few strains of rodents and a few other species (Denton, 1982; Rowland & Fregly, 1988a), and is dependent on the vehicle for the salt.

SODIUM APPETITE

Hormonal Mechanisms

An appetite for sodium is defined as an increase in the intake of a solution (usually hypertonic) of NaCl above some normal or baseline level. It may be induced by a diversity of treatments in Wistar or Sprague-Dawley rats (Table 1). These treatments activate the peripheral renin-angiotensin-aldosterone axis (Fregly & Rowland, 1985). The issues of whether and how angiotensin reaches the brain, and the critical sites involved in sodium appetite are still unresolved (see Rowland & Fregly 1988b; Schulkin, Marini, & Epstein, 1989). Other hormones that are released during sodium deficiency may act synergistically with angiotensin in

Table 1

SELECTED LIST OF TREATMENTS THAT INCREASE THE INTAKE OF NaCl SOLUTIONS IN VARIOUS STRAINS OF RAT

Experimental treatment	S-D	F344	Dahl (S&R)
Adrenalectomy	Yes[a]	Yes	ND
Administration of			
Mineralocorticoids	Yes[a]	Yes	Yes
Converting enzyme inhibitor	Yes[a]	Yes[a]	Yes[b]
Acute sodium depletion	Yes	Yes	ND
Diuretics (chronic)	Yes[a]	ND	ND
Angiotensin II (acute)	Yes	Yes	ND
Polyethylene glycol	Yes	Yes	ND

Note. Data for Sprague-Dawley (S-D) and Fischer 344 (F344) rats are from "Sodium Appetite: Species and Strain Differences and Role of Renin-Angiotensin-Aldosterone System" by N.E. Rowland and M.J. Fregly, 1988a, *Appetite, 11*, pp 143–178. Copyright 1988 by Academic Press Inc. (London) Ltd. Adapted by permission. Dahl rats were outbred from Brookhaven stock by Harlan Labs.
[a]Preference threshold concentration was also lowered.
[b]Increased NaCl intake in the R, but not the S subline. ND indicates this has not been determined.

stimulating sodium appetite. These include aldosterone, adrenocorticotrophic hormone (ACTH), and the hormones of pregnancy and lactation (Denton 1982; Epstein 1986; Stricker, 1983). There are also some species and strain differences in the induction of NaCl appetite; for example, inhibitors of angiotensin converting enzyme are behaviorally ineffective in hamsters and Dahl S rats, despite elevations of plasma renin activity (Rowland & Fregly, 1988a, 1988c, unpublished data). Salt-avoiding strains of mice increase their NaCl intake during pregnancy and lactation, acute sodium depletion, and hypovolemia, but not during administration of either deoxycorticosperone acetate (DOCA) or angiotensin I converting enzyme inhibitors, chronic access to sodium free diet, or after adrenalectomy (Denton, McBurnie, Ong, Osborne, & Tarjan, 1988; McBurnie, Denton, & Tarjan, 1988; Rowland & Fregly, 1988c). The reasons for the above appearance of sodium appetite under some conditions and not others has, as yet, eluded physiologic explanation.

Gustatory Aspects

Sodium appetite has most commonly been studied in rats using hypertonic solutions of NaCl that are highly nonpreferred under baseline conditions. The hormones of sodium depletion increase the acceptability of these solutions (Berridge, Flynn, Schulkin, & Grill, 1984). A mechanism for this may involve a decrease in the responsiveness of gustatory fibers that are sodium specialists (Kosten & Contreras, 1985), and/or the switch of some initially sweet specialist units in the brain to responding to salt (Jacobs, Mark, & Scott, 1988; Scott, this volume). In the former case, concentrated salt would be less readily perceived, and in the latter case, salt solutions would taste sweet during sodium deficiency. In this respect, sodium depletion in humans apparently enhances the pleasantness of ingested salt solutions (and a dissipation within minutes of the dysphoric effects of deprivation such as lethargy and cramps), but was *not reliably preceded by salt craving* even though the subjects were aware of their physiologic status (McCance, 1936).

There is another aspect of sodium appetite that was discovered early (Richter, 1939). Rats with a need for sodium showed an increased appetite for very dilute solutions of NaCl, as manifest by a downward shift in the preference threshold concentration (Rowland & Fregly, 1988a). In adrenalectomized rats, the behavioral preference threshold is similar to the threshold concentration of NaCl producing a chorda tympani response (Nachman & Pfaffman, 1963; Pfaffman & Bare, 1950). Increased sensitivity to a stimulus (in this case, the taste of sodium) following a relative deprivation of that stimulus (from the perspective of a taste bud, a decreased concentration of salivary sodium to which it is adapted) is a common biological finding. It makes adaptive sense insofar as most animals probably become sodium deficient gradually because the availability of food and/ or its sodium content change slowly and because mammals have highly efficient physiologic mechanisms for sodium retention (Denton, 1982). In order to find better sources of sodium, animals may need to migrate up a shallow concentration gradient of NaCl in food and/or ground water. While salt licks of relatively high mineral content (not only sodium) provide dramatic examples of appetite, they are by no means the only or maybe even the most common way in which animals or humans (Paque, 1980) solve the problem of sodium balance. Even the use of salt licks by animals seems to involve a fair amount of learned ritual (Denton, 1982).

Salivary sodium concentration may play a role in salt taste (McBurney & Pfaffman, 1963). In general, as the body is depleted of salt, salivary sodium concentration decreases and salt preference thresholds decrease (Rowland & Fregly, 1988a). Although it is not clear whether human fetuses can taste salt, it is clear that they swallow copious amounts of amniotic fluid (mean concentration of $Na^+ = 0.126$ M) during gestation and are exposed to maternal hormonal changes (Weiffenbach, Daniel, & Cowart, 1980).

In order to more directly assess the role of salivary sodium in salt intake, Thrasher & Fregly (1980) infused various concentrations of NaCl into the parotid duct of rats whose salivary glands had been removed. They found that as the concentration of the "artificial saliva" was increased, voluntary intake of NaCl decreased. Vance (1965) had earlier reported a transient increase in NaCl intake in the first week after salivarectomy in rats, followed by normalization. In recent studies in this lab, we have found that the basal preference for 0.3 M NaCl is reduced one month after removal of salivary glands (compared with intact rats), but that a near normal salt appetite is induced by treatment with either DOCA or furosemide.

Overconsumption of Salt and Persistence of Appetite

One of the sodium appetite puzzles that is studied in the laboratory with high concentrations of NaCl is that rats generally drink far more NaCl than is needed to meet their sodium deficit. For example, rats acutely depleted of body sodium (through treatment with a diuretic and sodium-free diet) often drink 5–10 times their urinary sodium loss during the treatment within the first few minutes of restored access to NaCl (Rowland & Fregly, 1988a). This sodium is later lost in urine and so the intake, although it subserves homeostasis, is wasteful. Previous studies have also noted a conspicuous inability of ingested or absorbed salt to turn off salt appetite (Wolf, Schulkin, & Simson, 1984) although absence of salt absorption promotes increased oral intake (Tordoff, Schulkin, & Friedman, 1987).

It is unlikely that behavioral excesses would be either adaptive or reinforced in the wild. For example, either actual or anticipated danger might truncate visits to a salt lick, and so rapidity of consumption may have been a genetically selected trait. In another scenario, sheer volume may limit the rate of repletion when only very dilute NaCl sources are available. In either instance, it is clear from several laboratory studies that rats are able to learn about the locations of salt sources when they are not depleted, and can immediately use that knowledge to obtain salt (Dickinson, 1986; Krieckhaus & Wolf, 1968).

Several investigators have noted that salt intake often remains elevated, maybe indefinitely, once the physiologic depletion is removed (Frankmann, Dorsa, Sakai, & Simpson, 1986; Leavitt, 1975; Sakai, Frankmann, Fine, & Epstein, 1989). Leavitt (1975) found that persistence was all-or-none, occurring in some but not all individuals, and studies in our lab tend to support this view. Further, informal observations of F344 rats found them persisting in 0.15 M NaCl intake several days after the removal of angiotensin converting enzyme inhibitor from their powdered food. We also found that changing to pelleted food and a few days' hiatus in salt access reversed their salt preference to a strong aversion (Rowland, 1988).

This needs more careful investigation because the only theoretical account for persistence (Sakai et al., 1989) suggests that passive exposure to the hormones of sodium depletion permanently sensitize the brain substrates for sodium intake (Epstein, 1986). If this is the case, simply changing the texture of food or transiently removing salt solution should be irrelevant. If, instead, the persistence is found to be dependent upon constancy of one or more elements of the environment, then sodium intake does not have a unitary representation within the brain, but has several discrete or loosely connected representations. Preliminary data along these lines come from an unpublished study (Rowland, 1988) in which I found that prior depletions of sodium followed by ingestion of concentrated NaCl, similar to the experimental design of Sakai et al. (1989), did not increase the intake of lower concentrations of NaCl during persistence tests. Clearly, more work needs to be done on aspects of generalization of salt appetite, in regard to the important issue of whether high voluntary salt intakes in humans are, in part, the result of incidental sodium depletions in ontogeny.

Dilute NaCl Solutions and NaCl Appetite

Having now reviewed aspects of the overconsumption of salt during and after sodium depletions, I will now consider how concentrations of salt affect salt appetite. In one study, male Sprague-Dawley rats were adapted to drinking distilled water and either 0.015 M, 0.03 M, or 0.3 M NaCl solution ad libitum. They were then depleted of sodium with furosemide and a sodium-free diet (Sakai et al. 1989). The amount of sodium that was lost in the urine during the depletion period was in the range 1–2 mEq for all of the rats. Access to NaCl was restored 24 hr after furosemide was restored and at the start of the night phase because, in other studies, we have found that NaCl appetite is expressed preferentially at night (Rowland & Fregly, 1988a). The mean intakes of NaCl are shown in Table 2. In the first hour, the volume intake was highest for the high NaCl concentration (water intakes were minimal in all groups for the first hour). Despite the fact that the 0.3 M group drank 2–3 times their estimated deficit in this first hour, they continued to drink large amounts of NaCl throughout the night. The 0.015 and 0.03 M groups drank NaCl throughout the night and into the next day, repairing their deficit within 24 hr. Blood was taken from parallel groups of rats. The results indicated that rats with access to 0.03 M NaCl took 12–24 hr to normalize

Table 2
MEAN INTAKES OF NaCl SOLUTIONS OF VARYING CONCENTRATIONS
FOLLOWING ACUTE SODIUM DEPLETION IN SPRAGUE-DAWLEY RATS

Concentration of NaCl	Time (hr) of NaCl access				24 hr NaCl intake (mEq)
	1	3	12	24	
0.015 M	8	26	53	83	1.24
0.03 M	12	22	45	67	2.01
0.30 M	14	19	36	37	11.10

Note. Values shown are for 6–8 rats; water was available. Access started at lights off in a 12:12 hr cycle.

correlates of plasma volume, while rats drinking 0.3 M NaCl were volume expanded within 1 hr and remained so for at least 24 hr.

Thus sodium appetite after acute sodium depletion is excessive, in part, because concentrated solutions of NaCl are offered. When dilute NaCl is offered, the intake is more need-related, for at least 24 hr. It is likely this is also true for spontaneous preference and intake because total solute intake is clearly not a regulated variable (Fregly, Harper, & Radford, 1965). Other species of animals differ with respect to the various aspects in the induction and termination of salt intake in relation to body sodium status (Rowland & Fregly, 1988a) and more comparative work is needed.

Parallels Between Salt and Carbohydrate Appetite

Finally, it is of interest to note some parallels between NaCl preference and the intake of carbohydrate solutions. The elective intake of both sweet and nonsweet (polycose) sugar solutions increases with concentration and generally involves a net increase in caloric intake and subsequent obesity (Sclafani, 1980). Additionally, as is the case for NaCl, rats appear to treat a carbohydrate in solution as a separate commodity from the same carbohydrate in solid form (Mook, Brane, & Whitt, 1983). This, coupled with the evidence for innate preference for both sweet and salt tastes (Lipsitt, this volume; Weiffenbach et al., 1980), suggests that behavioral processes underlying both sweet and salt preferences may have more similarities than differences.

CONCLUSIONS AND PROSPECTS

Sodium depleted mammals accept and ingest NaCl (or LiCl which has a similar taste) solutions and, less readily, foods rich in NaCl (Rowland & Fregly, 1988a). The preference for sodium solutions is often conferred a special innate status. In view of accruing evidence from a variety of ingestive feats by neonate humans

(Lipsitt, this volume) and rodents (Hall, in press), and parallels with sweet intake, it is not clear to me that this unique status is justified. Sensory factors have major determining roles in the acceptability and intake of NaCl and, conversely, the role of postingestive factors in satiation of salt appetite appears to be quite weak. There are some robust species and strain differences in preference and appetite that require further study. With regard to mechanism, several hormones appear to act to stimulate sodium seeking and intake. The amount consumed does not appear to be simply related to the deficit, and may vary as a function of concentration of the NaCl as well as ease of availability. More work is needed on both peripheral and central mechanisms of salt satiation. It is evident that sodium salts naturally occur with other flavors (e.g., in food), and sodium depletion is sufficient to allow associative learning of a salt-paired tastes (Bertino & Tordoff, 1988; Fudim, 1978; Krause & LoLordo, 1986). The interplay of such associative factors with the mechanisms noted above is also an area in need of more work. Although my own work and this review have focussed mainly on physiologic signals in animals, very little is known about the way in which such signals or their modulation by experience interact with structural and cultural aspects of both the proximal and distal environment.

References

Beauchamp, G. K. (1987). The human preference for excess salt. *American Scientist, 75,* 27–33.

Beauchamp, G. K. & Bertino, M. (1985). Rats (*Rattus norvegicus*) do not prefer salted food. *Journal of Comparative Psychology, 99,* 240–247.

Bernstein, I. L. (1988). Development of salt aversion in the Fisher-344 rat. *Developmental Psychobiology, 21,* 663–670

Bernstein, I. L., & Courtney, L. (1987). Salt preferences in the preweaning rat. *Developmental Psychobiology, 20,* 443–453.

Bertino, M., Beauchamp, G. K., & Engelman, K. (1983). Long-term reduction in dietary sodium alters the taste of salt. *American Journal of Clinical Nutrition, 36,* 1134–1144.

Bertino, M., & Tordoff, M. G. (1988). Sodium depletion increases rats' preferences for salty food. *Behavioral Neuroscience, 102,* 565–573.

Berridge, K. C., Flynn, F. W., Schulkin, J., & Grill, H. J. (1984). Sodium depletion enhances salt palatability in rats. *Behavioral Neuroscience, 98,* 652–660.

Bird, E., & Contreras, R. J. (1987). Maternal dietary NaCl intake influences weanling rats' salt preferences without affecting taste nerve responses. *Developmental Psychobiology, 20,* 111–130.

Carpenter, J. A. (1956). Species differences in taste preferences. *Journal of Comparative and Physiological Psychology, 49,* 139–144.

Contreras, R. J., Kosten, T., & Frank, M. E. (1984). Activity in salt taste fibers: Peripheral mechanism for mediating changes in salt intake. *Chemical Senses, 8,* 275–288.

Cowart, B. J., & Beauchamp, G. K. (1986). Factors affecting acceptance of salt by human infants and children. In M. R. Kare & J. G. Brand (Eds.), *Interaction of the chemical senses with nutrition,* (pp. 25–44). New York: Academic Press.

Denton, D. A. (1982). *The hunger for salt.* Berlin: Springer.

Denton, D. A., McBurnie, M., Ong, F., Osborne, P., & Tarjan, E. (1988). Na deficiency and other physiological influences on voluntary Na intake of BALB/c mice. *American Journal of Physiology, 255,* 1025–1034.

Dickinson, A. (1986). Re-examination of the role of instrumental contingency in the sodium-appetite irrelevant incentive effect. *Quarterly Journal of Experimental Psychology, 38B,* 161–172.

Epstein, A. N. (1986). Hormonal synergy as the cause of salt appetite. In G. deCaro, A. N. Epstein & G. Massi (Eds.), *The physiology of thirst and sodium appetite* (pp. 395–404). New York: Plenum Press.

Ferrell, F., Lanou, A., & Gray, S. D. (1986). Salt level in weaning diet affects saline preference and fluid intake Dahl rats. *Hypertension, 8,* 1021–1026.

Frankmann, S. P., Dorsa, D. M., Sakai, R. R., & Simpson, J. B. (1986). A single experience with hyperoncotic colloid dialysis persistently alters water and sodium intake. In G. deCaro, A. N. Epstein, & M. Massi (Eds.), *The physiology of thirst and sodium appetite (pp. 115–121). New York: Plenum Press.*

Fregly, M. J., Harper, J. M., & Radford, E. P. (1965). Regulation of sodium chloride intake by rats. *American Journal of Physiology, 209,* 287–292.

Fregly, M. J., & Rowland, N. E. (1985). Role of renin-angiotensin-aldosterone system in NaCl appetite of rats. *American Journal of Physiology, 248,* R1–R11.

Fudim, O. K. (1978). Sensory preconditioning of flavors with a formalin-produced sodium need. *Journal of Experimental Psychology: Animal Behavior Processes, 4,* 276–285.

Galef, B. G. (1986). Social interaction modifies learned aversions, sodium appetite, and both palatability and handling-time induced dietary preference in rats (*Rattus norvegicus*). *Journal of Comparative Psychology, 100,* 432–439.

Grimsley, D. L., & Starnes, E. C. (1979). Salt seeking by means of food and fluid selection in adrenalectomized rats. *Physiological Psychology, 7,* 295–298.

Hall, W. G. (in press). The ontogeny of ingestive behavior: Changing control of components in the feeding sequence. In E. M. Stricker (Ed.), *Neurobiology of food and fluid intake.* New York: Plenum Publishing Corp.

Hill, D. L. (1987). Susceptibility of the developing rat gustatory system to the physiological effects of dietary sodium deprivation. *Journal of Physiology* (London), *393,* 413–424.

Hill, D. L., & Przekop, P. R. (1988). Influences of dietary sodium on functional taste receptor development: A sensitive period. *Science, 241,* 1826–1828.

Hoshishima, K., Yokoyama, S., & Seto, K. (1962). Taste sensitivity in various strains of mice. *American Journal of Physiology, 202,* 1200–1204.

Jacobs, K. M., Mark, G. P., & Scott, T. R. (1988). Taste responses in the nucleus tractus solitarius of sodium-deprived rats. *Journal of Physiology, 406,* 393–410.

Kosten, T., & Contreras, R. J. (1985). Adrenalectomy reduces peripheral neural responses to gustatory stimuli in the rat. *Behavioral Neuroscience, 99,* 734–741.

Krause, J. M., & LoLordo, V. M. (1986). Pavlovian conditioning with ingested saline solution as the US. *Animal Learning and Behavior, 14,* 22–28.

Krieckhaus, E. E., & Wolf, G. (1968). Acquisition of sodium by rats: Interaction of innate mechanisms and latent learning. *Journal of Comparative and Physiological Psychology, 65,* 197–201.

Leavitt, M. L. (1975). The phenomenon of permanent Na^+ appetite in rats. Unpublished doctoral dissertation, University of Iowa.

McBurney, D. H., & Pfaffman, C. (1963). Gustatory adaptation to saliva and sodium chloride. *Journal of Experimental Psychology, 65,* 523–529.

McBurnie, M., Denton, D., & Tarjan, E. (1988). Influence of pregnancy and lactation on Na appetite of BALB/c mice. *American Journal of Physiology, 255,* R1020–R1024.

McCance, R. A. (1936). Experimental sodium chloride deficiency in man. *Proceedings of the Royal Society, Series A, 119,* 245–268.

Midkiff, E. E., Fitts, D. A., Simpson, J. B., & Bernstein, I. L. (1985). Absence of sodium chloride preference in Fischer-344 rats. *American Journal of Physiology, 249,* R438–R442.

Moe, K. E. (1986). The ontogeny of salt preference in rats. *Developmental Psychobiology, 19,* 185–196.

Mook, D. G., Brane, J. A. & Whitt, J. A. (1983). "De-satiation": The reinstatement of feeding in glucose-satiated rats. *Appetite, 4,* 125–136.

Nachman, M., & Pfaffman, C. (1963). Gustatory nerve discharges in normal and sodium deficient rats. *Journal of Comparative and Physiological Psychology, 56,* 1007–1011.

Paque, C. (1980). Saharan Bedouins and the salt water of the Sahara: A model for salt intake. In M. R. Kare, M. J. Fregly, & R. A. Bernard (Eds.), *Biological and behavioral aspects of salt intake* (pp. 31–47). New York: Academic Press.

Pfaffman, C., & Bare, J. K. (1950). Gustatory nerve discharges in normal and adrenalectomized rats. *Journal of Comparative and Physiological Psychology, 43,* 320–328.

Richter, C. P. (1939). Salt taste thresholds for normal and adrnealectomized rats. *Endocrinology, 24,* 367–371.

Rowland, N. E. (1988). [Persistance of salt appetite in rats]. Unpublished raw data.

Rowland, N. E., & Fregly, M. J. (1988a). Sodium appetite: Species and strain differences and role of renin-angiotensin-aldosterone system. *Appetite, 11,* 143–178.

Rowland, N. E., & Fregly, M. J. (1988b). Comparison of the effects of the dipeptidyl peptidase inhibitors captopril, ramipril, and enalapril on water intake and sodium appetite of Sprague-Dawley rats. *Behavioral Neuroscience, 102,* 953–960.

Rowland, N. E., & Fregly, M. J. (1988c). Characteristics of thirst and sodium appetite in mice *(Mus musculus). Behavioral Neuroscience, 102,* 969–974.

Rowland, N. E., & Fregly, M. J. (1990). Thirst and sodium appetite in Dahl rats. *Physiology & Behavior, 47,* 331–335.

Sakai, R. R., Frankmann, S., Fine, W. B., & Epstein, A. N. (1989). Prior episodes of sodium depletion increase the need-free sodium intake of the rate. *Behavioral Neuroscience, 103,* 186–192.

Schulkin, J., Marini, J., & Epstein, A. N. (1989). A role for the medial region of the amygdala in mineralocorticoid induced salt hunger. *Behavioral Neuroscience, 103,* 178–185.

Sclafani, A. (1980). Dietary obesity. In A. J. Stunkard (Ed.), *Obesity* (pp. 166–181). Philadelphia, PA: Saunders.

Stricker, E. M. (1983). Thirst and sodium appetite after colloid treatment in rats: Role of ther renin-angiotensin-aldosterone system. *Behavioral Neuroscience, 97,* 725–737.

Thrasher, T. N., & Fregly, M. J. (1980). Factors affecting salivary sodium concentration, NaCl intake, and preference threshold and their interrelationship. In M. R. Kare, M. J. Fregly & R. A. Bernard (Eds.), *Biological and behavioral aspects of salt intake* (pp. 145–165). New York: Academic Press.

Tordoff, M. G., Schulkin, J., & Friedman, M. I. (1987). Further evidence for hepatic control of salt intake in rats. *American Journal of Physiology, 253,* R444–R449.

Vance, W. B. (1965). Observations on the role of salivary secretions in the regulation of food and fluid intake in the white rat. *Psychological Monographs, 79* (Whole No. 598), 1–22.

Weiffenbach, J. M., Daniel, P. A., & Cowart, B. J. (1980). Saltiness in developmental perspective. In M. R. Kare, M. J. Fregly, & R. A. Bernard (Eds.), *Biological and behavioral aspects of salt intake,* (pp. 13–29). New York: Academic Press.

Wolf, G., Schulkin, J., & Simson, P. E. (1984). Multiple factors in the satiation of salt appetite. *Behavioral Neuroscience, 98,* 661–673.

CHAPTER 8

CHAPTER 8

PERCEPTION OF THE ODOR OF ANDROSTENONE: INFLUENCE OF GENES, DEVELOPMENT, AND EXPOSURE

GARY K. BEAUCHAMP AND CHARLES J. WYSOCKI

The odor of a substance is a critical component of its flavor. While there has been a substantial number of studies on the development and modification of human taste sensitivity and preference (Beauchamp & Cowart, 1985; Cowart, 1981; Cowart & Beauchamp, 1985; Weiffenbach, 1977), and considerable work on similar topics involving foods (Birch, this volume), the study of olfaction from a developmental and experiential perspective has lagged. Methodological difficulties may partially account for this (see Schmidt & Beauchamp, 1988). Recently, we have conducted a series of studies on the development and modification of human response to the odor of androstenone. These studies serve to illustrate the role of genetic variation in the determination of individual differences in sensitivity to odors, developmental changes in response to odors, and the effects of exposure on the perception of odors. While androstenone is not a major volatile in most foods, these studies may also serve as a model for the analysis of sensory responses to other common food odors.

ANDROSTENONE

Androstenone (5α-androst-16-en-3-one) is a steroid found abundantly in male pigs where it stimulates assumption of the lordosis position in receptive females (Reed, Melrose, & Patterson, 1974). It is also found in human secretions and excretions (Bird & Gower, 1983; Brooksbank, Brown, & Gustafsson, 1974; Claus & Asling, 1976), more abundantly in males than in females. Finally, it also occurs in some foods: pork products, truffles, and celery.

The odor of androstenone is described variously as urinous, sweaty, musky, like sandalwood, or having no smell. While there are a number of reports that this or related odors alter human behavior, act as a sexual attractant, or have special effects on emotions and sexual responses (Benton, 1982; Cowley, Johnson, & Brooksbank, 1977; Filsinger, Braun, Monte, & Linder, 1984; Filsinger, Braun, & Monte, 1985; Kirk-Smith, Booth, Carroll, & Davies, 1978; Van Toller, Kirk-Smith, Wood, Lombard, & Dodd, 1983), these remain controversial and tentative. Our particular interest in the odor stemmed from the extreme variation in sensitivity to it among adults. Previous studies have shown that many otherwise normal adults cannot detect this odor at vapor saturation, while others are exquisitely sensitive to it; it is estimated that about 50% of individuals are anosmic (Labows & Wysocki, 1984). Not only is there vast variation in threshold levels, but different individuals appear to experience the odor as having different qualities. Based on this variation, genetic studies seemed likely to be particularly fruitful. Consequently, we first employed the classic twin method to probe for a genetic basis underlying the large individual differences in sensitivity.

GENETICS

To evaluate the possibility that individual differences in perception of androstenone might be due to genetic differences between individuals, detection thresholds for androstenone and pyridine (the odor of spoiled milk; a substance to which almost no one exhibits a specific anosmia) were determined in 17 identical twin pairs and 21 fraternal twin pairs (Wysocki & Beauchamp, 1984). Threshold determinations were accomplished with an ascending concentration two-sample (odor vs. blank) forced-choice procedure (see Figure 1). Details concerning odor purity, exact testing procedures, determination of zygosity, and statistical procedures can be found in the original publication (Wysocki & Beauchamp, 1984).

The results were straightforward: Identical twin pairs were more similar in androstenone sensitivity than were fraternal twin pairs. Specifically, 100% of the identical twin pairs were either both sensitive to the smell of androstenone or both were insensitive to the smell of androstenone (sensitivity was arbitrarily defined at the antimode of the bimodal threshold/concentration histogram). Only 61% of the fraternal twins were concordant. There was no evidence for a genetic influence on pyridine sensitivity.

This initial study seemed to suggest a rather simple and elegant model system. Sensitivity to androstenone has a major genetic component; perhaps genetic differences between individuals can explain all phenotypic variance in this trait. More recent genetic studies, however, indicate a complex mode of inheritance (Pollack et al., 1982; Wysocki, Dorries, & Beauchamp, unpub-

Work described in this chapter was supported by NIH NS-22014.

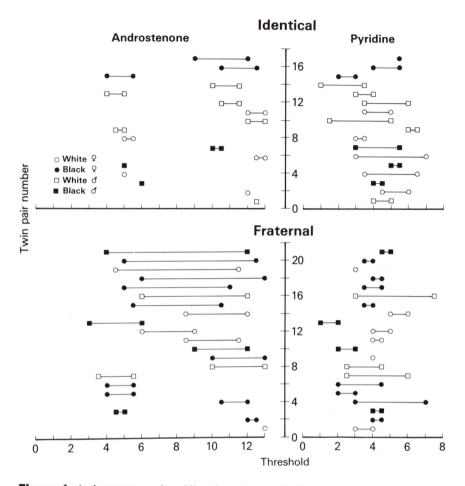

Figure 1 Androstenone and pyridine detection thresholds for each member of 17 identical twin pairs and 21 fraternal twin pairs. Pair mates are connected by horizontal lines. A single entry for a twin pair indicates identical thresholds for each. The data are plotted by decreasing discordance for androstenone. In step 12, the concentration of androstenone in mineral oil was 3.67 mM and in step 8, the concentration of pyridine in mineral oil was 0.372 mM. For each odorant, decreasing concentration series were prepared by serial binary dilution.

lished). Moreover, developmental and exposure studies now demonstrate that this apparent simplicity was an illusion.

DEVELOPMENT

Young Children

The initial developmental study of androstenone sensitivity and hedonics (Schmidt & Beauchamp, 1988) was incidental to a more general interest in olfaction in infancy and childhood, a neglected area. The few published experiments that have focused on this issue suggest that children are sensitive to odorants (Cernoch & Porter, 1985; Engen & Lipsitt, 1965; Engen, Lipsitt, & Kaye, 1963; Mac-Farlane, 1975; Rovee, 1969), but that their hedonic experience of odors is quite different than that of adults. In several different paradigms, children less than 5 years old have failed to respond differentially to odors that are judged by adults to have different hedonic values (Lipsitt et al., cited in Engen, 1982; Peto, 1936; Stein, Ottenberg, & Roulet, 1958).

Based on these and other related observations, some investigators have concluded that young children do not have aversions to odors that adults find offensive (Peto, 1936; Stein et al., 1958), that they are generally more tolerant of odors than adults (Moncrieff, 1966), or that the range of hedonic odor experience is more limited for children than adults (Engen, 1974). Furthermore, the apparent absence of odor aversions in young children has led to the suggestion that there are no inherently unpleasant odors, and that all hedonic reactions to odor are acquired through associational learning processes (Engen, 1974; Schmidt & Beauchamp, 1988).

These conclusions may be premature. Several recent studies are consistent with the proposition that offensive odor reactions begin in early infancy (Chernoch & Porter, 1985; Self, Horowitz, & Paden, 1972; Steiner, 1977, 1979). Furthermore, methodological and technical difficulties in evaluating odor hedonics in young children could be involved in the earlier failures to elicit offensive responses. In light of these considerations, we (Schmidt & Beauchamp, 1988) investigated 3-year-olds' (31–39 months) hedonic reactions using a method designed to minimize potential methodological artifacts and increase olfactory sampling by the child. The test was a forced-choice categorization procedure (good odor vs. bad odor). A testing session was introduced as a "smell game" with one simple rule: "good" things (things the subject liked) should be given to a stuffed toy of Big Bird and "bad or yucky" things (things the subject did not like) were to be given to a stuffed toy of Oscar the Grouch. Both characters are from "Sesame Street," a popular children's TV program with which all subjects were familiar. Children were told that they would be asked to smell something and if they liked the smell they should point to Big Bird, but if they did not like the smell they should point to Oscar the Grouch ("so that he could throw it in his trash can"). A comparable sample of adults was also evaluated in an identical manner.

Subjects were tested with nine chemical stimuli selected to represent a wide range of odor qualities and hedonic values. To minimize the possibility that intensity as opposed to quality differences could influence hedonic judgments, the odors were approximately matched for perceived intensity by adults and included: C-16 aldehyde (strawberry), phenylethylmethylethyl carbinol (PEMEC-floral), L-carvone (spearmint), methyl salicylate (wintergreen), eugenol (cloves), amyl acetate (banana), butyric acid (strong cheese/vomit), pyridine (spoiled milk), and of most interest in the current context, androstenone.

The overall results of this study can be summarized quite simply: Children and adults exhibited a very similar pattern of preferences and aversions. Odors the adults judged as good were generally judged good by the children and vice versa. Thus even children as young as 3 years old have distinctive, reliable preferences and aversions for odors.

Children and adults did differ, however, in affective judgments concerning androstenone. A greater proportion (13 of 14) of the children reported this odor as bad compared with the adults (10 of 17). The proportion of adults reporting the odor as bad is consistent with the approximately 50% anosmia found in the twin study described previously as well as in other studies. This is clearly not the case for the children. That this age difference in response to androstenone was not due to a general response bias is shown by the different pattern of responses to pyridine. All of the adults judged pyridine as bad while this was true for only 71% of the 3-year-olds.

We tentatively concluded that most or perhaps all 3-year-olds can detect the odor of androstenone. This result implies that between childhood and adulthood some proportion of individuals lose their ability to detect androstenone. In the next study, we investigated this developmental change in older children.

Older Children and Adolescents

In this study (Dorries, Schmidt, Beauchamp, & Wysocki, 1989), androstenone and pyridine thresholds were measured in subjects aged 9–20 years old and in a group of older adults. Descriptive and hedonic responses to these two odors plus PEMEC and a no-odor control (mineral oil diluent) were also obtained from these subjects and an additional group of 6- to 8-year-olds. A total of 247 individuals was tested. For threshold determination, a forced-choice ascending series of paired trials very similar to that described above was used. Following threshold testing, subjects were given the highest concentration of each odor and the control and then, using a standard face-scale, were asked to provide hedonic judgments. Further detail can be found in Dorries et al. (1989).

The results of this study are complex and only some will be discussed here. Consistent with the developmental work described above, we found a significant increase with age in the proportion of subjects, particularly males, insensitive to androstenone. The proportion of males insensitive to androstenone tripled between the ages of 9–14 and 15–20 years of age. Furthermore, among those males who could smell androstenone, the average sensitivity declined. Among females, the pattern was somewhat different. Though less extreme, there was a tendency for there to be a greater proportion of insensitive females at the older ages suggesting that some females also lose their ability to detect androstenone. In contrast to the males, however, among those females that could smell androstenone, greater sensitivities were apparent in older individuals.

Hedonic ratings also indicated a developmental change in perception of androstenone odor (Figure 2). Consistent with our work with 3-year-old children, no child in the youngest group rated androstenone as good and almost 67% rated

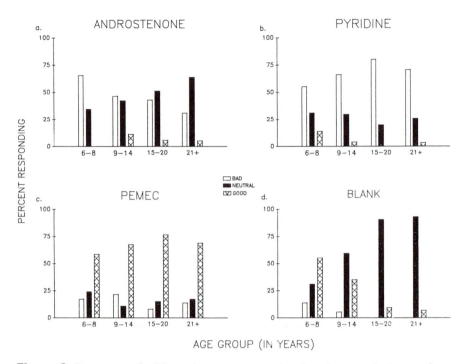

Figure 2 Percentage of subjects, by age group, rating the odorant as bad, neutral, or good when presented with (a) the highest concentration of androstenone (the value used in Figure 1), (b) a high concentration of pyridine, (c) undiluted phenylethylmethylethyl carbinol (PEMEC), and (d) a mineral oil blank (control).

it as bad. Since these same children tended to rate the control as good, it can be concluded that a large proportion of the 6- to 8-year olds detected androstenone and perceived it as a bad smell. Furthermore, this percentage declined with age. These data, combined with the large survey done through the National Geographic Society (Wysocki & Gilbert, 1988), generally support the hypothesis that the probability of detecting and disliking the odor of androstenone declines with age. They further suggested that this decline may be most apparent, at least for males, at or near adolescence. Thus individual differences in perception of the odor of androstenone must involve developmental factors interacting with genetic variation. Experience with the odor has now been shown to influence sensitivity, further complicating the story.

EXPERIENCE

During the course of other studies, one of us, who was initially insensitive to androstenone, experienced what appeared to be induced sensitivity; after a period of intermittent contact with the compound, a distinct odor could be perceived. To explore this, individuals were selected who were anosmic to it. Repeated measures of the threshold sensitivity (as described above) to pyridine, amyl acetate, and androstenone were obtained. Adult subjects in the experimental group individually sniffed androstenone and amyl acetate (each at the highest concentration used in these studies; see Figure 1) continuously for 3 minutes, 3 times/day, for a 6-week period. Subjects assigned to the control group were tested weekly, but they did not sniff the odor samples between sessions.

An ability to perceive androstenone was induced in half (10 of 20) of the subjects systematically exposed to it; none of the 18 control subjects exhibited evidence of a comparable shift in sensitivity (Wysocki et al., 1989; Figure 3). The qualities described by those whose perception was induced were varied. We were unable to discover any other differences between the 10 subjects who became sensitive to the odor and the 10 who did not.

What was altered in individuals who developed a sensitivity to the odor remains in question. One hypothesis, presuming a peripheral locus of effect, is that among some individuals who are insensitive to androstenone receptors do exist and extended exposure induces clonal expansion or selection of such receptors in a manner analogous with immune response to antigen. The consequent change in the receptor number or type would thus raise the odorant stimulation to the level of conscious perception. While this is an attractive idea, the data cannot exclude more central changes following exposure, for example, in the olfactory bulb or elsewhere in the central nervous system (Kucharski, Johanson, & Hall, 1986; Wilson, Sullivan, & Leon, 1987).

DISCUSSION

Human variation in response to the odor of androstenone is seen to be affected by genes, development, and individual experience. While studies in each of these realms have been initiated, it is not yet possible to comprehend the patterns underlying what appears to be almost contradictory data. How can experience influence a trait that appears to have such a large genetic component? Is induced sensitivity a permanent change? Why do only about half of the insensitive individuals become sensitive following exposure? What characterizes the individuals who appear to lose sensitivity to the odor as they age? Why do they tend to be adolescent males? We cannot answer these questions now, but a few salient points concerning human responsiveness to odors and flavors raised by the data merit mention.

The sensory worlds of children and adults, and males and females, may be characterized by striking differences. While it is clear that there is some general agreement among all individuals concerning which tastes and odors are good and which ones are bad (see Pangborn, Guinard, & Davis, 1988; Schmidt & Beauchamp, 1988), substantive differences do exist. For example, current work suggests that very young infants (less than 4 months old) do not preferentially consume NaCl, probably because they cannot detect it in the same way adults do (Beauchamp, Cowart, & Moran, 1985). Studies with the bitter substance phenylthiocarbamide (PTC) and its congeners indicate vast individual differences in bitter perception due to genetic differences, but here too there is a hint that these

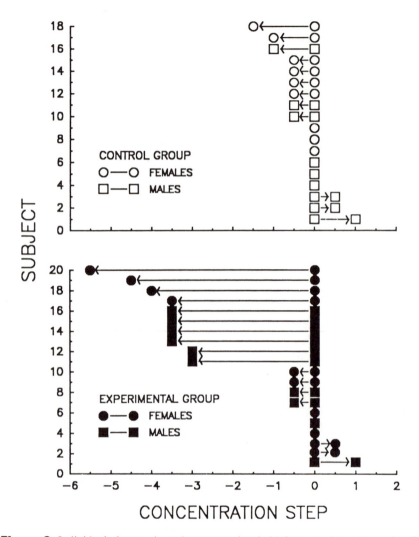

Figure 3 Individual changes in androstenone threshold from session 1 to session 7 for all subjects tested. Zero represents the individual's score at session 1; all subjects were insensitive to androstenone at the beginning of the experiment. A shift in the negative direction indicates a decrease in the threshold for detection of androstenone (i.e., increased sensitivity to the odorant). Half of the experimental subjects, but none of the control subjects, demonstrated a marked shift (≥ 3 steps) in sensitivity to androstenone.

differences may interact with individual experience (Fisher & Griffin, 1964). There is extensive literature on specific anosmia, of which androstenone insensitivity is only one example (Amoore, 1971; Amoore, 1977). Since flavors are usually complex mixtures of odors, tastes, and other sensory attributes, individual differences in the ability to perceive odors will result in subtle and perhaps not so subtle variations in perception of food flavors. Finally, sex differences in response to odors, with females generally exhibiting superiority, have been reported in many studies. The causal factors underlying these differences and their possible practical consequences remain to be elucidated.

Even amongst those individuals who could detect androstenone odor, there were differences in its quality and affective tone. Engen (1974) emphasized the importance of learning in the determination of odor pleasantness. Current data suggest that developmental changes and individual differences in the perceived pleasantness of odors may also derive from nonexperiential causes. Generally, individuals who are more sensitive to androstenone are more likely to label it as unpleasant (Dorries et al., 1989) and anecdotal evidence indicates that very sensitive individuals find it unpleasant at their very lowest level of detection.

Is the induction of sensitivity to an odor by exposure to it a novelty of androstenone or is it a much more common phenomenon? There is little in the literature to help answer this question. Modest increases in sensitivity to odor have been found with repeated threshold testing (Rabin & Cain, 1986) but these have been attributed to cognitive and performance factors rather than changes in absolute sensitivity. Much needs to be done in this area both with other odors where specific anosmias exist as well as with odors all people can detect. It should be noted, however, that no change in sensitivity to amyl acetate was observed in our study even though this too was sniffed daily. Perhaps more exposure to this odor is required. In this regard, it is interesting to speculate that expert tasters and smellers (e.g., wine tasters, perfumers, etc.) may, as a consequence of repeated exposure, increase their sensitivity to the substances of their expertise. Furthermore, while there is a general decline in odor sensitivity with age (Gilbert & Wysocki, 1987), perhaps this could, in part, be prevented through intensive exposure to flavors and odors. These speculations must also take into account powerful, anecdotal evidence that constant exposure to odors, for example in work places, appears to result in a lowered rather than heightened sensitivity to those substances; this issue needs formal study. Clearly, much remains to be worked out.

SUMMARY

The odor of androstenone provides a fascinating subject for study. Vast individual differences in perception of this odor are influenced by genes, factors associated with age, perhaps endocrine changes, and exposure history. These studies have illustrated the complexity of the human response to odors and flavors, and have highlighted the singularity of individual experience. Future work with androstenone, on both mechanistic and practical levels, could provide fundamental insights into the nature of chemosensory perception.

References

Amoore, J. E. (1971). Olfactory genetics and anosmia. In L. M. Beidler (Ed.), *Handbook of sensory physiology: Chemical senses,* (pp. 245–246). New York: Springer.

Amoore, J. E. (1977). Specific anosmia and the concept of primary odors. *Chemical Senses and Flavor, 2,* 267–281.

Beauchamp, G. K., & Cowart, B. J. (1985). Congenital and experiential factors in the development of human flavor preferences. *Appetite 6,* 357–372.

Beauchamp, G. K., Cowart, B. J., & Moran, M. (1985). Developmental changes in salt acceptance in human infants. *Developmental Psychobiology, 19,* 75–83.

Benton, D. (1982). The influence of androstenol—a putative human pheromone—on mood throughout the menstrual cycle. *Biological Psychology, 15,* 249–256.

Bird, S., & Gower, D. B. (1983). Estimation of the odorous steroid, 5α-androst-16-en-3-one, in human saliva. *Experientia, 39,* 790–792.

Brooksbank, B. W. L., Brown, R., & Gustafsson, J. A. (1974). The detection of 5α-androst-16-en-3-Ol in human male axillary sweat. *Experientia, 30,* 864–865.

Cernoch, J. M., & Porter, R. H. (1985). Recognition of maternal axillary odors by infants. *Child Development, 56,* 1593–1598.

Claus, R., & Asling, W. (1976). Occurrence of 5α-androst-16-en-3-one, a boar pheromone, in man and its relationship to testosterone. *Journal of Endocrinology, 68,* 483–484.

Cowart, B. J. (1981). Development of taste perception in humans: Sensitivity and preference throughout the life span. *Psychological Bulletin, 90,* 43–73.

Cowart, B. J., & Beauchamp G. K. (1985). Factors affecting acceptance of salt by human infants and children. In M. R. Kare & J. G. Brand (Eds.), *Interaction of the chemical senses with nutrition* (pp. 25–44). New York: Academic Press.

Cowley, J. J., Johnson, A. T., & Brooksbank, B. W. L. (1977). The effect of two odorous compounds on performance in an assessment-of-people test. *Psychoeuroendocrinology, 2,* 159–172.

Dorries K. M., Schmidt, H. J., Beauchamp, G. K., & Wysocki C. J. (1989). Changes in sensitivity to the odor of androstenone during adolescence. *Developmental Psychobiology, 22,* 423–436.

Engen, T. (1974). Method and theory in the study of odor preferences. In J. Johnston, D. Moulton, & A. Turk (Eds.), *Human response to environmental odors* (pp. 121–141). New York: Academic Press.

Engen, T. (1982). *The perception of odors.* New York: Academic Press.

Engen, T., & Lipsitt, L. P. (1965). Decrement and recovery of responses to olfactory stimuli in the human neonate. *Journal of Comparative and Physiological Psychology, 59,* 312–316.

Engen, T., Lipsitt, L. P., & Kaye, H. (1963). Olfactory responses and adaptation in the human neonate. *Journal of Comparative and Physiological Psychology, 56,* 73–77.

Filsinger, E. E., Braun, J. J., & Monte, W. C. (1985). An examination of the effects of putative pheromones on human judgments. *Ethology and Sociobiology, 6,* 227–236.

Filsinger, E. E., Braun, J. J., Monte, W. C., & Linder, D. E. (1984). Human (*Homo sapiens*) responses to the pig (*Sus scrofa*) sex pheromone 5-α-androst-16-en-one. *Journal of Comparative Psychology, 98,* 220–223.

Fisher, R., & Griffin, F. (1964). Pharmacogenetic aspects of gustation. *Jahrgang, 6,* 673–686.

Gilbert, A. N., & Wysocki, C. J. (1987). National Geographic smell survey: The results. *National Geographic, 122,* 514–525.

Kirk-Smith, M., Booth, D. A., Carroll, D., & Davies, P. (1978). Human social attitudes affected by androstenol. *Research Communications in Psychology, Psychiatry and Behavior, 3,* 379–384.

Kucharski, D., Johanson, I. B., & Hall, W. G. (1986). Unilateral olfactory conditioning in 6-day-old rat pups. *Behavioral and Neural Biology, 46,* 472–490.

Labows, J. N., & Wysocki, C. J. (1984). Individual differences in odor perception. *The Perfumer and Flavorist, 9,* 21–26.

MacFarlane, A. (1975). Olfaction in the development of social preferences in the human neonate. *Ciba Foundation Symposium, 33,* 103–117.

Moncrieff, R. W. (1966). *Odour preferences*. London: Leonard Hill.

Pangborn R. M., Guinard, J. X., & Davis R. G. (1988). Regional aroma preferences. *Food Quality and Preference, 1,* 11–19.

Peto, E. (1936). Contribution to the development of smell feeling. *British Journal of Medical Psychology, 15,* 314–320.

Pollack, M. S., Wysocki, C. J., Beauchamp, G. K., Braun, D., Jr., Calloway, C., & Dupont, B. (1982). Absence of HIA association or linkage for variations in sensitivity to the odor of androstenone. *Immunogenetics, 15,* 579–589.

Rabin, M. D., & Cain, W. S. (1986). Determinants of measured olfactory sensitivity. *Perception and Psychophysics, 39,* 281–286.

Reed, H. B. C., Melrose, D. R., & Patterson, R. L. S. (1974). Androgen steroids as an aid to detection of oestrus in pig artificial insemination. *British Veterinary Journal, 130,* 61–67.

Rovee, C. K. (1969). Psychophysical scaling of olfactory response to the aliphatic alcohols in human neonates. *Journal of Experimental Child Psychology, 7,* 245–254.

Schmidt, H. J., & Beauchamp, G. K. (1988). Adult-like odor preferences and aversions in 3-year-old children. *Child Development, 59,* 1136–1143.

Self, P. A., Horowitz, F. D., & Paden, L. Y. (1972). Olfaction in newborn infants. *Developmental Psychology, 7,* 349–363.

Stein, M., Ottenberg, P., & Roulet, N. (1958). A study of the development of olfactory preferences. *American Medical Association Archives of Neurological Psychiatry, 80,* 264–266.

Steiner, J. E. (1977). Facial expressions of the neonate infant indicating the hedonics of food-related chemical stimuli. In J. M. Weiffenback (Ed.), *Taste and development: The genesis of sweet preference* (pp. 173–189). Washington, DC: U.S. Government Printing Office.

Steiner, J. E. (1979). Oral and facial innate motor responses to gustatory and to some olfactory stimuli. In J. H. A. Kroese (Ed.), *Preference behavior and chemoreception* (pp. 247–262). London: Human Information Retrieval.

Van Toller, C., Kirk-Smith, M., Wood, N., Lombard, J., & Dodd, G. H. (1983). Skin conductance and subjective assessments associated with the odour of 5α-androstan-3-one. *Biological Psychology, 16,* 85–107.

Weiffenbach, J. M. (1977). Sensory mechanisms in the newborn's tongue. In J. M. Weiffenback (Ed.), *Taste and development: The genesis of sweet preference* (pp. 205–211). Washington DC: U.S. Government Printing Office.

Wilson, D. A., Sullivan, R. M., & Leon, M. (1987). Single-unit analysis of postnatal olfactory learning modified olfactory bulb out patient response patterns to learned attractive odors. *Journal of Neuroscience, 7,* 3154–3162.

Wysocki, C. J., & Beauchamp, G. K. (1984). Ability to smell androstenone is genetically determined. *Proceedings of the National Academy of Sciences, USA, 81,* 4899–4902.

Wysocki, C. J., Dorries, K. M., & Beauchamp, G. K. (1989). Genetic inability to perceive androstenone is reversed by exposure. *Proceedings of the National Academy of Sciences USA, 86,* 7976–7978.

Wysocki, C. J., & Gilbert, A. N. (1989). The National Geographic smell survey: The effects of age are heterogeneous. In C. L. Murphy, W. S. Cain & D. M. Hegsted (Eds.), Nutrition and the chemical senses in aging: Recent advances and current research needs (pp. 12–28). New York: New York Academy of Sciences. *Sensory Forum, 39,* 1–3.

CHAPTER 9

THE CONTROL OF FOOD INTAKE BY YOUNG CHILDREN: THE ROLE OF LEARNING

L. L. BIRCH

As a member of a mammalian species, a child makes the transition from suckling to eating and drinking during the first years of life. This transition involves (a) a shift from a single to multiple food sources, (b) increased opportunities for self-control of food intake by the child, and (c) new social contexts for eating, involving peers and adult caretakers. With respect to learning, these transitions imply changes in the cues present in the feeding context. Particularly during these early years, eating occurs at frequent intervals each day, providing many opportunities for learning. For the first few months after birth, an infant grows rapidly, nourished by a single food source. The successful functioning of this initial system is reflected in the fact that an infant's weight typically doubles in 4–6 months and triples in 1 year. During these months, infants are introduced to the foods of the adult diet of their culture. Over the next few years, several changes occur that are relevant to developmental changes in feeding behavior: independence increases, the growth rate slows, a great deal of knowledge regarding the rules of cuisine—the meanings of food and the purposes of eating—is acquired, and food preferences and aversions are developed.

The purpose of this review is to present current evidence regarding the contribution of learning and experience to the dramatic developments in the control of food intake that occur during the first few years of children's lives. I also define the areas in which we lack information regarding the developmental changes that occur in food acceptance patterns, and the extent to which they are shaped by learning. Questions concerning the physiology of feeding and the role of learning in feeding in animals will not be discussed, and the interested reader is referred to other chapters in this book (Booth, Capaldi, and Sclafani, this volume). The contributions of culture and cuisine are unique to human feeding. This implies that there are no appropriate animal models to aid in our understanding of the interactions of culture and biology in the development of human eating behavior.

The developmental changes in food acceptance patterns that occur during the first few years of life include: (a) alterations in infant and maternal factors contributing to the control of food intake during the first months of life; (b) the emergence of neophobia and its reduction through repeated experience; (c) the acquisition of conditioned preferences and aversions, through the associative conditioning of food cues to the social contexts and physiological consequences of eating; (d) learning about when to eat and when to stop eating, including the conditioning of meal initiation and satiety; and (e) the acquisition of cuisine rules and the affective reactions that apparently accompany knowledge of these rules. Cuisine rules regulate appropriateness (what substances are foods), food and flavor combinations, and when it is appropriate to consume particular foods. Children also learn which of the many cues available to them are relevant in the initiation, maintenance, and termination of eating. Each of these developmental factors are addressed below.

INFANT AND MATERNAL FACTORS IN CONTROL OF FOOD INTAKE

Changes that occur in the patterns of feeding during the first year or so of life provide evidence for early learning and experience in modifying food acceptance patterns. Few experimental studies exist, however, so the evidence is sparse and far from definitive. In one controlled study Fomon (1974) fed infants formulas varying in caloric density. Caloric intake was positively correlated with the caloric density of the formulas prior to 40 days of age. After that time, the infants began to show evidence of caloric compensation: infants fed the low-caloric density formulas consumed greater volumes than those on the high-caloric density formulas. The fact that this pattern did not emerge until about 6 weeks suggests that either the maturation of some innate mechanism or responsiveness was modified by learning (repeated experience with consuming a formula of a particular caloric density). Unfortunately, Fomon does not report information regarding feeding size and feeding intervals that would suggest how this compensation was accomplished.

The attitude of the adult caretaker can profoundly influence the infant's intake, both in terms of meal size and meal interval. However, recent research provides evidence for the role played by the infant in the control of intake. In an investigation of maternal and infant factors contributing to the regulation of feeding in early infancy, Neville, et al. (1988) investigated milk availability in breast-feeding mothers immediately following the cessation of a feed. They reported that more human milk was available than was consumed by the infant, suggesting that feeding size was determined by the infant and not limited by maternal factors. These results are consistent with those of Dewey and Lonnerdal (1986), who reported that in 6- to 21-week-old infants, intake was determined by the infant, and not limited by the mother's milk production. However, although these data suggest that the infant, not the mother, is in control of feeding size, the data do not suggest what factors influence feeding size and interval, and the extent to which these variables may be influenced by learning and experience.

To investigate the development of behavioral control of feeding in early infancy, especially the relationship between feeding size and pre- and postprandial feeding intervals, we analyzed data on the diurnal feeding patterns of 24 solely breast-fed infants, ranging from 2 to 12 weeks of age (Matheny, Birch, & Picciano, in press). Milk intakes and feeding interval data were obtained from 3-day dietary assessments at 2, 4, 6, 8, and 12 weeks. Quantity of milk was obtained by pre- and postweighing of the infants. Mothers also recorded the time and duration of each feeding. At all five time points, the strongest relationships ($p < .001$) were between feeding size and preprandial interval ($r = .46, .47, .41, .39,$ and $.43$, at 2, 4, 6, 8, and 12 weeks, respectively), although more moderate but significant relationships ($p < .01$) with postprandial interval were noted at all but 8 weeks ($r = .25, .17, .17, -.02,$ and $.17$, respectively). During this period, there was no evidence of a developmental shift in the feeding size–feeding interval relationship from the preprandial to the postprandial relationship typically reported for mature organisms (LeMagnen, 1985). Such a shift would reflect a developmental change from a reactive to an anticipatory pattern of feeding.

Changes in feeding patterns during infancy and a discussion of the role of learning in producing these changes have been presented by Wright (1987). He reported that at 2 months, breast-fed infants were taking their largest meal in the morning, following a long, overnight interval. However, this pattern had altered by 6 months, with the infants taking their largest feeding in the evening, prior to the overnight fast. These data, in combination with data from our 2- to 12-week-olds, suggested that a transition in the feeding size–feeding interval relationship may be occurring between 3 and 6 months, and that this shift from a reactive to an anticipatory pattern was mediated, at least in part, by learning and experience. However, the existing evidence is suggestive, and additional research on this topic is needed.

NEOPHOBIA AND ITS EFFECTS ON EARLY FOOD ACCEPTANCE PATTERNS

Data obtained from a series of experiments conducted with 2- to 5-year-olds in our laboratory revealed that by the age of 2 children are neophobic. This response was similar to the neophobia often observed in other omnivores. In general, other things being equal, young children show a preference for familiar foods over novel foods. This neophobia can be reduced through repeated exposure. However, there is very little information available on the emergence and developmental course of this neophobic response during infancy and very early childhood.

Anecdotal evidence suggests that neophobic responses may not exert an influence on feeding until after the first year of life, Davis (1928, 1939), in describing the initial responses of the infants (most of whom were under 1 year old when they began to participate in her self-selection studies), reported no hint of neophobia: ". . . they tried not only the food but chewed hopefully on the clean spoon, dishes, the edge of the tray, or a piece of paper on it. Their faces showed expressions of surprise, followed by pleasure, indifference, or dislike. All the articles on the list . . . were tried by all, but within the first few days, they began to reach eagerly for some and to neglect others. Never again did any child eat so many of the foods as in the first weeks of the experimental period" (1939; pp. 260–261).

As Rozin (1976) pointed out, as omnivores we need variety in our diet and must seek it out. On the other hand, novel foods are potentially dangerous and should be approached and sampled with caution. Neophobia often dissipates, however, when repeated samplings of a novel food are not followed by negative consequences; novel foods become an accepted part of the diet. For the young child who is being introduced to the adult diet of their culture, many foods are novel and can elicit a neophobic response. During this transitional introductory period, the adaptive value of the neophobic response must be weighed against the child's need for variety in the diet. Unfortunately, most parents are unaware that this initial rejection of a new food often reflects a transitory neophobia, which can frequently be reduced through repeated exposure. Adult caretakers often interpret this initial rejection as reflecting the child's fixed and immutable dislike of the new food. Rather than presenting the new food again, parents often remove that food from the child's diet, thus eliminating the possibility that the neophobic response will be reduced, and thereby failing to broaden the variety of foods the child will accept.

The experiments we conducted on the effects of repeated exposure on the reduction of neophobia in 2- to 5-year-olds indicated that repeated exposure to initially novel foods can lead to enhanced preference, with correlations between exposure frequency and preference greater than .90 (Birch & Marlin, 1982). The results of a recent experiment are shown in Figure 1. Preschool children ($N=39$) were repeatedly exposed to one of three versions of an initially novel food (sweetened, salty, or plain tofu). We examined the effects of exposure on preference for all three versions. Preferences for similar novel foods were also obtained to investigate possible generalization of an acquired preference. The children had 15 exposures and their preferences were assessed prior to exposure and after 15 exposures. Preference increased only for the exposed food, regardless of whether it was sweet, salty, or plain. However, experience with one version did not produce generalized liking for all versions. To the contrary, preference for the other versions of the food actually declined significantly. For the children who were exposed to plain tofu, that version became more preferred, while preference for the flavored versions declined, and the same pattern was noted in the preferences of the children exposed to the flavored versions. The acquired preferences

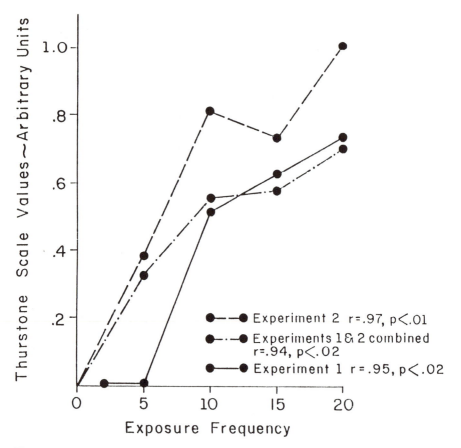

Figure 1 Food preference as a function of experience.

were restricted to the particular food/flavor complex. The declines in preference noted for the other versions of the food suggested that, through experience with eating the food, the children were learning whether or not it was appropriate to add salt or sugar to it. Repeated exposure to one novel food produced no generalization to other, similar novel foods. The results indicated that children typically require experience with tasting the food on about 10 occasions before changes in acceptance begin to appear. In other research, we varied the type of exposure (looking and smelling vs. tasting and ingesting) to determine whether tasting and ingestion are necessary to produce changes in preference judgments based on taste (Birch, McPhee, Shoba, Pirok, & Steinberg, 1987). Results indicated that exposure must include experience with the modality that is relevant to the preference judgments. For example, while looking at the novel foods enhanced visual judgments, such exposure had no effect on taste judgments. Unfortunately for parents, the results revealed that only repeated tastings of the novel foods produced enhanced flavor preferences, simply looking at and smelling the novel foods was not sufficient.

In the laboratory, neophobia and its reduction through repeated exposure contributed to determining which foods are accepted and which foods are rejected. At this point it is not clear how robust such effects are relative to other forms of learning that contribute to the development of food acceptance patterns. Eating is a socially and biologically relevant activity, and experience with food is typically associated with social contexts and physiological consequences. We have obtained evidence that the affective quality of the social context in which the experience with the novel food occurs also shapes the development of food acceptance patterns (Birch, Zimmerman, & Hind, 1980). There is also evidence that physiological feedback can produce conditioned preferences and conditioned satiety (Birch & Deysher, 1985, 1986; Birch, McPhee, Steinberg, & Sullivan, 1990). Novel foods are particularly associable: Conditioned aversions are readily formed to novel foods.

ACQUIRED FOOD PREFERENCES: CONTRIBUTIONS OF ASSOCIATIVE CONDITIONING AND SOCIAL LEARNING

In considering the opportunities for learning, the repetitive nature of eating can provide many opportunities for reinforced trials. What are the effects of repeatedly consuming a food in a particular social context? In our culture, children are expected to dislike spinach. However, this sterotypic dislike is culturally specific; Japanese children are expected to like and eat spinach (S. Salamon, personal communication). These types of expectations shape child feeding practices employed by adults.

The results of a series of experiments we conducted to investigate the effects of child feeding practices on the development and modification of food preferences revealed that child feeding practices shape children's food acceptance patterns (Birch et al., 1980; Birch, Marlin, & Rotter, 1984; Birch, McPhee, Shoba, Steinberg, & Krehbiel, 1987). For example, in our culture adult caretakers attempt to increase children's consumption of vegetables. One strategy that is used to induce children to consume these nutritionally desirable foods is to force the child to eat the vegetables in order to obtain extrinsic rewards (e.g., dessert). In a related maneuver, parents often use palatable, preferred foods as rewards for children's performance of desired behaviors. In experiments designed to investigate the effects of these child feeding practices on the acquisition of food preferences, the general approach was to assess the children's preferences for a set of foods, and to select one food that was neither strongly preferred nor strongly disliked for repeated presentation in a social context. Following a number of exposures to the target food in a social context, preferences were reassessed. The results of these experiments were clear: repeatedly associating a food with a distinctive social context systematically changed the children's preferences, in either a positive or negative direction, depending on the social context employed.

The data relevant to the interpretation of what produced these effects were less clear.

In two experiments, (Birch, Birch, Marlin, & Kramer, 1982; Birch, Marlin, & Rotter, 1984), we investigated the effects of having preschool children consume a food in order to obtain a reward (i.e., "drink your milk and then you can . . . [have access to an attractive reward]"). Results indicated that this feeding practice produced significant negative shifts in preference. The second of these experiments was designed to obtain information regarding the processes responsible for these effects, and included conditions designed to test possible extrinsic motivation and response deprivation hypotheses regarding the previously observed negative shifts in preference. Results indicated that having children consume foods in order to obtain rewards produced negative shifts in preference across all contingency conditions, regardless of whether the amounts consumed were greater than, equal to, or less than baseline amounts, or a tangible reward or verbal praise was provided contingent upon consumption. This implies that neither an extrinsic motivation interpretation nor a response deprivation interpretation was necessary to account for the negative effects on preference. Another possibility was that the coercive nature of this child feeding strategy generated negative emotions which became associated with the food.

A related experiment was designed to investigate the effects of the use of foods in the reward component of a contingency. Results revealed that when we presented foods repeatedly as rewards or in conjunction with positive, adult attention, these foods became highly preferred by the children (Birch, Zimmerman, & Hind, 1980). An interpretation of these findings was that food cues were being associated with the positive or negative affect generated by the social contexts. Although the processes responsible for these effects are not yet fully understood, it is clear that such practices can have unintended and negative effects on the quality of the child's diet: Preferences for highly palatable (typically high fat, high sugar) foods are enhanced, while nutritionally desirable foods can become even more disliked.

There is limited evidence that child feeding practices that impose external controls on feeding, either by forcing the child to consume more than is wanted or restricting access to food, may affect the etiology of individual differences in the control of food intake, particularly the extent to which intake is determined by hunger and satiety and by external factors (Birch et al., 1987; Costanzo & Woody, 1985). Parents use contingencies to increase and to restrict children's intake. While these are clearly two divergent tactics, a common assumption underlies both approaches: The adult believes that the child is unable to select and consume a nutritionally adequate diet without external control by the parent.

An extreme example of the role of parental beliefs about feeding on children's food intake has recently been reported by Pugliese, Weyman-Daum, Moses, and Lifshitz (1987). They described seven reported cases of nonorganic failure to thrive among middle-class U.S. children 7 to 22 months old. This nonorganic failure to thrive was a direct result of parents restricting the child's food intake, based on health beliefs. These children, from middle- and upper-income families, were all below the 5th percentile for weight. Parental health beliefs included concern that the child would become obese or develop cardiovascular disease, and the pursuit of a "healthy" diet. In these cases, access to food in general or to calorically dense "junk" foods was restricted, resulting in devastating consequences for the children. Case history information suggests that these children could have continuing difficulties in the control of food intake as a result of this early experience with deprivation (Satter, 1987). Longitudinal study of these children could provide information on the extent to which these parental practices to control feeding produce long-term effects on the development of individual differences in the control of food intake.

Middle-class Americans live in a culture of plenty that values thinness. Although the parental beliefs espoused by the parents in Pugliese et al.'s (1987) research may have had particularly extreme consequences, other evidence suggests that their beliefs may not be that different from those of many other concerned parents. For example, in a recent informal survey of 2,000 parents of infants calling the Gerber Products' toll-free number, 57% said they were concerned that their babies would become overweight, and 70% indicated that their infant feeding practices were influenced by information about *adult* nutrition and dieting (Johnson, personal communication). They did not seem to appreciate that what is good for adults (e.g., low fat diets) may not be good for young children and infants.

The Pugliese et al. (1987) paper underscored the point that parents' ideas about what and how much children should eat are often wrong. In some cases, parents think that children are eating too much or too much of the wrong foods. In other instances, parents are concerned that their children are not eating enough or not enough of the right foods. In either case, the underlying assumption is that children cannot adequately control their intake, and that a responsible parent should make certain that children eat properly. These attempts to control children's intake usually involve the imposition of authoritarian external controls. The literature on the relationship between parental control and child outcomes suggests that these efforts can backfire, leading to unintended, negative consequences (Baumrind, 1971).

While there is scant evidence of such negative consequences in the development of the control of food intake, evidence regarding other aspects of child development indicates that the imposition of rigid, authoritarian parenting styles and a high degree of parental involvement typically interferes with the development of adequate self-controls. The central theme of this chapter is that the social context of feeding provides many opportunities for learning processes to modify intake patterns. The research reviewed above indicated that learning can modify preferences for specific foods. A related issue concerns whether learning also influences the control of food intake by altering cues that control the initiation, maintenance, and termination of eating. How might the social contexts of feeding affect the control of food intake? One possibility that has received some empirical support (see below) is that some of the many external and internal cues available in the environment are conditioned to food cues, producing conditioned meal initiation and satiety, as well as conditioned preferences and aversions. Another possibility is that child feeding practices provide the child with opportunities to learn which of the many internal and external cues available are relevant to the control of food intake. For example, if the child says "I'm full" and the parent imposes a contingency and says "Finish what's on your plate," the child may conclude that external cues, not internal cues indicating satiety are relevant in terminating a meal.

Recently, Constanzo and Woody (1985) presented a model for the development of obesity proneness in children that can help to explain how the psychosocial environment of feeding may interact with genetic predisposition to produce obesity in susceptible individuals. They argued that parents are not consistent in their parenting practices across the domains of children's development. Rather, parents tend to monitor and impose stringent external controls on the child if they see the child as potentially deviant (the obese parent who fears that the child will become obese in a society that values thinness), the parents themselves are involved in that aspect of development (i.e., health, slimness, beauty consciousness), or the parent doubts that the child's naturally occurring opportunities for learning will produce the desired outcome. Research on the effects of parenting style on children's cognitive and social development reveals that the imposition of external control impedes the development of adequate self-control in the very areas where the parent is most concerned. While there are data from prospective studies on children's social and cognitive development that support this view (Baumrind, 1971), the only data relevant to this relationship in the domain of feeding are retrospective. This research, intended to address the relationship between parental style and the etiology of individual differences in the control of food intake, is described below.

Morgan and Costanzo (1985) conducted a retrospective study of college students who were classified on a restraint scale (Herman & Polivy, 1980) which discriminated among individuals in terms of how diet-conscious they are, how much their weight fluctuates, and how much they chronically dieted and are concerned about their weight. Herman et al. have argued that restraint rather than degree of obesity was most useful in determining which individuals ate inappropriately and which individuals were the most "out of touch" with their physiological state.

To obtain evidence on how individuals' early experiences contributed to being out of touch with their physical state, Morgan and Costanzo (1985) asked their college student subjects questions regarding their parents' child feeding practices and the extent to which their parents were dieters and were concerned about their weight. This sample also completed a scale designed to measure individual differences in restraint. Restraint was a measure of the extent of the subject's concern with food, dieting, and weight control, the extent to which eating was cognitively controlled, and their history of weight fluctuations (Herman & Polivy, 1980). They found that the one factor that separated the restrained eaters from the rest of the college sample population was high parental control and influence on eating. Parental control over food intake was significantly and positively related to the student's degree of obesity. These data are provocative with respect to the relationships between early feeding practices and later individual differences in the control of food intake, and emphasize the need for prospective research on the etiology of individual differences in the control of food intake. Although we do not have longitudinal data on this issue, we have obtained experimental evidence relevant to the relationships between child feeding practices and individual differences in learned controls of food intake in early childhood.

In our research with 2- to 5-year-olds, we presented evidence that in the absence of adult coercion and control, children have some capacity to adequately control intake. Young children showed responsiveness to caloric density cues that resulted from differences in carbohydrate content, eating more following low-caloric density preloads than high-caloric density preloads (Birch & Deysher, 1985, 1986; Birch, McPhee, & Sullivan, 1989). This responsiveness has both unlearned and learned components. Subsequent research has revealed that adults' behavior can also influence the extent to which children show responsiveness to such caloric density cues (Birch, McPhee, Shoba, Steinberg, & Krehbiel, 1987).

To compare children's and adults' responsiveness to caloric density cues in the absence of opportunities for learning, 21 2½- to 5-year-olds and 26 adults ate two lunches, one week apart. The two lunches consisted of an opportunity to eat ad libitum from among a variety of foods—including sandwich quarters, fresh fruits, and vegetables—following a fixed volume of a pudding preload which had either 40 kcal/100 ml or 150 kcal/100 ml. The pattern of ad libitum consumption following the two preloads is presented in Figure 2. The children's total consumption across the two meals was nearly identical, with the children consuming significantly fewer kcals in the ad libitum portion of the lunch following the high-caloric density preload. In contrast, the adults showed no evidence of caloric compensation.

In two subsequent experiments employing a preloading protocol, children's responsiveness to caloric density cues was also investigated (Birch, et al., 1989). The central purpose of these experiments was to examine the time course of the effects of carbohydrates on the suppression of children's subsequent food intake. Children consumed fixed volumes of fruit-flavored drinks containing sucrose, aspartame, aspartame plus low glucose maltodextrin, or a water control. The opportunity for ad libitum consumption occurred following one of three time delays: immediately, after 30 minutes, or after 60 minutes. As shown in Figure 3, the results indicated that the children showed caloric compensation, but these patterns of compensation were not related to the delay intervals. Analysis of the ad libitum consumption patterns indicated that following the high-caloric density preloads, the children tended to compensate for the calories in the preloads by restricting or totally eliminating consumption of nonpreferred foods, while keep-

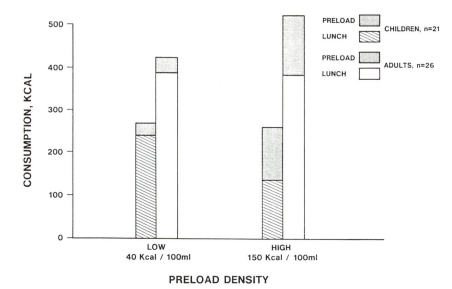

Figure 2 Ad libitum lunch consumption following high- and low-caloric density preload consumption by children and adults.

ing consumption of preferred foods relatively constant. Such a pattern can have negative consequences on the quality of children's diets by reducing variety in the diet and restricting the consumption of nonpreferred and nutritionally desirable foods.

CONDITIONED SATIETY AND CONDITIONED MEAL INITIATION

The research described in the previous section indicates that in the absence of adult control strategies, children can be responsive to cues that arise from the physiological consequences of eating. The formation of associations between food cues and the physiological consequences of eating those foods allow the individual to learn to anticipate the consequences of eating familiar foods, and adjust their intake accordingly. The existence of such conditioned satiety was suggested by the fact that eating usually stops well before postingestive cues signaling satiety develop (Le Magnen, 1955; Stunkard, 1975). At this point there is ample evidence for such conditioning in animal models (Booth, 1972; Tordoff & Friedman, 1986), and much current research focuses on the nature of the unconditioned stimulus in such learning.

Booth has presented evidence for conditioned satiety and state dependent conditioned preferences in human adults (Booth, Lee, & McAleavey, 1976; Booth, Mather, & Fuller, 1982). We have also obtained evidence for the conditioning of food cues to consequences in young children. In the experiments we conducted with young children (Birch & Deysher, 1985; Birch, McPhee, Shoba,

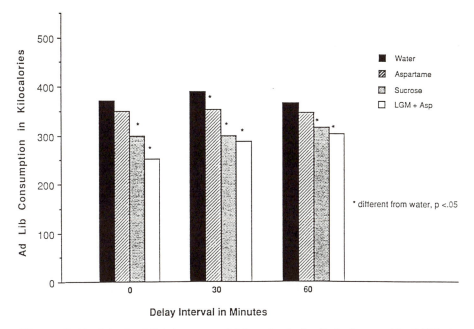

Figure 3 Food intake following sweet drink preloads for 2- to 3-year-olds. LGM + Asp = aspartame + glucose maltodextrin.

Steinberg, & Krehbiel, 1987), the children were given repeated experience with eating a series of pairs of two-part snacks consisting of a fixed volume preload and a variety of foods in the ad libitum portion. Within each pair of snacks, one preload was high in calorie density, the other low in caloric density. Caloric density was varied through the addition of low glucose maltodextrin to the high-caloric density preload. For each child, each preload density was always accompanied by the same distinctive flavor (e.g., low calorie apricot yogurt vs. high calorie strawberry yogurt). Following pairs of conditioning trials, extinction test trials were administered in which the preloads were isocaloric or of intermediate caloric density. The results (see Figure 4) indicated that the children learned to associate food cues with consequences, because when the caloric density differences had been removed during extinction and only the flavor cues were present to control intake, they continued to eat more following the flavor that had been previously paired with the low-caloric density preload. Thus in the absence of adult controls, children showed a degree of responsiveness to internal cues, and can learn to anticipate the caloric consequences of eating familiar foods.

The findings described above suggest that under some conditions, children can be responsive to internal cues resulting from caloric density differences. However, additional research indicates that the social context in which this experience occurs can influence the extent to which children respond to internal cues resulting from caloric density differences. In this research, we essentially repli-

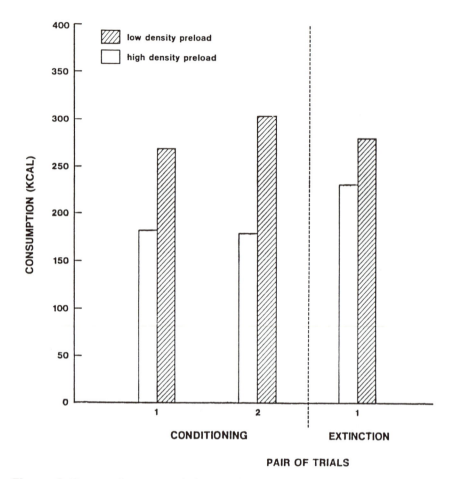

Figure 4 Consumption patterns during conditioning and extinction test snacks.

cated the conditioned satiety experiments just described, except that the children received the pairs of conditioning trials in one of two social contexts: One was designed to focus the children on the internal cues of hunger and satiety as determinants of eating, while the other was intended to emphasize external cues, such as the time of day and the amount of food remaining on the plate. In addition, in the external cues context, the children were rewarded for eating. Following the pairs of conditioning trials in one of the two social contexts, the children in both contexts had identical extinction test trials. In these test trials, the social context cues were removed. The preloads used during the extinction test trials were isocaloric and were of the same flavors as the preloads used in the conditioning trials in order to determine whether flavor cues had controlled intake. The results indicated that the children who were focused on internal cues of hunger and satiety showed clear evidence of conditioning, while those for whom external cues were salient showed no evidence of conditioning. These results, in combination with those from the previous research, suggested that although children are capable of being responsive to internal cues and that such cues can serve as the basis of conditioning, the social context in which experience occurs is very salient and can interfere with conditioning using food cues and consequences. My interpretation of these findings is that they provide limited experimental evidence supporting the relationship between parenting style and child outcome described by Costanzo et al. (1985) for the domain of feeding: The imposition of powerful external controls by adult caretakers seems to impede the development of internal controls.

The evidence presented above suggests that, at least under some circumstances, learning influences meal size; satiety can be conditioned in children. This conditioning involves the association of food cues with the caloric consequences of eating those foods. Recently, we have obtained evidence that learning can also influence children's initiation of meals (Birch, McPhee, Sullivan, & Johnson, 1989). This research was inspired by Weingarten's (1983, 1984, 1985) findings indicating that meals could be initiated in sated rats in the presence of cues that had previously been associated with food and eating. In our research, children were exposed to a series of conditioning sessions and test sessions. A series of four experiments have now been completed, which differ somewhat in the details. In general, the children were given repeated opportunities to eat in the presence of distinctive cues (CS+) when moderately hungry. On other occasions, they had free play sessions that were repeatedly associated with another set of cues (CS−), and in which food was never presented. Following a series of pairs of such trials, we assessed the extent to which the CS+ cues could elicit eating in the children when relatively satiated. This was done in a series of test sessions over several days; we fed them ice cream preloads that were roughly equivalent to their ad libitum caloric intake during the CS+ training sessions (about 260 kcal). Immediately following consumption of the preloads, they were presented with the CS+ cues on some days and CS− cues on other days. In both cases, food was present. The results provided evidence that in the presence of the CS+ cues, the children ate more food and had shorter latencies to eating than in the CS− conditions. Thus the environmental cues previously associated with food and eating came to facilitate consumption when the children were relatively sated, providing additional evidence for how learning can modify the control of food intake.

ACQUISITION OF CUISINE RULES

Learning about eating also involves learning to distinguish edible from inedible substances. We know very little about how and when this learning occurs. Galef's research on how young rats learn this basic and essential distinction provides clear evidence for social factors, although not for direct instruction (Galef, 1985). As Rozin (in press) has pointed out, we also have culture to assist the child in making these distinctions, and indeed, these distinctions regarding edible and inedible substances do differ across cultural groups. There is relatively little research on how children learn what is and what is not food in their culture, and how they learn about the appropriateness of consuming foods in particular contexts and combinations.

Rozin and Fallon (Fallon & Rozin, 1983; Rozin & Fallon, 1980, 1981) have developed a taxonomy of food acceptance and rejection that includes three categories of reasons for acceptance or rejection of potential edibles (a) sensory affective factors, (b) anticipated consequences, and (c) ideational factors. Their research on the development of children's understanding and use of these categories has revealed a developmental sequence in the acquisition of these three categories (Fallon, Rozin, & Pliner, 1984). Sensory affective factors determine food acceptance or rejection during the first years of life. As indicated above, these sensory affective factors (like and dislike) can be modified through associative conditioning. The second and third categories begin to influence food intake at the end of the preschool period. This is not surprising, given that these latter categories require that the child has acquired knowledge and beliefs imparted by the culture about anticipated consequences (i.e., what is good for you and what is bad for you) and the origins of potential edibles and contaminants.

Cuisine rules also define when foods can be eaten: In our culture, certain foods are eaten at breakfast, others at lunch or dinner, still others as snacks or on special occasions. We have conducted some initial research on when an how these rules are acquired. In one study, we investigated the extent to which young children are aware of these cuisine rules and whether or not they influenced the children's food preferences. At least for adults, food preferences shift with time of day and with the extent to which the food is appropriately consumed at that time. While explicit teaching of such cuisine rules undoubtedly occurs, much of what children are learning about such cuisine rules seems to be inferred from repeated experience with what is appropriate. The limited information available suggests that through repeated exposure and the reduction of neophobia, and the associative conditioning of food cues to the contexts of eating, rules of cuisine are gradually constructed by the child. We have hypothesized elsewhere (Birch, Billman, & Richards, 1984) that these cuisine rules are supported and maintained by the affective reactions they come to elicit. That is, foods are most preferred at the time of day when it is appropriate to eat them: For most of us, hot dogs are more preferred at lunch or dinner than at breakfast, while the reverse pattern emerges for oatmeal.

To explore young children's acquisition of cuisine rules, we asked young children (3- to 5-year-olds) to sort a set of foods into "for breakfast" and "for dinner" categories, after giving us preference data on all the foods (Birch et al., 1984). The children were seen twice, once in the morning and once in the late afternoon. A group of adults also participated. Results revealed that even the young children had no trouble in categorizing the foods appropriately as for breakfast or for dinner (including standard breakfast items such as Cheerios™ and scrambled eggs, and familiar dinner foods such as pizza and macaroni and cheese), in the same manner as the adults. The adults' preferences showed clear time of day shifts, with foods being most preferred at the time of day when it was appropriate to consume them. The children showed time of day shifts in preference, indicating that although their experience with the foods was more limited, they had already acquired the adult-like pattern of preferring foods at the time of day when they were most appropriate. The relationship between the acquisition of affect and knowledge of cuisine rules is an area worthy of additional study.

A second study on the acquisition of cuisine rules was designed to examine the role of experience in the acquisition of preferences for food-flavorant combinations (Sullivan & Birch, 1990). This work was inspired by the research of Beauchamp et al. (1986) who reported that by about 2 years, children were showing a preference for salted over unsalted soup, while preferring unsalted to salted water. These findings suggested to us that with experience, preference for an added flavorant might become increasingly context specific, due to the fact that children typically have had experience with salted but not unsalted soup, and with plain water but not salted water. The purpose of the research was to test whether repeated experience with a food flavorant combination was sufficient to engender a relative preference for that combination, and to explore whether the effects of this experience could be applied to other food-flavorant combinations.

We chose a food unfamiliar to all of our 4-year-old subjects at the beginning of the experiment: tofu. The children were randomly assigned to receive repeated experience with only one of three versions of tofu; sweetened, salted, or plain. Preferences for these items and for other similar food–flavorant combinations were assessed before, during, and after their experience with the food. Their experience consisted of a series of 15 exposures to the food, two exposures per week, over a period of several weeks. In each case, the child was asked to take a small taste of the food. The results provided additional evidence for a mere exposure effect: Across all three groups, preference for the experienced food-flavorant combination was enhanced.

With respect to the question of generalization of preference, none was noted. In fact, the data provided clear evidence for context-specific preferences for the added flavorants. When we categorized the foods as either flavored (combining the sweet and salty exposure groups) or unflavored, similar patterns appeared in the data, although the specific preference changes were different. As shown in Figure 5, while the children in both groups showed increased preferences for the foods they had experienced, they also showed significant declines in preference for the novel food-flavorant combinations. For example, the children who had experience with either sweet- or salty-flavored tofu preferred plain tofu even less than when it was completely novel. The same pattern emerged from the data of the children who had repeated experience with plain tofu: While the plain version became more preferred with experience, the sweet and salty versions became even less preferred than when they were novel. These results

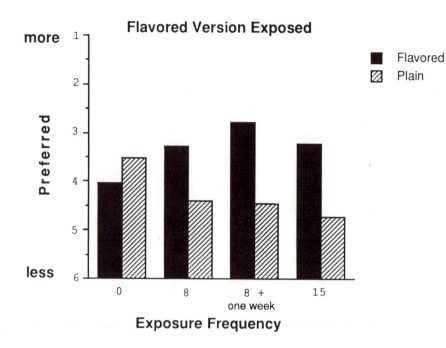

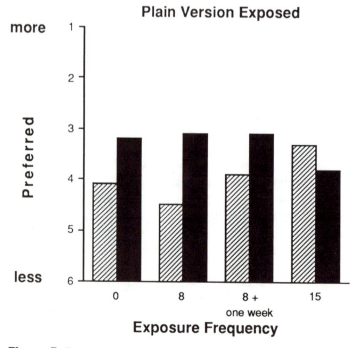

Figure 5 Food preference as a function of experience with plain and flavored foods.

indicated that, at least in the absence of an aversive presentation context or consequence, children come to like what we give them. In addition, experience seems to provide children with information about what is appropriate. Through inferring such rules from experience, children may be learning to dislike "inappropriate" food-flavor combinations.

SUMMARY AND CONCLUSIONS

In this chapter, evidence has been presented indicating a central role for learning in the development of food acceptance patterns during the first years of life. The young, omnivorous human must learn what is edible, what to like and dislike, which food combinations to eat, when to eat, how much to eat, and when to stop eating. During the suckling period, there is limited evidence that learning modifies diurnal patterning of feeding size and interval, and the relationship between these parameters. Subsequently, learning is central as the child is weaned and makes the transition to a more adult-like eating pattern. Upon introduction, many foods that are a familiar part of the adult diet of the culture may be initially rejected by the child, but repeated exposure reduces the child's neophobia, often resulting in acceptance. There is evidence that food cues can become associated with the social contexts of eating, producing either positive or negative changes in preference, depending on the valence of the social context. Children can also learn to associate food flavor cues with the physiological consequences of eating, acquiring preferences and aversions. In addition, the child's learned associations between food cues and the physiological consequences that result from eating foods differing in energy density can allow the child to adjust intake in response to anticipated differences in energy density. However, the evidence on the effects of child feeding practices indicates that the child's learning of associations between food cues and caloric consequences can be readily disrupted. Although the picture is far from complete, there is limited evidence that associative conditioning also contributes to when the child will initiate a meal. Learned rules about cuisine and acquired preferences influence which foods and food combinations are liked and consumed. Evidence also indicates that learning is involved in the conditioning of satiety and in controlling when eating stops.

References

Baumrind, D. (1971). Current patterns of parental authority. *Developmental Psychology Monograph, 4*(1), 1–103.

Beauchamp, G. K., Cowart, B. J., & Moran, M. (1986). Developmental changes in salt acceptability in human infants. *Developmental Psychobiology, 19*, 75–83.

Birch, L. L., Billman, J., & Richards, S. (1984). Time of day influences food acceptability. *Appetite, 5*, 109–112.

Birch, L. L., Birch, D., Marlin, D., & Kramer, L. (1982). Effects of instrumental eating on children's food preferences. *Appetite, 3*, 125–134.

Birch, L. L., & Deysher, M. (1985). Conditioned and unconditioned caloric compensation: Evidence for self-regulation of food intake by young children. *Learning and Motivation, 16*, 341–355.

Birch, L. L., & Deysher, M. (1986). Caloric compensation and sensory specific satiety: Evidence for self-regulation of food intake by young children. *Appetite, 7,* 323–331.

Birch, L. L., & Marlin, D. W. (1982). I don't like it; I never tried it: Effects of exposure on two-year-old children's food preferences. *Appetite, 3,* 353–360.

Birch, L. L., Marlin, D., & Rotter, J. (1984). Eating as the "means" activity in a contingency: Effects on young children's food preference. *Child Development, 55,* 532–439.

Birch, L. L., McPhee, L., & Sullivan, S. (1989). Children's food intake following drinks sweetened with sucrose or aspartame: Time course effects. *Physiology & Behavior, 45,* 387–396.

Birch, L. L. McPhee, L., Pirok, & Steinberg, L. (1987). What kind of exposure reduces childrens' food neophobia?: Looking versus tasting. *Appetite, 9,* 171–178.

Birch, L. L., McPhee, L., Shoba, B. C., Steinberg, L., & Krehbiel, R. (1987). "Clean up your plate:" Effects of child feeding practices on the development of intake regulation. *Learning & Motivation, 18,* 301–317.

Birch, L. L., McPhee, L., Steinberg, L. & Sullivan, S. (1990). Conditioned flavor preferences in young children. *Physiology & Behavior, 47,* 501–505.

Birch, L. L., McPhee, L., Sullivan, S., & Johnson, S. (1989). Conditioned meal initiation in young children. *Appetite, 13,* 105–113.

Birch, L. L., Zimmerman, S., & Hind, H. (1980). The influence of social affective context on preschool children's food preferences. *Child Development, 51,* 856–861.

Booth, D. A. (1972). Conditioned satiety in the rat. *Journal of Comparative and Physiological Psychology, 81,* 457–471.

Booth, D. A., Lee, M., & McAleavey, C. (1976). Acquired sensory control of satiation in man. *British Journal of Psychology, 67,* 137–147.

Booth, D. A., Mather, P., & Fuller, J. (1982). Starch content of ordinary foods associatively conditions human appetite and satiation, indexed by intake and eating pleasantness of starch-paired flavors. *Appetite, 3,* 163–184.

Costanzo, P. R., & Woody, E. Z. (1985). Domain-specific parenting styles and their impact on the child's development of particular deviance: The example of obesity proneness. *Journal of Social and Clinical Psychology, 3,* 425–430.

Davis, C. (1928). Self-selection of diet by newly weaned infants. *American Journal of Diseases of Children, 36,* 651–679.

Davis, C. (1939). Results of the self-selection of diets by young children. *The Canadian Medical Association Journal, 41,* 257–261.

Dewey, K. G., & Lonnerdal, B. (1986). Infant self-regulation of breast milk intake. *Acta Paediatrica Scandanavia, 75,* 893–898.

Fallon, A. E., & Rozin, P. (1983). The psychological bases of food rejections by humans. *Ecology of Food and Nutrition, 13,* 5–26.

Fallon, A. E. Rozin, P., & Pliner, P. (1984). The child's conception of food: The development of food rejection, with special reference to disgust and contamination sensitivity. *Child Development, 55,* 566–575.

Fomon, S. J. (1974). *Infant nutrition* (2nd ed.). Philadelphia: W. B. Saunders.

Galef, B. (1985). Socially induced diet preference can partially reverse a LiCl-induced diet aversion. *Animal Learning and Behavior, 13,* 415–418.

Herman, C.P., & Polivy, J. (1980). Restrained eating. In A. J. Stunkard (Ed.), *Obesity* (pp. 208–255). Philadelphia: W. B. Saunders.

Le Magnen, J. (1955). Sur le mécanisme d'établissement des appétits caloriques [On the mechanism establishing an appetite for calories]. *Comptes Rendus de l'Académie des Sciences, 240,* 2436–2438.

Le Magnen, J. (1985). *Hunger.* Cambridge, England: Cambridge University Press.

Matheny, R., Birch, L., & Picciano, M. F. (in press). Control of intake by human milk-fed infants: Relationship between feeding size and interval. *Developmental Psychobiology.*

Morgan, J., & Costanzo, P. R. (1985). *Factors discriminating restrained and unrestrained eaters: A retrospective self-report study.* Unpublished manuscript.

Neville, M. C., Keller, R., Seacat, J., Lutes, V., Neifert, M., Casey, C., Allen, J., & Archer, P. (1988). Studies in human lactation: Milk volumes in lactating women during the onset of lactation and full lactation. *American Journal of Clinical Nutrition, 48,* 1375–1386.

Pugliese, M. T., Weyman-Daum, M., Moses, N., & Lifshitz, M. (1987). Parental health beliefs as a cause of nonorganic failure to thrive. *Pediatrics, 80,* 185–182.

Rozin, P. (1976). The selection of foods by rats, humans, and other animals. In J. S. Rosenblatt, R. A. Hinde, E. Shaw, & C. Beer (Eds.), *Advances in the study of behaviour* (pp. 21–76). New York: Academic Press.

Rozin, P. (in press). Development in the food domain. *Developmental Psychology.*

Rozin, P., & Fallon, A. E. (1980). The psychological categorization of foods and non-foods: A preliminary taxonomy of food rejections. *Appetite, 1,* 193–201.

Rozin, P., & Fallon, A. E. (1981). The acquisition of likes and dislikes for foods. In Sohms, J. & Hall, R. L. (Eds.), *Criteria of food acceptance: How man chooses what he eats.* Zurich: Forster Verlag.

Satter, E. (1987). *How to get your kid to eat . . . but not too much.* Palo Alto, CA: Bull Publishing Co.

Stunkard, A. J. (1975). Satiety is a conditioned reflex. *Psychosomatic Medicine, 37,* 383–389.

Sullivan, S., & Birch, L. (1990). Pass the sugar; pass the salt: Experience dictates preference. *Developmental Psychology, 26,* 546–551.

Tordoff, M. G., & Friedman, M. I. (1986). Hepatic portal glucose infusions decrease food intake and increase food preference. *American Journal of Physiology, 20,* R192–R196.

Weingarten, H. (1983) Conditioned cues elicit eating in sated rats: A role for learning in meal initiation, *Science, 220,* 431–433.

Weingarten, H. (1984) Meal initiation controlled by learned cues: Basic behavioral properties. *Appetite, 5,* 147–158.

Weingarten, H. (1985) Stimulus control of eating: Implications for a two-factor theory of hunger. *Appetite, 6,* 387–401.

Wright, P. (1987). Hunger, satiety and feeding behavior in early infancy. In R. A. Boakes, D. A. Popplewell, & M. J. Burton (Eds.), *Eating habits: Food, physiology and learned behavior* (pp. 75–106). Chichester, England: Wiley.

PART FOUR

TASTE PREFERENCES AND LEARNING

CHAPTER 10

NUTRITIONALLY BASED LEARNED FLAVOR PREFERENCES IN RATS

ANTHONY SCLAFANI

The flavor of food, that is, its taste, smell, and texture, provides animals with important information as to whether a particular food item should be consumed or avoided. Animals respond to flavor cues based on inborn and learned preferences and aversions. For example, many species have an innate preference for sweet taste and an aversion to bitter taste. Animals can also learn to prefer or avoid foods based on their experiences with foods as well as their interactions with other animals (Barker, Best, & Domjan, 1977; Braveman & Bronstein, 1985). Because of their limited number of innate flavor preferences and aversions and the variety of foods in their diet, learning appears to play a major role in the food selection of omnivores such as rats and humans. There is extensive evidence that laboratory animals can readily learn to avoid foods that have toxic effects, but their ability to learn to prefer foods based on nutritional benefits is less well documented (Barker et al., 1977; Braveman & Bronstein, 1985). The paucity of experimental evidence for the conditioning of food preferences is surprising since in the real world most bouts of ingestion have positive rather than negative consequences.

This chapter will review recent research performed in my laboratory on nutrient-based conditioned flavor preferences (CFPs) in the rat. This work emerged from our studies on the hyperphagia-promoting effects of high-carbo-hydrate and high-fat diets (Sclafani, 1987, 1989). Analysis of the rat's appetite for carbohydrates and fats revealed that, in addition to their well-known preference for the sweet taste of sugar, rats have an innate preference for the taste of starch and probably for the flavor of fat (Ackroff, Vigorito, & Sclafani, 1990;

139

Sclafani, 1987; Vigorito & Sclafani, 1988). Other findings suggested that preferences for carbohydrates and fats are enhanced by the postingestive effects of these nutrients (Ackroff et al., 1989; Sclafani, 1987). This is not a new idea and several investigators have studied the postingestive conditioning of food preferences (Boakes & Lubart, 1988; Bolles, Hayward, & Crandall, 1981; Booth, 1985; Capaldi, Campbell, Sheffer, & Bradford, 1987; Holman, 1968; Le Magnen, 1969; Puerto, Deutsch, Molina, & Roll, 1976; Tordoff & Friedman, 1986). Nevertheless, the available evidence is incomplete and the role of postingestive nutritive feedback in the conditioning of appetite and food preferences remains poorly understood. We therefore initiated a program of research to address this issue using the conditioned flavor preference method.

GENERAL METHODS

The basic procedure used in most of our conditioning studies involved training rats, on alternate days, to associate one arbitrary cue flavor (the CS+) with a nutritive solution and a different cue flavor (the CS−) with a nonnutritive solution, a poorly absorbed nutritive solution, or nothing. The rat's preference for the two cue flavors was then assessed in a two-bottle choice test. The rats were exposed to 1–5 training–test cycles under either food-deprived or nondeprived conditions. The food-deprived animals were generally tested during short daily sessions (10–30 min/day), whereas the nondeprived animals were tested 23 hr/day. The results of the preference tests were summarized for this chapter in terms of the average percent of total intake consumed as CS+ solution during the two-bottle tests for each group. In those experiments that included multiple training–test cycles, the range of group mean percent CS+ intakes is presented for the repeated preference tests in order to emphasize the fact that conditioned preferences were not always obtained following the first training cycle.

Our work focused on two specific nutrients: Polycose® (Ross Laboratories), which is a form of hydrolyzed corn starch, and corn oil (Mazola®, Best Foods). Polycose was prepared as a solution at 8% to 32% (w/v) concentrations; the corn oil was prepared as an oil-water emulsion at 7.1% to 29% (w/w) concentrations. For cue flavors, most of the experiments used grape and cherry Kool Aid (.05% unsweetened mix; General Foods) dissolved in water; when additional flavors were needed, strawberry and orange Kool Aid were used. For half of the subjects, the CS+ solution was grape and the CS− solution was cherry; the CS flavors were reversed for the remaining subjects. Preliminary work indicated that these two flavors were isohedonic to rats but less preferred than plain water (Elizalde

The author gratefully acknowledges the contributions of Dr. Karen Ackroff, Graciela Elizalde, Dr. Francois Lucas, Jeffrey W. Nissenbaum, and Catalina Perez to the research described in this chapter, and to Dr. Ackroff and Dr. Lucas for their helpful comments on a draft of this chapter. The research was supported by grants from the National Institute of Diabetes and Digestive and Kidney Diseases (DK31135), the National Institute of Mental Health (MH43332), and the Research Foundation of the City University of New York.

& Sclafani, 1990a). In order to induce the rats to drink the CS solutions during the short-term tests, saccharin (0.2%) was added to the solutions; the saccharin-sweetened solutions are referred to as sCS+ and sCS−. In the long-term tests, both unsweetened (CS+, CS−) and sweetened (sCS+, sCS−) cue solutions were used. Depending upon the experimental paradigm, the CS flavors were presented in water or added to the nutrient solution.

CARBOHYDRATE CONDITIONING
Several studies have reported that rats learn to prefer flavors that are associated with carbohydrate solutions or carbohydrate-rich foods (Bolles et al., 1981; Booth, Lovett, & McSherry, 1972; Capaldi et al., 1987; Holman, 1975; Mather, Nicolaidis, & Booth, 1978; Mehiel & Bolles, 1984; Sherman, Hickis, Rice, Rusiniak, & Garcia, 1983; Simbayi, Boakes, & Burton, 1986; Tordoff & Friedman, 1986). However, reliable flavor preferences have not been obtained in all studies or with all conditioning procedures (Boakes, Rossi-Arnaud, & Garcia-Hoz, 1987; Deutsch, Molina, & Puerto, 1976; Koopmans & Maggio, 1978; Puerto et al., 1976; Revusky, Smith, & Chalmers, 1971; Simbayi et al., 1986). Furthermore, when positive results were obtained, the magnitude of the effect was typically modest (60–75% preference), and in some cases the nature of the reinforcer, (i.e., the taste or nutritive properties of the carbohydrate) was open to question. In view of these mixed results, we have reexamined carbohydrate-based conditioned flavor preferences using Polycose as the reinforcer. Our studies utilized a number of different testing paradigms in order to assess the generality of the conditioning effect (see Figure 1). The Polycose was either consumed by mouth (oral method) or delivered by intragastric infusion (gastric method).

Oral Methods

Simultaneous conditioning
In one of the simplest procedures used to produce CFPs, the CS+ flavor was added to a nutritive solution (i.e., the CS+) and it and the reinforcer were presented simultaneously; the CS− flavor was added to a nonnutritive solution or water. Following one-bottle training with these solutions, the rats' preference for the CS+ and CS− flavors was assessed in two-bottle tests (Figure 1, A). Several studies using this procedure have reported that rats learned to prefer flavors that had been added to glucose, sucrose, or hydrolyzed starch solutions (Booth et al., 1972; Capaldi et al., 1987; Fedorchak & Bolles, 1987; Holman, 1975; Mehiel & Bolles, 1984, 1988; Simbayi et al., 1986). Since conditioned preferences were obtained with "bland" starch solutions as well as with sweet sugar solutions, the preference was attributed to the nutritive rather than the taste properties of the carbohydrates. However, the assumption that starch solutions are bland to rats has proved to be incorrect, and it is now known that rats are very attracted to the taste of starch-derived polysaccharides (Sclafani, 1987). This new finding raises the possibility that the palatable taste of the starch may serve

FLAVOR PREFERENCE CONDITIONING PARADIGMS

ONE-BOTTLE TRAINING	TWO-BOTTLE TESTING

Oral Methods

A. Simultaneous

(30 min)	(10 min)
sCS+ / Nutrient sCS-	sCS+ vs. sCS-

B. Delayed

(10 min $\xrightarrow[60\ min]{10\ to}$ 30 min)	(10 min)
sCS+⟶ Nutrient sCS- ⟶ Nothing	sCS+ vs. sCS-

C. Real and Sham Feeding

(30 min)	(10 min)
CS+/ Nutrient (Real Fed) CS- / Nutrient (Sham Fed)	CS+/ Nutrient vs. CS- / Nutrient

Gastric Methods

D. Short-term

(10 min)	(10 min)
sCS+⟶ IG Nutrient sCS- ⟶ IG Water	sCS+ vs. sCS-

E. Long-term

(23 hr)	(23 hr)
CS+ ⟶ IG Nutrient CS- ⟶ IG Water	CS+ ⟶ IG Nutrient vs. CS- ⟶ IG Water

Figure 1 Schematic representation of the one-bottle and two-bottle testing procedures used in various flavor preference conditioning paradigms. CS+ and CS− refer to grape- or cherry-flavored solutions. sCS+ and sCS− refer to saccharin-sweetened grape- or cherry-flavored solutions. IG refers to intragastric infusion.

as a reinforcer for the conditioned flavor preference. Such flavor–flavor conditioning has been obtained with rats using sweet taste as the reinforcer (Holman, 1975).

We investigated the contribution of taste and postingestive factors in starch-conditioned flavor preferences using the drug acarbose (Elizalde & Sclafani, 1988). Acarbose is a glucosidase inhibitor which, when added to a Polycose solution, retards the digestion and absorption of the Polycose; acarbose does not alter the palatability of the solution, however (see Elizalde & Sclafani, 1988). Thus if rats learn to prefer a flavor added to a Polycose solution because of the postingestive nutritive effects of the carbohydrate, then adding acarbose to the solution should attenuate preference conditioning. This prediction was assessed by training two groups of food-deprived rats with sCS+ flavored Polycose solution and sCS− flavored water (Figure 1A). The POLY group was trained with a 16% Polycose solution; the POLY+A group was trained with a 16% Polycose solution containing acarbose (160 mg/100 ml solution). As indicated in Table 1, paradigm A, the POLY group displayed a 70–90% preference for the sCS+ flavor over the sCS−flavor. On the other hand, the POLY+A group did not develop a preference for the sCS+ flavor. These latter results indicated that it was the postingestive nutritive effect, not the palatable flavor of Polycose, that reinforced the acquisition of flavor preferences. The failure of the POLY+A group to display at least a weak preference for the sCS+ was somewhat surprising in view of findings that sweet taste and oily flavor can produce CFPs (Holman, 1975). This issue requires further investigation.

In a second study, two groups of rats were trained with sCS+ flavored 8% and 32% Polycose solutions (without acarbose; Elizalde & Sclafani, unpublished). During training, the 32% group consumed three times as much Polycose as did the 8% group (14.9 vs 4.7 kcal/30 min). Nevertheless, in the flavor preference test, the two groups displayed comparable preferences for the sCS+ over the sCS− (Table 1, paradigm B). Thus it appeared that the caloric content of the training solution, at least above some minimum, does not affect the magnitude of the conditioned preference obtained. These findings are of interest in light of differential conditioning effects obtained with 8% and 32% Polycose solutions using other training paradigms discussed below.

Delayed Conditioning

With the delayed conditioning procedure, the CS+ (flavored water) was presented alone for a short period and then, following a delay, the nutrient solution was presented (Figure 1, B). The ability of animals to develop flavor preferences when reinforcement is delayed is of interest for two reasons. First, in the normal process of ingestion and digestion, several minutes to hours elapse before the nutritive value of the food becomes available to the animal. Therefore, if the animal is to learn about the nutritive properties of food it must be able to develop flavor-nutrient associations over a delay. Second, it is well documented that rats can learn to avoid flavors that are associated with toxicosis over delays of up to

Table 1

SUMMARY OF FLAVOR PREFERENCES OBTAINED IN CARBOHYDRATE
CONDITIONING EXPERIMENTS

Paradigm	Flavor	Nutrient	Preference	Reference
Oral Methods				
Simultaneous				
A.	sCS	16% Polycose	70–90%	Elizalde & Sclafani, 1988
	sCS	16% Polycose + Acarbose	41–52%	
B.	sCS	8% Polycose	97%	Elizalde & Sclafani, unpublished
	sCS	32% Polycose	94%	
Delayed				
C. 10 min	sCS	16% Polycose	53–73%	Elizalde & Sclafani, 1988
10 min	sCS	16% Polycose (A)	69–83%	
D. 10 min	sCS	16% Polycose (A)	61–77%	Elizalde & Sclafani, 1988
30 min	sCS	16% Polycose (A)	51–79%	
60 min	sCS	16% Polycose (A)	52–78%	
Real and Sham Feeding				
E.	CS	8% Polycose	72–89%	Nissenbaum et al., 1988
	CS	32% Polycose	21–70%	
Gastric Methods				
Short-Term				
F.	pCS	14% Polycose (F)	73–77%	Nissenbaum & Sclafani, 1987; 1989
	pCS	14% Polycose (F) + Acarbose	40–47%	
G.	sCS	8% Polycose (F)	57–71%	Nissenbaum & Sclafani, 1989
	sCS	32% Polycose (F)	37–67%	
H.	sCS	8% Polycose (V)	75–76%	Nissenbaum & Sclafani, 1989
	sCS	32% Polycose (V)	63–70%	
Long-Term				
J.	CS	16% Polycose	96%	Sclafani & Nissenbaum, 1988
K.	CS	32% Polycose	78–98%	Elizalde & Sclafani, 1989

Notes: Flavor: CS = unsweetened Kool-Aid sCS = saccharin Kool-Aid, and pCS = Polycose Kool-Aid. Nutrient: (A) = Rats pre-exposed to Polycose + acarbose solution prior to training, (F) = Rats infused with fixed IG volume of 7 ml, and (V) = Rats infused with variable IG volume depending upon their oral CS intake. Preference scores represent the mean group percent CS+ intakes obtained in the two-bottle choice tests. The range of preference scores represents the lowest to highest mean percent CS+ intakes obtained in experiments that included multiple two-bottle choice tests.

several hours (see Barker et al., 1977; Braveman & Bronstein, 1985). If common learning mechanisms are involved in conditioned aversions and conditioned preferences, then animals should be able to acquire conditioned flavor preferences when reinforcement is delayed.

In an early study, Holman (1975) reported that rats learned to prefer a flavor that was reinforced after a 30-min delay by the presentation of a 20% glucose solution. In subsequent studies, however, either no preferences or weak preferences were obtained for flavors that were reinforced with the delayed presentation of glucose, sucrose, or starch solutions (Boakes et al., 1987; Capaldi et al., 1987; Simbayi et al., 1986) The difficulty in obtaining conditioned preferences over a delay may result because the animal associates the reinforcing postingestive effective of the nutrient with the flavor of the nutrient rather than with the CS+ flavor; that is, the nutrient flavor may overshadow the CS+ flavor (see Boakes & Lubart, 1988; Simbayi et al., 1986). According to this interpretation, delayed conditioning should be facilitated if the animals had previously learned that the flavor of the nutrient is not associated with postingestive reinforcement.

To test this prediction, we used the POLY and POLY+A groups described in the previous section (Elizalde & Sclafani, 1988). In this new experiment, the rats were presented with a novel sCS+ (e.g., orange-flavored saccharin solution) for 10 min followed by a 10-min delay and the flavored Polycose solution from their previous training (acarbose was now eliminated for the POLY+A group). On alternate days, the rats were given a novel sCS− (e.g, strawberry-flavored saccharin solution) for 10 min. The POLY+A rats, unlike the POLY rats, had previously learned that the flavor of the Polycose solution was not associated with rapid caloric repletion. Therefore, when now given a novel sCS+ followed by the Polycose solution without acarbose, the POLY+A rats should more readily attribute the postingestive effects of the Polycose to the novel sCS+ flavor as compared to the POLY rats. This is exactly what happened. The two-bottle preference tests revealed that both groups learned to prefer the sCS+ flavor over the sCS− flavor, but the conditioned flavor preference developed faster and was more robust in the POLY+A group than in the POLY group (Table 1, paradigm C).

In a second experiment, we determined whether rats would learn a flavor preference over delays longer than 10 min (Elizalde & Sclafani, 1988). To facilitate conditioning, the rats were first given experience with a Polycose + acarbose solution. They were then divided into three groups and trained to associate an sCS+ flavor with a 10-, 30-, or 60-min delayed presentation of a 16% Polycose solution (without acarbose). As indicated in Table 1, paradigm D, all three groups developed preferences for the sCS+ flavor over the sCS− flavor. Contrary to our expectation, there was no reliable effect of the delay interval; that is, the maximum sCS+ preferences (77–79%) obtained with the 10-min, 30-min, and 60-min delays were comparable. Whether delays longer than 60 min would interfere with conditioning remains to be determined.

There findings, in confirmation of previous results (Boakes et al., 1987; Capaldi et al., 1987; Holman, 1975) demonstrated that flavor preference conditioning can be obtained with the delayed presentation of a nutrient, and that conditioning is enhanced when the animals have previously learned that the flavor of the nutrient is not associated with postingestive reinforcement. Note, however, that the maximum preferences obtained with the delayed conditioning procedure (77–83%) were less than those obtained with the simultaneous procedure (90–97%) (Table 1). The increased effectiveness of the simultaneous conditioning procedure may occur because with this method the animal associates the CS+ with the palatable flavor of the nutrient as well as with the nutrient's postingestive effects (Holman, 1975).

Real and Sham Feeding

In the above studies we manipulated the postingestive effects of Polycose using the drug acarbose. Another way of doing this involves the sham-feeding preparation. With this preparation, rats are fitted with a gastric cannula which, when opened, causes ingested food to drain out the stomach (sham feeding); with the cannula closed, ingested food is normally digested and absorbed (real feeding). If the postingestive effects of normally digested and absorbed foods are rewarding, then rats should learn to prefer the flavor of real-fed food to the flavor of sham-fed food. Van Vort and Smith (1983) tested this prediction using flavored milk diets. They observed that when the amount of milk real and sham fed was equated, the animals did not acquire a preference for the real-fed milk. This finding is surprising since conditioned flavor preferences have been obtained with milk diets using other testing procedures (e.g., Puerto et al., 1976).

To determine if the results obtained by Von Vort and Smith (1983) were due to the real-and sham-feeding procedure or to the particular diet they used, we attempted to condition flavor preferences by having rats real and sham feed flavored Polycose solutions (Nissenbaum, Sclafani, Vigorito, & Cassouto, 1988). The food-deprived rats were trained to real feed a CS+ flavored Polycose solution on some days and sham feed the same amount of a CS− flavored Polycose solution on other days (Figure 1, C). In subsequent two-choice tests, the rats' preference for the CS+ and CS− flavored Polycose was determined. Rats trained with an 8% Polycose solution displayed a preference for the real-fed solution in the first preference test, and this preference increased to 89% by the third test (Table 1, paradigm E). However, rats trained with a 32% Polycose solution initially tended to avoid the real-fed Polycose solution, and only after five test cycles did they display a reliable preference (70%) for the real-fed solution (Table 1, paradigm E). Why the 32% solution was less effective than the 8% solution in producing a CFP is not known, particularly since these concentrations produced comparable preferences in the oral-simultaneous experiment described above. It would appear that the consumption of relatively large meals of concentrated starch has aversive as well as positive effects and the aversive effects are expressed more under some training procedures than others. In view of these findings, the failure of Van Vort and Smith to obtain a preference for the real-fed food may be related to the concentration of the milk diet used in their study.

Gastric Methods

Short-Term Conditioning

Another approach to the study of food preference conditioning is to provide the nutrient via a route that bypasses the oral cavity. In this way the flavor of the nutrient can be eliminated as a factor in the conditioning process. Several studies have paired cue flavors with intragastric, intraduodenal, intraperitoneal, or intravenous infusions of glucose but the results have been inconsistent. That is, while some have obtained significant preferences (≈ 65–75%) (Mather et al., 1978; Sherman et al., 1983; Tordoff & Friedman, 1986), others have reported either no preferences or even aversions for flavors paired with glucose infusions (Deutsch et al., 1976; Koopmans & Maggio, 1978; Puerto et al., 1976; Revusky et al., 1971). The difficulty in obtaining reliable conditioned flavor preferences in these experiments may be related to the use of hypertonic glucose solutions. Such solutions can have aversive osmotic consequences which would counteract the positive reinforcing effect of the glucose (Booth, 1985).

Polycose has a much lower osmolarity than glucose at isocaloric concentrations; we therefore investigated whether intragastric (IG) infusions of Polycose would reinforce flavor preferences in rats (Nissenbaum & Sclafani, 1987, 1989). In our first experiment, food-deprived rats were trained to drink grape- and cherry-flavored 2% Polycose solutions during 10 min/day sessions. (In these early experiments, 2% Polycose rather than .2% saccharin was used to enhance the palatability of the CS solutions; the CS-flavored Polycose solutions are referred to as pCS.) Following one flavor (pCS+), the rats were infused IG with 14% Polycose, while following the other flavor (pCS−) they were infused with water; infusion volumes were 7 ml (Figure 1, D). In subsequent two-bottle tests, the rats displayed a significant preference (73–77%) for the pCS+ over the pCS− (Table 1, paradigm F). The same procedure was used in a second experiment except that acarbose was added to the IG Polycose infusion. In this case the rats did not acquire a preference for the pCS+ flavor (Table 1, paradigm F). These results demonstrated that IG Polycose can reinforce flavor preferences and that flavor conditioning is blocked if Polycose digestion is inhibited with acarbose.

In the next experiment, we compared the flavor conditioning effects of IG infusions of 8% and 32% Polycose (Nissenbaum & Sclafani, 1989). The procedure used was similar to that described above except that saccharin-sweetened CS solutions were used. Conditioned flavor preferences were obtained with both IG infusions, but the effect developed more rapidly with the 8% Polycose than with the 32% Polycose IG infusions (Table 1, paradigm G). Furthermore, the rats initially displayed a mild avoidance of the sCS+ reinforced with the 32% Polycose infusion.

In a follow-up experiment naive rats were conditioned with 8% and 32% Polycose infusions using a modified procedure (Nissenbaum & Sclafani, 1989). That is, rather than infusing the rats with a fixed IG load (7 ml) at the end of the 10-min training sessions, the rats were infused during the session, and the amount infused was determined by the rat (i.e., approximately 1 ml was infused for each 1 ml of CS consumed orally). With this procedure, both the 8% and 32% Polycose infusions produced rapid conditioning and the flavor preference produced by the 32% concentration was only slightly and nonsignificantly less than that produced by the 8% Polycose (Table 1, paradigm H). Note that when allowed to control the size of their IG load, the rats tested with 8% Polycose received infusions of 6.9–9.2 ml whereas the rats tested with 32% Polycose received infusions of 4.5–5.1 ml. This latter finding suggested that the 7 ml IG load of 32% Polycose used in the previous experiment was too large and probably produced some discomfort; this would explain why the rats displayed an initial aversion to the sCS+.

Long-Term Conditioning

In the experiments reviewed above, the animals were conditioned during short-term training sessions under food-deprived conditions. To determine if flavor preference conditioning is possible in nondeprived rats and to assess the influence of such conditioning on long-term food preference and intake, we developed a chronic, intragastric infusion preparation (Sclafani & Nissenbaum, 1988). With this "electronic esophagus" technique, animals were implanted with two gastric catheters and were automatically infused with a nutrient solution or water as they drank flavored water from drinking spouts; approximately 1.3 ml were infused for each 1 ml orally consumed. The flavored water and lab chow were available ad libitum 23 hr/day; the animals and equipment were serviced during the remaining 1 hr/day. With this system the rats, by their voluntary drinking behavior, determined the size, number, and type (nutrient or water) of IG infusions received each day.

In our first experiment (Sclafani & Nissenbaum, 1988), the rats were given one cue flavor (CS+) paired with IG infusions of 16% Polycose on training days 1 and 3, and another cue flavor (CS−) paired with IG water infusions on training days 2 and 4 (Figure 1, E). On days 5 and 6, the rats were given access to both flavors paired with their respective infusions. In two-bottle tests, the rats displayed an overwhelming preference (96–98%) for the CS+ flavor over the CS− flavor (Table 1, paradigm J). The rats continued to prefer the CS+ (99%) during a 4-day extinction test when both the CS+ and CS− were paired with IG water infusions. The rats also strongly preferred the CS+ to plain water (89%). This latter finding demonstrated that the rats had acquired a true preference for the CS+ rather than an aversion to the CS−.

These results were confirmed and extended in a second study in which rats were conditioned with IG infusions of 32% Polycose (Elizalde & Sclafani, 1990a). When compared to the results obtained with the 16% Polycose infusions, the preference was somewhat slower to develop; the rats, however, eventually displayed a 98% preference for the CS+ over the CS− (Table 1, paradigm K). Furthermore, the rats maintained this preference during a 14-day extinction test during which both CS flavors were paired with IG water infusions. As in the previous experiment, the rats also displayed a robust preference (94%) for the CS+ over water. Note that in the two-bottle tests, naive rats avoided the unsweetened CS flavors in favor of water. Thus the IG Polycose infusions converted a mild flavor aversion to a strong flavor preference.

Although the rats in these experiments acquired a strong preference for the flavor paired with IG Polycose, surprisingly their acceptance of the flavor did not increase. That is, the rats consumed no more of the CS+ solution than plain water in one-bottle tests. This cannot be attributed to an inhibitory effect of the IG Polycose infusions because when saccharin was added to the CS+ solution the rats substantially increased their CS+ intake and therefore their IG Polycose intake (Elizalde & Sclafani, 1990a). It may be that because the CS+ was an unpalatable flavor to begin with, pairing it with IG Polycose increased its palatability enough to produce a strong flavor preference but not enough to increase its acceptance. According to this interpretation, if more palatable CS flavors are used, than the IG Polycose infusions might increase flavor acceptance (i.e., total intake) as well as flavor preference. We are currently investigating this possibility.

FAT CONDITIONING

Compared to the extensive literature on carbohydrate appetite in rats, there are relatively few studies on fat appetite. Early research indicated that there is a learning component to fat appetite (Carlisle & Stellar, 1969; Hamilton, 1964) and recent findings obtained in my laboratory suggested a similar conclusion (Ackroff et al., 1990). In our experiments, rats consumed comparable amounts of nutritive and nonnutritive oil emulsions (corn oil and mineral oil) in one-bottle tests (30 min/day) and when food deprived, the rats increased their intake of the two emulsions to the same degree. In two-bottle tests, the food-deprived rats initially displayed only a mild preference for the corn oil emulsion, but over the course of several test sessions they developed a strong corn oil preference. This latter finding suggested that the rats learned to prefer the corn oil as they associated the flavor of the oil with its postingestive nutritive effects. We explored this possibility using CFP procedures.

Oral Methods

Simultaneous Conditioning

If, as proposed above, the rat's appetite for corn oil is enhanced by the postingestive consequence of the nutrient, then rats should acquire a preference for a cue flavor added to a corn oil emulsion. Furthermore, rats should acquire a much weaker preference, if any, for a cue flavor added to a nonnutritive mineral oil emulsion. We evaluated these predictions by training two groups of food-deprived rats with sCS+ flavored oil emulsion and sCS− flavored water (Elizalde & Sclafani, 1990b). For the CO group, the emulsion contained 7.1% corn oil whereas for the MO group, the emulsion contained 7.1% mineral oil. As indicated in Table 2, paradigm A, both groups developed a preference for the sCS+ flavor, although the preference was greater for the CO group than for the MO group.

The sCS+ preference displayed by the MO group appeared to represent a form of flavor-flavor conditioning since it was unlikely that the mineral oil emulsion had a beneficial postingestive consequence for the food-deprived rats.

Table 2

SUMMARY OF FLAVOR PREFERENCES OBTAINED IN FAT CONDITIONING
EXPERIMENTS

Paradigm	Flavor	Nutrient	Preference	Reference
Oral Methods				
Simultaneous				
A.	sCS	7.1% corn oil	89–94%	Elizalde & Sclafani, 1990b
	sCS	7.1% mineral oil	71–78%	
Delayed				
B. 10 min	sCS	7.1% corn oil	58–80%	Elizalde & Sclafani, 1990b
10 min	sCS	7.1% mineral oil	44–46%	
Gastric Methods				
Short-Term				
C.	sCS	7.1% corn oil	48–61%	Lucas & Sclafani, 1989
Long-Term				
D.	CS	7.1% corn oil	50–59%	Lucas & Sclafani, 1989
	CS	14.5% corn oil	58%	
	CS	29% corn oil	42%	
E.	CS	14.5% corn oil (R)	70–84%	Lucas & Sclafani, 1989
	sCS	14.5% corn oil (R)	95%	
F.	CS	14.5% corn oil (P)	58–61%	Lucas & Sclafani, 1989
G.	sCS	14.5% corn oil	67–76%	Lucas & Sclafani, 1989

Notes: Flavor: CS = unsweetened Kool-Aid; and sCS = saccharin Kool-Aid. Nutrient: (R) = Rats given restricted access to chow and CS solutions, and (P) = preingested corn oil emulsion. Preference scores represent the mean group present CS+ intakes obtained in the two-bottle choice tests. The range of preference scores represents the lowest to highest mean percent CS+ intakes obtained in experiments that included multiple two-bottle choice tests.

If this interpretation is correct, then presumably flavor-flavor conditioning contributed to the preference displayed by the CO group. The fact that the corn oil emulsion conditioned a stronger preference than the mineral oil emulsion may be due to the combined effects of flavor-flavor and flavor-nutrient conditioning.

Mehiel and Bolles (1988) have also obtained a conditioned preference for a cue flavor added to a corn oil emulsion. However, they concluded that flavor-flavor conditioning played little or no role in this effect because CFPs were obtained with a variety of nutrients that differed in palatability (i.e., isocaloric solutions of sucrose, Polycose, ethanol, and corn oil). Nevertheless, their data suggested that the magnitude of the CFP effect was related to nutrient palatability.

Delayed Conditioning

The effectiveness of corn oil and mineral oil emulsions in producing CFPs was further investigated using a delayed conditioning procedure (Elizalde & Sclafani, 1990b). This was of interest because data reported by Holman (1975) indicated that flavor-nutrient conditioning is possible over a delay whereas flavor-flavor conditioning is not. Using the paradigm outlined in Figure 1, B, two new groups of rats were trained to associate an sCS+ with the 10-min delayed presentation of a 7.1% corn oil or mineral oil emulsion. As summarized in Table 2, paradigm B, the CO group acquired a signifcant sCS+ preference whereas the MO group failed to develop an sCS+ preference. Note that the maximum sCS+ preference displayed by the CO group was less than that obtained in the simultaneous conditioning experiment cited above (80% vs. 94%); this is consistent with the results obtained with Polycose.

Thus corn oil can produce flavor preferences using both simultaneous and delay conditioning paradigms, whereas mineral oil is effective only with the simultaneous conditioning procedure. The CFPs produced by mineral oil appear to be reinforced by the flavor of the oil, whereas the CFPs produced by corn oil appear to be reinforced by both the orosensory and nutritive properties of the oil.

Gastric Methods

Short-Term Conditioning

The role of nutritive conditioning in fat appetite is questioned by reports that IG infusions of fat do not produce flavor preferences in rats (Deutsch et al., 1976; Gonzalez & Deutsch, 1985; Maggio & Koopmans, 1982; Ramirez, 1984). In fact, in some cases significant aversions were produced by IG fat infusions (Deutsch et al., 1976; Ramirez, 1984). However, it may be that, as with carbohydrates, under certain conditions infusions of fat directly into the stomach can have aversive consequences that counteract the nutrient's postingestive rewarding effects. We therefore attempted to condition flavor preferences with IG fat infusions using the procedures found effective in our Polycose conditioning experiments (Lucas & Sclafani, 1989).

The rats in the short-term conditioning experiment were food deprived and were trained to associate a CS+ with an IG infusion of corn oil emulsion (7.1%), and a CS− with an IG water infusion (Figure 1, D). The IG loads (7 ml) were delivered at the end of the 10-min drinking sessions. In two-bottle choice tests, the rats displayed a significant preference for the sCS+ flavor, although the magnitude of the effect was not very strong ($\approx 60\%$; see Table 2, paradigm C). Perhaps with other infusion parameters (e.g., slower infusion rate, variable rather than fixed load, different fat concentrations) stronger flavor preferences would be obtained. Nevertheless, the positive results are noteworthy in view of the lack of preferences obtained in previous studies.

Long-Term Conditioning
In our carbohydrate conditioning studies, the most robust preferences were obtained using the long-term IG conditioning procedure. We therefore employed this paradigm and the electronic esophagus technique to further evaluate the postingestive rewarding effect of corn oil emulsions (Lucas & Sclafani, 1989).

The rats in the first experiment were given ad libitum access to food (chow) and were trained with a CS+ paired with IG infusions of a corn oil emulsion and a CS− paired with IG water infusions; the emulsions contained 7.1%, 14.5%, or 29% corn oil (Figure 1, E). In the two-bottle choice tests, the rats tended to prefer the CS+ when it was paired with the 7.1% and 14.5% emulsions, and to avoid the CS+ when it was paired with the 29% emulsion, but these effects were not significant (Table 2, paradigm D). In an attempt to enhance flavor conditioning, the rats were retained with new CS flavors (orange and strawberry) and a 14.5% emulsion, but were now given restricted access to chow (2 hr/day) and the CS solutions (20 hr/day). With this procedure the rats developed a significant preference for the CS+ (70–84%; Table 1, paradigm E). The preference was substantially increased when the rats were given additional training with saccharin-sweetened CS solutions; they now displayed a 95% preference for the sCS+ over the sCS−. The rats continued to display a strong sCS+ preference (92%) when subsequently tested under ad libitum feeding conditions.

Two additional experiments were conducted to determine if IG corn oil could produce a CFP in nondeprived rats (Lucas & Sclafani, 1989). Naive rats were trained as above with unsweetened CS solutions and a 14.5% corn oil emulsion except that the emulsion was "preingested." That is, donor rats were sham fed corn oil emulsion and the fluid collected from their stomachs was infused IG into the experimental animals. Preingested oil was used because previous findings suggested that mixing dietary fat with salivary and gastric secretions facilitated fat digestion and the conditioning of flavor preferences (Puerto et al., 1976). However, the preingested oil emulsion proved to be no more effective than regular corn oil; that is, only a weak and nonsignificant flavor preference was obtained (Table 2, paradigm F). The same nondeprived rats were then retrained with IG infusions of a plain 14.5% corn oil emulsion paired with new CS flavors (orange and strawberry) which, in this case, were sweetened with saccharin. Under these test conditions, the animals acquired a significant preference for the sCS+ over the sCS− (67–76%; Table 2, paradigm G). Furthermore, they continued to prefer the sCS+ during a 4-day extinction test when both the sCS+ and sCS− were paired with IG water infusions.

Thus under the same conditions in which IG Polycose infusions produced strong CFPs (ad libitum food, unsweetened cue solutions), isocaloric corn oil infusions were ineffective. However, significant flavor preferences were conditioned by the fat infusions when the animals were food deprived, and/or trained with sweetened CS solutions. Food deprivation may have facilitated conditioning because it increased the animal's caloric need and the saliency of postingestive feedback provided by the IG fat infusions. Note that when food was freely available, the animals probably consumed chow and the CS+ solution in the same meals and the calories provided by the chow may have obscured the nutritional benefit associated with the CS+ solution. Adding saccharin to the CS solutions may have enhanced flavor conditioning because it increased the rats' intake of the CS+ solutions and therefore the amount of fat infused IG. It is also possible that saccharin facilitated conditioning by increasing the salience of the CS flavors and/or triggering cephalic digestive reflexes (see Lucas & Sclafani, 1989).

DISCUSSION

The experiments summarized above document the ability of rats to acquire flavor preferences based on the postingestive, nutritive properties of carbohydrates and fats. Other findings not reviewed here demonstrated that rats can also develop preferences for flavors associated with proteins (Baker, Booth, Duggan, & Gibson, 1987; Gibson & Booth, 1986). These nutrient-based preferences were obtained in a variety of experimental paradigms and with both food-deprived and nondeprived animals. Furthermore, while the magnitude of the preferences varied depending upon the training paradigm used, remarkably strong flavor preferences (≥95%) were obtained in some experiments (long-term IG conditioning) and once established these preferences were very resistant to extinction.

In contrast to the positive results reported here and in other recent studies are experiments that failed to obtain conditioned flavor preferences (Boakes et al., 1987; Deutsch, et al., 1976; Koopmans & Maggio, 1978; Puerto et al., 1976; Revusky et al., 1971; Simbayi et al., 1986). At least some of these negative findings can be attributed to the specific training procedures used. For example, as discussed above, with the delayed conditioning procedure, the flavor of the nutrient may interfere with the establishment of a CFP. Also the specific cue flavors used may be an important factor; some flavoring agents may be less effective as CSs than others (see Elizalde & Sclafani, 1988). Experiments that involve intragastric, intraduodenal, or intravenous infusions are the most problematic since nutrients delivered by nonoral routes may not be normally processed by the gastrointestinal system (see Booth, 1985; Deutsch, 1987). Furthermore, the size, concentration, and/or rate of infusion may be excessive and, as a result, the infusions may produce discomfort which would counteract the rewarding effects of the nutrients. In our experiments, the strongest preferences were obtained when the animals controlled the size and frequency of the IG nutrient infusions. For these reasons, the failure to obtain conditioned flavor preferences in some experiments should not detract from the positive results obtained in many other experiments.

To date, much of the research on nutrient-based CFPs has focused on establishing the existence of the phenomenon. This issue is no longer in doubt and research attention can now turn to the physiological and behavioral mechanisms mediating CFPs and the role of CFPs in food selection and energy regulation. In particular, much remains to be learned about the nature and source of the postingestive signals generated by food that reinforce CFPs.

On a conceptual level, the rewarding quality of food has been attributed to the food's caloric value (Mehiel & Bolles, 1988; Sherman et al., 1983) or to its satiating effects (e.g., Booth, 1985; Rozin & Zellner, 1985). However, some data suggest that animals can discriminate between the postingestive effects of different macronutrients (Deutsch, 1987; Gibson & Booth, 1986). For example, IG protein loads but not carbohydrate loads are reported to suppress the rat's preference for a flavor previously paired with IG protein infusions (Baker et al., 1987). Also, the results reviewed above suggest that isocaloric loads of carbohydrate and fat are not equally effective in conditioning flavor preferences. Note that if a primary function of postingestive conditioning in omnivores is to facilitate the selection of a balanced diet, then flavor preferences should be determined by the specific nutritive value of foods rather than their energy or satiating value.

On a mechanistic level, relatively little is known about the specific neural and/or hormonal signals that mediate conditioned flavor preferences. Some studies suggest that nutrient "sensors" in the stomach and liver are involved (Deutsch, 1983; Tordoff & Friedman, 1986); nutrient signals may also originate in the intestinal tract. Other recent experiments have investigated the role of hormones (e.g., insulin, cholecystokinin) in nutrient-based CFPs, but the findings to date have been inconsistent (Mehiel, 1989; Perez & Sclafani, 1989; VanderWeele & Deems, 1989).

In conclusion, the findings reviewed in this chapter clearly demonstrate that rats can learn to prefer foods based on the postingestive, nutritional consequences of the foods. Food preference conditioning along with aversion conditioning is most likely an important determinant of the "nutritional wisdom" of animals.

References

Ackroff, K., Vigorito, M., & Sclafani, A. (1990). Fat appetite in rats: The response of infant and adult rats to nutritive and non-nutritive oil emulsions. *Appetite*. In press.

Baker, B. J., Booth, D. A., Duggan, J. P., & Gibson, E. L. (1987). Protein appetite demonstrated: Learned specificity of protein-cue preference to protein need in adult rats. *Nutrition Research, 7*, 481–487.

Barker, L. M., Best, M. R., & Domjan, M. (Eds). (1977). *Learning mechanisms in food selection.* Waco, TX: Baylor University Press.

Boakes, R. A., & Lubart, T. (1988). Enhanced preference for a flavour following reversed flavour glucose pairing. *Quarterly Journal of Experimental Psychology, 40*, 49–62.

Boakes, R. A., Rossi-Arnaud, C., & Garcia-Hoz, V. (1987). Early experience and reinforcer quality in delayed flavour-food learning in the rat. *Appetite, 9*, 191–206.

Bolles, R. C., Hayward, L., & Crandall, C. (1981). Conditioned taste preferences based on caloric density. *Journal of Experimental Psychology: Animal Behavior Processes, 7*, 59–69.

Booth, D. A. (1985). Food-conditioned eating preferences and aversions with interoceptive elements: Conditioned appetites and satieties. *Annals of the New York Academy of Sciences, 443*, 22–41.

Booth, D. A., Lovett, D., & McSherry, G. M. (1972). Postingestive modulation of the sweetness preference gradient in the rat. *Journal of Comparative and Physiological Psychology, 78*, 485–512.

Braveman, N. S., & Bronstein, P. (Eds.). (1985). Experimental assessments and clinical applications of conditioned food aversions. *Annals of the New York Academy of Sciences, 443*, 1–441.

Capaldi, E. D., Campbell, D. H., Sheffer, J. D., & Bradford, J. P. (1987). Conditioned flavor preferences based on delayed caloric consequences. *Journal of Experimental Psychology: Animal Behavior Processes, 13*, 150–155.

Carlisle, H. J., & Stellar, E. (1969). Caloric regulation and food preference in normal, hyperphagic, and aphagic rats. *Journal of Comparative and Physiological Psychology, 69*, 107–114.

Deutsch, J. A. (1983). Dietary control and the stomach. *Progress in Neurobiology, 20*, 313–332.

Deutsch, J. A., Molina, F., & Puerto, A. (1976). Conditioned taste aversion caused by palatable nontoxic nutrients. *Behavioral Biology, 16*, 161–174.

Elizalde, G., & Sclafani, A. (1988). Starch-based conditioned flavor preferences in rats: Influence of taste, calories, and CS-US delay. *Appetite, 11*, 179–200.

Elizalde, G., & Sclafani, A. (1990a). Flavor preferences conditioned by intragastric Polycose: A detailed analysis using an electronic espohagus preparation. *Physiology & Behavior, 47*, 63–77.

Elizalde, G., & Sclafani, A. (1990b). Fat appetite in rats: Flavor preferences conditioned by nutritive and non-nutritive oil emulsions. *Appetite.* In press.

Fedorchak, P. M., & Bolles, R. C. (1987). Hunger enhances the expression of calorie-but not taste-mediated conditioned flavor preferences. *Journal of Experimental Psychology: Animal Behavior Processes, 13*, 73–79.

Gibson, E. L., & Booth, D. A. (1986). Acquired protein appetite in rats: Dependence on a protein-specific state. *Experientia, 42*, 1003–1004.

Gonzalez, M. F., & Deutsch, J. A. (1985). Intragastric injections of partially digested triglyceride suppress feeding in the rat. *Physiology & Behavior, 35*, 861–865.

Hamilton, C. L. (1964). Rat's preference for high fat diets. *Journal of Comparative and Physiological Psychology, 58*, 459–460.

Holman, E. W. (1975). Immediate and delayed reinforcers for flavor preferences in the rat. *Learning and Motivation, 6*, 91–100.

Holman, G. L. (1968). Intragastric reinforcement effect. *Journal of Comparative and Physiological Psychology, 69*, 432–441.

Koopmans, H. S., & Maggio, C. A. (1978). The effects of specified chemical meals on food intake. *American Journal of Clinical Nutrition, 31*, S267–S272.

Le Magnen, J. (1969). Peripheral and systemic actions of food in the caloric regulation of intake. *Annals of the New York Academy of Sciences, 157*, 1126–1157.

Lucas, F., & Sclafani, A. (1989). Flavor preferences conditioned by intragastric fat infusions in rats. *Physiology & Behavior, 46*, 403–412.

Maggio, C. A., & Koopmans, H. S. (1982). Food intake after intragastric meals of short-, medium-, or long-chain triglyceride. *Physiology & Behavior, 28*, 921–926.

Mather, P., Nicolaidis, S., & Booth, D. A. (1978). Compensatory and conditioned feeding responses to scheduled glucose infusions in the rat. *Nature, 273*, 461–463.

Mehiel, R. (1989). Rats learn to like flavors paired with CCK [Abstract]. *Proceedings of the Eastern Psychological Association Meeting, 60*, 39.

Mehiel, R., & Bolles, R. C. (1984). Learned flavor preferences based on caloric outcome. *Animal Learning and Behavior, 12*, 421–427.

Mehiel, R., & Bolles, R. C. (1988). Learned flavor preferences based on calories are independent of initial hedonic value. *Animal Learning and Behavior, 16*, 383–387.

Nissenbaum, J. W., & Sclafani, A. (1987). Conditioned flavor preferences produced by intragastric Polycose infusions in rats. *Proceedings of the Eastern Psychological Association Meeting, 58*, 62.

Nissenbaum, J. W., & Sclafani, A. (1989). *Flavor preferences conditioned by intragastric Polycose: Effects of Polycose concentration and infusion rate.* Manuscript submitted for publication.

Nissenbaum, J. W., Sclafani, A., Vigorito, M., & Cassouto, K. (1988). Conditioned flavor preferences in sham-feeding rats. *Proceedings of the Eastern Psychological Association Meeting, 59*, 18.

Perez, C., & Sclafani, A. (1989). Is satiety rewarding? The case of CCK. *Proceedings of the Eastern Psychological Association Meeting, 60*, 39.

Puerto, A., Deutsch, J. A., Molina, F., & Roll, P. (1976). Rapid rewarding effects of intragastric injections. *Behavioral Biology, 18*, 123–134.

Ramirez, I. (1984). Behavioral and physiological consequences of intragastric oil feeding in rats. *Physiology & Behavior, 33*, 421–426.

Revusky, S. H., Smith, M. H., Jr., & Chalmers, D. V. (1971). Flavor preference: Effects of ingestion-contingent intravenous saline or glucose. *Physiology & Behavior, 6*, 341–343.

Rozin, P., & Zellner, D. (1985). The role of Pavlovian conditioning in the acquisition of food likes and dislikes. *Annals of the New York Academy of Sciences, 443*, 189–202.

Sclafani, A. (1987). Carbohydrate taste, appetite, and obesity: An overview. *Neuroscience and Biobehavioral Reviews, 11*, 131–153.

Sclafani, A. (1989). Dietary-induced overeating. *Annals of the New York Academy of Sciences, 575*, 281–289.

Sclafani, A., & Nissenbaum, J. W. (1988). Robust conditioned flavor preference produced by intragastric starch infusions in rats. *American Journal of Physiology, 255*, R672–R675.

Sherman, J. E., Hickis, C. F., Rice, A. G., Rusiniak, K. W., & Garcia, J. (1983). Preferences and aversions for stimuli paired with ethanol in hungry rats. *Animal Learning and Behavior, 11*, 101–106.

Simbayi, L. C., Boakes, R. A., & Burton, M. J. (1986). Can rats learn to associate a flavour with the delayed delivery of food? *Appetite, 7*, 41–53.

Tordoff, M. G., & Friedman, M. I. (1986). Hepatic-portal glucose infusions decrease food intake and increase food preference. *American Journal of Physiology, 251*, R192–R196.

VanderWeele, D. A., & Deems, R. O. (1989). Insulin, sham feeding, real feeding, glucostasis and flavor preferences in the rat. *Annals of the New York Academy of Sciences, 575*, 582–584.

Van Vort, W., & Smith, G. P. (1983). The relationship between the positive reinforcing and satiating effects of a meal in the rat. *Physiology & Behavior, 30*, 279–284.

Vigorito, M., & Sclafani, A. (1988). Ontogeny of Polycose and sucrose appetite in neonatal rats. *Developmental Psychobiology, 21*, 457–465.

CHAPTER 11

HUNGER AND CONDITIONED FLAVOR PREFERENCES

ELIZABETH D. CAPALDI

A common assumption in theories of motivation is that the "value" of food increases with increasing hunger. "Depriving a rat of food, or depriving a person of the opportunity to affiliate with other people will increase the value of food or other people . . . the production of a need which has always been regarded as a basic motivation producing operation, can be viewed simply as a means of giving a particular goal an especially high value" (Bolles, 1972, p. 403).

One way of testing this assumption is to measure the preference for food and food related cues under varying levels of hunger. For example, Cabanac (1971) reported that pleasantness ratings of sweet tastes declined after the human subjects consumed sugar solutions. He proposed that the pleasantness of food varied with usefulness to the body. Revusky (1967) reported one of the few animal experiments directly concerned with showing that the higher the hunger the greater the value of food. He showed that rats preferred a flavor they had previously consumed under high food deprivation to a flavor consumed previously under low deprivation, whether they were tested under high or low deprivation.

In both Cabanac's and Revusky's studies, the food consumed under high food deprivation was consumed shortly before a meal or large amount of food was given, while the food consumed under low food deprivation was consumed shortly after a meal. Many other variables thus differed between the high and low food deprivation conditions besides hunger level: the high deprivation food was given prior to the meal and thus could become a cue for the large meal, whereas the low deprivation food was given during digestion of the meal and thus could be associated with these effects. The low deprivation flavor was given soon after the consumption of a particular food, so short-term sensory specific satiety effects could also influence the low deprivation food experience (e.g., Rolls, Rolls, Rowe, & Sweeney, 1981).

We were interested in whether preference for a flavor consumed under high food deprivation would be greater than the preference for a flavor consumed under low food deprivation when the flavors were given separately from the daily feeding. As will be seen later, we found that under these conditions animals prefer a flavor they previously consumed under low deprivation to one that they had previously consumed under high deprivation.

In our studies, a small amount of food delivered the flavors and foods were given separately from the daily feeding. Under these conditions, the rats preferred the distinctive flavor they had when they were less hungry. If, however, a distinctive flavor cued an amount of food, large enough to eliminate or significantly reduce hunger, that flavor was preferred to a flavor they had consumed when less hungry.

GENERAL METHODS

In our experiments on hunger and conditioned food preferences, we fed the rats every other day in the late afternoon or evening. Conditioning experiences with flavors were given in the morning. The flavor paired with low deprivation was given on even numbered days, the morning after the rats received their evening 35 gm of food. The flavor paired with high deprivation was given on odd numbered days. The rats used were 77–90-day-old Sprague-Dawley males. Their normal, daily ad libitum intake was approximately 35 gm of lab chow. Thus neither flavor immediately preceded or followed feeding, however, the low-deprivation flavor was experienced under a lower level of hunger than the high-deprivation flavor. Typically, we employed 20 days of training (although we have used as few as six and obtained the same results). The flavors were dissolved in a sweet solution so the rats would consume them. Flavor cues consisted of 1% cinnamon (2% imitation cinnamon flavoring mixed with 100% ethanol) or 1% wintergreen (2% imitation wintergreen flavoring mixed with 100% ethanol). In our first experiment we dissolved the two flavors in either .15% saccharin or 8% sucrose. The rats consumed all of the cue solutions. The rats were then given a choice between two flavors in solution (a two-bottle test), one flavor had been paired with low deprivation and one flavor had been paired with high deprivation. The deprivation schedule was maintained during testing so that the tests would be given under both high and low deprivation. The results were the same under both deprivation conditions (Capaldi & Myers, 1982; Capaldi, Myers, Campbell, & Sheffer, 1983).

This research was supported in part by Grant MH 39453 from the National Institute of Mental Health. The final experiment was part of an unpublished doctoral dessertation by D. E. Myers, "Taste preferences and aversions based upon rats' internal deprivation state," Purdue University, 1982.

EARLY RESULTS

Table 1 shows the results from two experiments of this design. In the first experiment, the flavors were dissolved in 5 ml of solution (saccharin or sucrose) and there were six training days; in the second experiment, the flavors were dissolved in 10 ml of solution (saccharin or sucrose) and there were 20 training days. The preference for the flavor that was paired with each deprivation (e.g., preference for the flavor paired with low deprivation = ml of that flavor consumed/ml consumed of both flavors) is shown. The higher the number, the greater the preference. We always obtained the same results analyzing absolute consumptions but it was more convenient to view one number for each group rather than two. As can be seen, the rats preferred the flavor associated with *low* deprivation, and this preference was greater when the flavors were dissolved in saccharin rather than sucrose.

TWO HYPOTHESES

Because the preference was greater when the flavors were given in saccharin, our first hypothesis was that some aversive effects of consuming a sweet, noncaloric solution when very hungry accounted for our conditioned flavor preferences. That is, the rats were avoiding the flavor experienced under high deprivation because it was associated with the aversive effects of eating a sweet noncaloric solution. Perhaps a cephalic phase insulin release produced by consuming a sweet substance is unpleasant unless followed by calories (e.g., Geiselman & Novin, 1982; Powley, 1977). Or perhaps the sweet solution alters the disposition of metabolic fuels towards storage and away from oxidation. This reduction in oxidation may

Table 1

PREFERENCES FOR FLAVORS PAIRED WITH LOW OR HIGH DEPRIVATION IN EXPERIMENTS 1 AND 2

Vehicle used	Low deprivation[a]	High deprivation[b]
Experiment 1[c]		
5 ml .15% saccharin	.60	.40
5 ml 8% sucrose	.50	.50
Experiment 2[d]		
10 ml .15% saccharin	.59	.41
10 ml 8% sucrose	.54	.46

[a]Preference for flavor paired with low deprivation = ml of that flavor consumed/ml of both flavors consumed.
[b]Preference for flavor paired with high deprivation = ml of that flavor consumed/ml of both flavors consumed.
[c]Preference for flavor paired with low deprivation was significantly greater than preference for flavor paired with high deprivation for saccharin group, $p < .02$.
[d]Preference for flavor paired with high deprivation was significantly greater than preference for flavor paired with low deprivation for saccharin group, $p < .01$.

be aversive unless followed by a large amount of food (e.g., Tordoff & Friedman, 1989a, 1989b, 1989c, 1989d).

Our second hypothesis was that some aspect of feeding is more pleasant under low deprivation than under high deprivation. Perhaps food tastes better under low deprivation. Rats under high deprivation may eat too rapidly to properly experience or appreciate taste.

Experiments Relevant to the Hypotheses

The first manipulations we tried were to increase the number of calories or the caloric density of the solutions used to deliver the flavors (Capaldi, Myers, Campbell, & Sheffer, 1983; Experiments 3 and 4). If receiving a noncaloric or low-calorie solution under high deprivation is aversive, increasing calories may reverse the preference. We tried two different manipulations using sweet solutions: we increased the ml of sucrose given with the flavors from 5 ml to 40 ml to increase the number of calories accompanying the taste and we added 1% or 20% Polycose® (a minimally sweet glucose polymer) to saccharin to deliver the flavors. Increasing the amount of solution increased the number of calories, increasing the concentration of the Polycose increased the density of calories, which may be more important than the number (e.g., Bolles, Hayward, & Crandall, 1981). Table 2 shows that in neither case did we produce a preference for the flavor associated with high deprivation.

Table 2

PREFERENCES FOR FLAVORS PAIRED WITH LOW OR HIGH DEPRIVATION IN EXPERIMENTS 3 AND 4

Vehicle used	Low deprivation[a]	High deprivation[b]
Experiment 3[c]		
40 ml .15% saccharin	.78	.22
40 ml 8% sucrose	.54	.46
Experiment 4[d]		
5 ml .15% saccharin		
+ 1% Polycose	.60	.40
5 ml .15% Saccharin		
+ 20% Polycose	.56	.44

[a]Preference for flavor paired with low deprivation = ml of that flavor consumed ÷ ml of both flavors consumed.
[b]Preference for flavor paired with high deprivation = ml of that flavor consumed ÷ ml of both flavors consumed.
[c]Preference for flavor paired with low deprivation was significantly greater than preference for flavor paired with high deprivation, $p < .001$, difference larger with saccharin, $p < .001$.
[d]Preference for flavor paired with low deprivation was significantly greater than preference for flavor paired with high deprivation, $p < .01$, no interaction with concentration of Polycose.

The mean amount consumed of the 40 ml offered to rats given sucrose was 39.96 ml on high deprivation days and 39.69 ml on low deprivation days; for rats given saccharin it was 39.73 ml on high deprivation days and 35.5 ml on low deprivation days. The lower consumption of saccharin on low deprivation days produced significant differences associated with deprivation, saccharin versus sucrose and the interaction of deprivation with saccharin versus sucrose (Fs(1,20) = 16.5, 17.5 and 12.7 respectively; $ps < .01$).

In all cases the preference was for the flavor associated with low deprivation although the preference was reduced when sucrose was used to deliver the flavors rather than saccharin and when a higher concentration of Polycose was added to the saccharin. These findings are not consistent with the hypothesis that the preference for a flavor experienced under low deprivation is due to an unpleasant reaction produced by noncaloric, sweet substances because increasing the calories from 1.54 (in 5 ml of 8% sucrose) to 3.8 (in 5 ml of 20% Polycose) or to 12.32 (in 40 ml of 8% sucrose) did not reduce the preference for the low deprivation flavor (or aversion to the high deprivation flavor).

To determine if we could obtain the same findings with nonsweet caloric foods, our next experiment (Experiment 5) used greasy-flavored wet mashes to deliver the flavors paired with deprivations. Feedings of 35 gm were given every other night at 8:00 p.m. The afternoon after a feeding the animals were considered to be under low deprivation and the afternoon after no feeding they were considered to be under high deprivation.

The high calorie diet consisted of 70% ground lab blox and 30% solid Crisco® shortening, the low-calorie diet used unscented Vaseline® petroleum jelly instead of Crisco. Flavor mashes were 28.57% cinnamon (2% cinnamon oil in 100% ethanol dissolved as a 50% solution in deionized water) or 28.57% wintergreen (2% wintergreen oil in 100% ethanol dissolved as a 50% solution in deionized water).

To equate caloric consumption across groups, Group Lo received the low-calorie diet in the afternoon and the high-calorie diet in the evening, Group Hi received the opposite. Both groups received flavored chow in the afternoon and unflavored chow in the evening. Ten days after the deprivation schedule began there were 20 days of training during which rats received 5 gm of the appropriate flavored chow at 12:30 p.m. and 5 gm of the appropriate unflavored chow at 6 p.m. During training, the 8:00 p.m. feeding was reduced to 25 gm. No food remained in any of the cages by the following morning. Four days of testing consisted of a 15 min two dish choice between 40 gm each of the two flavored chows. Test chow was a 70% ground lab blox, 15% Crisco, 15% Vaseline mixture. Left and right positions were reversed in the middle of each test.

Table 3 shows the results of this experiment. The preference for the flavor associated with low deprivation was significantly greater than the preference for the flavor associated with high deprivation (F(1,36) = 8.57, $p < .01$) and this did not vary with type of chow.

This result is very important. It shows our basic finding of greater condi-

Table 3

PREFERENCES FOR FLAVORS PAIRED WITH LOW OR HIGH
DEPRIVATION IN EXPERIMENT 5

Vehicle used	Low deprivation[a]	High deprivation[b]
High fat chow	.56	.44
Low fat chow	.59	.41

[a]Preference for flavor paired with low deprivation = ml of that flavor consumed ÷ ml of both flavors consumed.
[b]Preference for flavor paired with high deprivation = ml of that flavor consumed ÷ ml of both flavors consumed.

tioned preferences for flavors experienced under low rather than high deprivation is not limited to sweet substances or to low calorie substances. Neither chow was sweet and both were highly caloric (27.46 calories in 5 gm of high fat chow, 13.7 in 5 gm of low fat chow).

These findings show that a greater preference for a flavor given under low deprivation than under high deprivation is not limited to flavors given in noncaloric sweet substances. Even when flavors are given along with a fairly large number of calories, rats prefer a flavor received under low deprivation to that received under high deprivation. It is still possible though, that the hypothesis that a small amount of food or food cues in the absence of food are unpleasant under high hunger conditions is correct. Perhaps with the strong degree of hunger we are using only a large meal is rewarding—5 gm of mash may not be enough. We will return to this idea in the general discussion section of this chapter.

Our second hypothesis was that some aspect of eating may be more pleasant under low deprivation than under high deprivation. It seems unlikely, although not impossible, that caloric repletion is more rewarding under low deprivation than under high deprivation. If this were the factor that accounted for our results, the preference for the low deprivation flavor would be greater when calories accompanied the flavors, that is, with sucrose or Polycose, not with saccharin. But our effect is bigger with saccharin than with sucrose, or with Polycose combined with saccharin. This suggests that the sensory aspects of feeding may be responsible for our results, that the sensory effects of ingesting at least saccharin may be more rewarding under low deprivation than under high deprivation. Scott (this volume) had shown that afferent activity evoked by sweet tastes is affected by internal state. Our data suggest that the reduced intensity of saccharin's sweet taste with lower hunger may be more pleasant than the taste of saccharin under high hunger.

If taste quality or intensity varies with deprivation and rats prefer the low deprivation taste, apparently the taste differences produced by deprivation are greater with saccharin than with sucrose. Perhaps this is because sucrose is more palatable than saccharin. In our experiments, the rats always drank more sucrose than saccharin, independent of any other variable. The rats may have liked the sucrose so much that they drank a lot of it in test regardless of the previous hunger level associated with the flavor. Also, the palatability of sucrose may be so high that there were no noticeable taste differences as a function of deprivation level during training, so no differential taste preferences were conditioned to the flavors.

If so, reducing the palatability of sucrose by using a lower concentration may recruit a preference for the flavor given under low deprivation. Capaldi et al., (1983) showed that this is indeed the case: A clear preference for the low deprivation flavor emerged if the flavors were delivered in 1% sucrose rather than 8% sucrose.

In our next experiment (Experiment 6) we asked whether training *and* testing with 8% sucrose prevented a conditioned flavor preference due to deprivation level. Rats were trained with flavors delivered in either .15% saccharin, 8% sucrose, or water. Test solutions were .15% saccharin, 8% sucrose or water. Table 4 shows the results of the experiment. The rats preferred the flavor associated with low deprivation if training and testing used saccharin solutions (as was reported in prior experiments). However, if training or testing or both were given with sucrose this preference was eliminated. Apparently the reinforcing effect of sucrose solutions does not vary with deprivation so no differential preferences were conditioned when sucrose was used in training. There was also no preference when saccharin was used in training and sucrose was used in testing. This suggests that the high palatability of sucrose masks the conditioned preference formed with saccharin training. When a highly preferred food was used, such as 8% sucrose, the food was so enjoyable that there was no difference in preference

Table 4

PREFERENCES FOR FLAVORS PAIRED WITH LOW OR HIGH
DEPRIVATION IN EXPERIMENT 6

Vehicle used		Low deprivation[a]	High deprivation[b]
Training Group	*Test Group*		
saccharin	saccharin	.55	.40
	sucrose	.50	.49
	water	.54	.45
sucrose	saccharin	.53	.47
	sucrose	.46	.54
	water	.45	.54

[a]Preference for flavor paired with low deprivation = ml of that flavor consumed ÷ ml of both flavors consumed.
[b]Preference for flavor paired with high deprivation = ml of that flavor consumed ÷ ml of both flavors consumed.

produced by deprivation. Likewise, it would be expected that differences in deprivation may not affect the enjoyment of very bad food.

Both of our hypotheses assumed that deprivation per se had an effect on flavor preferences. In addition, relationship to feeding may also have had an effect on flavor preferences. A flavor consumed shortly before a large meal when very hungry may come to be preferred because it precedes the large meal. This is the procedure used by Revusky (1967) who found a flavor consumed shortly before a large meal ("high deprivation") was preferred to one consumed shortly after that meal ("low deprivation"). Similarly, Cabanac (1971) showed that the pleasantness ratings of sweet tastes decline after a meal.

Our final experiment (Experiment 7) measured conditioned flavor preferences as a function of deprivation when the flavors were given separately from feeding versus shortly before and after feeding (Myers, 1982). There are many procedural differences between studies giving flavors shortly before and after feeding and our studies giving flavors separate from feeding. Deprivation schedule may be particularly important. We used the same deprivation schedule for all of the rats. The rats were fed 35 gm of chow every other day for 20 days. For 60 rats, the flavors were given separate from feeding: the flavors were given at 9:05 a.m. and 35 gm of food was given at 3:00 p.m. on odd-numbered days. Therefore the low and high deprivation cues for these groups were received at approximately 18 and 42 hours, respectively, after food was given. For groups in which feeding and flavors were paired, the 35 gm food ration was given on odd-numbered days at 9:00 a.m. On these days, the high deprivation flavor was presented at 8:30 a.m. (47.5 hours since food was last delivered) and removed 20 min later (10 min prior to the receipt of 35 gm of food). The low deprivation flavor was given 60 min after food was given and remained in the cage until the next morning. For 10 rats within each of the two feeding groups, the flavors were presented in one of six possible concentrations of sweet solutions: .15% saccharin, .05% saccharin, .015% saccharin, 4% sucrose + .1% saccharin, 4% sucrose + .05% saccharin or 4% sucrose. There were 8 test days on each of which rats were presented with 45 ml of their two training solutions for 20 min. The results of this experiment are shown in Table 5.

As can be seen, three variables were important in determining whether or not there was a preference for the flavor associated with low deprivation. First, this preference was greater if the flavors were given separate from feeding ($F(1,96)$ + 12.88 $p < .001$). Second, this preference was greater if the flavors were given in saccharin rather than sucrose ($F(1,96) = 31.43$ $p < .001$). Finally, the preference for the flavor associated with low deprivation was greater with higher concentrations of saccharin ($F(2,96) = 4.13$ $p < .02$). There were no higher order interactions.

This experiment confirmed the theory from cross experiment comparisons that the relationship to feeding is important in determining the effects of deprivation on conditioned flavor preferences. The preference for the flavor associated

Table 5

PREFERENCES FOR FLAVORS PAIRED WITH LOW OR HIGH
DEPRIVATION IN EXPERIMENT 7

Vehicle used	Low deprivation[a]	High deprivation[b]
With feeding		
4% sucrose	.44	.56
4% sucrose + .05% saccharin	.49	.51
4% sucrose + .1% saccharin	.50	.50
.015% saccharin	.56	.44
.05% saccharin	.54	.46
.15% saccharin	.60	.40
Separate		
from feeding[c]		
4% sucrose	.51	.49
4% sucrose + .05% saccharin	.51	.48
4% sucrose + .1% saccharin	.56	.44
.015% saccharin	.62	.38
.05% saccharin	.58	.36
.15% saccharin	.73	.27

[a]Preference for flavor paired with low deprivation = ml of that flavor consumed ÷ ml of both flavors consumed.
[b]Preference for flavor paired with high deprivation = ml of that flavor consumed ÷ ml of both flavors consumed.
[c]Preference for flavor associated with low deprivation was significantly greater than preference for flavor associated with high deprivation. Difference in preference just missed significance ($F(1,36)=3.32$, $.05 < p < .1$).

with low deprivation was much greater when flavors were given separately from feeding rather than shortly before or after feeding.

Rats also preferred the flavor associated with low deprivation when the flavors came shortly before and after feeding and when saccharin was used to deliver flavors. Only when sucrose was used to deliver flavors, was there a greater preference for the flavor consumed under high deprivation. This procedure is similar to the one used by Revusky (1967) who measured preference for grape juice and milk after they had previously preceded or followed feeding. Thus the greater preference for a flavor consumed under high deprivation seems limited to the use of nutritive flavors that shortly precede and follow feeding.

GENERAL DISCUSSION

Cabanac (1971) coined the term *alliesthesia* to refer to the effects of internal signals on the pleasantness produced by external cues. The pleasantness of food cues was assumed to be increased by hunger because of the increased usefulness of food to the body. Our results suggest that the pleasantness of food cues is not increased by hunger alone. When food cues are given separately from feeding, the pleasantness of food cues seems to be decreased by increased hunger.

One reason this may be is that when food cues are given separately from feeding, no large meal follows these cues. We suggested earlier that food cues or a small amount of food may be unpleasant unless followed by a large amount of food because of various physiological effects of the small amount of food (Powley, 1977; Tordoff & Friedman, 1989a, 1989b, 1989c, 1989d). Even though in our experiments we increased the calories quite a bit (the highest number being 27.46 calories in 5 gm of high fat mash), this amount may be insufficient to satisfy the strong hunger we produced. A cue that shortly preceded the 35 gm feeding may be preferred because the 35 gm feeding is sufficient to appreciably reduce the amount of hunger present after 38 hours without food. In Revusky's (1967) study, a large feeding followed the flavor cue and the flavor cue was given after 23 hours without food. Under these conditions a flavor associated with high deprivation (and the subsequent large feeding) was preferred to a flavor that followed the large feeding. Both the time without food (high deprivation) and the large subsequent feeding may be necessary to produce a preference for a flavor given under high deprivation.

Even when a large feeding followed the flavor given under high deprivation, the rats preferred the flavor given *after* feeding not before, when saccharin was used to deliver the flavors. Tordoff and Friedman (1989a, 1989b, 1989c, 1989d) showed that saccharin increases food intake and that a flavor given in saccharin is unpleasant unless followed by food. Capaldi, Campbell, Sheffer, and Bradford (1987), showed that a flavor given in saccharin after feeding was preferred to a flavor given in saccharin without food. Thus, saccharin was more pleasant when followed or preceded by food than when given without food. Our last experiment showed that pleasantness is greater for saccharin that follows rather than precedes food. Tordoff and Friedman (1989a, 1989b, 1989c, 1989d) suggested saccharin alters the disposition of metabolic fuels towards storage and away from oxidation. Food provides fuel to counteract this reduction in oxidation. Thus a flavored saccharin given prior to food is more pleasant than a flavored saccharin given alone and, presumably, a flavor given in saccharin after eating is more pleasant than one given before eating because there is no period of saccharin without fuel when saccharin follows food, while when saccharin precedes food there is a food free period.

When sucrose is used to deliver flavors, rats tend to prefer the flavor given under low deprivation. Rats prefer flavors given in saccharin and mashes, however, when the flavors are given separately from feeding. However, when flavored sucrose shortly precedes and follows feeding, the rats prefer the flavor that precedes feeding. What is going on here? We think two different factors are involved in this result.

One factor that varies with whether flavors precede or follow the daily feeding is degree of hunger. In our experiments the low-deprivation flavor was given typically about 14 hours after the rat had been given 35 gm. Typically all of the food had been consumed at least 30 min prior to the low-deprivation flavor and often longer. The high-deprivation flavor was given 24 hours later. In studies of alliesthesia in humans, the high hunger test is given only a few hours after feeding and the low hunger test is given immediately after feeding. In Revusky's study, the high-deprivation flavor was given 135 min before feeding (22.5 hours after feeding the day before) and the low-deprivation flavor was given shortly after feeding. Perhaps rats prefer flavors received 14–24 hours after eating (our low-deprivation flavor, Revusky's high-deprivation flavor) to those received 48 hours after eating (our high-deprivation flavor) and those received immediately after feeding (Revusky's low-deprivation flavor). Figure 1 shows this postulated relationship.

Capaldi et al., (1983) investigated preferences between a flavor received 25 hours after being fed 35 gm and one received 110 min after being given 35 gm when the food was still in the cages. When sucrose was used to deliver the flavors, rats preferred the flavor given 25 hours after being fed 35 gm to that given 110 min after the feeding. This is consistent with the relationship shown in Figure 1. When flavors were given in saccharin, Capaldi et al. (1983) found that rats preferred the flavor given 110 min after feeding to that given 25 hours later. This is to be expected because, as explained above, rats prefer to have food when they have saccharin.

If a meal is given (i.e., a large amount of food), the inverted U function shown in Figure 1 may change to a linear increasing function. Eating may be more and more pleasant with increasing hunger if enough food is given to remove the hunger. When a relatively small amount of food is given, eating is more pleasant the lower the hunger. This occurred even when the flavors were given in a fairly substantial meal (5 gm of high fat mash, 27.46 calories). However, our high hunger was also very high. Perhaps this amount of food would be more pleasant at a medium level of hunger versus a very low level. In general, we are suggesting that the effect of hunger on the pleasantness of eating varies with the amount of food and maybe with other characteristics of the food as well. When hunger is very high, food cues without food or small amounts of food seem to be unpleasant. Food cues (smell, taste) increase human reports of hunger (Wooley, Wooley & Dyrenforth, 1979) and so very well might be unpleasant. Perhaps providing food cues or a small amount of food increase hunger and therefore are aversive when initial hunger is very high. Or, as we have also suggested, the taste of food may be more pleasant under low hunger conditions because very hungry animals may eat too fast to experience or appreciate taste.

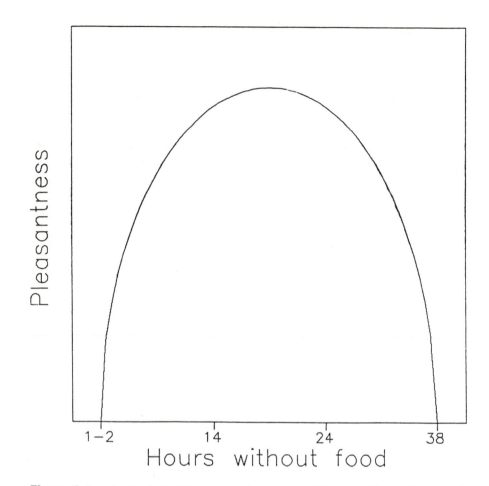

Figure 1 Postulated relationship between pleasantness of flavors and hours without food during training when the flavors are given in small amounts of food or sweet caloric solutions. Relative positions of points and 1 hr versus 24 hr and 14 hr versus 38 hr have been empirically illustrated.

The main point of this chapter is to show that it is overly simplistic to say food cues are more pleasant the higher the hunger. Under some conditions, food cues are less pleasant the higher the hunger.

References

Bolles, R. C. (1972). Reinforcement, expectancy, and learning. *Psychological Review, 79,* 394–409.

Bolles, R. C., Hayward, L., & Crandell, C. (1981). Conditioned taste preferences based on caloric density. *Journal of Experimental Psychology: Animal Behavior Processes, 7,* 59–69.

Cabanac, M. (1971). The physiological role of pleasure. *Science, 173,* 1103–1107.

Capaldi, E. D., Campbell, D. H., Sheffer, J. D., & Bradford, J. M. (1987). Nonreinforcing effects of giving "dessert" in rats. *Appetite, 9,* 99–112.

Capaldi, E. D., & Myers, D. E. (1982). Taste preferences as a function of food deprivation during original taste exposure. *Animal Learning & Behavior, 10,* 211–219.

Capaldi, E. D., Myers, D. E., Campbell, D. H., & Sheffer, J. D. (1983). Conditioned flavor preferences based on hunger level during original flavor exposure. *Animal Learning & Behavior, 11,* 107–115.

Geiselman, P. J., & Novin, D. (1982). The role of carbohydrates in appetite, hunger and obesity. *Appetite, 3,* 203–223.

Myers, D. E. (1982). *Taste preferences and aversions based on rats' internal deprivation state.* Unpublished doctoral dissertation, Purdue University, West Lafayette, IN.

Powley, T. L. (1977). The ventromedial syndrome, satiety, and a cephalic phase hypothesis. *Psychological Review, 84,* 89–126.

Revusky, S. H. (1967). Hunger level during food consumption: Effects on subsequent preference. *Psychonomic Science, 7,* 109–110.

Rolls, B. J., Rolls, E. T., Rowe, E. A., & Sweeney, K. (1981). Sensory specific satiety in man. *Physiology and Behavior, 27,* 137–142.

Tordoff, M. G., & Friedman, M. I. (1989a). Drinking saccharin increases food intake and preference-I. Comparison with other drinks. *Appetite, 12,* 1–10.

Tordoff, M. G., & Friedman, M. I. (1989b). Drinking saccharin increases food intake and preference-II. Hydrational factors. *Appetite, 12,* 11–21.

Tordoff, M. G., & Friedman, M. I. (1989c). Drinking saccharin increases food intake and preference-III. Sensory and associative factors. *Appetite, 12,* 23–36.

Tordoff, M. G., & Friedman, M. I. (1989d). Drinking saccharin increases food intake and preference-IV. Cephalic phase and metabolic factors. *Appetite, 12,* 37–56.

Wooley, S. C., Wooley, O. W., & Dyrenforth, S. R. (1979). Theoretical, practical, and social issues in behavioral treatments of obesity. *Journal of Applied Behavior Analysis, 12,* 3–25.

CHAPTER 12

FOOD AVERSION LEARNING: ITS IMPACT ON APPETITE

ILENE L. BERNSTEIN AND CYNTHIA L. MEACHUM

It is likely that conditioned taste aversions (CTAs) constitute the most well documented learned response where tastes are concerned (Garcia, Hankins, & Rusiniak, 1974; Riley & Tuck, 1985). Yet this volume contains remarkably light coverage on this topic, and that does not appear to be due to any oversight on the part of the editors. Actually, it is due to the minimal interaction between people interested in CTAs and people interested in factors regulating food intake (Bernstein & Borson, 1986). As a consequence, we believe that many studies which purport to be examining the effects of some chronic treatment or surgical intervention on basic mechanisms of food intake regulation may actually be examining the impact of food aversion learning on food intake. In this chapter, we review the evidence that has led us to conclude that the role of food aversion learning in the changes in food intake occurring as a result of experimental treatments has been underestimated. We will also speculate about whether aversion learning mechanisms in humans are sometimes triggered under "inappropriate circumstances" such that they generate or contribute to clinical anorexia syndromes.

TUMOR-INDUCED ANOREXIA

Our interest in food aversion learning and anorexia was originally generated by studies conducted on animals bearing experimental tumors (Bernstein & Sigmundi, 1980). Like their human counterparts, such animals often develop severe anorexia and exhibit significant loss of body weight. The causes of this appetite and weight loss are not well understood. Food aversion learning became implicated in the tumor anorexia syndrome when we found that anorexic tumor-bearing animals displayed a profound distaste for the specific "target" diet they had been

Table 1
FOOD PREFERENCE AND INTAKE IN TUMOR-BEARING RATS

	Tumor	Control
Mean 24 hr food intake (g) Before preference test	9.9[a]	15.7
Preference for target diet (AIN[b] intake/total food intake)	.11[a]	.48
Mean 24 hr food intake (g) During preference test	18.3	17.4

[a]Difference between tumor-bearing and control rats: $p < .05$ From "Tumor Anorexia: A Learned Food Aversion?" by I. L. Bernstein and R. A. Sigmundi, July 18, 1980, *Science, 209,* p. 417. Copyright 1989 by the AAAS. Reprinted by permission.
[b]AIN = American Institute of Nutrition diet

eating while the tumor was growing (See Table 1). Furthermore, the food intake of these animals increased immediately upon the introduction of a new food (Bernstein & Sigmundi, 1980). These findings suggested that one reason why anorexic, tumor-bearing rats displayed a loss of appetite and weight was that they developed strong aversions to the available food. This suggestion implies that if nonaversive foods were available, anorexia symptoms would be alleviated. To test this, we examined whether the provision of a sequence of new foods to tumor-bearing rats would be associated with elevations in food intake (Bernstein, Treneer, Goehler, & Murowchick, 1985).

Frequent changes in the diet available to tumor-bearing rats were found to lead to a significantly greater intake of those foods than when a single, initially highly palatable food was available for the entire 2½ week measurement period. The enhancement of intake under conditions of diet variety was substantially greater in the tumor-bearing animals than in the control animals. These results indicated that when learned food aversions could be prevented, or when aversive foods were replaced by new, nonaversive ones, the impact of aversion conditioning on food intake of tumor-bearing animals was reduced.

CHRONIC LiCl INFUSIONS AND ANOREXIA

The observations made in tumor-bearing animals prompted us to reexamine general aspects of food aversion learning and anorexia. We were struck by certain unusual features of this learning, notably that because the conditioned stimulus (CS) and unconditioned stimulus (UCS) were chronic, there was no apparent temporal contiguity between tasting the food and experiencing illness. This pattern of CS–UCS exposure seemed unlikely to foster strong learning, yet the evidence for specific, associative food aversion conditioning was quite convincing. We were interested in examining this learning more systematically. However,

Preparation of this chapter supported in part by NIH Grant CA26419.

because tumors introduce hard to control variables which complicate an experimental analysis, they were not a good experimental treatment. For example, we do not know when the tumors begin to generate the biochemical signals responsible for diet aversions, and the signal output is unlikely to be constant because the disease is progressive.

Consequently, to address basic questions about food aversion learning more systematically in a chronic illness paradigm, we developed a model system in which a chronic UCS was introduced by infusing lithium chloride (LiCl) over an 8-day period through implantable infusion pumps (Bernstein & Goehler, 1983a). This allowed us to simulate a chronic pattern of illness or discomfort while having control over parameters such as UCS onset and offset.

In order to assess the contribution of learned aversions to anorexia symptoms, we needed to distinguish between depressions in food intake that were the direct result of the LiCl infusion and those that were secondary to the development of learned aversions. This distinction is important because LiCl and most UCSs capable of supporting taste aversion learning can, by themselves, cause perturbations of food intake. To separate associative from nonassociative effects of LiCl infusion, the food intake of animals consuming their familiar maintenance diet was compared to that of animals consuming a novel diet (Bernstein & Goehler, 1983a). (Familiar tastes are relatively resistant to the development of learned food aversions, whereas novel tastes rapidly become the target of such aversions [Revusky & Bedarf, 1967]). Thus even though drug infusions were the same in both groups, the likelihoods of forming strong aversions were quite different because the group with a novel diet had a more salient target. We could therefore distinguish between effects of nonspecific malaise induced by these treatments and associative learning effects.

We found that drug infusions lowered food intake substantially in animals consuming a novel diet, whereas those consuming familiar chow were only minimally affected (See Figure 1). Furthermore, significant aversions to the target diet were evident after the novel diet–drug association but not after chow–drug pairing. These findings provided evidence that learned aversions can be acquired when exposure to the CS is continuous and the UCS is chronic. Though this paradigm differs from the usual design of learned taste aversion experiments, the demonstration of significant aversions to the novel but not the familiar diet indicated important commonalties between the two procedures (Revusky & Bedarf, 1967). Hence, these results support the notion that when experimental treatments produce chronic illness, the association of that illness with the available diet (particularly if it is relatively novel) fits a model of aversion conditioning. Interestingly, in the present study LiCl by itself, due to its slow infusion rate, had minimal effects on food intake, at least in the familiar diet group. Yet the drug infusion was sufficient to produce significant aversions to the novel diet, and those aversions appeared to have led to significant declines in food intake. It appears, from these data, as though learned aversions can dramatically affect food intake when the now-aversive food is the only food available.

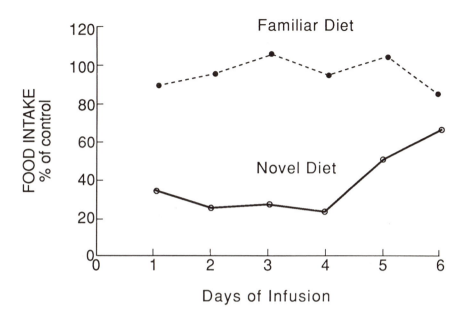

Figure 1 Mean daily food intake during LiCl infusions expressed as a percentage of the intake of control animals on comparable diets. Groups were consuming either a novel diet (C-21) or a familiar diet (Wayne lab chow). From "Chronic Lithium Chloride Infusions: Conditioned Suppression of Food Intake and Preference" by I. L. Bernstein and L. E. Goehler, 1983, *Behavioral Neuroscience, 97,* p. 292. Copyright 1983 by the American Psychological Association. Reprinted by permission.

The impact of aversion learning on food intake was consistent with the known potency of CTAs. These findings raised the question of whether other experimental treatments which produce anorexia also produce learned food aversions. A number of years ago Rozin and Kalat (1971) convincingly proposed learned diet aversions as an explanation for certain nutrient-deficiency anorexias. Until recently, however, there has been little work conducted to extend their findings beyond the nutrient-deficiency paradigm. Table 2 provides a list of experimental conditions which are associated with declines in food intake and body weight, and which are now known to lead to the development of aversions to foods or tastes made available during the experiments. It is likely that this is only a partial list. The extent to which learned diet aversions occur in situations in which chronic treatments, such as surgery or repeated drug injections, depress food intake is unknown at this point. This will remain the case until investigators become sensitive to this issue and routinely test for the development of aversions to the available diet. Certainly there has been an awareness by most investigators in this area of the need to address the issue of nonspecific malaise. This is sometimes dealt with by assessing the specificity of a treatment by measuring water as well as food intake. CTA procedures are also used widely to test for aversiveness of experimental treatments. However, our findings raise the possibil-

Table 2

EXAMPLES OF TREATMENTS KNOWN TO BE ASSOCIATED WITH ANOREXIA
AND LEARNED FOOD AVERSIONS

Vitamin deficiencies	[Rozin & Rodgers, 1967; Rozin, 1967]
Amino acid imbalances and deficiencies	[Simson & Booth, 1974 a & b; Rogers & Leung, 1977; Treneer & Bernstein, 1981]
Tumors	[Bernstein & Sigmundi, 1980; Bernstein & Fenner, 1983]
Subdiaphragmatic vagotomy	[Bernstein & Goehler, 1983b; Sclafani & Kramer, 1985]
Intestinal bypass surgery	[Sclafani, Kramer, & Koopmans, 1985]
Area postrema lesions	[Tomoyasu & Kenney, 1986]
Estrogen infusions	[Bernstein, Treneer, Goehler, & Murowchick, 1985]
Fenfluramine administration	[Carlton & Rowland, 1988; Barnfield & Clifton, 1989]

ity that aversions may be acquired in a chronic design even though no aversions
would have been evident in a more traditional CTA test.

TARGETS OF FOOD AVERSIONS

What is the relevance of these findings to real world clinical problems and to the
design of laboratory studies? Well, that depends rather critically on what foods
can become the targets of learned food aversions (LFAs). If, for example, very
familiar foods (like standard laboratory chow) are resistant to the development of
aversions, then laboratory studies in which chow is used as the standard diet
would not be affected by this conditioning. Initially, it did appear that lab chow
was relatively immune to the conditioning of aversions as, in our diet novelty
studies, we were rarely able to detect chow aversions in experimental groups
(Bernstein et al., 1985). However, there remained the possibility that chow
aversions existed in these animals but went undetected because our preference
tests were not sensitive enough to reveal them. Why would this be? In these tests
we typically provided a novel alternative diet to the animals and if, as has been
claimed, poisoned animals develop enhanced neophobia (Domjan, 1977) we may
have been pitting a chow aversion against neophobia in our preference tests and
the neophobia predominated. In an effort to deal with this issue we ran a study
in which animals received preexposure to the alternative diet for several weeks
before the beginning of a food aversion conditioning study (Bernstein, unpublished observation). The alternative diet was then removed and Wayne lab chow

was made available during LiCl infusions. We found aversions to Wayne lab chow when it was offered to the experimental animals in a choice test with the preexposed alternative (preference for Wayne chow: LiCl infusion group = .22; control group = .44; $p <$ .05, one-tailed). Thus it appears that aversions to familiar chow may be detected after chronic aversion conditioning. They are likely to develop more slowly and to be milder than those acquired to a novel diet, but they do occur.

Even more problematic than familiar diets are new diets, such as nutritionally defined diets, which may be an important part of an experimental protocol. It would appear prudent to preexpose animals to such diets for some time before beginning experimental treatments. However, this procedure, although retarding the development of aversions, may not completely eliminate their acquisition.

The issue of targets for aversions is particularly important clinically because humans have so much choice in what they can eat. It would appear that the development of aversions to a food or a number of foods would simply lead people to choose something else to eat. On the other hand, when symptoms are pervasive, and generalization broad, there may well be clinical situations in which learned food aversions develop to a wide array of foods in a person's diet and contribute significantly to a loss of appetite. Data are not yet available on the extent to which learned food aversions contribute to clinical appetite problems, although the possibility of such a contribution cannot be excluded simply because of differences in humans' feeding opportunities.

MECHANISMS RESPONSIBLE FOR ANOREXIA AFTER AVERSION CONDITIONING

When the available diet has become a target of a learned aversion, animals display significant declines in food intake and body weight. What are the mechanisms responsible for this effect? One way to answer this question is to consider what we know about food aversion learning itself. In the typical CTA paradigm the dependent measure is "solution preference" in a one- or two-bottle test. Experimenters are generally able to conclude from such tests that a shift in palatability has occurred. Diet palatability is known to influence food intake and body weight regulation and a strong dislike for the available diet could lead animals to reduce their intake. However, animals with unpalatable but otherwise nontoxic diets rarely show changes in food intake and body weight which are as dramatic as those observed in our chronic food aversion conditioning studies.

Another possibility which needs to be considered is that through classical conditioning, the conditioned aversive taste comes to elicit behaviors and sensations that are similar to those produced by the unconditioned stimulus. In spite of the vast amount of published work on CTAs, we know relatively little about conditioned responses that may be triggered by CS tastes paired with, for example, LiCl (Gustafson, Garcia, Hankins, & Rusiniak, 1974; Parker, 1982). One obvious problem in examining conditioned responses (CRs) of this type is that animals with strong CTAs manage rather successfully to avoid coming into contact with conditioned aversive tastes and thus they may avoid the triggering of classically conditioned responses. The other problem is that rats, the species of choice for CTA studies, don't retch or vomit—a response which would be a likely CR. In contrast, the coyote, a species that does vomit in response to LiCl and other toxic treatments, has been reported to show a classically conditioned response of retching to a CS (taste) (Gustafson et al., 1974).

Recent studies in our lab have begun to characterize conditioned responses to tastes paired with LiCl (Meachum & Bernstein, in press). In these studies, rats were implanted with intraoral cannulae to allow delivery of taste solutions without a consummatory response on the part of the animal. Five min infusions of saccharin solution were followed by LiCl injections. Initial studies have focused on behavioral responses—those which follow the LiCl treatments (unconditioned responses; URs) and those which become conditioned to the saccharin delivery (CRs).

LiCl delivery was accompanied by a very distinctive postural response which was associated with reductions in activity. That unconditioned response was described by Parker (1982) as "lying on belly" and involved a flattened body with head on the floor or even below the bars of our experimental chambers. This response is easily distinguished from freezing, sleeping, or dozing, which are also reductions in motor activity. Our results indicated clear parallels between the behaviors which followed LiCl treatments and the behaviors which followed the delivery of a LiCl-paired taste solution. For example, in rats receiving high doses of LiCl, lying on belly represented the dominant behavior in the hour after injection and grooming behavior was almost completely suppressed. Similarly, rats exposed to an intraoral infusion of saccharin which had previously been paired with LiCl, spent most of their time lying on belly and virtually no time grooming. The similarity between these unconditioned and conditioned behavior patterns was consistent with the hypothesis that responses are conditioned during taste aversion acquisition and that the CRs are similar to those which are generated by the drugs used for conditioning.

These findings have important implications in terms of the mechanisms responsible for the anorexia evident in the chronic learned food aversion paradigm. Animals with a strong aversion to the only available food have to either be hungry all the time or expose themselves to the aversive CS and experience the aversive CRs which follow such exposure. This conflict and the symptoms conditioned to eating may well contribute significantly to the observed anorexia and weight loss. Our work in identifying specific unconditioned and conditioned responses is in its early stages, and our next step will be the consideration of the types of CRs which characterize chronic aversion paradigms such as LiCl infusions or transplantable tumors. Nonetheless, these initial findings provide new information about taste aversion conditioning and suggest a powerful mechanism whereby such conditioning can have an impact on appetite.

References

Barnfield, A. M. C., & Clifton, P. G. (1989). Flavour aversions conditioned by dl-fenfluramine: A volume independent mechanism. *Psychopharmacology, 98,* 108–112.

Bernstein, I. L., & Borson, S. (1986). Learned food aversions: A component of anorexia syndromes. *Psychological Review, 93,* 462–472.

Bernstein, I. L., & Fenner, D. P. (1983). Learned food aversions: Heterogeneity of animal models of tumor-induced anorexia. *Appetite, 4,* 79–86.

Bernstein, I. L., & Goehler, L. E. (1983a). Chronic lithium chloride infusions: Conditioned suppression of food intake and preference. *Behavioral Neuroscience, 97,* 290–298.

Bernstein, I. L., & Goehler, L. E. (1983b). Vagotomy produces learned food aversions in the rat. *Behavioral Neuroscience, 97,* 585–594.

Bernstein, I. L., & Sigmundi, R. A. (1980). Tumor anorexia: A learned food aversion? *Science, 209,* 416–418.

Bernstein, I. L., Treneer, C. M., Goehler, L. E., & Murowchick, E. (1985). Tumor growth in rats: Conditioned suppression of food intake and preference. *Behavioral Neuroscience, 99,* 818–830.

Carlton, J., & Rowland, N. E. (1988). Effect of dexfenfluramine on taste preferences and aversions in rats. *Appetite, 10,* 221–225.

Domjan, M. (1977). Attenuation and enhancement of neophobia for edible substances. In L. Barker, M. Best, & M. Domjan (Eds.), *Learning mechanisms in food selection* (pp. 151–179). Waco, TX: Baylor University Press.

Garcia, J., Hankins, W. G., & Rusiniak, K. W. (1974). Behavioral regulation of the milieu interne in man and rat. *Science, 185,* 824–831.

Gustafson, C. R., Garcia, J., Hankins, W. G., & Rusiniak, K. W. (1974). Coyote predation control by aversive conditioning. *Science, 184,* 581–583.

Meachum, C. L., & Bernstein, I. L. (in press). Conditioned responses to a taste CS paired with LiCl administration. *Behavioral Neuroscience.*

Parker, L. A. (1982). Nonconsummatory and consummatory behavioral CRs elicited by lithium- and amphetamine-paired flavors. *Learning and Motivation, 13,* 281–303.

Revusky, S. H., & Bedarf, E. W. (1967). Association of illness with prior ingestion of novel foods. *Science, 155,* 219–220.

Riley, A. L., & Tuck, D. L. (1985). Conditioned taste aversions: A behavioral index of toxicity. *Annals of the New York Academy of Sciences, 443,* 272–292.

Rogers, Q. R., & Leung, P. M. B. (1977). The control of food intake: When and how are amino acids involved? In M. R. Kare & O. Maller (Eds.), *The chemical senses and nutrition* (pp. 213–249). New York: Academic Press.

Rozin, P. (1967). Thiamine and specific hungers. In C. F. Code (Ed.), *Handbook of physiology: Alimentary canal* (pp. 411–431). Baltimore, MD: Waverly Press.

Rozin, P., & Kalat, J. W. (1971). Specific hungers and poison avoidance as adaptive specializations of learning. *Psychological Review, 78,* 459–486.

Rozin, P., & Rodgers, W. (1967). Novel diet preferences in vitamin-deficient rats and rats recovered from vitamin deficiency. *Journal of Comparative and Physiological Psychology, 63,* 421–428.

Sclafani, A., & Kramer, T. H. (1985). Aversive effects of vagotomy in the rat: A conditioned taste aversion analysis. *Physiology & Behavior, 34,* 721–725.

Sclafani, A., Kramer, T. H., & Koopmans, H. S. (1985). Aversive consequences of jejunileal bypass in the rat: A conditioned taste aversion analysis. *Physiology & Behavior, 34,* 709–719.

Simson, P. C., & Booth, D. A. (1974a). Dietary aversion established by a deficient load: Specificity to the amino acid omitted from a balanced mixture. *Pharmacology, Biochemistry and Behavior, 2,* 481–485.

Simson, P. C., & Booth, D. A. (1974b). The rejection of a diet which has been associated with a single administration of an histidine-free amino acid mixture. *British Journal of Nutrition, 31,* 285–296.

Tomoyasu, N., & Kenney, N. J. (1986). Development of food aversion after area postrema ablation. *Appetite, 7,* 305.

Treneer, C. M., & Bernstein, I. L. (1981). Learned aversions in rats fed a tryptophan-free diet. *Physiology & Behavior, 27,* 757–760.

CHAPTER 13

LEARNED ROLE OF TASTES IN EATING MOTIVATION

DAVID BOOTH

The ingestive reflex to solutions of sugars or saccharin has provided a model of eating motivation that remains highly influential in and out of psychology. The continuing predominance of this idea that a liking for pure sweetness is a paradigm of appetite is extraordinary because it has long been demonstrated that sweeteners and other flavors usually motivate ingestion by learned mechanisms that are specific to context. Everyday experience supports this theory. For most people, plain sweet water is not a drink or a food. Sweetness is palatable only at specific levels in particular foods and drinks. Moreover, experiments conducted 20 years ago demonstrated that, even in rats, as earlier research had indicated (Le Magnen, 1955), preference for any particular level of sweetness can be learned by caloric conditioning (Booth & Lovett, 1968; Booth, Lovett, & McSherry, 1972).

Psychological research on learning processes over the last two decades has also made much use of saccharin solutions. It is thus somewhat paradoxical that such research has neglected the fact that ingestive motivation is frequently highly positive. It appears that attention to normal palatability was diverted by the ease with which an aversion to saccharin could be conditioned in the rat by poisoning. As a result, experimenters have tried to build theories of eating on concepts such as bait shyness (Garcia, Hankins, & Rusiniak, 1974) and learned disgust, that is the avoidance of a food item that is considered to have been contaminated (Rozin & Fallon, 1987). These views have been dominant despite the fact that by the early 1970s there was abundant evidence that after the omission of only one meal, strong preferences for odors, tastes, and other sensory cues could be conditioned by nutritionally beneficial consequences (Booth, 1985), and with delays between conditioned stimulus (CS and unconditioned stimulus (US) that were long enough to allow some absorption of the nutrients (Simson & Booth, 1973). Such findings cannot be ignored on the grounds that only slight preferences, if any, could be conditioned by incomplete recovery from the extreme malaise that conditions saccharin aversions (Zahorik, 1979).

A striking indication of the strength of preference learning is that it is not just the sweet or salty taste of a food that appeals to the eater. A food's initially aversive bitterness or sourness can be equally essential to its subsequent attractiveness (e.g., chocolate, coffee, oranges, pineapples). Indeed, we often acquire cravings for other innately aversive but nongustatory chemical stimulations such as the astringency of brews of tea, the bite of alcohol, or the stinging sensation from ginger or paprika.

EXPERIENCE-INDEPENDENT REACTIONS TO TASTES

Innate Preferences and Aversions

A liking for sweetness is congenital in human beings, rats, perhaps other omnivorous mammals, and many invertebrates. A weak saltiness, once it can be tasted, and the taste of glutamate (umami) also seem to be liked without experience. Bitterness, sourness, and intense saltiness are innately disliked as soon as the relevant gustatory receptors are fully functioning.

An innate egestive reflex to plant alkaloids that taste bitter presumably functions to protect generalist feeders from poisoning throughout life. The reflexive ingestion of sugars, however, has yet to be scientifically explained. We recently suggested that the sweet reflex arose to meet the requirements peculiar to infant suckling and has nothing to do with mature ingestion (Booth et al., 1987). If this is so, then the congenital preference for sweetness should not be used as a paradigm for eating and drinking. This new theory is expounded in more detail in the following section.

Innate Appetite

When a rat is in sodium deficit, it likes even a strong salty taste. Such a need-dependent taste preference has commonly been called an appetite or hunger for the nutrient whose repletion would naturally be signalled by the taste. This sodium appetite is innate in the rat although it is potentiated by experience.

The notion of a sugar appetite, however, is without foundation. Facilitatory effects of food deprivation on sweetener ingestion have not been distinguished from general drive. An allegedly postingestional suppression of people's perception of sweetness by sugar proved to have a large element of taste preference habituation (Wooley, Wooley, & Dunham, 1972). The postingestional satiating actions of sugars are general to foodstuffs and not specific to reactions to sweetness or carbohydrates, in people (Booth, Campbell, & Chase, 1970; Ducleaux, Feisthauer, & Cabanac, 1973) or in rats (Booth et al., 1972).

It has usually been supposed that the pleasure that sugary foods give before their hypertonicity nauseates us (Booth et al., 1972; Cabanac & Fantino, 1977) had survival value as incentives to eat the calories, carbohydrate or micronutrients available from ripe fruit. This is most implausible. A hungry primate needs no extra encouragement to eat fruit that has softened and changed color. For the sweet preference to be functional in this way there has to be reproductive advantage in a liking for the taste of the higher sugar level when the fruit ripens. If, alternatively, it is proposed that a liking for honey is functional, then ancestors of such species must have survived by raiding bees' nests.

The new proposal is that the "sweetness receptor" and the innate ingestive reflex to its stimulation are only side effects of some function crucial to reproductive success. The liking for sugar benefits plants that exploit animal mobility to spread their seeds. The proposed vital role for the reflex evoked by sweeteners is to counter the unpalatability that mother's milk otherwise would have (Booth, Conner, & Marie, 1987). This aversiveness of milk would arise as follows.

The bitterness receptors connected to the egestive reflex pattern are tuned to a great variety of poisonous, nitrogenous compounds in plants. The inevitable result is that the nitrogen in amino acids also stimulates these receptors. Many amino acids and peptides do indeed have a bitter taste. How then can an infant be prevented from spitting out milk that is rich in proteins, glycoproteins, amino sugars, and free amino acids, thereby endangering its growth, its immunity from infection, and even its survival?

What is required are receptors that are sensitive to the aliphatic hydroxyl and carbonyl groups in the essential amino acids and amino sugars and that suppress amino group detection or elicit ingestive movements that suppress egestion. Indeed, some amino acids are sweet or bittersweet. The unique prevalence of both bitterness and sweetness in this family of nutritionally essential molecules can hardly be without functional significance. I propose that their function is to stop protein being rejected in infancy. This results in aldehydic polyols (sugars) being "superreleasers" via the antibitter receptors. The noteworthy absence of a sweetness preference in carnivorous mammals fits this account rather well, in that the young of obligate carnivores do not need an overwhelming aversion to the taste of plant alkaloids and so have no incidental aversion to protein.

In addition, there is some evidence that the most abundant amino acid, glutamate, stimulates receptors that are different from those sensitive to the other four classical tastants. This too would help to counter any tendency of essential proteinaceous materials to recruit the aversion to dangerous bitterness.

UNLEARNED EXPERIENCE-BASED MODIFICATION

We turn next to experience-dependent ingestive motivation. Our attention cannot be limited to learning or full-blown associative processes.

Stimulus-Specific Satiety

Recent experience of eating can temporarily alter reactions to foods. Such a transient, food-induced suppression of eating motivation is known as *satiety*.

Some postingestional actions of foods already mentioned induce satiety which is not specific to the sensory features of foods. This applies to the more extreme sating effects, including oversatiety and nausea, which are likely to be largely unlearned reactions.

The concept of nutrient-specific satiety presupposes a stimulus-specific satiation mechanism that identifies a source of the nutrient. Such nutritional specificity of satiety should not be confused with differences in the degree or the time course of suppression of eating motivation due to the postingestional action of different nutrients. The notion of innate nutrient-specific satieties (or hungers) is highly problematic. Such a phenomenon could arise only if there were a sensory characteristic that had once been an ecologically valid cue to the nutrient. Furthermore, for an innate satiety to have been functional, an excess of the nutrient must be dangerous. Except for salt, there is no evidence for any stimulus-specific aversion when an excess of a nutrient is signalled by the digestive tract or tissues. The nutrient specificity of nutritionally conditioned stimulus-specific satiation (Booth, 1972b) remains to be tested.

There is, however, clear evidence for another mechanism of stimulus-specific satiation. This is caused by recent exposure to sensorily similar foods (Rolls, this volume). No decline in intensity of sensation is required, and so this satiety has the characteristic of habituation. There is no evidence of dependence on the context or number of the earlier exposures and so the habituation is presumably nonassociative. The decrement in eating motivation depends on fully sensing the food, as during ingestion (although it is not clear whether gastrointestinal stimulation is also necessary). However, this satiation may be specific to some conceptual category of food (i.e., more like boredom than like simple habituation to sensory characteristics). The possibility of taste-specific satiation has yet to be satisfactorily distinguished from habituation to all of the previously ingested food's salient characteristics.

The contributions of habituation, postingestionally triggered nausea, and conditioned satiation to the cloying effect of sweetness have yet to be disconfounded. Why rats switched from ingesting sugar via a sweet concentrated solution to taking it mainly from a dilute solution was examined in detail for evidence of a transient decline of sweetness preference after ingesting sugar (as has been reported in human subjects), but no clear evidence for such "alliesthesia" (sugar-specific satiation) was found (Booth et al., 1972). Rather, the switch arose from the conditioning of aversions and preferences to the tastes of stronger and weaker solutions respectively.

Long-Term Taste Habituation

Both neophobic reactions and innate or acquired ingestive reactions to tastes might, in principle, be subject to long-term habituation (ie, faster decrements in response with successive periods of exposure, and perhaps less spontaneous recovery). Careful analysis of these possibilities for sweetness or other tastes remains to be done. Behavioral (Mook & Wagner, 1989) and neurophysiological (Scott & Giza, 1987) data point to the possibility that sweet taste strength innately drives a batch of ingestive movements as much as movement-to-movement rate. So it is important to look for habituation of lick or bite number or amount ingested and not just the momentary strength of motivation, such as the rated pleasantness of the food.

Repeated exposure to novel foods that taste sweet or salty increases preferences for those foods (Birch, this volume). In such experiments, preschoolers and adults have been tested on several sweet and sometimes nonsweet foods and drinks and so were likely to react to sensory characteristics other than sweetness, although habituation to different specific levels of sweetness was not excluded. The induction of salt preference by exposure to salt-containing foods in 6-month-old infants may involve simple habituation of taste neophobia, but by 12 months these preferences have become contextualised to other features of a food (Harris & Booth, 1987), pointing to more complex stimulus learning as discussed below.

On the other hand, in affluent societies used to highly varied meals, adults find a menu uninteresting if it is repeated too frequently. Major staple foods within the menus, such as potatoes and bread, seem to be an exception to this, however. It has been suggested that blandness in a subsistence diet can prejudice appetite in the long term but studies of such phenomena during famine relief, for example, need to allow for the culturally alien character of some relief foods.

It is clear from our discussion above that experimental psychology has hardly begun to scratch the surface of even the most primitive effects of experience on reactions to taste.

TASTES AND LEARNING

Most of the research on behavioral reactions to tastes and other orosensory stimuli has used amount of the flavored diet consumed as the measure of the behavior. Intake and even ingestion are not in themselves behavior; they are the results of the control of movement patterns by external and internal circumstances. A motivational disposition or behavioral tendency is not a movement pattern or a physical effect such as the passage of material down the throat; it is a relationship between the situation and the intended or involuntary movements that would normally yield ingestion. Eating motivation consists of stimulus-response relationships in all its aspects, be they the momentary integrative orocline (ingestive tendency in response to current stimuli; Booth, 1981), a stable palatability, an uncontextualised preference or aversion, an appetite or a satiety, or a culturally meaningful eating habit.

Thus intake preference measures have a great advantage for present purposes. They monitor rather sensitively the behavioral reactions to taste that may be affected by experience. At the same time, they assess the role of modification of taste reactions in controlling eating and drinking. It is, however, crucial to the causal analysis of eating motivation to measure the relationship between tastant variations and intake variations, not just to present a sweet test diet and observe intake or a pleasantness rating (Booth, 1990).

Sweetness Reward

There has been an unfortunate tendency to refer to palatability as reward. In psychology, a reward quite clearly means a reinforcer of instrumental behavior. This terminology therefore encourages a view of ingestive behavior as an operant. Analysis of autoshaping clearly shows that innate food-oriented movements function as respondents in learning. The reflex nature of ingestive and egestive movements casts further doubt on an operant analysis. Of course, all unconditioned respondents and their conditionability are likely to be "instrumental" in the sense of serving a function, but the issue is whether they are commonly under the control of response reinforcement contingencies in the individual's previous experience. Electrical self-stimulation of the brain is based on such reinforcement of instrumental responses; "reward" has been a more acceptable label for this phenomenon than "pleasure," but in this case behavioral analysis has not been sufficiently directed to the distinction between associative reward and motivational selection among learned responses (Booth, 1987b). Behavioral relationships between brain stimulation reward and food's function as a reward of behavior other than eating have deepened the confusion between elicitative and associative effects of food stimuli.

That is, the motivating effect of sweetness should not be called reward. Nevertheless, sweetness can function as an instrumental reward as well. Saccharin-rewarded lever pressing is the classic counterexample to the drive-reduction theory of reinforcement. Also, sweetness has a so-called rewarding (i.e., stimulus reinforcing, classical conditioning, or unconditioned stimulus associative) effect on the selection and intake of odorised solutions in rats (Holman, 1975) and tea flavors in people (Zellner, Rozin, Aron, & Kulish, 1983).

Calorically Conditioned Sweetness Preference

The first demonstration that experience of caloric repletion conditions a taste preference arose from the analysis of rats' switching from concentrated to dilute glucose (Booth et al., 1972). Part of the explanation was irrelevant to the control of caloric intake, in that a strongly hypertonic solution conditioned aversion, even if it yielded many calories. What emerged that is relevant was that the dilute glucose was consumed in great quantities because of a preference conditioning effect of its calories. Calories were disconfounded from tonicity in the final conclusive experiments by Booth et al. (1972) by the first published use in psychology of a maltodextrin or glucooligosaccharide preparation. Maltodextrins are one type of partly hydrolysed starch, a polysaccharide of purely glucose subunits. All maltodextrins are highly soluble but the variety used was low in glucose and maltose, and hence in tonicity and sweetness. Ingestion of a concentrated solution of maltodextrin yielded rapid absorption of glucose calories without the osmotic effects of glucose in the digestive tract. In two ranges of malto-dextrin concentration, Booth et al. (1972) showed that a higher concentration conditioned a greater preference to whatever sweetness it was associated with, relative to a different level of sweetness paired with a lower maltodextrin concentration.

It must be noted that the high oligosaccharide content gives concentrated maltodextrin solutions a bulky as well as a syrupy texture. Maltodextrin prepara-tions also typically smell of the starch of origin [e.g., maize (U.S.) or potato (U.K.)]. Claims that glucose polymers have a taste other than sweetness must exclude these strong tactile and olfactory stimuli, as well as the taste of maltose and modulatory effects of salts in the carbohydrate preparation.

The preference conditioning was shown not to arise from any taste, texture, or smell of maltodextrin preparations. So long as hypertonic solutions were avoided, glucose, in greater concentrations, conditioned sweetness preferences relative to lower concentrations, as did sugar loaded directly into the stomach (Booth et al., 1972). Furthermore, rapid intravenous infusion of glucose condi-tions preference for the odor in the chow eaten before and during the early part of infusion (Mather, Nicolaidis, & Booth, 1978). Gastric infusion of maltodextrin has subsequently been shown to reinforce strong flavor preferences (Sclafani, this volume).

Subsequent claims to have conditioned preferences calorically by starch are unfounded (Bolles, Hayward, & Crandall, 1981). The concentration ratio of 2:1 used was insufficient to condition a substantial differential preference, let alone the differently based learning of sensory control of meal size (Booth, 1972b) that was initially sought. The observed selection of the odor paired with more concen-trated starch can be attributed to an aversion that had been conditioned to the alternative flavor by the poor texture of the chalk diluent (Booth, 1972a). A more plausible candidate for caloric conditioning of preferences results from pairing a flavor with alcohol in quantities that are unlikely to be intoxicating (Sherman, Hickis, Rice, Rusiniak, & Garcia, 1983) and at a concentration that would, if anything, be aversively astringent (Mehiel & Bolles, 1984).

Caloric conditioning was shown by Booth et al. (1972) to be capable of making a lower level of sweetness become preferred to a higher level of sweet-ness. This reversed the initial preference gradient, in which increasing vigor of ingestive reflex is seen in innate response to increasing concentrations of sugar. This result has the most profound implications for understanding the relationships of food perception to food preferences. These implications are developed in the remainder of this chapter.

The conditioned preference reversal is entirely consonant with the concept of a stimulus generalization decrement. The learned response is strongest to the particular stimulus presented during training. A different wavelength of color or a different orientation of a line will produce less of a response. The greater the difference from the training stimulus, the weaker will be the learned performance. Thus a stronger than trained sweetness is liable to produce a weaker preference, as a result of incomplete generalization. A weaker sweetness would also produce a weaker preference but because of its difference from the trained sweetness, not because of its weaker elicitation of the innate reflex. Thus the slope of the decrement in learned response on the low sweetness side may be steeper or flatter than that of the innate weakening. Furthermore, if stimulus control is entirely learned, then a given size of difference above or below the trained sweetness level should have the same effect on responding as a result of generalization decrement. This is the basis in learning theory for the hedonic triangle, described below. (It should be noted that this account neglects the possibility of stimulus intensity dynamism, a somewhat obscure phenomenon that might be a drive effect of high intensities of any stimulus.)

The predicted symmetrical decrement in preference around the learned maximum provides the basis for a measure of the innateness of any particular sweetness preference (Booth et al., 1987). If the decline in preference above the maximum is less than it is below it, or does not occur at all but is asymptotic, then the innate reflex has not been totally suppressed by learned responding to sweetness. The lack of a "break point" (preference maximum) in pleasantness ratings of increasing concentrations of sweetener is thus evidence of reversion to the infantile response and of a poor measure of learned drink sweetness preferences.

The caloric conditioning of preferences is not restricted to tastes, any more than is the toxic conditioning of aversions (Baker & Booth, 1989; Pain & Booth, 1968). Odorous oils or food flavor essences that sometimes are gustatorily indiscriminable have indeed become the norm in recent years.

Nutritionally Conditioned Preferences for Odors

Caloric effects of carbohydrates, ethanol, and perhaps fats are not the only reinforcers or unconditioned stimuli (USs) in taste, odor, or (jointly) flavor preference conditioning. Repletion of amino acid deficiency provided the first demonstration of nutritional conditioning of odor preference (Booth & Simson, 1971). Omission of protein from no more than the last meal is sufficient to make intragastric protein amino acid mixtures effective at conditioning odor preferences in the rat and in human subjects (Booth & Gibson, 1988). Possibly such mild incipient deficiencies of certain other nutrients (e.g., some vitamin or mineral) will prove sufficient to permit conditioning of strong preferences. The evidence for innateness of sodium appetite might be worth reexamining from this viewpoint.

Other Preference-Inducing Associative Effects of Experience

The USs are not confined to nutrients either. Emotionally significant events also reinforce preference. Preschoolers come to prefer a food that has been paired with adult approval or with peers' food choices (Birch, this volume). Preference for the flavor of a nonnutritive soda was increased in schoolchildren by one pairing with relief from mild anxiety (S. Campbell & D. A. Booth, unpublished data).

THE HEDONIC TRIANGLE

The stimulus generalization decrement from a preferred taste or an appetite configuration that has been learned is based on recognition of the learned stimulus (e.g., CS^+ or S^D) and discrimination from it. The motivating effect of the learned stimulus configuration does not fully generalize to another stimulus because it is discriminably different from it. This gives the theory of signal detection an elementary application that was foreseen by Fechner, albeit in a subjectivist context; he speculated that perception of the strength of the stimulus and of differences between stimuli involved the same mental process. There is no reason why this principle should not apply to the vigor of any human or animal response, including overt ingestion or ingestive choice, as well as to the psychophysicists' intensity ratings.

The implication is that the responses in tasks of rating sensation magnitudes should be linear against a cumulation of equally discriminable differences. Hedonic responses to a familiar motivating situation should also change linearly with objective dissimilarity. However, the motivational function of a tastant in food, for example, is unlikely to be monotonically increasing with concentration because the difference from the learned stimulus can be in directions of greater as well as less intensity. Hence, the generalization decrement from a conditioned preference stimulus should form an isosceles triangle.

This fundamental theoretical mechanism for learned peak intensities of food stimuli might be called the *hedonic triangle* or, more descriptively, the linear folded function for a determinant of acceptance and appetite (Booth et al., 1987; Booth, Conner, & Gibson, 1989). Above an optimum intensity, the motivation to ingest declines with the same slope against perceived stimulus differences as it rises from below peak preference.

The asymmetric and flat-topped inverted U often reported for preference data is attributable to artifacts of stimulus units that are not equally discriminable, and test situations that are not fully motivating in features other than the stimulus dimension plotted (Booth, Thompson, & Shahedian, 1983; Booth et al., 1987). No person's preference for sweetness in a familiar food or drink that we have so far tested has been reliably distinguishable from an isosceles triangle of degrees of preference plotted against levels of sweetener scaled in units having constant discriminability. This does not just confirm that the hedonic U is artifactual. The consistent observation of the triangle predicted for a conditioned stimulus is also strong evidence that all normal adult eating motivation stimulated by sweetness is entirely learned.

The same conclusion applies to salty and bitter preferences in foods. We have yet to test sourness, but there is no reason to expect it to be different from other tastes, textures, aromas, or colors. We have found responses controlled by all these modalities to be colinear above and below the ideal point for the individual in the food or drink tested (Booth & Blair, 1988; Conner et al., 1988a; Griffiths et al., 1984).

CONTEXTUALIZATION OF LEARNED TASTE PREFERENCES

The conditioned taste stimulus is not an isolated physical entity. Palatability is not a property of a food nor is it a set of ingestive movements. The learned reaction to a taste in a food does not depend solely on the precise level of the tastant relative to the habituated or conditioned level. It also depends on other tastes and sensed constituents of the food and indeed sometimes on aspects of the eating situation.

Taste Mixtures

It is hard to think of any food or drink that does not combine at least two tastes. Sourness and sweetness are both needed to approach a passable lemon flavor. Monosodium glutamate needs sodium chloride to be reminiscent of chicken flavor. Vegetables to which we add some salt sell better with some sugar added also. Even when flavored and colored, nothing is purely sweet—a sour, bitter, or salty note is also needed. That is to say, conventionally learned gustatory preferences are typically for mixtures.

Thus the learned taste is multidimensional. There is an integrated hedonic triangle, with a joint ideal point and a combination tolerance characteristic. There are two or more analytical gustatory hedonic triangles but there has to be a decision on how to combine them (Booth et al., 1987; Booth & Blair, 1988). Ideal points and tolerated ranges vary across subjects and so the most precise judgments, in the subject's familiar range of judgment, will require different stimulus ranges chosen to suit each subject. Still more serious in its methodological implications, the combination rule may be qualitatively idiosyncratic. Thus the only fundamentally safe analysis is subject by subject, as has been advocated in some quarters for studies of learned performance. Then the sensitivity of the integral judgment to each of the two or more physical stimuli can be calculated and the decision rule identified as the principle of combination that is most predictive of overall response.

The same approach will carry forward recent advances in the analysis of mixtures of tastants having a similar taste, such as sugars or artificial sweeteners. Even when the interest is in the combination of stimuli into an unconscious perception or a described sensation, rather than into preference, the fundamental issue is still the discriminativeness among levels of tastants shown by an integrated judgment relative to identified norms (Booth & Blair, 1988; Booth, Conner, & Gibson, 1989).

Dietary Configurations

Most food identities are more than mixtures of tastes. Something as simple as lemonade has a more genuine flavor with a slight aroma of lemon oil. Most fruit flavors depend on color and odor as well as taste. Even tonic water (sweetened quinine solution) has to be carbonated. The many nuances of texture and of its change during mastication are no less important in the recognition and acceptability of a food.

Indeed, the heart of the viewpoint presented here is that the liking for a food, and indeed the whole motivation to eat, is a multimodal recognition process. In a given context, the better the salient characteristics of an item of the diet match those of a configuration that has been habituated and nutritionally and socioaffectively conditioned, the stronger will be the motivation to ingest that item.

This approach exposes incoherent assumptions behind many traditional issues about food perceptions and preferences. All salient characteristics of foods are crucial. Taste cannot be regarded as globally any more or less important than another sensory modality, certainly not from what people say in response to a direct question to that effect, let alone from speculations about neuronal connections in the brain. Neither innateness of behavioral reactions to taste nor the strength of physiological reactions to taste stimulation make any more feasible a genetic analysis specific to taste preferences in familiar foods, because these are experientially determined behaviors (Booth, 1988b). Taste sensitivity may decline with age but this does not necessarily give rise to any predictable effect on food preferences, intake, or nutrition, for people's habits will adapt their preferences to changed sensations (Booth et al., 1989).

The relative importance of taste in food preferences is not a scientific issue. What is important to a person about a taste in a foodstuff is the objective performance characteristics of its hedonic triangle in that context, that is, how much of the tastant is preferred (the ideal point) and how little of a difference in tastant level makes a difference to preference (the sensitivity of choices). The marketer or cook may make taste historically important or unimportant, depending on where in the individual's range of tolerance they put the level of tastant in the foodstuff provided. There is no meaning to relative psychological importance in grams tolerated of this or that sweetener or bittering agent, aroma molecule, colorant, or texturiser.

The limited discriminability of taste differences opens up the possibility of a method of reducing the prevalence of excessive salt intake and sugar intake rather than relying on a determined minority to take up low-salt and low-sugar versions of foods. A global reduction of salt or sugar in a food or drink by one-fifth would not be noticeable by even the least tolerantly motivated (Conner et al., 1988a; Conner, Haddon, Pickering, & Booth, 1988). Habitual consumption of the reduced salt or sugar variant would then adapt taste preferences down, permitting a further reduction. Continued marketing of the currently most popular of a wide range of preferred levels or even of higher levels serves only to maintain a tradition, instead of rapidly adapting consumers to lower levels by experience, modifying the effect of taste on food choice.

Appetites and Satieties

Finally, the learned ingestive reaction to tastes and other food features is often dependent on learned cues in the internal or external environment at the moment of performance. This is a learned appetite for the contextual features of the controlling stimulus configuration (e.g., a protein need in the case of protein appetite) (Baker, Booth, Duggan, & Gibson, 1987). If the learned reaction is aversive, the effect is a satiety (Booth, 1972b).

It should be emphasized again that these reactions are the momentary motivation to ingest. Such a dispositional response to the whole stimulus situation can control meal size (satiety) as well as food selection (palatability). From this dispositional viewpoint, it is not surprising that nutritional USs, able to condition food preferences at the start of meals (Booth & Davis, 1973; Booth & Simson, 1971) and prolong greatly the maintenance of ingestion during a meal (Booth, 1972b, 1988a; Gibson & Booth, 1989), are also capable of conditioning elicitation of intake (Weingarten, 1983). In this context, such conditioning of meal-taking raises the neglected question of its dependence on internal states (Booth, 1985).

The initiation, maintenance, termination, and sustained inhibition of ingestion can all be given different names but there is no reason to expect totally distinct mechanisms to be involved in each overt effect. Such assumptions have permeated many discussions of intake control, thus disconnecting them from the classic psychological conceptions of motivation as competing or time-sharing dispositions (Booth, 1972a, 1976; Booth et al., 1972). The implications of this dispositional approach are well illustrated by the behavioral mechanism by which hypothalamic administration of norepinephrine (NE) induces the eating of a meal (Matthews, Gibson, & Booth, 1985). It is widely thought that the NE gates out satiety, partly on the grounds that low doses increase the size of a meal already started. Indeed, behavioral analysis of NE-induced meals has shown that they can be explained only by a blockade of conditioned, food-specific, meal-size reduction (Gibson & Booth, 1986; Matthews et al., 1985).

Acquired preference for the richer nutrient in the hungry state at the start of the meal was demonstrated in the replications of satiation conditioning by Booth and Davis (1973). That appetite was conditioned to mixtures of saccharin with either quinine or citric acid. Tastant-odorant mixtures have also been used in satiation and appetite conditioning experiments (Booth, 1977). Most often, however, we have used odorants as conditioned stimuli, so that intake preferences can include conditioning of approach as well as of maintained ingestion. There are also more odors to choose from and less of an innate motivation to be controlled out. Furthermore, there are no indications from nutritional conditioning experiments that tastes are any better or worse as CSs than odors or textures to rats or primates.

Thus when we find taste preferences vary with context, we should look at past personal experience for the most likely explanation. Generally speaking, appetites and food preferences will have been induced by eating habits. The appetites will, in turn, help to sustain those habits. Yet the original acquisition of the habits will have been based on caloric and other reinforcers delivered by the initial interaction between lifestyle and culture, including the foods provided by the economy and technology that fit widespread eating habits.

For example, breakfast cereals are liked best (or only) at breakfast time by many people. The stage in the day and/or perhaps the fasting state has become an element with the food's features in that breakfast appetite CS, much as a rat can be conditioned to eat to a sound cue (Weingarten, this volume). Furthermore, these cereals are usually eaten with a large portion of sugar. This liking for these foods in this context and strongly sweetened is cultural in origin: the Scots, for example, traditionally have salt and no sugar with cooked breakfast cereal.

We find that there is not a unitary sweet tooth among English people. There are two families of likings for highly sweetened foods, one for desserts, snack foods, and soft and hot drinks and the other for sweet vegetables and fruit (Conner & Booth, 1988; Conner et al., 1988b). Presumably, many people snack on confectionary and sweetened drinks, but a minority in Britain snack on carrots, tomato soup, and fruit juice instead.

There are major practical implications of this learned appetite for drinks and their food accompaniments between meals. The "snacking sweet tooth" has not been associated with overweight as such (Conner & Booth, 1988.) Nevertheless, theory and evidence point to habitual consumption of energy in and with drinks after and between meals as a major cause of overweight (Booth, 1988c; Blair, Booth, Lewis, & Wainwright, 1989). So it is not surprising if some obese people prefer sugar/butter fat mixtures having the level of sweetness commonly associated in the U.S. with cream fillings and toppings and if such formulations are regarded as "danger foods" by those concerned about their shape (Booth, 1988a; Drewnowski, this volume). It follows from the contextual learning principles that consumption of energy-free drinks and low-calorie, tasty, solid accompaniments between meals would make a major contribution to the prevention of obesity and success in weight control.

Normally, the motivation to eat has been conditioned to bodily signals of caloric depletion as well as to calorific foods (Booth, 1980, 1985; Booth & Davis, 1973). Mild cues such as a nearly empty stomach are probably sufficient for motivation of normal strength (Booth, 1972c; Davidson, 1987). However, a motivation to eat convenience foods, for example, could as readily be conditioned to bodily sensations of repletion (Gibson & Booth, 1989) or to emotional states of anxiety, sadness, and anger (although this has yet to be demonstrated). This then provides a basis for acquiring snack food cravings, bingeing habits, and emotional overeating (Booth, 1988a). When this motivation is strong enough to rise to consciousness, it can be conventionally rationalized (Booth, 1980, 1987a). Some overeating may also have on instrumental basis, motivated by attempts at mood control.

LEARNING, COGNITION, AND APPLICATIONS
A fundamental implication of the approach is that learned stimulus control and object perception can no longer be treated as separate specialisms in psychology. In the study of eating and other psychological phenomena, it is not far from fundamental discovery to application, and indeed back again; with ecologically valid experimental designs, there is no distance at all.

References

Baker, B. J. & Booth, D. A. (1989). Preference conditioning by concurrent diets with delayed proportional reinforcements. *Physiology & Behavior, 46,* 585–591.

Baker, B. J., Booth, D. A., Duggan, J. P., & Gibson, E. L. (1987). Protein appetite demonstrated: Learned specificity of protein-cue preference to protein need in adult rats. *Nutrition Research, 7,* 481–487.

Blair, A. J., Booth, D. A., Lewis, V. J., & Wainwright, C. J. (1989). The relative success of official and informal weight reduction techniques: Retrospective correlational evidence. *Psychology and Health, 3,* 195–206.

Bolles, R. C., Hayward, L., & Crandall, C. (1981). Conditioned taste preferences based on caloric density. *Journal of Experimental Psychology: Animal Behavior Processes, 7,* 59–69.

Booth, D. A. (1972a). Caloric compensation in rats with continuous or intermittent access to food. *Physiology & Behavior, 8,* 891–899.

Booth, D. A. (1972b). Conditioned satiety in the rat. *Journal of Comparative and Physiological Psychology, 81,* 457–471.

Booth, D. A. (1972c). Taste reactivity in satiated, ready to eat and starved rats. *Physiology & Behavior, 8,* 901–908.

Booth, D. A. (1976). Approaches to feeding control. In T. Silverstone (Ed.), *Appetite and food intake* (pp. 417–478). West Berlin: Abakon Verlagsgesellschaft/Dahlem Konferenzen.

Booth, D. A. (1977). Appetite and satiety as metabolic expectancies. In Y. Katsuki, M. Sato, S. F. Takagi, & Y. Oomura (Eds.), *Food intake and chemical senses* (pp. 317–330). Tokyo: University of Tokyo Press.

Booth, D. A. (1980). Acquired behavior controlling energy intake and output. In A. J. Stunkard (Ed.), *Obesity* (pp. 101–143). Philadelphia, PA: W. B. Saunders.

Booth, D. A. (1981). Momentary acceptance of particular foods and processes that change it. In J. Solms & R. L. Hall (Eds.), *Criteria of food acceptance: How man chooses what he eats* (pp. 49–68). Zurich: Forster.

Booth, D. A. (1985). Food-conditioned eating preferences and aversions with interoceptive elements: Learned appetites and satieties. *Annals of the New York Academy of Sciences, 443,* 22–37.

Booth, D. A. (1987a). Cognitive experimental psychology of appetite. In R. A. Boakes, M. J. Burton, & D. A. Popplewell (Eds.), *Eating habits* (pp. 175–209). Chichester: Wiley.

Booth, D. A. (1987b). Book review: J. R. Stellar & E. Stellar, The neurobiology of motivation and reward. *Psychological Medicine, 17,* 521–522.

Booth, D. A. (1988a). Culturally corralled into food abuse: The eating disorders as physiologically reinforced excessive appetites. In K. M. Pirke, W. Vandereycken, & D. Ploog (Eds.), *The psychobiology of bulimia nervosa* (pp. 18–32). Heidelberg: Springer-Verlag.

Booth, D. A. (1988b). Mechanisms from models—actual effects from real life: The zero-calorie drink-break option. In D. A. Booth, J. Rodin, & G. L. Blackburn (Eds.), *Sweeteners, appetite and obesity* (pp. 94–102). London: Academic Press.

Booth, D. A. (1990). Mood- or nutrient-conditioned appetites: Cultural and physiological bases for eating disorders. *Annals of the New York Academy of Sciences, 575,* 122–135.

Booth, D. A., & Blair, A. J. (1988). Objective factors in the appeal of a brand during use by the individual consumer. In D. M. H. Thomson (Ed.), *Food acceptability* (pp. 329–346). London: Elsevier Applied Science.

Booth, D. A., Campbell, A. T., & Chase, A. (1970). Temporal bounds of postingestive glucose-induced satiety in man. *Nature, 228,* 1104–1105.

Booth, D. A., Conner, M. T., & Gibson, E. L. (1989). Measurement of food perception, food preference, and nutrient selection. *Annals of the New York Academy of Sciences, 561,* 226–242.

Booth, D. A., Conner, M. T., & Marie, S. (1987). Sweetness and food selection: Measurement of sweeteners' effects on acceptance. In J. Dobbing (Ed.), *Sweetness* (pp. 143–160). London: Springer-Verlag.

Booth, D. A., & Davis, J. D. (1973). Gastrointestinal factors in the acquisition of oral sensory control of satiation. *Physiology & Behavior, 11,* 23–29.

Booth, D. A., & Gibson, E. L. (1988). Control of eating behaviour by amino acid supply. In G. Heuther (Ed.), *Amino acid availability and brain function in health and disease* (pp. 259–266). Berlin: Springer-Verlag.

Booth, D. A., & Lovett, D. (1968). Postingestive modulation of palatability in the control of food intake. *Abstracts: Third International Conference on the Regulation of Food and Water Intake, Philadelphia, PA, September, 1968.*

Booth, D. A., Lovett, D., & McSherry, G. M. (1972). Postingestive modulation of the sweetness preference gradient in the rat. *Journal of Comparative and Physiological Psychology, 78,* 485–512.

Booth, D. A., & Simson, P. C. (1971). Food preferences acquired by association with variations in amino acid nutrition. *Quarterly Journal of Experimental Psychology, 23,* 135–145.

Booth, D. A., Thompson, A. L., & Shahedian, B. (1983). A robust, brief measure of an individual's most preferred level of salt in an ordinary foodstuff. *Appetite, 4,* 301–312.

Conner, M. T., & Booth, D. A. (1988). Preferred sweetness of a lime drink and preference for sweet over nonsweet foods, related to sex and reported age and body weight. *Appetite, 10,* 25–35.

Conner, M. T., Booth, D. A., Clifton, V. J., & Griffiths, R. P. (1988a). Individualized optimization of the salt content of white bread for acceptability. *Journal of Food Science, 53,* 549–554.

Conner, M. T., Haddon, A. V., Pickering, E. S., & Booth, D. A.. (1988b). Sweet tooth demonstrated: Individual differences in preference for both sweet foods and foods highly sweetened. *Journal of Applied Psychology, 73,* 275–280.

Davidson, T. L. (1987). Learning about deprivation stimuli. *Behavioral Neuroscience, 101,* 198–208.

Ducleaux, R., Feisthauer, J., & Cabanac, M. (1973). Effets du repas sur l'agrément d'odeurs alimentaire et non alimentaire chez l'homme [Effects of a meal on the pleasantness of food and nonfood odors in human subjects]. *Physiology & Behavior, 10,* 1029–1033.

Garcia, J., Hankins, W. G., & Rusiniak, K. W. (1974). Behavioral regulation of the milieu interne in man and rat. *Science, 185,* 824–831.

Gibson, E. L., & Booth, D. A. (1986). Feeding induced by injection of norepinephrine near the paraventricular nucleus is suppressed specifically by the early stages of strong postingestional satiety in the rat. *Physiological Psychology, 14,* 98–103.

Gibson, E. L., & Booth, D. A. (1989). Dependence of carbohydrate-conditioned flavor preference on internal state in rats. *Learning and Motivation, 20,* 36–47.

Griffiths, R. P., Clifton, V. J., & Booth, D. A. (1984). Measurement of an individual's optimally preferred level of food flavor. In J. Adda (Ed.), *Progress in flavor research* (pp. 81–90). Amsterdam: Elsevier.

Harris, G., & Booth, D. A. (1987). Infants' preference for salt in food: Its dependence upon recent dietary experience. *Journal of Reproductive and Infant Psychology, 5,* 97–104.

Holman, E. W. (1975). Immediate and delayed reinforcers for flavor preference in rats. *Learning and Motivation, 6,* 91–100.

Le Magnen, J. (1955). La satiété induite par les stimuli sucrés chez le rat blanc [Satiety induced by sweet stimuli in rats]. *Comptes Rendus des Séances de la Société de Biologie, Paris, 149,* 1339–1342.

Mather, P., Nicolaïdis, S., & Booth, D. A. (1978). Compensatory and conditioned feeding responses to scheduled glucose infusions in the rat. *Nature, 273,* 461–463.

Matthews, J. W., Gibson, E. L., & Booth, D. A. (1985). Norepinephrine-facilitated eating: Reduction in saccharin preferences and conditioned flavor preferences with increase in quinine aversion. *Pharmacology Biochemistry and Behavior, 22,* 1045–1052.

Mehiel, R., & Bolles, R. C. (1984). Learned flavor preferences based on caloric outcome. *Animal Learning and Behavior, 12,* 421–427.

Mook, D. G., & Wagner, S. (1989). Orosensory suppression of saccharin drinking in rat: The response, not the taste. *Appetite, 13,* 1–13.

Pain, J. F., & Booth, D. A. (1968). Toxiphobia to odors. *Psychonomic Science, 10,* 363–364.

Rozin, P., & Fallon, A. (1987). A perspective on disgust. *Psychological Review, 94,* 23–41.

Scott, T. R., & Giza, D. (1987). Neurophysiological aspects of sweetness. In J. Dobbing (Ed.), *Sweetness* (pp. 21–32). London: Springer-Verlag.

Sherman, J. E., Hickis, C. F., Rice, A. G., Rusiniak, K. W., & Garcia, J. (1983). Preferences and aversions for stimuli paired with ethanol. *Animal Learning and Behavior, 11,* 101–106.

Simson, P. C., & Booth, D. A. (1973). Effect of CS-US interval on the conditioning of odour preferences by amino acid loads. *Physiology & Behavior, 11,* 801–808.

Weingarten, H. P. (1983). Conditioned cues elicit eating in sated rats: A role for learning in meal initiation. *Science, 220,* 431–433.

Wooley, O. W., Wooley, S. C., & Dunham, R. B. (1972). Calories and sweet taste: Effects on sucrose preference in the obese and nonobese. *Physiology & Behavior, 9,* 765–768.

Zahorik, D. M. (1979). Learned changes in preferences for chemical stimuli: Asymmetrical effects of positive and negative consequences, and species differences in learning. In J. H. A. Kroeze (Ed.), *Preference behaviour and chemoreception* (pp. 233–245). London: IRL Press.

Zellner, D. A., Rozin, P., Aron, M., & Kulish, C. (1983). Conditioned enhancement of human liking for flavor by pairing with sweetness. *Learning and Motivation, 14,* 338–350.

PART FIVE

TASTE PREFERENCES, EXPERIENCE, AND OBESITY

CHAPTER 14

THE ROLE OF SENSORY-SPECIFIC SATIETY IN FOOD INTAKE AND FOOD SELECTION

BARBARA J. ROLLS

As a food or drink is consumed, the pleasantness of its sensory qualities or its palatability declines. The changing hedonic responses to foods and drinks have been referred to as both alliesthesia and sensory-specific satiety. I will first describe the characteristics of these phenomena and will then focus on how sensory-specific satiety influences food intake and food selection.

ALLIESTHESIA

"A given stimulus can induce a pleasant or unpleasant sensation depending on the subject's internal state" (Cabanac, 1971, p. 1107). Cabanac (1971) proposed the word *alliesthesia* to describe this phenomenon. Thus in relation to food intake, the pleasantness of a particular food's or nutrient's taste or smell is determined by the organism's need for it. Cabanac (1971) demonstrated that judgements of the pleasantness of sucrose solutions changed slowly as the solutions were ingested in small portions over time. As the sucrose solution was consumed, the need for sucrose declined and so the pleasantness of the taste of sucrose decreased. Furthermore, gastric intubation of glucose decreased the pleasantness of sweet solutions but not salty solutions; gastric loads of hypertonic saline decreased the pleasantness of salty solutions but did not influence the response to sweet solutions (Cabanac & Duclaux, 1970). These studies support the hypothesis that changes in the internal state are important factors in the decrease in the sensation of pleasantness, or negative alliesthesia (Cabanac, 1979).

SENSORY-SPECIFIC SATIETY

While Cabanac's studies of alliesthesia served to focus attention on the changing
hedonic response to foods, the idea that palatability changes was not new. We
should give Aristotle (translation, 1973) credit for this idea since he described
the way that the flavors and smells of foods can change with man's internal state
of repletion: "these smells are pleasant when we are hungry, but when we are sated
and not requiring to eat, they are not pleasant" (p. 75). Yudkin in 1956 described
specific satiety in which consumption of a particular food leads to an unpleasant
sensation which is relieved by consumption of another food of a different nutrient
composition. The focus was still on the nutrients in foods as the determinants of
the changing hedonic response. However, Le Magnen, also in 1956, described
an experiment in which rats ate 72% more when presented with a variety of
chows—which differed only in that they had different odors—than when presented
with chow with just one odor. He called this phenomenon *sensory-specific satiety*
and thus introduced the idea that satiety can be for the sensory properties of
foods rather than their nutritional composition (Le Magnen, 1967). This view
was extended to humans with the finding that ingestion of a noncaloric, sweet
solution of cyclamate was just as effective in decreasing the pleasantness of 20%
sucrose as was glucose (Wooley, Wooley, & Dunham, 1972).

When we started our studies of the changing hedonic response to foods, we
were not sure whether specific satieties would occur for the sensory properties of
foods, the nutritional composition, or both. Our experiments on human eating
behavior have been guided by the belief that the studies should be conducted with
real foods, rather than with solutions, as had often previously been the case.
Although this means some loss of purity of design, it also means the results are
more likely to be relevant to normal eating. We also believe that studies of eating
in normal weight, nondieting individuals should precede those in which abnormal
eating is being defined.

Thus to investigate the specificity of satiety, we tested normal weight,
nondieting young men and women. Before being offered lunch, they were asked
to taste and rate the pleasantness of eight different foods. They were then given
one of these foods to eat ad libitum and, after finishing, they again rated the
foods they had sampled before the meal. We found that the pleasantness of the
taste of the food eaten in the meal decreased significantly more than that of the
foods not eaten. Thus satiety appeared to be specific to the food that had been
consumed. We then became interested in whether such changes in the hedonic
response to foods would be related to the amount eaten subsequently. To test this,
the subjects were given an unexpected second course just after they completed
the second series of ratings. If the subjects were given the same food in the
second course that they had consumed in the first course, their intake fell to
about half that eaten in the first course, whereas if they were given a different
food, intake was the same in the second course as it was in the first course. The
changes in taste were found to be significantly correlated with the amount eaten
in the second course (Rolls, Rolls, Rowe, & Sweeney, 1981).

We were interested in how this specificity of satiety might operate in a varied meal of successive courses (Rolls, van Duijvenvoorde, & Rolls, 1984). One question was whether as subjects became more satiated over the meal, the specific changes in liking for the foods consumed would give way to a general decrease in the palatability of all foods. Another question was whether intake in the successive courses was related to changes in the pleasantness of the food to be consumed.

Normal weight, nondieting males and females were tested twice at lunch time. On one occasion, they were given a varied meal consisting of four successive courses (sausages, bread and butter, chocolate dessert, and bananas). On the other occasion, they were given a meal which consisted of just one of the foods offered previously. Subjects rated the pleasantness of the taste of the eight foods at the start of each course. We found that the pleasantness of the taste of the eaten foods decreased rapidly, whereas the pleasantness of the foods which had not been eaten changed little. These pleasantness changes correlated significantly with the amount of a particular food that was eaten in the subsequent course. Energy intake was elevated by 60% in the varied meal, and this is probably because of the lack of change in the pleasantness of foods that had not yet been eaten. Therefore, sensory-specific satiety was still seen after eating four different courses in a meal, and there was no overall reduction in the pleasantness of foods that had not been consumed. However, it seems likely that situations could be found (i.e., a very large and varied meal) in which an overall reduction in the liking for all foods would be seen. Personal experience indicates that it may require a very large amount of food leading to feelings of nausea and bloatedness before one refuses to eat at least small amounts of a particularly delicious sweet. Imagine resisting a homemade chocolate truffle at the end of a rich multicourse French meal!

Nutrient-Specific Satiety

Thus far we have not addressed the issue of whether the hedonic changes are due to the nutrient composition or the sensory properties of the ingested food. In the four course meal just described, the biggest decrease in pleasantness was for the eaten food; however, there were some interactions so that some of the uneaten foods decreased in pleasantness (see Figure 1). The basis of the interaction appeared to be that consumption of sweet foods caused some decline in the pleasantness of other sweet foods but had little effect on savory or salty foods, whereas the consumption of savory or salty foods decreased the pleasantness of other savory or salty foods but not sweet foods. However, the savory foods were higher in fat content, so it is not clear whether such interactions took place on the basis of differences in flavor, or whether specific macronutrients may also be involved (Rolls et al., 1984).

To determine the role of different macronutrients in the changing hedonic responses to foods, we offered subjects equicaloric amounts of foods high in one macronutrient and low in other major nutrients (Rolls, Hetherington, & Burley,

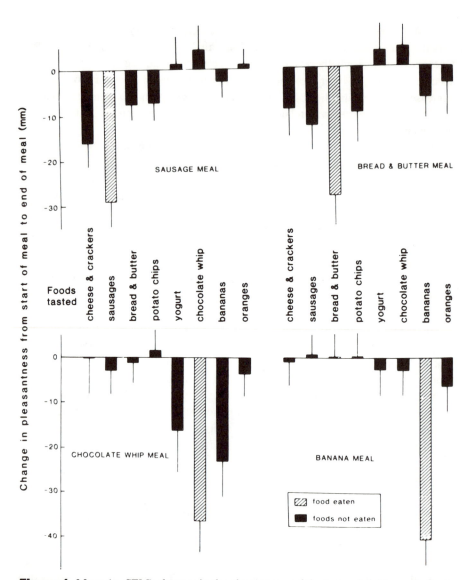

Figure 1 Mean (± SEM) changes in the pleasantness of the taste of eight sample foods (i.e., foods tasted) from the start to the end of four different meals. The eaten foods (hatched bars) declined the most in pleasantness. From "Pleasantness Changes and Food Intake in a Varied Four-Course Meal" by B. J. Rolls et al., 1984, *Appetite, 5,* p. 344. Copyright 1984 by Academic Press Inc. (London) Ltd. Reprinted by permission.

1988b). To test for interactions due to similarities in composition, each test food was paired with a food—tasted but not eaten—that was similar in nutrient composition but had different sensory properties. As expected, the largest change in the pleasantness of the taste occurred with the food eaten in the test meal. There were no significant differences among changes between the uneaten food with the same composition as that eaten and foods with different nutrient compositions. All of the uneaten foods showed little change in palatability following the test meals. When a varied meal was offered 2 hours after these preloads, the type of nutrient in the load did not affect the proportions of nutrients selected. Thus these data do not support the hypothesis that hedonic changes are due to the nutrient composition of the foods. However, we should bear in mind that negative results are never as convincing as positive results, so it is possible that in other contexts nutrient-specific satiety might be observed.

Sensory Stimulation and Satiety

We have conducted a number of studies which indicated that the sensory stimulation accompanying ingestion, rather than just the nutritional consequences of ingestion, was an important influence on the changing hedonic response, hence the terminology "sensory-specific satiety" (Rolls et al., 1988b; Rolls, Laster, & Summerfelt, 1989).

An obvious way to separate sensory and nutritive influences on pleasantness ratings is to compare the effects of foods with different energy content but similar sensory qualities. We have compared the effects of consuming a virtually noncaloric gelatin dessert or soup with the consumption of higher calorie versions of the same foods (Figure 2). Subjects did not detect that the two versions of the foods were different. Following a test meal in which subjects ate as much as they wanted of these foods, the time course and magnitude of the decrease in the

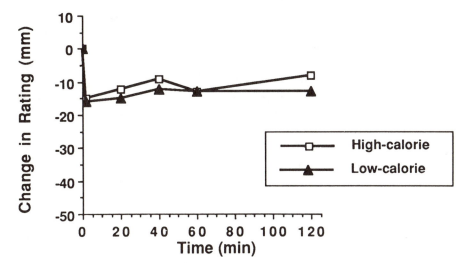

Figure 2 Mean changes in the pleasantness of the taste of high-calorie or low-calorie gelatin dessert from just prior to eating the gelatin dessert to 120 min postconsumption. From "Hunger and Food Intake Following Consumption of Low-Calorie Foods" by B. J. Rolls et al., 1989, *Appetite, 13* p. 122. Copyright 1989 by Academic Press Inc. (London) Ltd. Reprinted by permission.

pleasantness of the taste, texture, smell, and appearance of the eaten foods were not affected by the calories consumed (Rolls et al., 1988b; Rolls et al., 1989). A similar result was obtained when subjects ate high- and low-calorie versions of pudding (Rolls et al., 1989). Birch and Deysher (1986) also found in 2- to 5-year-old children that the decrease in preference for pudding following its consumption did not depend on its caloric density.

Time Course of Sensory-Specific Satiety

Alliesthesia for sweet solutions appears to develop slowly after ingestion so that the largest changes in pleasantness are seen 45 to 60 min after starting to slowly ingest sucrose (a 50 ml sample with 10 g sucrose was ingested every 5 min) (Cabanac, 1979). On the other hand, we have observed that large changes in the pleasantness of the taste of a food which had been eaten to satiety were seen 2 min after the termination of eating and that the magnitude of these changes did not alter over the next 20 min (Rolls et al., 1981). It may be that there are two separate phenomena: alliesthesia which depends on postingestive changes and sensory-specific satiety resulting from sensory stimulation accompanying ingestion. In another experiment, we examined this issue further by measuring the time course of the changes in ratings of the pleasantness of the taste, smell, texture, and appearance of three different foods—cheese on crackers, soup, gelatin dessert—after they had been eaten to satiety (Hetherington, Rolls, & Burley, 1989). For all of the sensory variables measured and all foods consumed, the greatest decline in pleasantness occurred 2 min after consumption ended. There was some indication that the initial palatability of the foods affected the time course of changes in that during the hour after consumption, there was some recovery in the pleasantness of the taste and texture of the most palatable of these foods (cheese on crackers) (Hetherington & Rolls, 1989). We speculated that both the palatability and the amount consumed affected the time course of sensory-specific satiety. However, since changes in the pleasantness of the foods occurred rapidly for all sensory variables studied, and since the magnitude of these changes did not increase over time, we concluded that the development of sensory-specific satiety was related primarily to the sensory stimulation accompanying ingestion as opposed to the postabsorptive effects of consuming these foods. But the fact that pleasantness did not always return to baseline after an hour indicated that changes in the need for nutrients may also influence hedonic responses.

Varied Sensory Properties and Food Intake

If satiety is specific to particular properties of foods, then during a meal, more should be consumed if a variety of foods is available than if just one food is presented. We found in a series of experiments that variety in a meal can increase energy intake. Varying just the sensory properties of foods while keeping the nutritional composition constant will increase food intake (Rolls & Hetherington, 1989).

Variations in the flavor of food can enhance intake. Successive courses of cream cheese sandwiches with very distinctive flavors (salt, curry, and combined saccharin and lemon) enhanced intake by 15% when compared to another test where subjects were offered only the favorite flavor (Rolls, Rowe, & Rolls, 1982). It is perhaps critical that the sandwiches were of different basic tastes since no intake enhancement was seen with three different sweetened, fruit flavors of yogurts (Rolls et al., 1981) or three different flavors of chocolates (Rolls et al., 1982). This lack of effect was probably because all of the foods were sweet as well as of the same type.

Variations in the shape of food, affecting both the appearance and texture, can also affect intake. Intake was enhanced by 14% when successive courses of three different shapes of pasta were compared with the successive presentation of a favorite shape (Rolls et al., 1982). When just the appearance of a food was different, as in a test in which children were offered different colored candies, neither the successive nor simultaneous presentation enhanced intake (Rolls et al. 1982).

Thus when the flavor or shape of foods was varied, the enhancement of intake was around 15% over three successive courses. When more properties of the foods differed, the enhancement was greater (Rolls & Hetherington, 1989). It is likely that intake was enhanced because of sensory-specific satiety, as was discussed in the study of intake and subjective sensations over a four course meal (Rolls, van Duijvenvoorde, & Rolls, 1984).

Mechanisms of Sensory-Specific Satiety

An obvious question is whether the decrease in the pleasantness of foods is simply due to a decrease in the intensity of the sensory properties with ingestion. Behavioral studies in humans indicate that there is no simple relationship between consumption and the intensity of food-related smells and tastes (E.T. Rolls, Rolls, & Rowe, 1983). Also, electrophysiological studies of brain cells in unanesthetized, behaving monkeys indicated that sensory-specific satiety did not appear to be related to changes in the sensory processing of responses to foods, but was related to brain areas controlling motivation and the reward value of foods (E. T. Rolls, 1984; Yaxley, Rolls, Sienkiewicz, & Scott, 1985).

It would not be adaptive to have food consumption lead to a decreased ability to taste foods. Since it is more likely that sensory-specific satiety involves changes in mechanisms concerned with the reward value of foods, we (Hetherington & Rolls, 1990) investigated the effect of blocking the endogenous opioid system, which may play a role in the pleasure associated with eating. Fantino, Hosotte, and Apfelbaum (1986) found that naltrexone, which blocks the opioid system, reduced the rated pleasantness of sweetened water (i.e., it produced an effect very similar to alliesthesia). We were interested to see if we could induce a similar decrease in the pleasantness of the taste of a highly palatable food such as chocolate ice cream. In normal weight young men, we found that a dose of naltrexone (50 mg) similar to that which decreased the pleasantness of sweet solutions had no effect on the pleasantness of the taste of chocolate ice cream or a variety of other foods, nor did it affect the sensory-specific satiety which was seen after ad libitum consumption of the ice cream. Thus we did not see any convincing evidence that the endogenous opioid system was involved in sensory-specific satiety, although it is possible that a different type of test with a different blocking agent might yield more positive results.

The influence of sensory-specific satiety on food intake may be mediated by some other physiological variables. For example, the presentation of new foods may stimulate the release of insulin, which in turn would increase food intake (Louis-Sylvestre, 1983).

It is likely that at least part of the specificity of satiety stems simply from the knowledge that a particular food has been consumed. Since we learn how much of a food is appropriate to satisfy hunger in various situations (Booth, Mather, & Fuller, 1982), it seems likely that when this limit is exceeded, the pleasantness of a food will be reduced. Thus we propose that the changing hedonic response to foods is a complex response resulting from the sensory stimulation accompanying ingestion, the knowledge that a particular food has been consumed, and finally, after some delay, changes in the need for particular nutrients (alliesthesia).

Role of Sensory-Specific Satiety in Food Selection

The studies by Davis (1928, 1939) on food selection by newly weaned infants indicated that when a number of foods were available, the normal strategy was to eat a varied and balanced diet. In adults, there is also a tendency to eat varied meals. This consumption of a variety of foods in adults could be due to learning about culturally accepted meal patterns and the need for a nutritionally balanced diet, or it could be due to changes in the relative palatability of foods as eating proceeds (which, as stated above, might be affected by learning as well as by sensory factors and the internal state).

Individuals normally eat in a manner that maintains palatability in a meal. Thus the order in which subjects eat foods and the distribution of drinks within a meal appear as strategies to optimize oropharyngeal stimulation provided by foods. When subjects were offered bread with five different spreads, the individual preferences for the spreads predicted the order in which the foods were consumed. Meals started with foods of medium palatability and ended with those of high palatability. Water tended to be taken between foods of different flavors (Bellisle & Le Magnen, 1980, 1984).

If palatability is to be optimized in a meal, the specific decrease in the pleasantness of a food as it is consumed will encourage a shift away from that food to another which has remained palatable. Thus a major effect of sensory-specific satiety is to encourage the consumption of a variety of foods during a meal.

The way that sensory-specific satiety affects food selection could turn out to be complex in that the changes in pleasantness are not limited to the food that has been consumed. Some uneaten foods also decline, possibly because they have a similar taste or other sensory properties or because they are considered to be of the same type. We have already suggested that interactions can take place on the basis of taste so that, for example, consumption of one sweet food decreases the pleasantness of the taste of other sweet foods. Although such interactions may occur on the basis of taste or flavor, they may not be seen if other sensory properties of the foods are very different. We found in a recent study that consumption of tomato soup did not affect the palatability of a tomato-based casserole. Presumably, the differences in texture, appearance, etc. overrode the similarity due to the tomato base (Rolls, Fedoroff, Guthrie, & Laster, 1990).

Foods of the same type also interact. For example, following consumption of orange gelatin dessert, ratings of the pleasantness of the taste of raspberry gelatin dessert declined similarly and more than any of the other foods rated. Also, following ingestion of tomato soup, a similar decrease in the ratings of the taste of consomme was observed (Rolls, Hetherington, & Burley, 1988a). This type of interaction may be due to beliefs about the similarities between foods (i.e., the way in which foods are grouped together, as well as to similarities in their sensory qualities). Understanding the way in which foods interact to affect palatability should be of benefit in the future by allowing people to design meals with optimal palatability.

We (Hetherington & Rolls, 1988, 1989) have recently applied the theory that sensory-specific satiety can affect food selection to the study of the aberrant food intake of individuals with eating disorders. In anorexia nervosa, it appears that beliefs about foods override the normal controls of eating. Patients have strong views about high-calorie foods being dangerous and low-calorie foods being safe for consumption. Thus in a lunch, we fed normal weight, nondieting women and women with anorexia nervosa a first course of cottage cheese, which is usually considered a safe food by the eating disordered population. We followed this course with a self-selection lunch in which the only low-calorie food available was cottage cheese. The normal subjects showed sensory-specific satiety for the cottage cheese after the first course and as predicted did not select cottage cheese as part of their lunch. The anorexics also showed sensory-specific satiety for the cottage cheese (Figure 3), but nevertheless most of them chose to eat cottage cheese as part of their lunch.

We have proposed that sensory-specific satiety is a relatively short lived phenomenon that would have its primary effect on the selection of foods within a single meal (Rolls, 1986). There are longer term effects in which changes in the palatability of foods persist from meal to meal and even from day to day. These are referred to as monotony effects. Such long-term effects are probably due to cognitions (i.e., knowledge that a particular food was recently consumed and a memory of its sensory properties). If there is a cognitive component to the phenomenon we refer to as sensory-specific satiety, it is possible that it and monotony effects are a continuum rather than distinct phenomena. As was mentioned in the description of the time course studies, it is not yet clear what factors affect the recovery of palatability after consumption. We have not seen complete recovery to baseline over the 1–2 hrs that we examined (Hetherington et al., 1989). In studies of repeated daily consumption of very palatable snack foods (chocolate, corn and potato snacks) over several weeks, we did not see a decline in the initial palatability of the snacks at the start of each snacking session (Rolls, unpublished raw data). Some foods appear to be spared from monotony effects. For example, staple foods such as bread, cereals, and dairy products as well as tea, coffee, and sweets, can be eaten every day without a loss of acceptability (see Rolls,, 1986). Clearly, trying to understand why some foods remain acceptable with repeated consumption is a major challenge not only for research scientists but also for the food industry.

Sensory-Specific Satiety and Food Intake

By calling the changing hedonic response to a food sensory-specific *satiety,* we imply that the phenomenon is involved in limiting food intake. This effect is most likely to be seen in situations where a variety of foods is available. We have found that subjects tended to stop eating a particular food before it was rated below the neutral point on visual analog scales (Rolls, Rolls, Rowe, & Sweeny, 1981); thus the decline in palatability limited consumption of the food being eaten if another food was available to satisfy hunger. Although this has not been systematically investigated, it seems likely that sensory-specific satiety will have much less impact on intake when only one food is available and hunger persists. An indication of this is the persistent consumption of liquid diet that is seen in animals with a gastric fistula through which the ingested food drains before absorption (Young et al., 1974). Clearly in this case, the sensory stimulation without a concomitant reduction in hunger does not stop ingestion. This serves to emphasize the point that sensory-specific satiety is only one of many factors that will act to terminate eating. There are undoubtedly complex interactions between these factors which will determine when consumption of a particular food ends.

Our studies of food intake in eating disorders are consistent with the hypothesis that sensory-specific satiety plays a role in food intake (Hetherington & Rolls, 1988, 1989). We found that patients with bulimia nervosa showed little decrease in the pleasantness of a food as it was consumed (Figure 3) and sometimes showed an increase. This could help to explain why they continue to eat a food during a binge. On the other hand, patients with anorexia nervosa showed a sharp decline in the pleasantness of a food after consuming only small amounts (Figure 3). This could help to explain their low food intake.

Sensory-Specific Satiety and Body Weight

The amount consumed in a meal will depend to some extent on the number of food items available. The enhancement of food intake by variety depends on sensory-specific satiety for particular foods as they are consumed. Looking be-

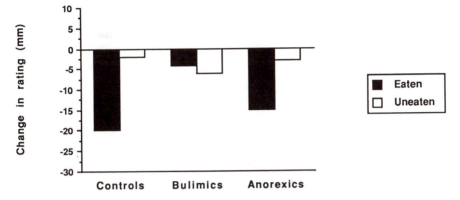

Figure 3 Mean changes in the pleasantness of the taste of the eaten food (cottage cheese or cheese on crackers, data combined) and the uneaten foods (i.e., all foods that were tasted and rated) from the initial rating to 2 min after the first course by normal weight, nondieting controls, and individuals with bulimia nervosa or anorexia nervosa. From "Sensory-Specific Satiety and Food Intake in Eating Disorders" by M. Hetherington and B. J. Rolls, 1988, in B. T. Walsh (Ed.), *Eating Behavior in Eating Disorders*, p. 153. Copyright 1988 by American Psychiatric Press. Adapted by permission.

yond single meals, it is possible that body weight maintenance may depend in part on the availability of a varied and palatable diet. Experiments in which rats were fed a varied diet support this view (see Rolls & Hetherington, 1989, for review).

In studies on the effects of the consumption of a monotonous liquid diet, it was found that obese subjects (Hashim & Van Itallie, 1965) and normal weight individuals (Cabanac & Rabe, 1976) voluntarily restricted intake and lost weight. There was also some evidence that if the diets that were freely available were very varied and palatable, there may be weight gain. In a hospital setting, the provision of a plentiful and varied supply of palatable food led to overeating and weight gain over 3- to 6-day periods in both obese (Porikos, Booth, & Van Itallie, 1977) and normal weight subjects (Porikos, Hesser, & Van Itallie, 1982). Apart from these few studies, we know little about the effects of variety in the diet on the control of body weight in humans. It is possible that with continual stimulation over days with a smorgasbord or platter service, if body weight increased, cognitive or physiological mechanisms might enable individuals to resist the stimulating influence of variety on appetite. On the other hand, there is such a large variety of foods available in Western countries, it may be that this provides a constant stimulus to some individuals and contributes to overeating and obesity. Only by further controlled studies will the role of sensory-specific satiety and variety in body weight regulation in humans be understood.

CONCLUSIONS

Sensory-specific satiety can affect food intake and selection; however, more studies are required to understand how changes in palatability affect both normal and abnormal eating behaviors. Palatability is one of the many influences on food intake and its effects can be moderated by hunger and beliefs about foods. More studies are required not only to understand the mechanisms underlying sensory-specific satiety, but also the way in which it interacts with other factors to affect food intake and selection in health and disease.

References

Aristotle. (1973). *De sensa* [The senses]. (G.R.T. Ross, Trans.). New York: Arno Press.

Bellisle, F., & Le Magnen, J. (1980). Patterns of food intake in mixed flavor meals and patterns of water intake during mixed and single flavor meals in humans. Paper presented at the Seventh International Conference on the Physiology of Food and Fluid Intake.

Bellisle, F., & Le Magnen, J. (1984). The structure of meals in humans: Eating and drinking patterns in lean and obese subjects. *Physiology & Behavior, 27,* 649–658.

Birch, L. L., & Deysher, M. (1986). Caloric compensation and sensory specific satiety: Evidence for self-regulation of food intake by young children. *Appetite, 7,* 323–331.

Booth, D. A., Mather, P., & Fuller, J. (1982). Starch content of ordinary foods associatively conditions human appetite and satiation indexed by intake and eating pleasantness of starch-paired flavours. *Appetite, 3,* 163–184.

Cabanac, M. (1971). Physiological role of pleasure. *Science, 173,* 1103–1107.

Cabanac, M. (1979). Sensory pleasure. *Quarterly Review of Biology, 54,* 1–29.

Cabanac, M., & Duclaux, R. (1970). Specificity of internal signals in producing satiety for taste stimuli. *Nature, 227,* 966–967.

Cabanac, M., & Rabe, E. F. (1976). Influence of a monotonous diet on body weight regulation in humans. *Physiology & Behavior, 17,* 675–678.

Davis, C. M. (1928). Self selection of diet by newly weaned infants. *American Journal of Diseases of Children, 36,* 651–679.

Davis, C. M. (1939). Results of the self-selection of diets by young children. *Canadian Medical Association Journal, 41,* 257–261.

Fantino, M., Hosotte, J., & Apfelbaum, M. (1986). An opioid antagonist, naltrexone, reduces preference for sucrose in humans. *American Journal of Physiology, 251,* R91–R96.

Hashim, S. A., & Van Itallie, T. B. (1965). Studies in normal and obese subjects with a monitored food dispensing device. *Annals of the New York Academy of Sciences, 131,* 654–661.

Hetherington, M., & Rolls, B. J. (1988). Sensory-specific satiety and food intake in eating disorders. In B. T. Walsh (Ed.), *Eating Behavior in Eating Disorders.* (pp. 143–159). Washington, DC: American Psychiatric Association Press.

Hetherington, M., & Rolls, B. J. (1989). Sensory-specific satiety in anorexia and bulimia nervosa. In L. H. Schneider, S. J. Cooper, & K. A. Halmi (Eds.), The Psychobiology of Human Eating Disorders: Preclinical and Clinical Perspectives. *Annals of the New York Academy of Sciences, 575,* 387–398.

Hetherington, M. M., & Rolls, B. J. (1990). Effects of naltrexone on ingestive behavior. *FASEB Journal, 4,* A399.

Hetherington, M., Rolls, B. J., & Burley, V. J. (1989). The time course of sensory-specific satiety. *Appetite, 12,* 57–68.

Le Magnen, J. (1956). Hyperphagie provoquée chez le rat blanc par altération du mécanisme de satiété périphérique [Hyperphagia induced in the white rat through the alteration of the mechanism of peripheral satiety]. *Comptes rendus des séances de la société de biologie et de ses filiales, 150*, 32-35.

Le Magnen, J. (1967). Habits and food intake. In C. F. Code (Ed.), *Handbook of Physiology* (pp. 11-13). Washington, DC: American Physiology Society.

Louis-Sylvestre, J. (1983). Phase céphalique de secrétion d'insuline et variété des aliments au cours du repas chez le rat [Cephalic phase secretion of insulin and the variety of food choices during a meal in the rat]. *Reproduction, Nutrition, Development, 23*, 351-356.

Porikos, K. P., Booth, G., & Van Itallie, T. B. (1977). Effect of covert nutritive dilution on the spontaneous intake of obese individuals: A pilot study. *American Journal of Clinical Nutrition, 30*, 1638-1644.

Porikos, K. P., Hesser, M. F., & Van Itallie, T. B. (1982). Caloric regulation in normal weight men maintained on a palatable diet of conventional foods. *Physiology & Behavior, 29*, 293-300.

Rolls, B. J. (1986). Sensory-specific satiety. *Nutrition Reviews, 44*, 93-101.

Rolls, B. J. (1990). [Decline in initial palatability of snacks]. Unpublished raw data.

Rolls, B. J., Fedoroff, I. C., Guthrie, J. F., & Laster, L. J. (in press). Foods with different satiating effects in humans. *Appetite*.

Rolls, B. J., & Hetherington, M. (1989). The role of variety in eating and body weight regulation. In R. Shepherd (Ed.), *Handbook of the Psychophysiology of Human Eating* (pp. 57-84). Chichester, England: John Wiley & Sons Ltd.

Rolls, B. J., Hetherington, M., & Burley, V. J. (1988a). The specificity of satiety: The influence of foods of different macronutrient content on the development of satiety. *Physiology & Behavior, 43*, 145-153.

Rolls, B. J., Hetherington, M. & Burley, V. J. (1988b). Sensory stimulation and energy density in the development of satiety. *Physiology & Behavior, 44*, 727-733.

Rolls, B. J., Laster, L. J., & Summerfelt, A. (1989). Hunger and food intake following consumption of low-calorie foods. *Appetite, 13*, 115-127.

Rolls, B. J., Rolls, E. T., & Rowe, E. A. (1982). The influence of variety on food selection and intake in man. In L. M. Barker (Ed.), *Psychobiology of Human Food Selection* (pp. 101-122). Westport, CT: A.V.I. Publishing Co.

Rolls, B. J., Rolls, E. T., Rowe, E. A., & Sweeney, K. (1981). Sensory specific satiety in man. *Physiology & Behavior, 27*, 137-142.

Rolls, B. J., Rowe, E. A., & Rolls, E. T. (1982). How sensory properties of foods affect human feeding behavior. *Physiology & Behavior, 27*, 137-142.

Rolls, B. J., Rowe, E. A., Rolls, E. T., Kingston, B., Megson, A., & Gunary, R. (1981). Variety in a meal enhances food intake in man. *Physiology & Behavior, 31*, 21-27.

Rolls, B. J., van Duijvenvoorde, P. M., & Rolls, E. T. (1984). Pleasantness changes and food intake in a varied four-course meal. *Appetite, 5*, 337-348.

Rolls, E. T. (1984). The neurophysiology of feeding. *International Journal of Obesity, 8* (Suppl. 1), 139-150.

Rolls, E. T., Rolls, B. J., & Rowe, E. A. (1983). Sensory-specific and motivation-specific satiety for the sight and taste of food and water in man. *Physiology & Behavior, 30*, 185-192.

Wooley, O. W., Wooley, S. C., & Dunham, R. B. (1972). Calories and sweet taste: Effects on sucrose preference in the obese and nonobese. *Physiology & Behavior, 9*, 765-768.

Yaxley, S., Rolls, E. T., Sienkiewicz, J., & Scott, T. R. (1985). Satiety does not affect gustatory activity in the nucleus of the solitary tract of the alert monkey. *Brain Research, 347*, 85-93.

Young, R. C., Gibbs, J., Antin, J., Holt, H., & Smith, G. P. (1974). Absence of satiety during sham feeding in the rat. *Journal of Comparative and Physiological Psychology, 87*, 795-800.

Yudkin, J. (1956, May 12). Man's choice of food. *Lancet*, 645-649.

CHAPTER 15

PALATABILITY AS A DETERMINANT OF EATING: FINICKINESS AS A FUNCTION OF TASTE, HUNGER, AND THE PROSPECT OF GOOD FOOD

PATRICIA PLINER, C. PETER HERMAN, AND JANET POLIVY

Our goal is to review the effects of palatability on food intake in humans, although we reserve the right to refer occasionally to the animal literature. In its simplest form, the issue is not a particularly interesting one since the conclusion is obvious—under ordinary circumstances, people eat more palatable than unpalatable food. However, it is possible to make the question more interesting and the answer less obvious by considering the relative effects of palatability on individuals differing in nutritional status. Thus our more specific question becomes does palatability differentially affect the amount of food consumed by individuals who are obese, underweight, dieting, hungry, or starving, in comparison to those who are of normal weight, not dieting, not hungry, or not starving? For the moment, and for the sake of convenience, we have lumped together groups who might be considered to be of "aberrant" nutritional status. For all but the first group (the obese), a seemingly obvious common characteristic is a chronic or acute low level of food intake. As for the obese, it has been argued that they too may be chronically deprived or biologically underweight (Cabanac & Duclaux 1970a; Nisbett, 1972); and even if they are not actually suppressing their weight, in many respects they resemble (behaviorally) those who are chronically deprived. To facilitate evaluation of the evidence, we will transform the question into an empirically verifiable proposition: In terms of amount eaten, individuals of aberrant nutritional status are more responsive to variations in palatablity than are

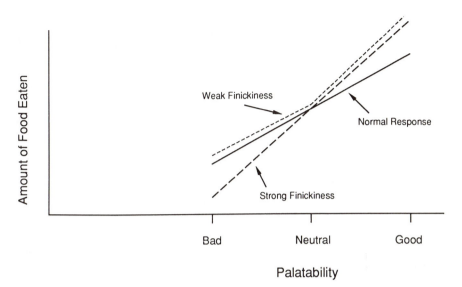

Figure 1 Two types of finickiness.

those of "normal" nutritional status. Or, to use a term perhaps more familiar to those who deal with the animal literature, the aberrant groups of interest are more finicky than are appropriate controls.

Evidence for differential finickiness is of two types. The first examines the difference in amount eaten of high and low palatable food, with greater finickiness represented by a larger difference score. The second examines the difference between groups at different levels of palatability; greater finickiness would be demonstrated if the aberrant groups ate more good tasting and/or less bad tasting food than controls. If our aberrant groups eat more good tasting food but no less bad tasting food, then their finickiness could be said to take a "weak" form, indicating that obese, underweight, dieting, hungry, and starving people eat more, but only if the food is highly palatable. If our aberrant groups eat more good tasting food and also eat less bad-tasting food, then their finickiness takes a "strong"form (see Figure 1). In examining the literature, whenever possible we have looked for evidence of differential finickiness in terms of both the within-groups difference score and the between-groups comparisons at each level of palatability; in some cases, however, our examination is curtailed by incomplete data presentation.

Two different animal literatures lead us to expect that individuals differing in nutritional status might be differentially responsive to variations in palatability.

This research was supported by grants from the Natural Sciences and Engineering Research Council of Canada and the Social Sciences and Humanities Research Council of Canada.

First, there is the research showing that rats with ventromedial hypothalamus (VMH) lesions become both obese and more finicky than controls, responding more positively to palatable food and more negatively to unpalatable food (Corbitt & Stellar, 1964; Cruce, Greenwood, Johnson, & Quartermain, 1974; Graff & Stellar, 1962; Teitelbaum, 1955). Second, it has been shown that food-deprived animals, contrary to the common sense notion that deprivation should make nonenergy-related aspects of food (such as taste) less important, are more finicky than nondeprived animals, eating more good tasting and less bad tasting food (Jacobs & Sharma, 1969). As for human eating behavior, Schachter (1971) explicitly predicts that obese individuals should be especially responsive to the external cue of taste and eat more palatable and less unpalatable food than normal individuals; much of the research we will review was designed specifically to test Schachter's theory. Nisbett, writing in 1972, after reviewing the human literature to that date, persuasively argued that the empirical resemblance between VMH-lesioned rats, food-deprived animals, and obese humans was not accidental and that similar aspects of their behavior, including finickiness, shared a common etiology—hunger.

Before we proceed, we must deal with two important "side" issues. Our proposition treats palatability conceptually as an independent variable, which potentially affects food intake differently in different groups. However, there is much literature treating palatability as a dependent variable and examining group differences in hedonic responses to various taste stimuli. The second issue concerns possible group differences in such nonhedonic aspects of taste perception as the ability to detect taste stimuli or the perception of their intensity. If such group differences exist, it follows that manipulations of palatability might be differentially detectable or perceived differently by various groups of subjects. Clearly, such hedonic or perceptual differences would make interpretation of intake data complicated, since intended variations in palatability might not be equivalent for the various groups.

In order to determine the existence of such possible differences, we surveyed the relevant taste perception and taste hedonics literatures, and present here our conclusions rather than the details of our review. The data pertaining to group differences in taste perception are unusually consistent. Taken as a whole, the research has not convincingly demonstrated differences either in the ability to detect or perceptions of intensity of the four basic tastes as a function of body weight, weight loss, or food deprivation.

The data are somewhat more complicated and less consistent when we consider the possibility of group differences in hedonic responses to taste stimuli. Most of the work in the area of hedonics has focussed on responses to sweet taste. While a few studies have purported to demonstrate an "aversion" to sweet taste in obese (as compared to normal) subjects (Enns, Van Itallie, & Grinker, 1979; Grinker, 1975, 1978; Grinker, Price, & Greenwood, 1976), these studies are unconvincing for several reasons and most studies have found no differences. The studies on the effects of weight loss and/or dieting on hedonic response to sweetness have shown all three possible patterns—an increase, a decrease, or no change. Much of the research on the effect of hunger on hedonic responses was conducted in the context of Cabanac's (1979) work on the negative alliesthesia for sweet taste which follows a glucose load in previously fasted subjects. These studies provide a clear demonstration that states of deprivation-satiation influence the palatability of sweet taste and would seem to provide just the sort of complication that would ambiguate interpretation of data on the effect of palatability on amounts consumed by hungry and nonhungry individuals. One additional fact makes the interpretive difficulty less acute; negative alliesthesia is fairly specific. For example, a glucose load substantially reduces the pleasantness of a sucrose solution, while a saline, lipid, or protein-lipid load does not (Cabanac & Duclaux, 1970b; Guy-Grand & Sitt, 1976). Thus to the extent that manipulations of hunger-satiety in the studies in the main body of our review do not require that subjects eat a food (to manipulate satiety) and then measure the amount eaten of the same or a similar food, negative alliesthesia would not appear to be a problem. Empirical justification for this lack of concern comes from a study in which subjects preloaded with one food did not rate other foods varying in palatability less positively than fasted ones (Nisbett, 1968).

In summary, after reviewing the available research on taste perception and taste hedonics, we do not believe that there are group differences that will compromise the interpretation of the literature on group differences in the effects of palatability on consumption which is the main focus of this chapter. Accordingly, we will now turn to the data relevant to the proposition that the aberrant groups are more finicky than are the appropriate controls. We will generally ignore the most consistent finding across these studies—that almost without exception, people eat more when the food is highly palatable than when it is not. That is, we will not bother to describe for each study the ubiquitous main effect of palatability. Our discussion will be organized in terms of the various relevant subject groups, beginning with comparisons of obese (and in one study, underweight) and normal weight subjects and then going on to studies involving dieting, hungry, and starving individuals.

OBESE-NORMAL COMPARISONS OF FINICKINESS

In the first study explicitly directed at weight differences in finickiness, Nisbett (1968) presented obese, normal, and underweight subjects with a highly palatable food (an excellent and expensive French vanilla ice cream) or an unpalatable food (an inexpensive vanilla ice cream liberally adulterated with quinine), instructing them to eat as much as they wished. In terms of the difference between the amount of good and bad ice cream eaten, the manipulation had the strongest effect on obese subjects, followed by normal and underweight subjects. For the obese-normal comparison, the effect occurred only with good ice cream: Obese subjects ate more good ice cream and the same amount of bad ice cream as normal weight subjects. There was no underweight-normal difference in the amount of good or bad ice cream eaten. In McKenna's (1972) study, obese and normal weight subjects were provided with either "extremely appetizing" or unappetizing cookies following an anxiety manipulation. The results for high anxiety conditions exactly replicated Nisbett's (1968) findings for obese and normal weight subjects, although in the low anxiety condition, there was no differential effect of the palatability manipulation on the two groups. In a conceptually similar study, Decke (cited in Schachter, 1971) presented obese and normal weight subjects with palatable and unpalatable (quinine-adulterated) milkshakes, permitting them to drink as much as desired in a "taste and rate" context. She obtained a marginally significant interaction between weight and palatability ($p = .07$); obese subjects responded more strongly to the manipulation, eating less bad and more good milkshake than normals.

Thus the three studies in which palatability was directly manipulated all found interactions between weight and palatablity indicative of greater finickiness in the obese. With respect to the separate comparisons for good and bad food, the proposition that the obese eat more good food than normals was statistically confirmed in two studies (McKenna, 1972; Nisbett, 1968) and nearly so in a third (Decke, 1971). The proposition that obese individuals eat less bad-tasting food than normals was not confirmed in two studies (McKenna, 1972; Nisbett, 1968) and was confirmed in the third (Decke, cited in Schachter, 1971).

In several other studies, palatability was not manipulated but defined in terms of subjects' behavior—their ratings or consumption. Price and Grinker (1973) obtained liking ratings for five types of crackers from massively obese subjects and normal controls during a "tasting" task. The slope of the function relating grams of crackers eaten to liking was significantly greater for obese subjects, who also ate significantly more crackers overall than normals and ate more at every point of preference. Similar results were obtained by Rodin, Slochower, and Fleming (1977) who measured intake of individually defined, highly palatable and unpalatable flavors of ice milk. In a study by Spiegel, Shrager, and Stellar (1989), weight and preference interacted in the same manner ($p = .09$); obese subjects ate more of the highly preferred and very slightly less of the nonpreferred food. Hill and McCutcheon (1975) served high and low preference test meals to obese and normal subjects, obtaining a significant interaction between weight and preference. Obese subjects ate more of the high preference food and less of the low preference food than did normals. Unfortunately, in neither this study nor the previous three were statistical comparisons made of the magnitudes of the differences in consumption between obese and normal subjects for the preferred and nonpreferred foods. Nisbett (1968), analyzing some unpublished data from a study by Schachter, Goldman, and Gordon (1968), compared amounts eaten of positively versus negatively rated crackers. For obese subjects, the discrepancy between the two was significant while for normals it was not; obese subjects ate nonsignificantly more of the positively rated crackers and nonsignificantly less of the negatively rated crackers than normals. Bellisle and Le Magnen (1981) presented five different test meals consisting of bites of bread topped with various spreads and considered the high and low palatability meals to be those at which the most and the least (on an individual subject basis) were consumed, respectively. Although normal subjects ate slightly more at both meals, there were no significant differences in the amounts consumed for either the high or the low palatability meals by obese and normal weight subjects. Ballard, Gipson, Guttenberg, and Ramsey (1980) examined the amount of food that children left over from prepackaged school lunches as a function of palatability (defined a priori in terms of food category) and weight. Overall, the children left five times as much of the foods in the designated unpalatable category, lending credence to the categorization. Palatability also interacted significantly with obesity in the now familiar manner; normal weight children left twice as much palatable food and the same amount of unpalatable food as obese children.

Analysis of palatable-unpalatable differences in these seven studies strongly supports the proposition that obese individuals are more responsive to variations in palatability than are those of normal weight. In terms of between groups comparisons, in none of the studies was there strong evidence for the proposition that obese subjects eat less unpalatable food than do normals. In none of the three cases in which the obese-normal difference was actually tested, was it significant (Ballard et al., 1980; Bellisle & Le Magnen, 1981; Nisbett, 1968), while in two of the remaining four studies, obese subjects actually ate more unpalatable food than did normals (Price & Grinker, 1973; Rodin et al., 1977). Evidence for the proposition that the obese eat more palatable food is more convincing; in all but one (Bellisle & Le Magnen, 1981) of seven studies, the data were in this direction and, when tested, it was significant in one of two cases (Ballard et al., 1980).

Several studies have examined obese and normal weight individuals in contexts in which the food is assumed (rather than manipulated or measured) to be low in palatability. Goldman, Jaffa, and Schachter (1968) found that obese students were significantly more likely than normals to drop out of a prepaid dormitory eating plan in which the food was described as being of "low quality." Hashim and Van Itallie (1965) reported that hospitalized obese subjects given only a bland, unappetizing liquid diet showed immediate precipitous drops in caloric intake from their pre-experimental baselines; this suppression lasted for periods ranging from a few weeks to a few months. In contrast, a few normal subjects, run for shorter periods, maintained their usual caloric intake. These results suggested that the obese (but not normals) refrain from eating if the only food available is low in palatability. However, it should be noted that motivation may have played a role here, since the obese subjects were in hospital to lose weight while the normal weight controls were in hospital to serve as controls. In a study using a similar liquid diet which was not done in a weight loss context, there were no differences between amounts consumed by obese and normal weight subjects (Wooley, 1971). In addition, Cabanac and Rabe (1976) showed that even subjects of normal weight decreased their ad libitum intake of a monotonous liquid diet over a 3-week period. Thus we cannot conclude that this research provides strong support for the notion that obese individuals eat less bad tasting food than normals.

Finickiness in Infants

A number of studies have measured neonates' intake of solutions varying in sweetness (e.g., Milstein, 1980). If we assume that increases in sweetness are functionally equivalent to increases in palatability, these studies come into our purview. While all of these studies were concerned with the effect of sweetness on the eating behavior of neonates varying in body weight, they nevertheless differed in a number of ways that make comparisons difficult. First, they differed widely in terms of their conceptualizations of weight, characterizing infants on the basis of birth weight, ponderosity (weight corrected for length), skinfold thickness, and forearm circumference. Second, these measures were sometimes used to create heavy, medium, or light categories, which do not necessarily correspond from study to study or even within the same study; in other cases, weight was treated as a continuous variable and was correlated with measures of consumption. Third, the measures of consumption also differed from study to study. In some cases, investigators measured the amount consumed during a regular feeding; in others, they measured the amount consumed during a brief time-limited test. In one study, the measure was not even consumption but rather pressure of the expressive component of the sucking response. Thus in many studies, the measure was better characterized as the avidity of eating rather than amount consumed. Fourth, in some cases, the food stimulus consisted of milk-based infant formula while in others infants were presented with simple solutions of various sugars in water. Finally, in some cases the data were presented in terms of the amounts of various stimuli consumed while in others infants were assigned difference scores based on the difference between consumption of plain water and a sweet stimulus. With these complications in mind, we will try to make some sense of the data. It will be useful to keep in mind that, although no independent measures of palatablity were obtained, we are probably dealing with palatability on the positive side of the continuum; in no case were infants presented with foods which had been adulterated to make them unpalatable. Thus the data are not really relevant to the proposition that the obese eat less bad tasting food than normals.

Nisbett and Gurwitz (1970) divided "full-term" infants into three groups on the basis of birth weight (heaviest: birthweight > 3,540 g, midpoint = 4,290 g; medium: birthweight 2,881–3,540 g, midpoint = 3,210 g; lightest: birthweight < 2,881 g, midpoint = 2,690 g). They then measured intake at one feeding where the babies were offered the hospital's standard formula and at another where a calorically identical but substantially sweeter tasting version was available. Confirming the notion that palatability covaries with sweetness, babies in all three groups consumed more of the sweetened formula. In addition, the effect of the palatability manipulation was greater for the heaviest group of infants (who consumed 28% more of the sweetened formula) in comparison to the medium and light infants combined (for whom the difference was 8%). It appeared that in comparison to the medium infants, the heavy infants consumed much more of the highly palatable and very slightly less of the less palatable formula. When weight corrected for length was used as the measure of obesity, it did not predict response to sweet taste. Desor, Maller, and Turner (1973) offered infants one of four concentrations of sucrose, glucose, fructose, or lactose and plain water, and measured the volume ingested. Heavier (birthweight > 3,175 g, midpoint = 3,563 g) babies showed a greater relative preference than lighter (birthweight < 2,722 g, midpoint = 2,535 g) babies for the sugar solution as compared to water, drinking slightly more water and substantially more sugar solution. In a comparison of two additional groups (heavier: birthweight > 3,486 g, midpoint = 3,782 g; lighter: birthweight < 3,175 g, midpoint = 2,737 g), weight was not related to relative preference. Engen, Lipsitt, and Robinson (1978) presented newborns with water and one of six glucose or sucrose solutions and measured the number of sucks of each in standard 6-min test periods. There was a significant correlation between birthweight and number of sucks per minute for the sweet solutions ($r=.32$, $n=93$) and a smaller, nonsignificant correlation for water ($r=.13$; the two correlations are not significantly different). Beauchamp and Moran (1982) tested neonates on 1-min consumption tests of plain water and two sucrose solutions, finding that intake of both sweetened solutions, but not plain water, was positively correlated with absolute weight and body mass index (BMI). To pursue these findings further, they selected the subjects in one of their subpopulations who were heaviest (M = 3,790 g), lightest (M = 2,440 g), and closest to the mean (M = 3,140), performed a two-way analysis of variance, and found an interaction between weight groups and solution. The lightest infants drank less of the sweetened water than did medium and heavy infants but the same amount of plain water. When the experimenters retested 69% of these babies at 6 months, placing each into his or her original weight group, there was no longer an interaction between weight and solution, nor was there any relationship between various measures of current body size (including weight gain) and amounts ingested of the various stimuli. Milstein (1980) measured the avidity (in terms of the expressive component of the sucking response) with which infants consumed constant amounts of three increasingly sweet glucose solutions and found that degree of fatness (as measured by BMI and skinfold thickness [SFT]) interacted with type of solution. Medium and heavy infants increased amounts consumed with increasing sweetness, while the thin infants showed little effect, decreasing slightly at the highest level of sweetness.

Overall, the data on infants' reactions to sweet solutions are consistent with the notion that responsiveness to palatability increases with increasing weight. It is difficult in these studies to designate particular groups of infants as obese, normal, or underweight since in some cases birthweight (uncorrected for length) was the basis for classification, whereas in others the data are presented as correlations between weight and consumption. There is some disagreement about exactly which aspect of weight is most strongly related to responsiveness. One study found that absolute weight was related while a ponderosity index (weight/length^3) was not (Nisbett & Gurwitz, 1970); another found that both were related (Beauchamp & Moran, 1982). Milstein's (1980) data showed a relationship using BMI and skinfold thickness but not using absolute weight. Two other studies (Desor et al., 1973; Engen et al., 1978) reported positive results for absolute weight but did not mention analyses using other measures. Furthermore, whereas one study found differences between the heavier infants on the one hand and medium and lighter ones on the other (Nisbett & Gurwitz, 1970), in three others it appears to be the lighter infants who are discrepant (Beauchamp & Moran, 1982; Desor et al., 1973; Engen et al., 1978). Despite these differences in details, however, it appears that in neonates responsiveness to sweet taste is positively related to some aspect of body weight. These data are probably not relevant to the question of response to bad tasting food, since the most unpalatable substance presented to infants in any of the studies was plain water; but the evidence strongly suggests that relatively heavier babies eat more good food than do relatively lighter ones.

Weight Suppression and Finickiness

The majority of studies examining responsiveness to palatability in adults have compared currently obese and normal subjects, but several others have looked at the effects of dieting and weight loss on finickiness. Rodin et al. (1977) measured the amount of individually defined, palatable and unpalatable ice milk consumed by a group of obese women before and after loss of at least 15% of body weight. In terms of the difference between amount of preferred and nonpreferred ice milk consumed, subjects were significantly more responsive to palatability after weight loss than before. The amount of palatable and unpalatable food eaten after weight loss increased by 26% and 8%, respectively; however, these differences were not tested statistically. Woody, Costanzo, Liefer, and Conger (1981) presented dieting and nondieting, normal weight subjects with palatable and unpalatable (quinine-adulterated) milkshakes after they had consumed no preload, a preload described as low in calories, or a preload described as high in calories. In the condition most conducive to disinhibited eating among dieters—that is, after eating a preload perceived as highly caloric—dieters showed a greater response to palatability than nondieters, eating significantly more palatable ice cream but the same amount of unpalatable ice cream. In the other two preload conditions, the two groups were not differentially responsive to palatability. Similarly, Herman, Polivy, and Werry (1989) gave palatable and quinine-adulterated milkshakes to dieters (who were not disinhibited) and nondieters and found they did not differ in finickiness. These three studies support the proposition that disinhibited (but not inhibited) dieters and people who have lost weight are more responsive to palatability than are appropriate controls; this responsiveness, however, is a matter of greater consumption of good food rather than lesser consumption of bad food.

Hunger and Finickiness

We come finally to the last set of studies in our review, those looking at the effect of hunger on responsiveness to palatability. We have ordered the studies roughly on the basis of how hungry subjects in the high hunger condition were, from least to most hungry. Again, we are concerned with interactions between palatability and hunger and with simple main effects of hunger for particular levels of palatability. Herman et al. (1989) asked moderately deprived (at least 3 hr) and nonhungry subjects to drink enough milkshake to "comfortably fill [themselves] up for the next part of the experiment." The milkshake was either very palatable or a quinine-adulterated version of the same drink. They obtained a significant interaction between palatability and hunger, such that hungry subjects drank slightly (but not significantly) more of the good tasting milkshake and significantly less of the bad tasting milkshake. Nisbett's (1968) study, described earlier, also included a manipulation of deprivation. Subjects came to the experiment food deprived (at least 4 hr), were either preloaded or not, and then had an opportunity to eat palatable or unpalatable ice cream. Unlike Herman et al. (1989), there was not a hint of an interaction between hunger and palatability: Hungry subjects ate significantly more good ice cream than full ones, and the difference for bad ice cream consumption was in the same direction and marginally significant.

Testing newborns immediately before and after a feeding, Desor, Maller, and Greene (1977) observed that deprivation increased consumption but not differentially for sweet solutions versus plain water. Subjects in a study by Bellisle, Lucas, Amrani, and Le Magnen (1984) received test meals consisting of high or low preference foods under conditions of high (15 hr) and low (1 hr) deprivation. Again, preference and hunger did not interact. In a pair of similar studies Hill (1974) and Hill and McCutcheon (1975) served test meals high and low in preference to subjects after 1 or 18 hr of food deprivation, and obtained no evidence for a hunger-preference interaction.

Seaton and Peryam (1970) studied soldiers on snowshoe treks in Greenland under conditions of high deprivation (a 10-day cycle with 2,400 kcal/day available) and low deprivation (4,800 kcal/day). They found that the correlation between average food preference and consumption was lower under high deprivation, suggesting a reduction rather than an increase in finickiness under conditions of hunger. Similarly, Keys, Brozek, Henschel, Mickelsen and Taylor (1950), in their study of semi-starvation, noted that "[i]ndividual food dislikes for such diet items as rutabagas and fish disappeared in the early part of the semi-starvation period" (p. 832). Presumably they meant that these dislikes ceased to affect food consumption since they then quoted the saying attributed to Horace, "Jejunus raro stomachus vulgaria temnit" (A hungry stomach rarely scorns common foods) (Keys et al., 1950, p. 832). Finally, the anecdotal literature on starvation (e.g. Berton, 1988; Keys et al., 1950) suggests that when in extremis, people will eat virtually anything, including such presumably unpalatable substances as human flesh, insects, moldy or rotten food, garbage, roots, and even clothing and shoes.

CONCLUSIONS

What can we make of these data? More specifically, what support is there for the empirical propositions we put forward earlier? Let us begin with the within-groups version of our proposition, that nutritionally aberrant groups are more responsive to variations in palatability than are normal controls. Overall, the data would appear to support the proposition. Of ten studies comparing obese and normal subjects, nine showed greater good food-bad food differences for obese subjects than for their normal counterparts. Neonates' reactions to sweet solutions also suggest that responsiveness to palatability increases with increasing weight. Of the three studies assessing dieters or those who had recently lost weight, two demonstrated greater responsiveness to palatability in those groups. The studies involving moderately food-deprived subjects show the weakest evidence for differential response to palatability. Of seven studies described, only one showed clear evidence for the effect. Finally, the studies on starving subjects (including the Greenland trekkers) and the anecdotal evidence on starvation suggest that palatability has less effect under conditions of extreme deprivation.

Reviewing the data once again, this time for evidence of between group differences in responses to good tasting and bad tasting food, it seems clear that in nearly all the cases in which group-palatability interactions were found, the nutritionally aberrant group ate more good tasting food than did the normal controls. Evidence for negative finickiness was much rarer. However, we would like to argue that despite the many studies examining finickiness in humans, negative finickiness has rarely been tested. With a few exceptions, to which we shall return, the unpalatable foods presented to subjects have not, in all likelihood, been bad tasting in an absolute sense; that is, they have not been on the negative side of some hedonically neutral point (or at least not very far from neutral), but rather have simply been relatively less palatable than the positive foods used. Thus as shown in Figure 1, most existing research has examined only the portion of the figure to the right of neutral; and of course, if one compares the expected consumption of a hedonically neutral food with that of a hedonically positive food, one would obtain the pattern of data shown in most studies—greater consumption of the highly palatable food and equal consumption of the less palatable food—regardless of whether the finickiness were weak or strong.

In a very few studies, however, otherwise good tasting food has been made truly unpalatable by the addition of quinine, which most people find clearly aversive in the quantities used. Let us examine these studies closely for evidence of negative finickiness. We first note that in the four studies in which quinine was used, the range of amounts used was enormous. In Nisbett's (1968) study, comparing obese and normal subjects, there was no sign of negative finickiness in the obese. However, Nisbett seems to have outdone himself in presenting to his subjects a concoction so vile that no researcher since has used a concentration of quinine nearly so high (2.5 g quinine/quart of ice cream). Woody et al. (1981), also finding no evidence for negative finickiness in dieters, used only half as much quinine (1.2 g quinine/quart of ice cream), but still offered their subjects a dish for which only someone suffering from a serious case of malaria could have any real affection. In both studies, the amount of ice cream eaten by all subjects receiving the doctored ice cream was only about 50 g, an amount which led Schachter (1971) to suggest, in discussing Nisbett's results, that they were simply eating the minimum amount possible while conforming to the experimental requirement to taste and rate. Decke (cited in Schachter, 1971) used only a fraction as much quinine (.04 g quinine/quart of milkshake) and found that obese subjects ate significantly less than normal weight subjects, and Herman et al. (1989), who added .24 g quinine/quart of milkshake, found that food-deprived subjects ate significantly less than nondeprived subjects. This pattern suggests that we may extend our figure depicting the relationship between palatability and amount consumed (Figure 1), beyond bad tasting food to the truly vile, where we might expect all subjects to eat equal amounts—basically nothing—or nothing beyond experimental requirements (see Figure 2).

Although there are only these two studies with strong evidence for negative finickiness, we are inclined to argue that it exists, but only within a relatively narrow range of negative palatability—somewhere between neutral and food so aversive that all subjects eat virtually nothing. Within this narrow range, at least two kinds of our nutritionally aberrant individuals (obese [Decke, 1971] and hungry [Herman et al., 1989]) show both positive and negative finickiness. As for the obese, Schachter's original theory predicted this outcome (Schachter, 1971). The obese were assumed to be unresponsive to internal cues, which vary

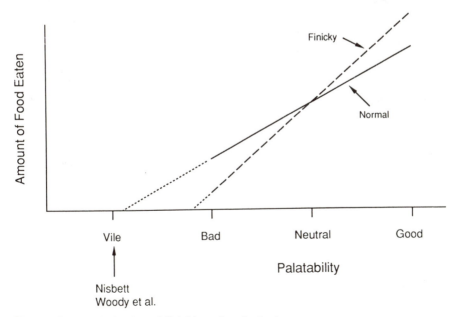

Figure 2 The elimination of finickiness by vile food.

as a function of nutritional status, and instead eat in response to external cues, factors related to food and eating but having nothing to do with nutritional status. Palatability was assumed to be an external cue, and positive palatability was expected to have an exaggerated positive effect on eating while negative palatability was expected to have an exaggerated negative effect. In the present context, this explanation is not very parsimonious since it doesn't account for the similar behavior of food-deprived individuals; but if we assume for the moment, following others (Cabanac & Duclaux, 1970a; Nisbett, 1972), that the obese are chronically food deprived, then it appears that food-deprived individuals, whether the deprivation be chronic or acute, not only eat more good tasting food but also eat less bad tasting food than those who are not deprived. There is nothing startling about food deprivation causing people to eat more good tasting food; many theories make this prediction. But that deprivation causes people to eat even less bad tasting food seems to fly in the face of common sense. People who are hungry, who are nutritionally "in trouble," should presumably be less likely to be deterred from eating by negative palatability, a seemingly nutrition-irrelevant aspect of food. Nevertheless, it is possible to make sense of this "paradoxical" finding; Nisbett (1972), for one, has already offered some potential solutions.

We begin with the premise that sweetness is innately palatable and that this reaction is adaptive since, under ordinary circumstances, sweet substances tend to be good sources of calories (Rozin & Vollmecke, 1986). To paraphrase Cabanac's dictum, "pleasant equals useful." Thus the hungry organism is especially motivated to eat good tasting food, and will eat more than usual if it is available. But if only bad tasting (i.e., less useful) food is available, the organism must make a decision: eat now or wait for something better (more useful). If good tasting food will be available in the not-too-distant future, then waiting may be a more beneficial strategy. If, however, bad taste signals not particularly useful, calorically dilute food, then filling up on it might actually reduce overall caloric intake by the hungry organism insofar as it inhibits its capacity to gorge on good tasting food when it becomes available. Thus when confronted with bad tasting food, the hungry animal, faced with an "eat now or wait for better" decision is biased in the "wait" direction as long as there is a reasonable likelihood of obtaining better food in the near future. Presumably, this is the situation that obtained in the two experiments in which evidence for negative finickiness was found (Decke, cited in Schachter, 1971; Herman et al., 1989). The acutely hungry and chronically hungry (obese) subjects, when faced with bad tasting food, ate little, exercising their option to wait for something better. It might be argued that missing a meal (as in Herman et al., 1989) is not enough of a threat to one's nutritional well-being to require extremely close attention to the caloric value of food as indexed by its palatability; nevertheless, it is possible that even short-term hunger may be interpreted as a prelude to long-term hunger, and therefore activate the defense of finickiness.

There are two situations in which we think organisms will be unlikely to make the "wait for better" decision, choosing instead to "eat now." Although

ordinarily they are confounded, it is possible to conceptualize them separately.
The first occurs when the organism is extraordinarily food deprived, near starvation. In such a case, even if there were a reasonable prospect of "good" food in
the near future, the organism might not be willing to gamble on waiting; death
might arrive before dinner. The second situation arises when there is virtually no
hope of better food, "waiting for better" is futile and the individual eats whatever
is available. In a sense, much of the anecdotal literature on starvation describes
situations in which both are true—individuals are near starvation and there is no
hope of better food (Berton, 1988; Keys et al., 1950). In such circumstances it
is no surprise to learn that people will eat even the inedible. Figure 3 depicts this
more complex view of eating as a function of palatability, degree of hunger, and
the probability of better food in the near future.

This explanation assumes that, in nature, taste, rather than simply being a
nutrition-irrelevant aspect of a food, conveys information about its nutritional
value. This information serves to help the organism make its "eat now or wait"
decision. It is also possible that palatability can provide useful information
regarding another characteristic of food—its safety. Bitterness, an innately unpalatable flavor, is often associated with the presence of toxicity, and the flavor and
odor of decay, also aversive to adult humans, may predict the presence of dangerous microorganisms. Although avoiding dangerous foods is probably a good idea
for everyone, hungry organisms may be particularly vulnerable to poisoning.
First, poisonous or contaminated foods may be more lethal when they are not

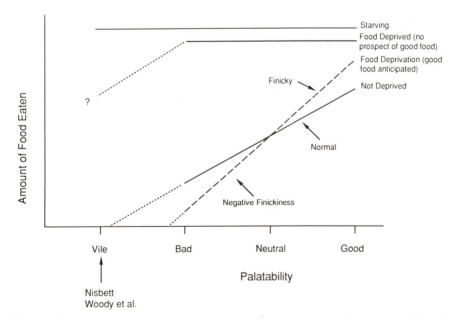

Figure 3 Finickiness as a function of palatability, hunger, and the prospect of good
food.

buffered by a full stomach of more benign material. Moreover, as Nisbett (1972) suggests, ingestion of lethal amounts of dangerous material is more likely in the case of an animal that is desperate to eat and therefore gorges itself. Thus, it would be in the interest of a hungry animal to be biased in the direction of caution, and palatability would convey information to help the organism make an "eat now or wait for safer" decision.

Our explanation of negative finickiness goes beyond Nisbett's (1972) primarily in that we have added some qualifications regarding how unpalatable the food must be, how hungry the organism must be, and how probable it must be that good tasting food will soon be available. If all these conditions are right, then the elusive negative finickiness may appear. Our view, building as it does on Nisbett's (1972) proposal, shares his reliance on highly speculative functionalistic arguments, which are notoriously slippery. Researchers are now faced with two questions: First, can they reliably demonstrate negative finickiness if (a) the food is unpalatable but not too unpalatable, (b) the organism is hungry but not too hungry, and (c) good tasting food is available but not right away? Second, can they provide a cogent explanation for the phenomenon, based (if necessary) on the function of the response, but preferably without having to depend entirely on the wisdom of nature's grand design?

References

Ballard, B. D., Gipson, M. T., Guttenberg, W., & Ramsey, K. (1980). Palatability of food as a factor influencing obese and normal-weight children's eating habits. *Behavior Research and Therapy, 18,* 598-600.

Beauchamp, G. K., & Moran M. (1982). Dietary experience and sweet taste preferences in human infants. *Appetite, 3,* 139-152.

Bellisle, F., & Le Magnen, J. (1981). The structure of meals in humans: Eating and drinking patterns in lean and obese subjects. *Physiology & Behavior, 27,* 649-658.

Bellisle, F., Lucas, F., Amrani, R., & Le Magnen, J. (1984). Deprivation, palatability, and the micro-structure of meals in human subjects. *Appetite, 5,* 85-94.

Berton, P. (1988). *The Arctic Grail.* Toronto, Canada: McClelland and Stewart.

Cabanac, M. (1979). Sensory pleasure. *Quarterly Review of Biology, 54,* 1-29.

Cabanac, M. & Duclaux, R. (1970a). Obesity: Absence of satiety aversion to sucrose. *Science, 168,* 496-497.

Cabanac, M., & Duclaux, R. (1970b). Specificity of internal signals in producing satiety for taste stimuli. *Nature, 227,* 966-967.

Cabanac, M., & Rabe, E. F. (1976). Influence of a monotonous food on body weight regulation in humans. *Physiology & Behavior, 17,* 675-678.

Corbitt, J., & Stellar, E. (1964) Palatability, food intake, and obesity in normal and hyperphagic rats. *Journal of Comparative and Physiological Psychology, 58,* 63-67.

Cruce, J. A. F., Greenwood, M. R. C., Johnson, P. R., & Quartermain, D. (1974). Genetic versus hypothalamic obesity: Studies of intake and dietary manipulations in rats. *Journal of Comparative and Physiological Psychology, 87,* 295-301.

Desor, J. A., Maller, O., & Green, L. S. (1977). Preference for sweet in humans: Infants, children, and adults. In J. M. Weiffenbach (Ed.), *Taste and development: The genesis of sweet preference* (pp. 161-172). Washington, DC: U.S. Government Printing Office.

Desor, J. A., Maller, O., & Turner, R. E. (1973). Taste in acceptance of sugars by human infants. *Journal of Comparative and Physiological Psychology, 84,* 496–501.

Engen, T., Lipsitt, L. P., & Robinson, D. O. (1978). The human newborn's sucking behavior for sweet fluids as a function of birthweight and maternal weight. *Infant Behavior and Development, 1,* 118–121.

Enns, M. P., Van Itallie, T. B., & Grinker, J. A. (1979). Contributions of age, sex, and degree of fatness on preferences and magnitude estimations for sucrose in humans. *Physiology & Behavior, 22,* 999–1003.

Goldman, R., Jaffa, M., & Schachter, S. (1968). Yom Kippur, Air France, dormitory food, and the eating behavior of obese and normal persons. *Journal of Personality and Social Psychology, 10,* 117–123.

Graff, H., & Stellar, E. (1962) Hyperphagia, obesity, and finickiness. *Journal of Comparative and Physiological Psychology, 55,* 418–424.

Grinker, J. (1975). Obesity and taste: Sensory and cognitive factors in food intake. In G. A. Bray (Ed.), *Obesity in perspective: Vol. 2 (pp. 73–80).* Washington, DC: Department of Health, Education, and Welfare.

Grinker, J. (1978). Obesity and sweet taste. *American Journal of Clinical Nutrition, 31,* 1078–1087.

Grinker, J., Price, J., & Greenwood, M. R. C. (1976). Studies of taste in childhood obesity. In D. Novin, W. Wywricka, & G. A. Bray (Eds.), *Hunger: Basic mechanisms and clinical implications.* New York: Raven Press.

Guy-Grand, B., & Sitt, Y. (1976). Origine de l'alliesthésie gustative: Effets comparés de charges orales glucosées ou protido-lipidiques [Origin of gustatory alliesthesia: Comparative effects of oral glucose or protein lipid loads]. *Comptes-rendus de l'Académie des Sciences de Paris, 282,* 755–757.

Hashim, S. A., & Van Itallie, T. B. (1965). Studies in normal and obese subjects with a monitored food dispensing device. *Annals of the New York Academy of Sciences, 131,* 654–661.

Herman, C. P., Polivy, J., & Werry, E. (1989). Short-term hunger increases finickiness in humans. Unpublished manuscript.

Hill, S. W. (1974). Eating responses of humans during dinner meals. *Journal of Comparative and Physiological Psychology, 86,* 652–657.

Hill, S. W. & McCutcheon, N. B. (1975). Eating responses of obese and non-obese humans during dinner meals. *Psychosomatic Medicine, 37,* 395–401.

Jacobs, H. L., & Sharma, K. N. (1969). Taste versus calories: Sensory and metabolic signals in the control of food intake. *Annals of the New York Academy of Sciences, 157,* 1084–1125.

Keys, A., Brozek, J., Henschel, A., Mickelsen, O., & Taylor, H. L. (1950). *The biology of human starvation.* Minneapolis, MN: University of Minnesota Press.

McKenna, R. J. (1972). Some effects of anxiety level and food cues on the eating behavior of obese and normal subjects: A comparison of the Schachterian and psychosomatic conceptions. *Journal of Personality and Social Psychology, 22,* 311–319.

Milstein, R. M. (1980). Responsiveness in newborn infants of overweight and normal weight parents. *Appetite, 1,* 65–74.

Nisbett, R. E. (1968). Taste, deprivation, and weight determinants of eating behavior. *Journal of Personality and Social Psychology, 10,* 107–116.

Nisbett, R. E. (1972). Hunger, obesity, and the ventromedial hypothalamus. *Psychological Review, 79,* 433–453.

Nisbett, R. E., & Gurwitz, S. (1970). Weight, sex, and the eating behavior of human newborns. *Journal of Comparative and Physiological Psychology, 73,* 245–253.

Price, J. M., & Grinker, J. (1973). Effects of degree of obesity, food deprivation, and palatability on eating behavior of humans. *Journal of Comparative and Physiological Psychology, 85,* 265–271.

Rodin, J., Slochower, J., & Fleming, B. (1977). Effects of degree of obesity, age of onset, and weight loss on responsiveness to sensory and external stimuli. *Journal of Comparative and Physiological Psychology, 91,* 586–597.

Rozin, P., & Vollmecke, T. A. (1986). Food likes and dislikes. *Annual Review of Nutrition, 6,* 433–456.

Schachter, S. (1971). *Emotion, obesity, and crime.* New York: Academic Press.

Schachter, S., Goldman, R., & Gordon, A. (1968). The effects of fear, food deprivation, and obesity on eating. *Journal of Personality and Social Psychology, 10,* 91–97.

Seaton, R. W., & Peryam, D. R. (1970). Hunger, food preference, and consumption. *Human Factors, 12,* 515–522.

Spiegal, T. A., Shrager, E. E., & Stellar, E. (1989). Responses of lean and obese subjects to preloads, deprivation and palatability. *Appetite, 13,* 45–69.

Teitelbaum, P. (1955). Sensory control of hypothalamic hyperphagia. *Journal of Comparative and Physiological Psychology, 48,* 156–163.

Woody, E. Z., Costanzo, P. R., Leifer, H., & Conger, J. (1981). The effects of taste and caloric perceptions on the eating behavior of restrained and unrestrained subjects. *Cognitive Research and Therapy, 5,* 381–390.

Wooley, O. W. (1971). Long-term food regulation in the obese and nonobese. *Psychosomatic Medicine, 33,* 436–444.

CHAPTER 16

TASTE AND FOOD PREFERENCES IN HUMAN OBESITY

ADAM DREWNOWSKI

Human obesity is a complex multifactorial disorder with a wide range of antecedents and predisposing factors. Experts agree that genetic, biological, psychological, and sociocultural factors all contribute in different ways to the development and maintenance of the obese state. In recent years, research in the area of human obesity has become more interdisciplinary, increasingly drawing on molecular genetics, nutritional epidemiology, social and behavioral sciences, and other aspects of public health (National Academy of Sciences, 1989; Surgeon General's Report, 1988).

Yet to many health practitioners and the general public, obesity is caused solely by overeating. The prevailing view is that obese people find palatable, sweet foods hard to resist, and are unable to follow a sensible low-calorie diet. Overeating is regarded as a bad habit that can be broken through a combination of behavior therapy, peer-group support, and nutritional counseling. Leading weight reduction programs in the U.S. offer weekly behavior therapy sessions in addition to providing clients with low-fat, no-sugar, reduced-calorie diets.

The view that overeating is largely a psychological problem had its roots in Skinnerian behaviorism. Early formulations (Stuart & Davis, 1972) viewed overeating as maladaptive behavior that could be reshaped or modified in the course of therapy. If the reinforcing properties of palatable food could be minimized or eliminated, then behavior could be channelled toward other rewarding activities. Among key components of behavior modification were increased awareness of eating patterns, reduced exposure to problem situations, reduced susceptibility to the determinants of eating, and the development of new adaptive responses to food (Stunkard & Berthold, 1985). One underlying assumption was that obese people were somehow more vulnerable than normal weight persons to good tasting foods, and often continued eating whether they were hungry or not. Establishing behavioral control over food cues was the first step toward successful weight loss.

Some support for the notion that obese people were hypersensitive to the sensory aspects of food was provided by studies in social psychology. At one point, obese people were said to be highly influenced by environmental factors and therefore more "external" than normal weight individuals (Schachter & Rodin, 1974). Rather than attend to the internal cues of hunger and satiety, the obese were thought to be guided by such external factors as the taste and sight of food and the number of palatable food cues present (Nisbett, 1968; Schachter & Rodin, 1974). This hypersensitivity to external food cues was the supposed result of chronic deprivation and dieting that maintained body weight below its physiological set-point. Enhanced responsiveness to sweet taste was accordingly thought to be a characteristic of all obese individuals (Cabanac & Duclaux, 1970). The externality hypothesis led some investigators to propose that obese humans (and VMH-lesioned rats) were "finicky," eating more of good tasting but less of bad tasting foods than their normal weight counterparts (Nisbett, 1968).

However, the externality hypothesis soon outlived its usefulness (Rodin, 1978). As subsequent studies demonstrated, the obese as a group were no more external than anyone else (Rodin, 1978; Rodin, 1981a). Further, while some obese people liked the sweet taste of sugar, others who were equally obese did not (Drewnowski, 1983). Nor was there evidence that the obese had increased their responsiveness to external cues following weight loss, as the set-point hypothesis would require (Rodin et al., 1976; Rodin, 1981b). Furthermore, the finicky VMH-lesioned rat, once the leading animal model of obesity, lost much of its early promise for human obesity research. Animal models in which genetic predisposition to obesity interacts with hyperphagia and nutrient dependence are now thought to be more promising as well as more relevant to the human condition.

The view of human obesity has also changed. The realization that some human obesities represented metabolic disease states meant that bad eating habits could no longer be advanced as the sole explanation for overweight. The current thinking is that human obesities resemble animal models in following a continuum ranging from those that are familial and possibly genetic to those that may be diet-induced (Sclafani, 1985). The expression of obesity in a given individual can be conceptualized in terms of an interaction between genetic predisposition and environmental variables, including the palatability and nutrient composition of the diet.

The role of taste and food preferences has thus acquired new importance in obesity research. While earlier studies concentrated on comparing obese patients with normal weight controls, the current emphasis is on the use of taste and food preferences to characterize different subgroups of human obesity. For example, studies on the role of central neurotransmitters and endogenous opioid peptides in food selection (Blass, 1987; Wurtman, 1984) suggest that individual differences in central metabolism may account for differences in behavior even within the obese population. Individual experience may also play a major role. While some taste and food preferences may be innate, others may be acquired in later life, possibly as a function of prior exposure to various types of diet. Taste and food preferences may also be modified by the metabolic or physiological status of the organism. Animal data indicate, for example, that preferences for dietary fats may increase following repeated cycles of weight loss and weight regain (Reed, Contreras, Maggio, Greenwood, & Rodin, 1988). Although human data are scarce, there are suggestions that the diet of some obese adults is not elevated in calories, but may be richer in fat.

ANIMAL MODELS

Studies with animals provide the best evidence for interaction between genetic and dietary factors in the expression of obesity. Genetic models including the ob/ob mouse and the obese (fa/fa) Zucker rat gain excess weight through overeating of any diet, even laboratory chow (Bray & York, 1971) Although Zucker rats will select the bulk of their calories from fat when given a choice (Castonguay & Stern, 1983) nutrient composition of the diet has little additional effect on the expression of obesity. Furthermore, hyperphagia is not essential for the development of obesity in the Zucker rat: Food restricted obese Zuckers will still deposit excess fat tissue at the expense of lean body mass.

In contrast, obesity promoted by high-fat diets, sucrose solutions, or the so-called cafeteria diet generally involves hyperphagia and is highly dependent on diet composition (Sclafani & Springer, 1976). The best results are typically obtained with diets containing high proportions of sugar and fat. As summarized in Table 1, several investigators have used combinations of chocolate chip cookies, marshmallows, peanut butter, and sweetened condensed milk. Although such diets are composed of ostensibly palatable foods—at least to us—the degree of hyperphagia may be limited, and weight gain in rats often occurs in the absence of pronounced overeating (Bray, 1988).

One explanation for the obesity-promoting effects of palatable diets without

Table 1

OBESITY-PROMOTING DIETS

Cafeteria diet	Lab chow plus cookies, salami, cheese, bananas, marshmallows, candy, peanut butter, and sweetened condensed milk (Sclafani & Springer, 1976).
Snack food diet	Liquid formula (sweetened condensed milk and Sustacal), sugared cereal, banana, marshmallow, salami, cheese wafers, peanut butter, cookies and lab chow (Gale, Van Itallie, & Faust, 1981).
High fat/sugar diet	Lab chow plus chocolate chip cookies and sweetened condensed milk (Drewnowski, Cohen, Faust, & Grinker, 1984).

hyperphagia may be that such diets differ in caloric density, nutrient composition, and variety from standard laboratory chow. In addition, such diets are often rich in fat. Current research shows that fat-based diets are more efficient in promoting obesity than are carbohydrate-based diets (Flatt, Ravussin, Acheson & Jequier, 1985). While excess carbohydrate calories are lost as heat, excess fat calories fail to stimulate thermogenesis and tend to be deposited as body fat (Salmon & Flatt, 1985; Schwartz et al., 1985). Recent studies from Japan further show that the timing of intake may be important: sugar and fat provided in a single meal result in greater deposition of adipose tissue than equicaloric amounts of fat and sugar provided at different times of day (Suzuki & Tamura, 1988).

There is also evidence for interactions between rat strains and nutrient composition of the diet. While some rat strains (e.g., Osborne-Mendel) are highly responsive to high-fat feeding, other strains are resistant to dietary manipulations (Schemmel, Michelsen, & Gill, 1970). The response of the Sprague-Dawley rat is highly variable: some rats become obese when provided with palatable diets, while others do not. The VMH-lesioned rat is something of an anomaly: the development of obesity in hypothalamic-lesioned rats requires hyperphagia, but is relatively independent of the nutrient composition of the diet.

HUMAN OBESITIES

Studies of human obesities increasingly suggest that obesity represents a variety of syndromes and not all obese people are alike (Bray, 1978). Some obesities clearly represent a familial trait. It has been known for some time that obese parents are likely to have obese children, and that the probability of childhood obesity depends on whether one or both parents are obese (Garn, 1985). However, since family members also share both diet and environment, the evidence for genetic as opposed to familial factors was weak. More compelling data for a genetic component in obesity have been provided by studies of body fat distribution of monozygotic and dizygotic twins (Bouchard, 1988), and from adoption studies correlating body build of offspring with those of natural and adoptive parents (Stunkard et al., 1986). Recent studies suggest further that age at onset of obesity may be linked to familial risk (the proportion of first-degree relatives who are also obese). Childhood-onset (age < 10) obesity had high familial risk (Price et al., 1990) and age at onset may prove to be a useful marker for genetic types of human obesity.

There is also evidence for an interaction between genetic predisposition to obesity and exposure to environmental stimuli. Differential responses of pairs of twins to overfeeding (Poehlman et al., 1986) suggested that both genetics and early feeding experience play a role in the etiology of human obesity. Overfeeding may not even be necessary. Recent studies indicated that a reduced rate of energy expenditure among obese adults (Ravussin et al., 1988) and among infants of obese mothers (Roberts, Savage, Coward, Chew, & Lucas, 1988) may be a risk factor for body weight gain. Dieting and weight loss may also have significant effects. Studies with rats (Brownell, Greenwood, Stellar & Shrager, 1986) and more recently with male wrestlers (Steen, Opplinger, & Brownell, 1988) suggest that experience in the form of multiple cycles of weight loss and weight regain may lead to increased metabolic efficiency and greater energy storage. It is unclear at this point whether weight cycling in humans results in increased fat deposition and enhanced selection of a high-fat diet.

The potential subcategories of human obesity are summarized in Table 2. Human obesities represent a heterogeneous group of syndromes, and the etiology and ontogeny of the disease may vary widely across individuals. Consequently, there is no reason to expect all obese people to share common personality profiles, eating styles, diet habits, or food preferences. Not surprisingly, such similarities have never been found: obese people show as much individual variability as do lean people. As summarized below, studies on preferences for sweet solutions in obesity have for the most part failed to find a connection between taste responsiveness and the extent of overweight.

SENSORY STUDIES
Since food palatability has always been equated with sweet taste, most studies on taste preference have been conducted with sugar solutions, lemonade, or KoolAid® of varying sweetness (Grinker, Hirsch, & Smith, 1972; Witherly, Pangborn, & Stern, 1980). A limited number of studies made use of "real" foods such as milkshakes, canned peaches, or ice cream (Pangborn & Simone, 1958; Moskowitz, Kluter, Westerling, & Jacobs, 1974). A more recent focus has been on the combined role of sugar and fat in determining sensory preferences for sweet dessert-type foods (Drewnowski & Greenwood, 1983). The new generation of stimuli, shown in Table 3, combines different levels of sugar and fat in such food models as milkshakes, soft white cheese, cake frostings, and ice cream

Table 2

TYPES OF HUMAN OBESITY

Criteria	Options	
Familial risk	Low	High
Age at onset	Childhood (< 10 yrs)	Juvenile (10–20 yrs)
		Adult (> 20 yrs)
Extent of overweight	Mild (120–150%)	Moderate (150–200%)
		Massive (200% +)
Body fat distribution	Lower body	Upper body
Weight cycling	No	Yes

Table 3
SENSORY STIMULI USED IN PAST STUDIES

Sensory stimuli	Study
Glucose solution	Rodin, Moskowitz, & Bray (1976)
Sucrose solution	Grinker, Hirsch, & Smith (1972)
Carbonated soft drinks	Drewnowski et al., (1982)
Lemonade, apricot nectar	Witherly et al., (1982)
Canned peaches	Pangborn et al., (1959)
Vanilla ice cream	Pangborn, (1957)
Chocolate milkshakes	Rodin, Moskowitz, & Bray (1976)
Milk, cream, and sugar	Drewnowski & Greenwood, (1983)
Cottage/cream cheese blends	Drewnowski et al., (1989)
Fromage blanc	Drewnowski et al., (1987)
Cake frostings	Drewnowski & Schwartz, (1989)

(Drewnowski, Brunzell, Sande, Iverius, & Greenwood, 1985; Drewnowski, Shrager, Lipsky, Stellar, & Greenwood, 1989; Drewnowski & Schwartz, 1990).

Sensory evaluation studies typically distinguish between stimulus threshold, intensity judgments, and acceptability or hedonic preference ratings (Moskowitz et al., 1974). While intensity judgments follow the logarithm of sucrose concentration, acceptability ratings for sweetness can be highly variable. Some subjects prefer, while others dislike, sugar solutions of increasing sweetness intensity. The average response typically follows an inverted-U shape as preferences first increase with increasing sugar concentration, reaching a maximum at around 8–10% sucrose. Preferences than decline as sweeter stimuli are judged as increasingly less pleasant. Higher sucrose breakpoints are generally observed with solid food as compared to liquid foods (Moskowitz et al., 1974).

Do sensory preferences correlate with body weight? Attempts to link the acceptability of sweet solutions with body weight status have been largely unsuccessful (Gilbert and Hagen, 1988; Thompson, Moskowitz, & Campbell, 1976). Studies using sucrose solutions, sweetened KoolAid®, and chocolate milkshakes found no consistent relationship between sweet taste preferences and obesity (Grinker et al., 1972; Rodin, Moskowitz, & Bray, 1976). Large-scale consumer studies found no relationship between body weight and hedonic preferences for increasing concentrations of sugar in such foods as apricot nectar, canned peaches, lemonade, or vanilla ice cream, (Pangborn & Simone, 1958). In studies comparing obese and normal weight subjects, individual variability of hedonic response was far greater than any between group differences (Pangborn, Bos, & Stern, 1985; Witherly, Pangborn, & Stern, 1980).

Preferences for Sugar and Fat Mixtures

Hedonic responses to sweet solutions are not always a good index of preference for sweet, high-fat foods. Most "sweets" and other desserts are solids rather than liquids, and often contain fat as the principal source of calories. The acceptability of such foods is determined both by their sugar and their fat content (Drewnowski et al., 1989).

Recent studies have addressed the role of fat in relation to food acceptance (Drewnowski, 1987; Pangborn, Bos, & Stern, 1985; Tuorila and Pangborn, 1988). Although studies with sugar solutions had failed to find a relationship between sweet taste preferences and overweight, such a relationship might well hold for dietary fats. One early hypothesis (Drewnowski et al., 1985) was that sensory preferences for sugar versus fat within the same food system may help discriminate between clinical populations of women patients at extremes of body weight. (Drewnowski et al., 1985; Drewnowski, Halmi, Pierce, Gibbs, & Smith, 1987).

A series of sensory evaluations using 20 different mixtures of milk, cream, and sugar was conducted with massively obese women patients and with emaciated young women hospitalized for anorexia nervosa (Drewnowski et al., 1985; Drewnowski, Halmi, Pierce, Gibbs, & Smith, 1987). Additional responses were obtained from groups of age-matched, normal weight female controls. Subject characteristics are summarized in Table 4.

The subjects rated each stimulus in turn for its sweetness, creaminess, and perceived fat content. They also rated the acceptability of each sample on a 9-point category scale. The use of a mathematical modelling technique known as

Table 4

SUMMARY OF SUBJECT DATA AND COMPOSITION OF BEST TASTING SUGAR AND FAT MIXTURES

Subject group	N	Age (yrs)	Weight (kg)	Sucrose (%)	Fat (%)
Obese	12	38.0	95.8	4.4	34.5
Reduced obese	8	32.7	67.9	10.1	35.1
Normal weight	15	30.1	58.8	7.7	20.7
Normal weight	16	19.1	57.7	9.1	28.7
Bulimic	7	19.4	56.8	15.3	27.9
Anorectic	25	17.2	40.5	12.7	16.5

Data from "Sweet Tooth Reconsidered: Taste Preferences in Human Obesity" by A. Drewnowski et al., 1985, *Physiology & Behavior, 35* and "Taste and Eating Disorders" by A. Drewnowski, K. A. Halni, B. Pierce, J. Gibbs, and G. P. Smith, 1987, *American Journal of Clinical Nutrition, 46.* Copyright 1985 by Pergamon Press, Inc. and 1987 by American Society for Clinical Nutrition. Reprinted by permission.

the Response Surface Method allowed us to predict the shape of hedonic response for a wide range of ingredient levels (Drewnowski & Greenwood, 1983).

The response profile to the sugar and fat mixtures was strongly interactive. Preference ratings for sweetened skim milk or unsweetened dairy products were relatively low. However, the sugar and fat combination produced a potentiation of hedonic response. The highest ratings were obtained for a mixture estimated as containing 8% sugar and 20% fat. As shown in Table 4, the composition of the best-liked mixture varied among subject groups. Obese women tended to prefer stimuli that were rich in fat but relatively low in sugar. In contrast, anorectic women liked sweet taste, but showed an aversion to the oral sensation of dietary fats.

Sugar and fat mixtures are not only uniquely palatable; studies with animals show that they may also be uniquely fattening (Suzuki & Tamura, 1988). However, two questions remain. The first is whether sensory preferences for sugar and fat mixtures are influenced by metabolic or physiologic variables. The second is whether taste preferences can serve as an accurate index of food acceptability and therefore food consumption.

Metabolic Factors

Food preferences and food cravings are sometimes thought to be triggered by physiological or metabolic events. For example, it has been proposed that most obese people crave carbohydrates because they suffer from a deficiency in central serotonin metabolism (Wurtman, 1984). Selective consumption of carbohydrate-rich snacks supposedly promotes satiety and relieves depression and fatigue, but it also leads to overeating and continued weight gain. Although the sensory properties of such snacks should be relatively unimportant, the most common targets of food cravings are typically mixtures of sugar and fat, including chocolate candy (Snickers® and M&M's®), chocolate cupcakes, chocolate chip cookies, cakes, frozen pastries, and other desserts. Cravings for sweet dessert type foods have been observed among obese patients, bulimic women, and depressed patients, including those suffering from the seasonal affective disorder (Rosenthal, Genhart, Jacobsen, Skwerer, & Wehr, 1987). Carbohydrate craving and weight gain were reported as side effects of amitryptiline treatment (Paykel, Mueller, & de la Vergne, 1973).

The involvement of opioid peptides, pleasure enhancing molecules manufactured by the human brain, may provide another explanation for food cravings. One early study in this area (Margules et al, 1978) showed that beta-endorphins were associated with overeating in genetically obese (ob/ob) mice and the obese (fa/fa) Zucker rats. Subsequent studies with rats and mice (Blass, 1987) linked intakes of sugar and fat with the endogeneous opioid peptide system. Morphine-injected animals selectively increased fat intake (Marks-Kaufman, 1982), while the opioid antagonist naltrexone blocked overeating induced by a palatable cafeteria diet. In a recent study, sensory preferences for mixtures of sugar and fat were reduced by opioid antagonist naloxone as was the consumption of sweet, high-fat snack foods (Drewnowski, Gosnell, Krahn, & Canum, 1989).

TASTE AND FOOD PREFERENCES

Sensory preferences for sweet, high-calorie foods are thought to play a major role in the development of human obesity. However, enhanced taste preferences for sugar and fat mixtures do not necessarily lead to overeating of all sweet desserts. Although taste factors are undoubtedly important in determining food acceptance, attitudes towards health, body weight, and dieting often override physiological and metabolic signals. In other words, taste is often tempered by experience.

It is a popular misconception that enhanced taste responsiveness naturally leads to overeating and thus to obesity. Although some early studies with laboratory rats used consumption as an index of palatability, more recent studies suggest that diet palatability and hyperphagia are not necessarily linked (Bray, 1988). Similarly, studies with human adults suggest that taste preferences alone are not a good index of food consumption (Mattes, 1985). People do not always eat more of the palatable than of the unpalatable foods, and there are many intervening steps between taste responsiveness, food acceptability, and food consumption. A distinction should also be made between short-term food intake, typically assessed using a single meal consumed under laboratory conditions, and the habitual long-term patterns of food consumption in real life.

Preferences for sugar and fat mixtures may be modulated by previous experience, or may be contingent on attitudinal or social variables, including attitudes toward body weight and dieting. Past experience may include positive postingestional consequences: the provision of calories is itself reinforcing to a hungry organism. In contrast, the aversion to fats in eating disorders may be linked to bouts of nausea and vomiting. Fats absorb the smells and odors of foods and provide a salient target of food aversion in both pregnant women and cancer patients undergoing chemotherapy (Midkiff & Berstein, 1985).

Food Choices and Food Consumption

What foods do overweight people say they like to eat? In a large study of U.S. Army personnel, Meiselman, Waterman, & Symington (1974) showed that overweight people selected red meat dishes rather than desserts. Clinical observations of obese patients suggested that self-reported food preferences of obese males typically included steaks and roasts, hamburgers, french fries, pizza and ice cream, while obese women listed bread, cake, cookies, ice cream, chocolate, pies, and other desserts.

It is not clear how self-reported food preferences relate to measures of intake. Assessing dietary intake of the obese is notoriously difficult (Lansky & Brownell, 1982). Most survey studies have used the 24-hr food recall as the principal measure of dietary intake. Overweight patients are known to underestimate daily calories and may engage in frequent and short-lived bouts of dieting. More detailed clinical studies using 3-day food records have produced inconsistent results. While some studies reported elevated consumption of sweet snacks among obese children and adults, other studies have reported the opposite.

There is no evidence at present that the diet of overweight people is rich in sweet foods. On the contrary, epidemiological studies have repeatedly observed an inverse correlation between sugar consumption and the degree of overweight (Glinsman, Irausquin, & Park, 1986). A nationwide survey of almost 1,000 adolescents (5–18 years) found no significant relationship between body fatness and self-reported intakes of sweet snacks (Morgan, Johnson, & Stampley 1983). Data from the Ten-State Nutrition Survey found no relationship between triceps skinfold of teenagers and reported intakes of sugar containing foods, including jams, honey, candies, and soft drinks (Garn, Solomon, & Cole, 1980). No data are available at this point on the subject of fat consumption among obese men and women.

Both obese and eating disorder patients are characterized by a high level of dietary restraint. The obese diet and evidently fail; the anorectic diet and succeed. Anorexia nervosa involves extreme caloric restriction and a severe loss of body weight. Bulimia nervosa is characterized by frequent eating binges that may be countered by fasting, purging, or self-induced vomiting to lose weight (Drewnowski, Halmi, Pierce, Gibbs, & Smith, 1987).

Unlike obese women, anorectic women show an aversion toward dietary fats. According to some reports, anorectic women were willing to eat vegetables, lettuce, fresh fruit, cheese, and sometimes eggs, but were disgusted by milk and meat (Russell, 1967). Attitudinal studies have confirmed that anorectic women report liking only those foods, which they also view as nutritious and low in calories (Drewnowski, Pierce, & Halmi, 1988). Among the top food choices were salads, vegetables, and fresh fruit. A study based on 24-hr food recalls (Beumont & Chambers, 1981) reported that anorectic patients ate a normal amount of carbohydrate but ate significantly less fat than normal weight controls.

Food preferences in bulimia appear to resemble those of some obese women. Clinical observations (Russell, 1979) have suggested that typical binge foods were bread, cakes, chocolate, yogurt, or cottage cheese. The patients ate up to 7 lb of food and the magnitude of an eating binge was estimated at 15–20,000 kcal. The chief binge foods included ice cream, bread, candy, doughnuts, soft drinks, salads and sandwiches, cookies, popcorn, milk, cheese, and cereal. (Abraham and Beumont, 1982; Rosen, Leitenberg, Fisher, & Khazam, 1986). Bulimic patients monitored in a hospital setting consumed mostly doughnuts, pies, sandwiches, chocolate candy, and carbonated beverages. In contrast, eating bouts not classified as binges included salads, vegetables and fruit, and diet soft drinks. According to most reports, eating binges typically included high fat, moderate carbohydrate and low protein foods. Taste preferences in bulimia (Drewnowski, Bellisle, Aimez, & Remy, 1987) are characterized by liking for sugar and limited acceptance of fat containing foods.

CONCLUSIONS

Taste responsiveness plays a central role in mediating the connection between metabolic status, food acceptance, and food consumption. On one hand, central and peripheral manipulations of metabolic status are reported to result in short-term changes in taste responsiveness and have been implicated in selected food cravings. On the other hand, taste responsiveness modified by experience is one of the key factors determining food acceptance and is likely to influence habitual food consumption. Further research needs to deal with the ways in which biological, psychological, and sociocultural variables determine the regulation of feeding in human obesity.

References

Abraham, S. F., & Beumont, P. J. V. (1982). How patients describe bulimia or binge eating. *Psychological Medicine, 12,* 625–635.

Beumont, P. J. V., & Chambers, T. L. (1981). The diet composition and nutritional knowledge of patients with anorexia nervosa. *Journal of Human Nutrition, 35,* 265–273.

Blass, E. M. (1987). Opioids, sugar and the inherent taste of sweet: Broad motivational implications. In J. Dobbing (Ed.), *Sweetness* [ILSI-Nutrition Foundation Symposium] (pp. 115–126). Berlin: Springer-Verlag.

Bouchard, C. (1988) Inheritance of human fat distribution. In C. Bouchard & F. E. Johnston (Eds.), *Fat Distribution During Growth and Later Health Outcomes: Current Topics in Nutrition and Disease: Vol. 17* (pp. 103–125). New York: Alan R. Liss.

Bray, G. A. (1978). Definition, measurement, and classification of the syndromes of obesity. *International Journal of Obesity, 2,* 99–112.

Bray, G. A. (1988). Controls of food intake and energy expenditure. In G. A. Bray, J. LeBlanc, S. Inoue, & M. Suzuki (Eds.), *Diet and Obesity* (pp. 17–35). Tokyo: Japan Scientific Societies Press/Basel, Switzerland: S. Karger Publishers Inc.

Bray, G. A. & York D. A. (1971). Genetically transmitted obesity in rodents. *Physiological Review, 51,* 598–646.

Brownell, K. D., Greenwood, M. R., Stellar, E. & Shrager, E. E. (1986). The effects of repeated cycles of weight loss and regain in rats. *Physiology & Behavior, 38,* 459–464.

Cabanac, M., & Duclaux, R. (1970). Obesity: Absence of satiety aversion to sucrose. *Science, 168,* 496–497.

Castonguay, T. W., & Stern, J. S. (1983). The effect of adrenalectomy on dietary component selection by the genetically obese Zucker Rat. *Nutrition Reports International, 28,* 725–730.

Drewnowski, A. (1983). Cognitive structure in obesity and dieting. In M. R. C. Greenwood (Ed.), *Obesity: Contemporary issues in clinical nutrition.* New York: Churchill Livingstone.

Drewnowski, A. (1987). Fats and food texture: Sensory and hedonic evaluations. In H. R. Moskowitz, (Ed.), *Food Texture* (pp. 217–250). New York: Marcel Dekker.

Drewnowski, A., Bellisle, F., Aimez, P., & Remy, B. (1987). Taste and bulimia. *Physiology & Behavior, 41,* 621–626.

Drewnowski, A., Brunzell, J. D., Sande, K., Iverius, P. H., & Greenwood, M. R. C. (1985). Sweet tooth reconsidered: Taste preferences in human obesity, *Physiology & Behavior, 35,* 617–622.

Drewnowski, A., Cohen, A., Faust, I. M., & Grinker, J. A. (1984) Meal-taking behavior is related to predisposition to dietary obesity in the rat. *Physiology & Behavior, 32,* 61–67.

Drewnowski, A., Gosnell, B., Krahn, D. D., & Canum, K. (1989). Sensory preference for sugar and fat: Evidence for opioid involvement. *Appetite, 12,* 206.

Drewnowski, A., & Greenwood, M. R. C. (1983). Cream and sugar: Human preferences for high-fat foods. *Physiology & Behavior, 30,* 629–633.

Drewnowski, A., Halmi, K. A., Pierce, B., Gibbs, J., & Smith, G. P. (1987). Taste and eating disorders. *American Journal of Clinical Nutrition, 46,* 442–450.

Drewnowski, A., Pierce, B., & Halmi, K. A. (1988). Fat aversion in eating disorders. *Appetite, 10,* 119-131.

Drewnowski, A., & Schwartz, M. (1990). Invisible fats: Sensory evaluation of sugar/fat mixtures. *Appetite, 14,* 203–217.

Drewnowski, A., Shrager, E. E., Lipsky, C., Stellar, E., & Greenwood, M. R. C. (1989). Sugar and fat: Sensory and hedonic evaluations of liquid and solid foods. *Physiology & Behavior, 45,* 177–183.

Flatt, J. P., Ravussin, E., Acheson, K. J., & Jequier, E. (1985). Effects of dietary fat on post-prandial substrate oxidation and on carbohydrate and fat balances. *Journal of Clinical Investigation, 76,* 1019–1024.

Garn, S. M. (1985). Continuities and changes in fatness from infancy through adulthood. In J. D. Lockhart (Ed.), *Current Problems in Pediatrics, 15,* 1–47.

Garn, S. M., Solomon, M. A., & Cole, P. E. (1980). Sugar-food intake of obese and lean adolescents. *Ecology of Food and Nutrition, 9,* 219–222.

Gilbert, D. G., & Hagen, R. L. (1988). Taste in underweight, overweight, and normal weight subjects before, during, and after sucrose ingestion. *Addictive Behaviors, 5,* 137–142.

Glinsman, W. H., Irausquin, H., & Park, Y. K. (1986). Evaluation of health aspects of sugars contained in carbohydrate sweeteners. *Journal of Nutrition, 116(11S),* S1–216.

Grinker, J. A., Hirsch, J., & Smith, D. V. (1972). Taste sensitivity and susceptibility to external influence in obese and normal-weight subjects. *Journal of Personality and Social Psychology, 22,* 320.

Lansky, D., & Brownell, K. D. (1982). Estimates of food quantity and calories: Errors in self-report among obese patients. *American Journal of Clinical Nutrition, 35,* 727–732.

Margules, D. L., Moisset, B., Lewis, M. J., Shibuya, H. & Pert, C. (1978). Beta-endorphin is associated with overeating in genetically obese mice (ob/ob) and rats (fa/fa). *Science, 202,* 988–991.

Marks-Kaufman, R. (1982). Increased fat consumption induced by morphine administration in rats. *Pharmacology Biochemistry & Behavior, 16,* 949–955.

Mattes, R. D. (1985). Gustation as a determinant of ingestion: Methodological issues. *American Journal of Clinical Nutrition, 41,* 672–683.

Meiselman, H. L., Waterman, D., & Symington, L. E. (1974). *Armed Forces food preferences.* (Tech. Rep. No. 75-63-FSL). Natick, MA: U.S. Army Natick Development Center.

Midkiff, E. E., & Bernstein, I. L. (1985). Targets of learned food aversions in humans. *Physiology & Behavior, 34,* 839–841.

Morgan, K. J., Johnson, S. R., & Stampley, G. L. (1983). Children's frequency of eating, total sugar intake and weight/height stature. *Nutrition Research, 3,* 635–652.

Moskowitz, H. R., Kluter, R. A., Westerling, J., & Jacobs, H. L. (1974). Sugar sweetness and pleasantness: Evidence for different psychophysical laws. *Science, 184,* 583–585.

National Academy of Sciences, Food and Nutrition Board. (1989). *Diet and health* Washington, DC: National Academy Press.

Nisbett, R. E. (1968). Taste, deprivation and weight determinants of eating behavior. *Journal of Personality and Social Psychology, 10,* 107–116.

Pangborn, R. M., & Simone, M. (1958). Body size and sweetness preference. *Journal of the American Dietetic Association, 34,* 924–928.

Pangborn, R. M., Bos, K. E., & Stern, J. (1985). Dietary fat intake and taste responses to fat in milk by under-, normal-, and overweight women. *Appetite, 6,* 25–40.

Paykel, E. S., Mueller, P. S., & de la Vergne, P. M. (1973). Amitryptyline, weight gain and carbohydrate craving: A side effect. *British Journal of Psychiatry, 125,* 501–507.

Poehlman, E. T., Tremblay, A., Depres, J. P., Fontaine, E., Perusse, L., Theriault, G., & Bouchard, C. (1986). Genotype-controlled changes in body composition and fat morphology following overfeeding in twins. *American Journal of Clinical Nutrition, 43,* 723–731.

Price, R. A., Stunkard, A. J., Ness, R. Wadden, T., Heshka, S., Kanders, B., & Cormillot, A. (1990). Childhood-onset (age < 10) obesity has high familial risk. *International Journal of Obesity, 14,* 185–195.

Ravussin, E., Lillioja, S., Knowler, W. C., Christin, L., Freymond, D., Abbott, W. G., Boyce, V., Howard, B. V., & Bogardus, C. (1988). Reduced rate of energy expenditure as a risk factor for body-weight gain. *New England Journal of Medicine, 318,* 467–472.

Reed, D. R., Contreras, R. J., Maggio, C., Greenwood, M. R., & Rodin, J. (1988). Weight cycling in female rats increases dietary fat selection and adiposity. *Physiology & Behavior, 42,* 389–395.

Roberts, S. B., Savage, J., Coward, W. A., Chew, B., & Lucas, A. (1988). Energy expenditure and intake in infants born to lean and overweight mothers. *New England Journal of Medicine, 318,* 461–466.

Rodin, J. (1978). Has the internal versus external distinction outlived its usefulness? In G. A. Bray, (Ed.), *Recent Advances in Obesity Research II* (pp. 75–85). London: Newman.

Rodin, J. (1981a). The current state of the internal-external hypothesis: What went wrong? *American Psychologist, 36,* 361–372.

Rodin, J. (1981b). Psychological factors in obesity. In P. Bjorntorp, M. Cairella, & A. N. Howard (Eds.), *Recent Advances in Obesity Research III* (pp. 106–123). London: J. Libbey.

Rodin, J., Moskowitz, H. R., & Bray, G. A. (1976). Relationship between obesity, weight loss, and taste responsiveness. *Physiology & Behavior, 17,* 391–197.

Rosen, J. C., Leitenberg, H., Fisher, C., & Khazam, C. (1986). Binge-eating episodes in bulimia nervosa: The amount and type of food consumed. *International Journal of Eating Disorders, 5,* 255–267.

Rosenthal, N. E., Genhart, M., Jacobsen, F. M., Shwerer, R. G., & Wehr, T. A. (1987). Disturbance of appetite and weight regulation in seasonal affective disorder. In R. J. Wurtman, & J. J. Wurtman (Eds.), *Human obesity. Annals of the New York Academy of Sciences, 499,* 216–230.

Russell, G. F. M. (1967). The nutritional disorder in anorexia nervosa. *Journal of Psychosomatic Research, 11,* 141–149.

Russell, G. F. M. (1979). Bulimia nervosa: An ominous variant of anorexia nervosa. *Psychological Medicine, 9,,* 429–448.

Salmon, D. M. W., & Flatt, J. P. (1985). Effect of dietary fat content on the incidence of obesity in ad libitum fed mice. *International Journal of Obesity, 9,* 443–449.

Schachter, S., & Rodin, J. (1974). *Obese humans and rats.* Potomac, MD: Lawrence Erlbaum Associates.

Schemmel, R., Mickelsen, O., & Gill, J. L. (1970). Dietary obesity in rats: Body weight and body fat accretion in seven strains of rats. *Journal of Nutrition, 100,* 1041–1048.

Schwartz, R. S., Ravussin, E., Massari, M., O'Connell, M., & Robbins, D. C. (1985). The thermic effect of carbohydrate versus fat feeding in man. *Metabolism, 34,* 285–293.

Sclafani, A. (1985). Animal models of obesity. In R. T. Frankle, J.Dwyer, L. Moragne, & A. Owen (Eds.), *Dietary treatment and prevention of obesity* (pp. 105–123). London: John Libbey.

Sclafani, A., & Springer, O. (1976). Dietary obesity in adult rats: Similarities to hypothalamic and human obesity syndromes. *Physiology & Behavior, 17,* 461–471.

Steen, S. N., Opplinger, R. A., & Brownell, K. D. (1988). Metabolic effects of repeated weight loss and regain in adolescent wrestlers. *Journal of the American Medical Association, 260,* 47–50.

Stuart, R. B., & Davis, B. (1972). *Slim chance in a fat world: Behavioral control of obesity.* Champaign, IL: Research Press.

Suzuki, M., & Tamura, T. (1988). Intake timing of fat and insulinogenic sugars and efficiency of body fat accumulation. In G. A. Bray, J. LeBlanc, S. Inoue, & M. Suzuki (Eds.), *Diet and obesity* (pp. 113–119). Tokyo: Japan Scientific Societies Press/Basel, Switzerland: S. Karger Publishers, Inc.

Stunkard, A. J., & Berthold, H. C. (1985). What is behavior therapy: A very short description of behavioral weight control. *American Journal of Clinical Nutrition, 41,* 821–823.

Stunkard, A. J., Sorensen, T. I. A., Hanic, C., Teasdale, T. W., Chakraborty, R. & Scholl, W. J. (1986). An adoption study of human obesity. *New England Journal of Medicine, 314,* 193–198.

The Surgeon General's Report on Nutrition and Health. (1988). (DHHS (PHS) Publication No. 88-50210). Washington, DC: U.S. Government Printing Office.

Thompson, D. A., Moskowitz, H. R., & Campbell, R. (1976). Effects of body weight and food intake on pleasantness ratings for a sweet stimulus. *Journal of Applied Psychology, 41,* 77–83.

Tuorila, H., & Pangborn, R. M. (1988). Prediction of reported consumption of selected fat-containing foods. *Appetite, 11,* 81–95.

Witherly, S. A., Pangborn, R. M., & Stern, J. S. (1980). Gustatory responses and eating duration of obese and lean adults. *Appetite, 1,* 52–63.

Wurtman, J. J. (1984). The involvement of brain serotonin in excessive carbohydrate snacking by obese carbohydrate cravers. *Journal of American Dietetic Association, 84,* 1004–1007.

CHAPTER 17

A ROLE FOR OPIATES IN FOOD REWARD AND FOOD ADDICTION

JACQUES LE MAGNEN

Studies on the palatability of foods are characterized by an excess of redundant and undefined terminology, confused concepts, and misleading methodology. The following words and expressions are alternatively used to refer to "the sensory stimulation to eat or not to eat," "palatability of foods," "preferences and aversions," "hedonic or incentive properties of foods," "pleasantness and un-pleasantness," "reinforcing values of foods," and lastly, "food reward." This chapter will outline the exact meaning of these terms in an attempt to eliminate the confusion introduced in the literature by their imprecise use.

THE MEANING OF WORDS

It is, or it should be unanimously agreed that the stimulation to eat results from the synergistic combination of two sets of information transmitted to the brain. The first set of information involves systemic or metabolic stimulus to eat giving rise to the brain arousal of hunger in a specific condition of body energy imbalance (Le Magnen, 1986). The other set of information is provided by the oro-sensory (sight, smell, taste, and textures) stimulation by the offered materials. This sensory activity (quality and intensity) is dependent on the stimulus-activity relationships of each involved sensory apparatus and on the brain processing of the sensory input; it is independent of their abilities to elicit or not elicit the oral intake of those materials. Some of these environmental factors effectively stimulate oral intake and determine, through their specific sensory activities, the amount eaten. Because their sensory activities elicit the feeding response, it is said that these foods are palatable. They are qualified as palatable or preferred by comparing their respective capacity to stimulate eating of enough food to alleviate the stimulation and therefore induce satiety. When food, a complex sensory stimulus in humans, is considered palatable it is subjectively perceived as pleasant. This pleasantness is called the "hedonic property of the food." It could be better designated "the hedonic aspect of the food" because it is not, contrary to the sensory activity per se, an intrinsic "property" of the food. Because it is admitted (somewhat confusingly) that behavioral responses exist and are "rewarded," food palatability and associated pleasantness are perceived as current rewards of the feeding response.

Other materials offered by the environment do not elicit intake. They either do not stimulate intake or, in a given state of systemic stimulation which stimulates response, antagonize or actively inhibit this response. These sensory stimuli that discourage intake are designated unpalatable or aversive. They are perceived in humans as unpleasant. These aversive feeding stimuli provide a "food punishment" analogous to pain or stressful stimuli in other behavioral performances.

This discussion of elementary notions and the meanings of words lead us to a definition of food palatability that raises questions about involved mechanisms. Palatability of foods is defined as being the "unlearned or learned sensory stimulation to eat." This stimulation is food- and sensory-specific, state-dependent, and state-specific.

Palatability is sensory-specific because it is dependent on a particular complex of one or more sensory activities of the food. It is also food-specific. A particular component of the sensory complex (e.g., sweetness or saltiness) and the type of food it is associated with determines whether the food is palatable or not. As shown by Beauchamp and Moran (1982), children learned early to prefer a sweet cake to a salty one, and a salty soup or meat to a sweet one. Palatability is state-dependent and state-specific. Alimentary stimuli and not female stimuli are attractive for hungry male rats and vice-versa. Many experiments have provided evidence that the palatability of sweet substances and the stimulation to eat or to drink by such substances are modulated by hunger and not by thirst, while the stimulation to drink a salty solution is specifically modulated by thirst and sodium depletion (Le Magnen, 1953a, 1953b).

Palatability or sensory stimulation to eat may be innate (i.e., exhibited at birth). These innate responses are either modified or reversed by learning. All other palatability responses are learned. As such, they are designated conditioned or learned taste (or flavor preferences or stimuli to eat). The process of learning is dealt with by Weingarten (chapter 3, this volume), Rowland (chapter 7, this volume), Sclafani (chapter 10, this volume), and Bernstein (chapter 12, this volume). Our early research helped lay the foundation for their work. During the early fifties, we demonstrated (a) that the palatability of food based upon an added flavor is learned, (b) that the primary reinforcer of this learning is the postingestive nutritive property of the food and its ability to relieve the current nutritive imbalance (i.e., to induce a persistent satiety, (c) that this learning explained that the palatability, contrary to sensory activity per se, is roughly adjusted to nutritive properties of associated foods, and (d) that two distinct learning processes occur, the first one modulating the initial stimulation to eat, the second one the sensory specific satiating capacity of the food (i.e., its contribution as an oro-pharyngeal stimulus to satiation [induction of satiety] (Booth, 1972; Le Magnen, 1956, 1959, 1968).

THE FOOD REWARD

What are the bases for the concept of food reward? In all learning or conditioning processes three elements are present and interacting: a specific behavioral arousal, also called motivation; external sensory stimuli coming from the goal object to be approached or avoided in the elicited performance; and a primary reinforcement generally represented by the postperformance abolition of the initial arousal by the correct performance. A confusion is introduced by the use of the word reward to designate both this postperformance reinforcement (i.e., postingestive), which is the cause of learning, and the sensory reward which is its effect. The result of all learning processes (arbitrarily separated in classical conditioning and instrumental learning) is the transfer of the reinforcing property to sensory stimuli associated with the primary reinforced performance. As secondary reinforcer or sensory reward the external stimuli acquire the property of a reward in the first meaning of the word inasmuch as it allows another response such as pressing a lever to be learned. The main question is thus raised: What are the brain mechanisms by which sensory afferents, mainly smell and taste afferents, have either innately or acquired through learning, the ability to make food palatable.

OPIATE AGONISTS-ANTAGONISTS AND FOOD INTAKE

The discovery by Hughes and Kosterlitz in 1975 of brain endogenous opioid peptides is among the most important findings in neurobiology, neurophysiology, and neurochemistry and their links with behavioral sciences. Soon it was reported by a large number of investigators that opiate mu receptor antagonists (primarily naloxone and naltrexone) inhibited eating and drinking (e.g., Le Magnen, Marfaing-Jallat, Miceli, & Devos, 1980). Naloxone injections, peripherally or centrally, were shown to reduce intake in various free-fed or moderately deprived animals. Meanwhile it was shown by a large number of other investigators that injected morphine and brain opioids (β-endorphin, enkephalin, etc.) and their analogues also modified food intake. Despite some discrepancies, the authors concluded that peripheral injections of moderate or high doses of morphine inhibited intake; conversely, central (intraventricular or into the ventromedial hypothalamus [VMH] or periventricular nucleus [PVN]) injections of morphine, brain opioids and their analogues facilitated feeding (McLaughlin, 1983; McLean & Hoebel, 1985; Tepperman & Hirst, 1982).

This series of studies should be interpreted with some caution. Hundreds of compounds (physiological agents and synthetic substances) have been injected either peripherally by various routes or centrally in lateral, 3rd or 4th ventricles or locally in various parts of the brain to test their effects on food intake. Almost all of these agents or substances were reported to either stimulate or reduce food intake. From this one observation, authors have often suggested that a compound is physiologically involved or acts on a system involved in the control of feeding. If the compound suppresses food intake, the substance is said to either suppress hunger or enhance satiety. If the compound facilitates intake, the substance is said to either enhance hunger or suppress satiety. Comparisons of effects in satiated and food-deprived rats were the only basis for these contradictory interpretations. Of course a number of methodological criteria have to be used to assess the actual interaction between the injected substance and the feeding mechanism. Actions on the performance, the state of vigilance, and the motor outcome must be eliminated. Other criteria and methods must be used to discriminate between the various actions on the multiple control systems which can lead to increases or decreases of food intake in various conditions regarding the food, the feeding schedule, the underlying metabolism, and so forth.

Opiates and Food Reward

We have provided evidence of the suppressing action of naloxone on the sensory stimulation to eat and suggested that brain-opioid release was the neurochemical basis for the sensory food reward (Le Magnen, Marfaing-Jallat, Miceli, & Devos, 1980).

Fed rats were offered, in a 30 min morning session on alternate days, a 0.1% saccharin solution or water. The last day of this alternate consumption of saccharin and water (both preceded by a control saline injection) was taken as baseline. Rats took a mean 17.2 ml saccharin solution and 11.1 ml water (p <0.001) and exhibited the palatability of the sweet fluid by their preference for this fluid over water. During the next 6 consecutive days, the same alternation was continued, each drinking session of saccharin and water being preceded by an injection of naloxone (1 mg/kg, I.P., 30 min before). Compared to the baseline, naloxone reduced the intake of both fluids, but had a larger effect on the saccharin solution so that there was no longer a difference in the intake of the two fluids. In other words, naloxone abolished the preference for a sweet solution versus water. During the next 6 days, when saline injections were again given prior to saccharin or water on alternating days, rats exhibited a progressive return to their initial preference for the saccharin solution (Figure 1). The same procedure using a glucose solution (5%) instead of saccharin gave the same result. Rats treated with naloxone drank the glucose solution as if it was water. In a similar short-term presentation, the drinking of a very dilute (0.0024%) quinine HCl solution was reduced 28.5% by naloxone and the difference with water intake was augmented. Thus the opiate antagonist made the mildly aversive solution more aversive. Lastly, in another group of rats, a glucose solution was made aversive using the classical conditioned taste aversion paradigm. The acquired aversion to water was observed after a control saline injection and naloxone (the control injection) appeared to enhance the aversive response. Thus the response to a sweet solution made aversive by conditioning was, under naloxone,

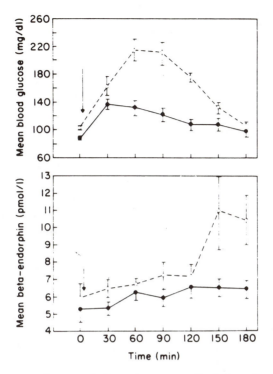

Figure 1 Mean serum glucose and plasma immunoreactive beta-endorphin with standard errors (*SE*) in obese and nonobese subjects following glucose ingestion. O———O, subjects (*N*=9); ●———●, controls (*N*=9). Arrow denotes ingestion of 100 g of glucose. From "Plasma Immunoreactive Beta-Endorphin Response to Glucose Ingestion in Human Obesity" by C. J. Getto et al., 1984, *Appetite, 5,* p. 331. Copyright 1984 by Academic Press Inc. (London) Ltd. Reprinted by permission.

identical to the response of the spontaneously aversive quinine solution. An opiate antagonist abolishes preference and specific palatability level of a sweet solution. In addition, the drug exaggerates the aversiveness of an aversive item; for example, it suppresses morphine analgesia and enhances nociceptive response.

These experiments were replicated and their results confirmed by Cooper (1985). Naloxone was also found to narrow the range of accepted and preferred concentrations of saccharin by rats, while morphine enlarged this range (Siviy, Calcagnetti, & Reid, 1982; Siviy & Ried, 1983). The saccharin preference-aversion curve was also shifted to the right (i.e., aversion direction) by naloxone. Cooper (1985) also confirmed our finding that naltrexone lowered the intake of a slightly aversive quinine solution. The dose-response curve of naloxone action on saccharin preference over water is consistent with the preceding result (Siviy & Reid, 1983). The dose of naloxone required to reduce the saccharin preference is related to the degree of saccharin preference (Lynch, 1986; Wu, 1981). Conclusive evidence that the opiate antagonist reduced intake of a sweet solution by acting on palatability and not on the gastro-intestinal feedback was recently provided (Kirkham & Cooper, 1988; Rockwood, 1982). The sham-drinking of a 30% sucrose solution was reduced by 50% by naloxone (1.25 mg/kg).

This phenomenon has been observed in humans (Fantino, Horsotte, & Apfelbaum, 1986): 60 mg naltrexone reduced only the self-reported and psychophysically determined pleasantness of taste and alimentary odor. The same dose had no effect on the pleasantness of other non food-related stimuli, regardless of their level of pleasantness. The reducing effect of naltrexone on the pleasantness of sweet taste was higher than the suppression induced by tubing 100 g of glucose in the stomach. Further, naltrexone potentiated the effect of glucose intubation.

All of these results with opiate antagonists suggest that an opioid somewhere in the brain is released by sensory stimulation and is a requisite of the action of this sensory stimulation in the control of intake (i.e., food reward). Further evidence for this is that consumption of highly palatable sucrose solutions induces analgesia that is comparable to that seen after the administration of morphine or β-endorphin, or during stress. In 10-day-old rats pups, the oral infusion of a sucrose solution augmented the latency of response of pain exhibited in hot plate and tail-flick tests. The same orally infused sucrose solutions also reduced the vocalization of pups isolated from the dam, as did the administration of morphine (Blass, Fitzgerald, & Kehoe, 1987). More direct confirmation of this palatability associated opiate release has been reported. The binding of injected 3H-etorphine in the hypothalamus was considerably reduced 20 min after the consumption of a highly palatable solution by rats. This was interpreted as an increased competitive displacement of the 3H ligand by increased opioid release; this is consistent with the observed decrease in β endorphin (but not dynorphin) content of the hypothalamus (Dum, Gramsch, & Hery, 1983). These effects can also be seen over long periods. Chronic intake of a saccharin solution (15 ml per day for 28 days) produced a loss of morphine-induced analgesia. This acquired morphine tolerance suggested that the chronic intake of a highly palatable solution, through chronic β-endorphin release, had induced opiate tolerance (Cohen, Lieblich, & Bergmann, 1984; Lieblich, Cohen, Ganchrow, Blass, & Bergmann, 1983). It is interesting to note that the elevation in refined sugar intake by Western people is often associated with an intolerance of pain and suffering.

Role of Opiates in Overeating Induced by Highly Palatable Foods and Stress

In humans, a biphasic rise of plasma β-endorphin concentration (presumably of pituitary origin) follows the ingestion of a meal. This rise of circulating β-endorphin, lasting from 5–60 min after the start of the oral meal, suggests a preabsorptive release of the peptide (Matsumura, Fukuda & Mori, 1982). Getto (Getto, Fullerton, & Carlson, 1984) confirmed this finding and in addition showed that this postmeal elevation of plasma β-endorphin was a specific response to the oral consumption of a glucose sweet solution (Figure 2).

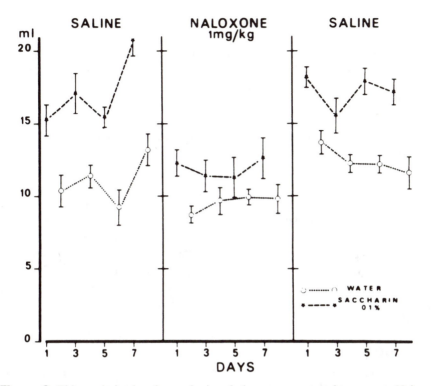

Figure 2 Thirty min intake of a saccharin solution versus water after an acute Naloxone (1 mg/kg) injection (central section) or after an injection of saline (pre- and postnaloxone controls). From "Pain Modulating and Reward Systems: a Single Brain Mechanism?" by J. Le Magnen et al., 1980, *Pharmacology Biochemistry & Behavior*, 12, p. 732. Copyright 1980 by Pergamon Press, Inc. Reprinted by permission.

It is well-known that a chronic feeding of rats by a choice of highly palatable foods (cafeteria regimen) produces a sustained hyperphagia leading to a reversible obesity (Sclafani & Gorman, 1977). It was shown that naltrexone, administered acutely at the beginning of the nocturnal period, inhibited the hyperphagia of rats eating a cafeteria regimen (Apfelbaum & Mandenoff, 1981). More convincingly, in chronic studies, the same authors showed that naltrexone suppressed the cafeteria diet-induced obesity through a reduction both of hyper-phagia and energy expenditure (Mandenoff, Fumeron, Apfelbaum, & Margules, 1982). The hyperphagia and body weight gain elicited in rats by a permanent choice of a 30% sucrose solution and the stock diet was not very different from the same responses to the cafeteria regimen. The sucrose lab chow diet produced high oral intake, weight gain, and an increase of O_2 consumption. These responses were blocked by naloxone (Marks-Kaufman, 1980).

Stress by tail-pinching produces overeating in rats. It has been repetitively found that this tail-pinch-induced overeating was achieved only on palatable foods or solutions (Marques, Fisher, Okrutny, & Rowland, 1979). Tail-pinching and other stresses induce a naloxone reversible analgesia (Levine, Wilcox, & Morley, 1982). Naloxone also prevents tail-pinch-induced eating (Betière, Baigt, Mandenoff, & Apfelbaum, 1984; Lowy, Maickel, & Yim, 1980; Morley & Levine, 1986). Interestingly, after 10 days of tail-pinching, naloxone precipitates a morphine-like withdrawal syndrome similar to repeated electric shock in mice (Christie & Chester, 1982).

It is thought that brain opioid release provoked by the tail-pinch stress, like morphine and other opioids centrally administered, facilitates eating of highly palatable items. Parallel results were obtained after other types of stresses were induced. After a swimming stress, 12 hr food-deprived rats increased intake of macronutrients in the following order: carbohydrates, proteins, and fats. Naloxone inhibited the augmented intake and the high fat diet more than any of the other macronutrients. The conclusion of the author was that opiates released by stress selectively augment intake of more palatable foods (Vaswani, Tejwani, & Mousa, 1983). After a cold water stress, rats increased their intake. Hypothalamic and circulating β-endorphin were reduced in the pituitary (Vaswani, Tejwani, & Mousa, 1983). Similar results were obtained by Davis, Lowy, and Yim (1983).

FOOD ADDICTION

The idea that humans could be addicted to food is an old one suggested by clinical observations of various kinds of eating disorders. Furthermore, clinicians commonly noted in obese patients that dieting induced syndromes of depression and hyperanxiety, sometimes resembling a morphine withdrawal syndrome. Also, during binge crises of bulimic subjects, patients looked for and preferred highly sweetened foods or beverages (Fullerton & Getto, 1985). Fullerton and Getto (1985) also showed that the oral intake of a glucose solution elicited an increase of plasma β-endorphin level.

The first suggestion involving opiates came from McCloy (McCloy & McCloy, 1979). These authors proposed that enkephalin is released in the duodenum by foods and, acting via the general circulation on the hypothalamus, is the basis for food reward and satiation. They suggested that overeating leading to an hypersecretion of duodenal enkephalin could lead to opiate tolerance, pushing the subject to eat more and more to obtain the same reward. The abstinence syndrome of dieters would then be a sign of this acquired opiate dependence. Experiments demonstrating that the chronic intake of a highly palatable fluid leads to a morphine tolerance strongly suggested that the opiate-related food rewards could also lead to a morphine-like dependence and therefore to a food addiction (McCloy & McCloy, 1979). We have carried out a preliminary experiment in this direction (Le Magnen, 1987).

Rats were maintained for three weeks on a cafeteria regimen during which time they gained weight. They were then returned to the stock diet and, 24 hr

later, naloxone (2 mg/kg) provided a morphine-like withdrawal syndrome including piloerection, head and whole body shaking, teeth chattering, and tremors.
The same naloxone injection in control rats maintained on the stock diet was
without any effect.

Addiction to particular foods could also be linked to the presence of opiate-
like substances (exorphins) or other addictive substances in the food. A gluten
hydrolysate containing an opiate-like material retards intestinal transit and ele-
vates plasma somatostatin concentration in humans, but no effect on intake and
feeding of satiety was observed (Morley & Levine, 1980). For example, in
humans, addiction to or craving for chocolate is well-known, it is probably due
to the action of theobromine. An abundant amount of recent literature also
supports the notion that alcohol addiction partially involves the direct action of
ethanol on brain opio-receptors.

Lastly, brain opioid and addictive processes have been implicated in anorexia nervosa. In nonobese humans and rats, food deprivation and fasting induced
analgesia (McGivern, Berka, Bernston, Walker, & Sandman, 1979). A depletion
of hypothalamic β-endorphin was found in 2- or 3-day fasted rats (Gambert et
al., 1980). In anorexia nervosa, voluntary dieting would produce this opioid
release. Its repetition would establish a progressive high tolerance to opiates
which, like naloxone, could product a long-lasting suppression of food reward
and enhance aversiveness to foods (Martazzi, 1980).

CONCLUSION

The results reviewed above suggest very strongly that oro-sensory stimulation by
foods is associated with hypothalamic and perhaps pituitary release of opioid
peptides, and that this elicited release underlies the specific involvement of some
of these sensory afferents in the stimulation to eat (food reward). Additional
findings suggest that critical sites include the lateral (LH) and paraventricular
(PVN) hypothalamic areas known to be involved in hunger arousal of feeding,
food and self-stimulation reward, and as terminal sites of sensory projections.
These areas are functionally dependent on opioid peptides and are rich in receptors. For example, naloxone blocks feeding elicited by LH electrical stimulation
(Carr & Simon, 1983). Self-stimulation of the same area is facilitated by both
food deprivation and the presence of a palatable food and this facilitation is
blocked by opiate antagonists (Katz & Roth, 1979). Effects of opiate agonists
and antagonists locally injected in VMH, PVN, or LH (Ono & Oomura, 1987;
Sikdar & Oomura, 1985) are consistent with this role of opiates as a basis for
sensory food reward.

Separate studies have suggested that dopaminergic mechanisms or hedonic
properties of foods are involved in food reward (Wise, 1978). Up to now, this
suggestion is based only upon a pharmacological approach, namely the effects of
antagonists. The same limited pharmacological action of agonists and antagonists
supports the finding of the putative involvement of serotoninergic pathways (Neill

& Cooper, 1988). What dopaminergic or serotoninergic systems in the brain are concerned with and how they can be linked with feeding mechanisms and food reward requires further investigation.

The role of opiates in the brain processing of sensory information and the modulation by learning of its role in behavioral outcome remains to be elucidated. A general conclusion that can be drawn is that reinforcement and reward, learning, and the mechanisms of memory are intrinsically incorporated at a neuronal level to the specific afferent-efferent circuitry governing each specific behavior.

References

Apfelbaum, M., & Mandenoff, A. (1981). Naltrexone suppresses in rats hyperphagia induced by high palatability diet. *Pharmacology Biochemistry & Behavior, 15,* 89–91.

Beauchamp, G. K., & Moran, M. (1982). Dietary experience and sweet taste preference in human infants. *Appetite, 3,* 139–152.

Bertière, M-Cl., Baigt, F. Mandenoff, A., & Apfelbaum, M. (1984). Stress and sucrose induced hyperphagia: Role of endogenous opiates. *Pharmacology & Behavior, 20,* 675–680.

Blass, E. M., Fitzgerald, E., & Kehoe, P. (1987). Interaction between sucrose, pain and isolation distress. *Pharmacology Biochemistry & Behavior, 26,* 483–489.

Booth, D.A. (1972). Conditioned satiety in rats. *Journal of Comparative Physiology and Psychology, 81,* 457–471.

Carr, M., & Simon, E. (1983). The role of opioids in feeding and reward elicited by LH electrical stimulation. *Life Science, 33,* 49–66.

Cohen, E. N., Lieblich, I., & Bergmann, F. (1984). Effects of chronically elevated intake of different concentrations of saccharin on morphine tolerance in genetically selected rats. *Physiology & Behavior, 32,* 1041–1043.

Cooper, S. J. (1985). Evidence for opiate receptor involvement in the consumption of a high-palatability diet in nondeprived rats. *Neuropeptides, 5,* 345–348.

Christie, M. J., & Chesher, G. B. (1982). Physical dependence on physiologically released endogenous opiates. *Life Science, 30,* 1173–1177.

Davis, J., Lowy, M., & Yim, G. (1983). Relationship between plasma concentrations of β-endorphin and food intake in the rat. *Peptides, 4,* 79–85.

Dum, J., Gramsch, C., & Hery, A. (1983). Activation of hypothalamic beta endorphin pool by reward induced by highly palatable food. *Pharmacology Biochemistry & Behavior, 18,* 443–446.

Fantino, M., Horsotte, J., & Apfelbaum, M. (1986). An opioid antagonist, naltrexone, reduces preference for sucrose in humans. *American Journal of Physiology, 251,* R91–R96.

Fullerton, D. T., & Getto, C. J. (1985). Sugar, opioids and binge eating. *Brain Research Bulletin, 14,* 673–680.

Gambert, S. R., Garthwaite, T. L., Pontzer, C. H., & Hagen, T. C. (1980). Fasting associated with decrease in hypothalamic beta-endorphin. *Science, 210,* 1271–1272.

Getto, C. J., Fullerton, D. T., & Carlson, I. H. (1984). Plasma immunoreactive beta-endorphin response to glucose ingestion in human obesity. *Appetite, 5,* 329–335.

Katz, R. J., & Roth, K. (1979). Tail-pinch induced stress arousal facilitates brain stimulation reward. *Physiology & Behavior, 22,* 193–194.

Kirkham, T., & Cooper, J. S. (1988). Attenuation of sham-feeding by naloxone is stereospecific: Evidence for opioid mediation in oro-sensory reward. *Physiology & Behavior, 43,* 845–847.

Le Magnen, J. (1953a). Activité de l'insuline sur la consommation spontanée de solutions sapides [Action of insulin on the spontaneous consumption of sapid solutions]. *Comptes-Rendus de la Société de Biologie (Paris)*, *147*, 1753–1757.

Le Magnen, J. (1953b). Nouvelles données sur le processus de régulation des consommations hydrique et saline chez le rat blanc [Further study on the regulatory process of water and saline consumptions in the rat]. *Comptes-Rendus de la Société de Biologie (Paris)*, *147*, 1675–1677.

Le Magnen, J. (1956). Effet sur la prise alimentaire du rat blanc des administrations postprandiales d'insuline et le mécanisme des appétits caloriques [Effect of postprandial administrations of insulin on food intake in the rat: Mechanism of caloric appetites]. *Journal de Physiologie (Paris)*, *48*, 789–802.

Le Magnen, J. (1959). Effet des administrations postprandiales de glucose sur l'établissement des appétits [Effect of postprandial administrations of glucose on the acquisition of appetites] *Comptes-Rendus de la Société de Biologie (Paris)*, *153*, 212–215.

Le Magnen, J. (1986). *Hunger.* Cambridge, MA: Cambridge University Press.

Le Magnen, J. (1987). Palatability: Concept, terminology and mechanism. In R. A. Boakes, D. A. Popplewel, & M. J. Burton (Eds.), *Eating habits* (pp. 131–154). New York: John Wiley & Sons Ltd.

Le Magnen, J., Marfaing-Jallat, P., Miceli, D., & Devos, M. (1980). Pain modulating and reward systems: A single brain mechanism? *Pharmacology Biochemistry & Behavior, 12*, 729–733.

Le Magnen, J., & Tallon, S. (1968). Préférence alimentaire du jeune rat induite par l'allaitement maternel [Food preference of the young rat induced by maternal lactation]. *Comptes-Rendus de la Société de Biologie (Paris)*, *162*, 387–390.

Levine, A. S., Wilcox, G., & Morley, J. (1982). Tail-pinch induced consummatory behaviors are associated with analgesia. *Physiology & Behavior, 28*, 659–664.

Lieblich, I., Cohen, E., Ganchrow, J. R., Blass, E. M., & Bergman, F. (1983). Morphine tolerance in genetically selected rats induced by chronically elevated saccharin intake. *Science, 221*, 871–873.

Lowy, M. T., Maickel, K. P., & Yim, G. K. W. (1980). Naloxone reduction of stress-induced feeding *Life Science, 26*, 2113.

Lynch, W.C. (1986). Opiate blockade inhibits saccharin intake and blocks normal preference acquisition. *Pharmacology Biochemistry & Behavior, 24*, 833–846.

Mandenoff, A., Fumeron, F., Apfelbaum, M., & Margules, D. L. (1982). Endogenous opiates and energy balance. *Science, 215*, 1536–1538.

Marks-Kaufman, R. (1980). Morphine selectively affects macronutrients intake in rats. *Pharmacology Biochemistry & Behavior, 12*, 329–330.

Marques, D., Fisher, A. E., Okrutny, M. S., & Rowland, N. E. (1979). Tail-pinch induced ingestion: Interaction of taste and deprivation. *Physiology & Behavior, 22*, 37–42.

Martazzi, M. (1980). *Mouse opiates model as a model of chronic anorexia nervosa.* Abstract presented at the International Conference on the Physiology of Food and Fluid Intake, Melbourne, Australia.

Matsumura, H., Fukuda, N., & Mori, H. (1982). Effect of a test meal, duodenal acidification and tetragastrin on the plasma concentration of β-endorphin-like immunoreactivity. *Regulatory Peptides, 4*, 173–189.

McCloy, G., & McCloy, R. (1979). Enkephalin, hunger and obesity. *Lancet, 1*, 156.

McGivern, R., Berka, C., Bernston, G. G., Walker, J. M., & Sandman, C. A. (1979). Effect of naloxone on analgesia produced by food deprivation. *Life Science, 25*, 885–888.

McLaughlin, C. L. S. (1983). Feeding by opiates injected into the PVN hypothalamus. *Peptides, 5*, 387.

McLean, S., & Hoebel, B. (1985). Meal stimulated increase of β-endorphin in the hypothalamus of Zucker obese and lean rats. *Physiology & Behavior, 35*, 891–896.

Morley, J. E., & Levine, A. S. (1980). Stress-induced eating is mediated through endogenous opiate. *Science, 296,* 1259.

Neill, G. C., & Cooper, S. (1988). Evidence for serotoninergic modulation of sucrose sham-feeding in the gastric fistulated rat. *Physiology & Behavior, 44,* 453–459.

Ono, T., & Oomura, Y. (1987). Morphine and enkephalin effects on hypothalamic glucosensitive neurons. *Brain Research, 175,* 208–212.

Rockwood, G. A. (1982). Naloxone modifies sugar water intake in rats drinking with an open gastric fistula. *Physiology & Behavior, 28,* 1175–1178.

Sclafani, A., & Gorman, A. N. (1977). Effects of age, sex, and prior body weight on the development of dietary obesity in adult rats. *Physiology & Behavior, 18,* 1021–1026.

Sikdar, S., & Oomura, Y. (1985). Selective inhibition of glucose sensitive neurons in rats LH by noxious stimuli and morphine. *Journal of Neurophysiology, 51,* 17–31.

Siviy, S. M., Calcagnetti, J., & Reid, L. D. (1982). Opioids and palatability. In B. G. Hoebel & D. Novin (Eds.), *Neural basis, of feeding and reward* (pp. 517–524). Haer Institute for Electrophysiological Research.

Siviy, S. M., & Reid, L. D. (1983). Endorphinergic modulation of acceptability of putative reinforcers. *Appetite, 4,* 249–257.

Tepperman, F. S., & Hirst, M. (1982). Concerning the specificity of opio-receptors responsible for food intake in rats. *Physiology & Behavior, 17,* 141–145.

Vaswani, K., Tejwani, G. A., & Mousa, S. (1983). Stress induced differential intake of various diets and water by rat: The role of the opiate system. *Life Science, 32,* 1983–1996.

Wise, R. A. (1978). Neuroleptics induced anhedonia in rats: Pimozide blocks reward quality of food. *Science, 201,* 222–224.

Wu, M. T. (1981). Dose-response relationship between Naloxone injections and intake of sucrose solutions. *Bulletin of Psychonomic Science, 17,* 101–103.

PART SIX

SOCIAL CONTEXT OF FOOD PREFERENCES

CHAPTER 18

THE IMPORTANCE OF SOCIAL FACTORS IN UNDERSTANDING THE ACQUISITION OF FOOD HABITS

PAUL ROZIN

Simplification is one of the great goals of science. It operates at both the level of theory and methodology. In theories concerning food intake and choice, the homeostatic model offers a simple framework for understanding. There is much truth in this model, but we now see it as only a partial explanation. There has been a consistent search for unidimensional solutions to complex problems: *the* satiety hormone, *the* single determinant of thirst or hunger, and so forth. Most investigators now recognize the multidimensional aspects of such complex phenomena as food intake and choice. There are still lapses into unidimensionality, however, though one often sees lapses in to unidimensionality, as when investigators claim that when there is no effect of elimination of a particular channel of information, it follows that this channel plays no role in the phenomenon in question. The view that food intake and choice are unlearned must also be modified, quite substantially as the papers presented at this symposium indicated. In this chapter I discuss why the learning principles now acknowledged to be involved in food intake and choice must be extended to include social factors as a major component.

Methodological simplicity involves stripping the phenomenon under study down to its bare essentials, in order to facilitate investigation. The danger in this process is that the context that is stripped away may be essential to understanding the phenomenon. As with simple theories, oversimplification of preparations can and does yield valuable information, but it may also lead to incomplete or misconstrued accounts. The freeing of feeding from its normal context, which has been characteristic of research on both animal and human feeding, has had both successes and problems.

One tactic has been to look at pure foods: sucrose or sodium chloride alone or in water are common examples.The results obtained with such studies, especially with humans, may not generalize to behavior with real foods. Thus sugar-water preferences imperfectly predict preference for sweetness in food contexts (Olson & Gemmill, 1981; Pangborn, 1980) although they do have some predictive value (Conner & Booth, 1988; see Cowart & Beauchamp, 1986 for similar findings in the area of sodium). There is a tendency in recent human food research to use real foods.

In both animal and human food research, there is a tendency to isolate the subjects from both social influence and other distractors. The typical food study in animals leaves the subject in a small cage with water and food sources, and virtually no other opportunities. Nicolaidis, Danguir, & Mather (1979) have shown that the number of meals eaten by a rat, a basic parameter of research in the field, drops substantially if the rat is given a small chamber for sleeping in its cage. The addition of conspecifics should have major effects on many food measures. Since many species, particularly humans, eat in social conditions, the cost of stripping away social factors may be the loss of important features of regulation and choice. Thus Galef's (1988; Galef & Beck, in press) remarkable findings on social influence on food choice in rats should have been discovered decades ago. They have changed our notions of the determinants of rat food preferences.

For humans, where the search and preparation of food, and its ingestion at meals are social occasions, food is a very social entity. Ingestion of food means taking something of the world into the body, and that something typically has a social history: it was procured, prepared, and presented by other humans. Food is a form of social exchange, and is imbued with special meanings in many cultures. The earliest significant events in the life of mammals include food at their center: the processes of nursing and weaning. From the very first, the taking of food is exquisitely social.

MODES OF ACTION OF SOCIAL FACTORS

I will first identify the ways in which social factors can influence eating, with humans as the target organism. This taxonomy derives from treatments of this issue by Galef (1976, 1985) and Birch (1987a, 1987b; Rozin, 1988).

A major source of social influence is *indirect*. Indirect social influences set the stage for or modulate the interpretation of food encounters. They do not require or include an immediate social presence (i.e., the presence of a conspe-

This chapter was prepared with the assistance of funding from the John D. and Catherine T. MacArthur Foundation Network for the study of health-related behaviors and from the Whitehall Foundation.

cific). These factors include beliefs, culinary traditions, and occasions that are established as part of the acquisition of culture.

Other social influences are *direct,* that is, they require the mediation of another organism, present on the occasion. In *inadvertent social agency,* the direct social presence is necessary, but is not specifically oriented to producing an effect. In *direct social agency,* the social agent participates in the learning task as an active teacher.

Indirect Social Agency

Beliefs and Attitudes

A small percentage of human beliefs and attitudes toward food result directly from our interaction with such foods. Beliefs that fat foods are unhealthy, that natural foods are healthy, and attitudes favoring shellfish and shunning worms as food derive from socially transmitted information. Conditioned taste aversions, a nonsocial phenomenon, are the only established mechanism for creating food dislikes in both humans and animals. The average person has one documentable food aversion, and a great many dislikes. Among the remaining large number of unexplained dislikes, social causes are bound to be important. Most critically, the meaning of food (source of nutrition and/or pleasure or a social or moral statement) is laid down by culture. For example, the great concern that Western people have about eating too much, and their preoccupation with dieting surely relates to the cultural ideal body image. There is a striking correspondence between the occurrence of anorexia and bulimia and the presence of a thin ideal.

Availability, Price, and the Setting of Occasions

Exposure is a recurrent and necessary, if not sufficient cause of food preferences (e.g., Pliner, 1982; Zajonc, 1968). Exposure itself is largely a product of culture. People are exposed to that subset of all possible foods that their ecology and culture supports. For example, the lack of exposure of many white, rural, midwestern Americans to bean curd or pork kidneys is not because the sources of these foods are ecologically unavailable, but because locals regard such things as "not food." Cost is also a major determinant of degree of exposure. Cultural valuation of a food may increase its price in the short term, but in the long term, it leads to improved methods of harvesting and processing, so that the food becomes more available. Many foods have lost their luxury status and have become commonplace; coffee and sugar are good examples of this transition. Technological advances, motivated by high demand, led to enormous increases in the availability (with concurrent price drop) of sugar for consumption and for mixture with a wide variety of foods (Mintz, 1985). This availability led to its widespread use as a sweetener for items, like coffee and chocolate, that were previously too bitter for wide acceptance.

Another mechanism for the development of food likes in humans involves Pavlovian association of a target food with another positive event, either postingestional (e.g., satiety: Booth, Mather & Fuller, 1982) or sensory (e.g., sweetness: Zellner, Rozin, Aron, & Kulish, 1983; see Rozin & Zellner, 1985 or Rozin & Vollmecke, 1986 for reviews). Such pairings are themselves nonsocial, but they may be socially engineered. For example, a possible route to the liking of unsweetened, black coffee is earlier experiences of coffee with cream and sugar. This coffee sweetening is made possible by cultural innovation (development of sugar technology), and is often staged by friends or parents, as a means of making coffee more attractive. Thus the pairings of coffee and sugar are scheduled in a social context.

The context within which a food is presented also affects the attitudes to it. Lolli, Serianni, Golder, and Luzzatto-Fegiz (1958) called attention to the fact that although alcohol consumption is quite high in Italy, there is relatively little alcohol abuse. They trace this to deeply rooted Italian attitudes toward alcohol as a food and as a part of meals. It is introduced to children early, in the context of a meal and a family event. This role for alcohol (wine in this case) places it in a situation where its absorption will be slower, and where it becomes a part of normal life, rather than a focus for rebellion from family values.

Universal Cultural Themes and the Social/Food Linkage: The Mouth Gateway to the Body, You Are What You Eat, and Contagion

Food is a social instrument for humans by virtue of the fact that more than one person is almost always involved with any food, from harvesting to ingestion. This social passage takes on added significance because of the existence of three probably universal patterns of thought. The first has to do with the special position of the mouth, as the dominant entry point to the body. People are sensitive to the status of their bodies, and cannot help but be concerned with what goes into them. The mouth is the gateway, so that there is great concern and strong feeling about what goes into the mouth (Rozin & Fallon, 1987; Rozin, Nemeroff, & Horowitz, 1990).

This concern becomes engaged in a more social sense when coupled with the belief that "you are what you eat." The view that a person takes on the physical, behavioral, and intentional properties of the food he eats is widespread in traditional culture (e.g., Frazer, 1890/1959). This belief seems entirely reasonable, in the absence of knowledge of the theory of digestion and the common small set of molecules that result after digestion from all foods. In our general experience, when two things combine, the product takes on the properties of both. You are what you eat, in a more subtle and unacknowledged form, seems to be held as a belief by educated Westerners, as well as members of other cultures. American undergraduates who read a cultural vignette about a group that consumes boar rate members of this culture as more boar-like, and less turtle-like than do other students who read an equivalent vignette in which turtle is mentioned as part of the diet, in place of boar (Nemeroff & Rozin, 1989). You are what you eat accounts, in part, for resistance to ingesting things that are offensive or that have other undesirable characteristics. But, with the exception of cannibals, it does not directly link humans to other humans via food.

That linkage is provided by a more general principle, the sympathetic magical law of contagion, explicated at the turn of the century by the anthropoligists Frazer (1890/1959) and Mauss (1902/1972)(see Rozin & Nemeroff, 1990 for a detailed exposition of this law). The law of contagion holds that "once in contact, always in contact," that is, when two objects come in contact, properties are permanently exchanged. Though originally expounded as a characteristic of "primitive" thinking, contagion clearly operates among Western, educated adults (Rozin, Millman, & Nemeroff, 1986; Rozin, Nemeroff, Wane, & Sherrod, 1989). For example, almost all of the people surveyed rejected wearing a sweater that had been worn by a disliked or unsavory person, or reject eating an apple bitten by same. On the positive side, a minority of people find clothing or food enhanced if it had been worn or tasted, respectively, by a loved or admired person.

The critical importance of contagion is that it links the human preparers or handlers of food to the eaters. Now you are what you eat holds not only for the food eaten, but for the previous contacts of that food. Food is now a loaded interpersonal message: grandma's soup can be better because it was made by grandma, and an enemy or a disliked person can convey bad fortune by contacting one's food.

The importance of these ideas in the food domain is illustrated by food attitudes in two nonWestern cultures, the Hua of Papua, New Guinea and Hindu Indians (see Rozin, 1990b) for a more detailed exposition of these two cultural examples).

Among the Hua of Papua, New Guinea (Meigs, 1978, 1984) food is the bearer of vital essence, or "nu," which is both a life force and a carrier of individual properties. It is good to eat food procured or prepared by those in a positive relation to ego; it both improves character and personality and increases good fortune. For example, it is desirable to consume food which an appropriate relative has spat upon. On the other hand, food from someone in a competitive position or an undesirable relation can cause harm. The Hua were cannibalistic within the memory of the older current villagers, and consumed their parents, after death; they would never consume killed warriors from another group, because of the hostile intent that would be conveyed. From before puberty to a few years postpuberty, Hua males are segregated, and are not allowed any contact with fertile females, for fear that the nu of these fertile females will feminize the young males. They are not allowed to consume any food procured or prepared by a fertile female. Meigs states that food and food transactions form the center of Hua conversation; indeed it was this fact that steered her ethnography in the direction of food.

Among Hindu Indians, a food's personal history carries social status and moral significance (Appadurai, 1981). Sharing food, or eating food made by a common third person, has a binding or homogenizing significance. Refusal to share establishes distance, or heterogenizes. Indeed, Marriott (1968) showed that the complex Hindu caste structure can be reconstructed simply from information on who can eat whose foods. Even within the family, the order of serving and rules about who can eat whose leftovers serve to maintain the family hierarchy, and reaffirm proper social relations between family members. The body is viewed as the temple for the soul, and eating is seen as a moral transaction in which food can serve as a fundamental link between humans and the gods. Thus, for example, Brahmin children rate "One of your family members eats beef regularly" as a more serious moral offense than "There was a rule in a hotel; Invalids and disfigured persons are not allowed in the dining hall" (Shweder, Mahapatra, & Miller, 1987).

In both India and New Guinea, contagion and you are what you eat play important roles in establishing personal linkages through the medium of food. Although these feelings also exist in the United States they are muted. To a large extent, we have decontextualized our food (just as our laboratory scientists have decontextualized feeding). We buy food in plastic wrap parcels, often frozen, with no record or information about their personal history. We have done what we can to make food impersonal, and so have lost much of its moral and social significance. But even in the United States, among the white rats of the human food world, food has social significance. It is the center of social occasions, such as evening dinner and holiday feasts. Dinner is the center of social life for many families. Among Americans, contagion is seen primarily in the emotion of disgust in response to animal products, while in India and New Guinea, the emotion of disgust is evoked primarily by human interactions.

Disgust and Social Ideation: The Human/Animal Distinction

We have identified the emotion of disgust as oriented to food rejection, at its core (hence the name, meaning bad taste, the facial expression centered around the nose and mouth, and nausea, a gastrointestinal sensation, as its most characteristic physiological feature) (Rozin & Fallon, 1987). Contagion is a critical feature of disgust; when a disgusting entity (e.g., a cockroach in the United States) touches an otherwise acceptable food, it renders that food inedible.

The expression of disgust does not depend on the presence of another person, but the entire emotion, and particularly the stimuli that elicit it, are culturally conditioned. Feces may be the only universal disgust, and even this strong aversion does not appear until after 1.5–2 years of life (Rozin, Hammer, Oster, Horowitz, & Marmara, 1986). The stimuli that elcit disgust, cross-culturally, are almost all animal products (Angyal, 1941; Rozin & Fallon, 1987). This relates to the general cultural theme that humans are not animals, and are to be clearly distinguished from animals. This theme, plus the you are what you eat principle, leads to an avoidance of animal foods so as not to become animal-like (Rozin & Fallon, 1987). This sequence of thought is explicit in the account of Hebrew animal prohibitions dating from the Old Testament (Grunfeld, 1982). The interesting question then becomes when and how certain animals or their parts become exempt, in specific cultures, from this prohibition. For the case of the Hebrews, one principle that seems to be involved is that excepted animals are not particularly animal-like (Grunfeld, 1982). The point of this discussion is that what may be the most powerful response humans have to food is conditioned in multiple and complex ways by cultural forces, though disgust may be manifested under solitary conditions.

Food and the Moral Domain: Moral/Physical Confusion

The "moral" status of food, and a confounding of physical health and moral thinking even among Westerners is illustrated by a simple example. When we ask American subjects why they reject drinking a glass of juice that just had a cockroach dipped into it, they almost invariably refer to the health risk, given that cockroaches are dirty and disease vectors. We then repeat this question, but stipulate that the cockroach involved is dead and sterilized. The degree of aversion remains very high, and subjects ultimately resort to the fact that "it's a cockroach." That is, it is "cockroachness," not health, that now accounts for their strong aversion. This is, in a sense, a switch from a physical to a moral explanation. Among Hindus, this moral aspect is more salient, so that a health explanation of attitudes to pollution is not felt to be necessary. In fact, if one was worried primarily about health issues in consuming foods contacted by lower castes, then one would avoid raw as opposed to cooked foods. In fact, one can purchase raw foods from lower-class people, but one cannot eat their cooked (microbially safe) food, because the cooked food has a lot of the lower caste persona or essence in it.

The tendency for Westerners to rely (superficially) on physical explanation, and/or to shun moral explanations, extends to scholars. Thus a popular explanation for the Hebrew pork taboo had to do with the avoidance of trichinosis, although this seems unlikely (the trichina is killed by cooking). Similarly, the common justification of the evolution of modern table manners in Europe (e.g., not eating from a common pot, not spitting at the table) has to do with hygiene. However, according to the social and historical analysis of Elias (1978), the driving force for these changes was social; being less animal-like and more like the upper classes.

SOCIAL FACTORS AS PART OF THE MECHANISM OF LEARNED FOOD PREFERENCES

Inadvertent Social Agency

Animal Studies

There is extensive literature on animal food preferences, dating back to Curt Richter (1943) and P. T. Young (1948) (reviewed in Booth, 1982; Rozin, 1976; Rozin & Schulkin, in press). The most rapid and robust effect is conditioned taste aversions, a phenomenon that does not engage social factors at all. The acquisition of preferences has been established many times, particularly in the laboratories of Bolles (Bolles, Hayward, & Crandall, 1981), Booth (e.g., Booth, Stoloff, & Nicholls, 1974) and Sclafani (Sclafani & Nissenbaum, 1988; Sclafani, this volume). Sclafani's most recent work reports the most striking effects in terms of rapidity and robustness, but there remains nothing as robust and rapid (usually one trial full preference reversal) as conditioned taste aversions. This had led to the suggestion (e.g., Rozin & Kalat, 1971; Rozin, 1976), that there is a bias to learn about negative events.

Although this generalization still has merit, the introduction of inadvertent social agencies has added a powerful new force for the creation of positive preferences. Galef and his colleagues (reviewed in Galef, 1988; Galef & Beck, in press) have produced robust effects in the direction of increasing preference from the simple expedient of exposing a target rat to a "demonstrator" who has already consumed a novel, target food. The positive effects seem to be produced primarily by an olfactory route; carbon disulfide on the breath of the demonstrator functions to enhance the value of food residues or odorants associated with that chemical (Galef, Mason, Preti, & Bean, 1988). These striking effects are observable only on the "positive" side. Galef has sought but has not found evidence of aversions induced by social factors. The absence of such effects is puzzling, from an adaptive point of view.

Human Studies

The modest-sized human literature on social factors in human food choice has concentrated on the positive (preference creation) side. These studies are reviewed by Birch (1987a, 1987b) and Rozin (1988). Briefly, early studies by Duncker (1938) showed that children would prefer a food if it was chosen by admired others, and Duncker (1938) and Marinho (1942) showed that children would prefer a food that was preferred by a fictional hero. These suggestions that child preferences were changeable by the intermediation of admired others were extended and confirmed in a series of studies by Leann Birch and her colleagues (reviewed in Birch, 1987a, 1987b). Preschoolers prefer a food that their peers select (Birch, 1980a). Approval by a significant adult (e.g., nursery school teacher) also causes an enhancement of preference that endures for weeks (Birch, Zimmerman, & Hind, 1980). Rewarding a child by use of a target food, or simply offering of the food a few times a day by the teacher, enhanced preference, in comparison to offering of the food in a nonsocial setting (e.g., leaving it in the locker). Birch interpreted these findings as indicating the importance of a positive social-affective context.

The importance of social factors is suggested by research on the acquisition of liking for innately unpalatable foods, such as chili pepper. A critical factor, as determined by interviews and observations in a traditional Mexican village, seems to be exposure to others ingesting the pepper, in the positive social-affective context of a meal in which a child observes older siblings and parents obviously relishing ingestion of the peppers (Rozin & Schiller, 1980; reviewed in Rozin, 1990a). It is interesting, in this regard, that attempts to establish chili preferences in animals have generally failed (Rozin, Gruss, & Berk, 1979). The only exceptions involved social mediation. Rozin and Kennel (1983) reported that two captive chimpanzees were trained to like chili pepper, in a very social situation in which they were fed chili crackers regularly by their trainer. Cases of two rhesus monkeys (Dua-Sharma & Sharma, 1980) and one dog (Rozin & Kennel, 1983) also involved the delivery of the food in the social context of a family meal. Finally, Galef (1989) has recently shown that his powerful rat social transmission mechanism holds for chili pepper as well. While months of solitary exposure to chili pepper do not induce a preference (Rozin, Gruss, & Berk, 1979), brief exposure to a conspecific who has consumed chili pepper induced a marked preference for it. Thus the animal literature on chili pepper strongly supports a social mediation model.

Mechanisms of Inadvertent Social Effects

There is no strong evidence implying a particular mechanism of action of social factors on preferences. More generally, the internalization or socialization process is not well understood. One account that makes contact with the nonsocial acquisition of preferences, invokes Pavlovian conditioning. On this view, evaluations of objects can change, in animals and humans, as a result of pairing of an event (e.g., a flavor) with an already positive or negative event. This process has termed *evaluative conditioning* (Martin & Levey, 1978). In food preferences, a target food (conditioned stimulus, CS) would be paired with a positive social event (unconditioned stimulus, US). Such a paradigm fits well with both Galef's social effects in animals (the carbon disulfide on the rat's breath, paired with the food odor) and with Birch's results on preschoolers (with social approval as the US). Tomkins (1963) has suggested particular pathways, including the idea that the facial expression in the subject is the US, and that it is induced by positive expressions in others. It is surprising how little is known, at present, about such an important process.

The Pavlovian perspective offers only one way of conceptualizing inadvertent social effects. Lefebvre and Palameta (1988) distinguished three modes of social influence involving inadvertent social agency: social facilitation, local enhancement, and observational learning. They provided criteria for observational learning, the most elaborate of the three, and demonstrated evidence for it in the food-finding behavior of feral pigeons. It seems likely that many of the examples of inadvertent social agency in humans involve observational learning, whether or not one wishes to place a Pavlovian interpretation upon this observation.

Active Social Agency: Teaching

In an extensive review of "tradition" and social effects on feeding in animals, Galef (1990) concluded that there is no evidence for active teaching in animals.

This is obviously not the case for humans. Parents, among others, are active forces in teaching children about foods, and, at least in American culture, parents attempt to shape children's food preferences.

Parents seem to have some insight into the process. A survey of feeding practices of American parents suggests that they are aware of the central importance of social factors in inducing preferences in their children; the two most popular techniques were engaging the child in the preparation of the food and exposing the child to displays of positive affect in association with the food (Casey & Rozin, 1989).

However, parent educative efforts may not always have the intended effect. Birch, Birch, Marlin, and Kramer (1982) have shown that rewarding ingestion of a target food has the long-term effect of decreasing the preference for that food. The interpretation is that while social approval indicated the valuation of the food in question by elders, rewarding the ingestion of the food indicated a lack of adult valuation of the food. A parent survey indicated that, in contrast to these findings, parents were more optimistic about the value of rewarding ingestion of a target food than about the efficacy of using the target food as a reward (Casey & Rozin, 1989).

The Family Paradox

In light of the major role of social factors in human food preferences, and in recognition of the fact that in the earlier years of life the family is the dominant influence on the child, one would predict strong family (particularly parent-child) resemblance in food preferences. One would also predict higher correlations with the mother, given her much more substantial traditional role in food preparation and feeding, and greater resemblance among same sex child-parent pairs, on the grounds of modeling. None of these three predictions seem to hold, a combination of results that I call the *family paradox* (Rozin, 1988, in press). The paradox is that given the strong role of social factors in general, the almost certain great importance of parental effects in establishing early culture-wide preferences, and the high amount of within culture variance in food preferences, family effects should be high, but they are not. I will briefly review the evidence for weak family effects in each of the three domains.

Correlations between parent and child food preferences run between 0 and .30 in the six studies that systematically examined this issue. Birch (1980), using preschoolers as the children, and Pliner (1983), using college students as the children, reported correlations for the pattern of preferences for a range of foods between children and parents, in comparison to the correlations between children and pseudoparents (randomly selected parents of other subjects in the sample). Birch found correlations for child-parents were only slightly higher than those for child-pseudoparent. Pliner found correlations for parent-child pairs for the pattern of preferences averaged in the .25 range for parent-child pairs, and were in the range of .10 for pseudoparent-child pairs. Pliner and Pelchat (1986) reported similar results. Rozin, Fallon, and Mandell (1984), Rozin (in press), and Logue, Logue, Uzzo, McCarty, and Smith (1988) used college or high school students and their parents as subjects, and food preference questionnaires. They reported correlations in the 0 to .30 range for particular foods or groups of foods (e.g., vegetables, junk foods).

One cause for the low correlations might be that parents may be discordant on a particular preference. If so, there is no reason to predict that a child should fall on the mid-parent value; it is not clear how one would expect a child to respond to a mixed message about a particular food. Rozin (in press) separately analyzed mid-parent-child food preference correlations for cases in which parents were concordant or discordant for the particular preference. Parent concordance did have a modest effect; the mean correlation across 12 ingestants (including beverages and cigarettes) was .11 for discordant parents and .18 for concordant parents. The great part of the variance remains unexplained.

Evidence on the superiority of mother effects is mixed. Rozin et al. (1984) and Rozin (in press) reported slightly higher mother-child than father-child correlations, and Logue et al. (1988) reported that most of their significant parent-child correlations occur in the mother-daughter pairing. On the other hand, Pliner (1983), Birch (1980b), Burt and Hertzler (1978), and Cavalli-Sforza, Feldman, Chen, and Dornbusch (1982) show no evidence favoring the mother. One reason for the lack of a mother effect may be that, at least at the level of selection of foods, mothers may be more influenced by their husband's preferences than by their own (Burt & Hertzler, 1978; Weidner, Archer, Healy, & Matarazzo, 1985).

The data on same-sex modeling are similarly mixed. Pliner (1983) reported a same sex effect, but Pliner and Pelchat (1986) in another survey, with younger children as the targets, failed to confirm this relationship. Rozin (in press) and Logue et al. (1988) found no evidence for a same sex effect, but found some indication that female children were more influenced by parents than were male children.

There is no simple explanation for this set of results, which is why I label them a paradox. It is possible that parent-child correlations would improve if they were established between fully mature children (e.g., 30-year-olds) and their parents. It is also likely that there are other social routes besides parents. Pliner and Pelchat (1986) reported much larger food preference correlations between siblings and there were probably major peer influences, as well as influences of adults other than parents and media influences. However, it remains a puzzle that cultural food preferences must be, in substantial part, communicated by parents, who seem at the same time quite ineffective at communicating their own.

CONCLUSIONS

The main thrust of this chapter has been to establish the importance of social factors, in understanding food in general, and specifically with respect to the acquisition of preferences. This chapter has been short on mechanisms because the literature is very thin here. The main research agenda in this area is to establish how social forces act, and why, as in the case of low parent-child resemblance, they are ineffective in some cases. There is a lot of work to be done.

References

Angyal, A. (1941). Disgust and related aversions. *Journal of Abnormal and Social Psychology, 36,* 393–412.

Appadurai, A. (1981). Gastro-politics in Hindu South Asia. *American Ethnologist, 8,* 494–511.

Birch, L. L. (1980a). Effect of peer model's food choices and eating behaviors on preschoolers food preferences. *Child Development, 51,* 489–496.

Birch, L. L. (1980b). The relationship between children's food preferences and those of their parents. *Journal of Nutrition Education, 12,* 14–18.

Birch, L. L. (1987a). Children's food preferences: Developmental patterns and environmental influences. In G. Whitehurst & R. Vasta (Eds.), *Annals of Child Development, Vol. 44* (pp. 171–208). Greenwich, CN: JAI.

Birch, L. L. (1987b). The acquisition of food acceptance patterns in children. In R. Boakes, D. Popplewell, & M. Burton (Eds.), *Eating Habits* (pp. 107–130). Chichester, England: Wiley,

Birch, L. L., Birch, D., Marlin, D. W., & Kramer, L. (1982). Effects of instrumental eating on children's food preferences. *Appetite, 3,* 125–134.

Birch, L. L., Zimmerman, S. I., & Hind, H. (1980). The influence of social-affective context on the formation of children's food preferences. *Child Development, 51,* 856–861.

Bolles, R. C., Hayward, L., & Crandall, C. (1981). Conditioned taste preferences based on caloric density. *Journal of Experimental Psychology: Animal Behavior Processes, 7,* 59–69.

Booth, D. A. (1982). Normal control of omnivore intake by taste and smell. In J. Steiner & J. Ganchrow (Eds.), *The determination of behavior by chemical stimuli. ECRO symposium.* (pp. 233–243.) London: Information Retrieval.

Booth, D. A., Mather, P., & Fuller, J. (1982). Starch content of ordinary foods associatively conditions human appetite and satiation, indexed by intake and eating pleasantness of starch-paired flavors. *Appetite, 3,* 163–184.

Booth, D. A., Stoloff, R., & Nicholls, J. (1974). Dietary flavor acceptance in infant rats established by association with effects of nutrient composition. *Physiological Psychology, 2,* 313–319.

Burt, J. V., & Hertzler, A. A., (1978). Parent influence on the child's food preference. *Journal of Nutrition Education, 10,* 127–128.

Casey, R., & Rozin, P. (1989). Changing children's food preferences: Parent opinions. *Appetite, 12,* 171–182.

Cavalli-Sforza, L. L., Feldman, M. W., Chen, K. H., & Dorbusch, S. M. (1982). Theory and observation in cultural transmission. *Science, 218,* 19–27.

Conner, M. T., & Booth, D. A. (1988). Preferred sweetness of a lime drink and preference for sweet over non-sweet foods related to sex and reported age and body weight. *Appetite, 10,* 25–35.

Cowart, B. J., & Beauchamp, G. K. (1986). The importance of sensory context in young children's acceptance of salty tastes. *Child Development, 57,* 1034–1039.

Dua-Sharma, S., & Sharma, K. N. (1980). Capsaicin and feeding responses in Macaca mulata: A longitudinal study. [Abstract]. International Conference on the Regulation of Food and Water Intake, Warsaw.

Duncker, K. (1938). Experimental modifications of children's food preferences through social suggestion. *Journal of Abnormal & Social Psychology, 33,* 489–507.

Elias, N. (1978). *The history of manners. The civilizing process: Vol. I*, (E. Jephcott, Trans.). New York: Pantheon Books. (Original work published 1939).

Frazer, J. G. (1890/1959). *The golden bough: A study in magic and religion*. New York: Macmillan. (reprint of 1922 abridged edition, edited by T. H. Gaster; original work published, 1890).

Galef, B. G. Jr. (1976). Social transmission of acquired behavior: A discussion of tradition and social learning in vertebrates. In J. S. Rosenblatt, R. A. Hinde, E. Shaw, & C. Beer (Eds.), *Advances in the Study of Behavior: Vol. 6* (pp. 77–100). New York: Academic Press.

Galef, B. G. Jr. (1985). Direct and indirect pathways to the social transmission of food avoidance. *Annals of the New York Academy of Sciences, 443*, 203–215.

Galef. B. G. Jr. (1988). Communication of information concerning distant diets in a social central-place foraging species: *Rattus norvegicus*. In T. Zentall & B. G. Galef, Jr. (Eds.), *Social learning: A comparative approach* (pp. 119–140). Hillsdale, New Jersey: Erlbaum.

Galef, B. G. Jr. (1989). Enduring social enhancement of rats' preferences for the palatable and the piquant. *Appetite, 13*, 81–92.

Galef, B. G. Jr. (1990). Tradition in animals: Field observations and laboratory analysis. In M. Bekoff & D. Jamieson (Eds.), *Methods, inference, interpretation and explanation in the study of behavior.* Boulder, CO: Westview Press.

Galef, B. G. Jr., & Beck, M. (in press). Diet selection and poison avoidance by mammals individually and in social groups. In E. M. Stricker (Ed.), *Handbook of Behavioral Neurobiology, Volume 10, Food and Water Intake,* New York: Plenum.

Galef, B. G. Jr., Mason, J. R., Preti, G., & Bean, N. J. (1988). Carbon disulfide: A semiochemical mediating socially-induced diet choice in rats. *Physiology & Behavior, 42*, 119–124.

Grunfeld, D. I. (1982). *The Jewish dietary laws. Volume One. Dietary laws regarding forbidden and permitted foods, with particular reference to meat and meat products (3rd edition).* London: Soncino Press (Original edition, 1972).

Lefebvre, L., & Palameta, B. (1988). Mechanisms, ecology, and population diffusion of socially learned, food-finding behavior in feral pigeons. In T. Zentall & B. G. Galef, Jr. (Eds.), *Social learning: A comparative approach* (pp. 141–164). Hillsdale, NJ: Erlbaum.

Logue, A. W., Logue, C. M., Uzzo, R. G., McCarty, M. J., & Smith, M. E. (1988). Food preferences in families. *Appetite, 10*, 169–180.

Lolli, G., Serianni, E., Golder, G. M., & Luzzatto-Fegiz, P. (1958), *Alcohol in Italian culture.* Glencoe, IL: The Free Press.

Marinho, H. (1942). Social influence in the formation of enduring preferences. *Journal of Abnormal and Social Psychology, 37*, 448–468.

Marriott, M. (1968). Caste ranking and food transactions: A matrix analysis. In M. Singer & B. S. Cohn (Eds.), *Structure and change in Indian society* (pp. 133–171). Chicago, IL: Aldine.

Martin, I., & Levey, A. B. (1978). Evaluative conditioning. *Advances in Behavior Research & Therapy, 1* 57–102.

Mauss, M. (1902/1972). *A general theory of magic* (R. Brain, Trans.). New York: W. W. Norton. (Original work published 1902).

Meigs, A. S. (1978). A Papuan perspective on pollution. *Man, 13*, 304–318.

Meigs A. S. (1984). *Food, sex, and pollution: A New Guinea religion.* New Brunswick, NJ: Rutgers University Press.

Mintz, S. W. (1985). *Sweetness and power.* New York: Viking.

Nemeroff, C., & Rozin, P. (1989). An unacknowledged belief in "you are what you eat" among college students in the United States: An application of the demand-free "impressions" technique. *Ethos. The Journal of Psychological Anthropology, 17*, 50–69.

Nicolaidis, S., Danguir, J., & Mather, P. (1979). A new approach of sleep and feeding behaviors in the laboratory rat. *Physiology & Behavior, 23*, 717–722.

Olson, C. M., & Gemmill, K. P. (1981). Association of sweet preference and food selection among four-to-five-year-old children. *Ecology of Food & Nutrition, 11,* 145–150.

Pangborn, R. M. (1980). A critical analysis of sensory responses to sweetness. In P. Koivistoinen & L. Hyvonen (Eds.), *Carbohydrate sweeteners in foods and nutrition.* (pp. 87–110) London: Academic Press.

Pliner, P. (1982). The effects of mere exposure on liking for edible substances. *Appetite, 3,* 283–290.

Pliner, P. (1983). Family resemblance in food preferences. *Journal of Nutrition Education, 15,* 137–140.

Pliner, P., & Pelchat, M. L. (1986). Children's feeding problems. *Appetite, 7,* 333–342.

Richter, C. P. (1943). Total self regulatory functions in animals and human beings. *Harvey Lecture Series, 38,* 63–103.

Rozin, P. (1976). The selection of food by rats, humans and other animals. In J. Rosenblatt, R. A. Hinde, C. Beer, & E. Shaw (Eds.), *Advances in the Study of Behavior, Volume 6* (pp. 21–76). New York: Academic Press.

Rozin, P. (1988). Social learning about foods by humans. In T. Zentall & B. G. Galef, Jr. (Eds.), *Social learning: A comparative approach* (pp. 165–187.) Hillsdale, NJ: Erlbaum.

Rozin, P. (1990a). Getting to like the burn of chili pepper: Biological, psychological, and cultural perspectives. In B. G. Green, J. R. Mason, & M. L. Kare (Eds.), *Chemical irritation in the nose and mouth* (pp. 231–269). New York: Marcel Dekker.

Rozin, P. (1990b). Social and moral aspects of eating. In I. Rock (Ed.), *The legacy of Solomon Asch: Essays in cognition and social psychology* (pp. 97–110). Potomac, MD: Lawrence Erlbaum.

Rozin, P. (in press). Family resemblance in food and other domains: The family paradox and the role of parental congruence. *Appetite.*

Rozin, P., & Fallon, A. E. (1987). A perspective on disgust. *Psychological Review, 94,* 23–41.

Rozin, P., Fallon, A. E., & Mandell, R. (1984). Family resemblance in attitudes to food. *Developmental Psychology, 20,* 309–314.

Rozin, P., Gruss, L., & Berk, G. (1979). The reversal of innate aversions: Attempts to induce a preference for chili peppers in rats. *Journal of Comparative and Physiological Psychology, 93,* 1001–1014.

Rozin, P., Hammer, L., Oster, H., Horowitz, T., & Marmara, V. (1986). The child's conception of food: Differentiation of categories of rejected substances in the 1.4 to 5 year age range. *Appetite, 7,* 141–151.

Rozin, P., & Kalat, J. W. (1971). Specific hungers and poison avoidance as adaptive specializations of learning. *Psychological Review, 78,* 459–486.

Rozin, P., & Kennel, K. (1983). Acquired preferences for piquant foods by chimpanzees. *Appetite, 4,* 69–77.

Rozin, P. Millman, L., & Nemeroff, C.. (1986). Operation of the laws of sympathetic magic in disgust and other domains. *Journal of Personality and Social Psychology, 40,* 703–712.

Rozin, P., & Nemeroff, C. J. (1990). The laws of sympathetic magic: A psychological analysis of similarity and contagion. In J. Stigler, G. Herdt & R. A. Shweder (Eds.), *Cultural psychology: Essays on comparative human development.* (pp. 205–232). Cambridge, England: Cambridge University Press.

Rozin, P., Nemeroff, C., & Horowitz, M. (1990). The borders of the self: The psychological microanatomy of the mouth. Submitted manuscript.

Rozin, P., Nemeroff, C., Wane, M., & Sherrod, A. (1989). Operation of the sympathetic magical law of contagion in interpersonal attitudes among Americans. *Bulletin of the Psychonomic Society, 27,* 367–370.

Rozin, P., & Schiller, D. (1980). The nature and acquisition of a preference for chili pepper by humans. *Motivation & Emotion, 4,* 77–101.

Rozin, P., & Schulkin, J. (in press). Food selection. In E. M. Stricker (Ed.), *Handbook of Behavioral Neurobiology, Volume 10, Food and water intake,* New York: Plenum.

Rozin, P., & Vollmecke, T. A. (1986). Food likes and dislikes. *Annual Review of Nutrition, 6,* 433–456.

Rozin, P., & Zellner, D. A. (1985). The role of Pavlovian conditioning in the acquisition of food likes and dislikes. *Annals of the New York Academy of Sciences. 443,* 189–202.

Sclafani, A., & Nissenbaum, J. W. (1988). Robust conditioned flavor preferences produced by intragastric starch infusions in the rat. *American Journal of Physiology (Regulatory, Integrative, Comparative Physiology), 24,* R672–R675.

Shweder, R.A., Mahapatra, M., & Miller, J. G. (1987). Culture and moral development. In J. Kagan & S. Lamb (Eds.), *The emergence of moral concepts in young children,* (pp. 1–82). Chicago, IL: University of Chicago Press.

Tomkins, S. S. (1963). *Affect, imagery, consciousness. Vol. II. The negative affects.* New York: Springer.

Weidner, G., Archer, S., Healy, B., & Matarazzo, J. D. (1985). Family consumption of low fat foods: Stated preference versus actual consumption. *Journal of Applied Social Psychology, 15,* 773–779.

Young, P. T. (1948). Appetite, palatability and feeding habit: A critical review. *Psychological Bulletin, 45,* 289–320.

Zajonc, R. G. (1968). Attitudinal effects of mere exposure. *Journal of Personality and Social Psychology, 9 (2),* 1–27.

Zellner, D.A., Rozin, P., Aron, M., & Kulish, C. (1983). Conditioned enhancement of human's liking for flavors by pairing with sweetness. *Learning & Motivation, 14,* 338–350.

INDEX